REVIEW 9

REVIEW

Volume 9   1987

Edited by

James O. Hoge
*Virginia Polytechnic Institute
and State University*

James L. W. West III
The Pennsylvania State University

University Press of Virginia

Charlottesville

THE UNIVERSITY PRESS OF VIRGINIA
Copyright © 1987 by the Rector and Visitors
of the University of Virginia

This journal is a member of (CELJ) the Conference of Editors of Learned Journals

First published 1987

ISSN 1090-3233
ISBN 0-8139-1160-5

Printed in the United States of America

The editorial assistants for volume 9 of REVIEW are LaVerne Maginnis and Debra Morris, both of The Pennsylvania State University.

PENNSTATE

Funding for *Review* is provided by the generous gifts of Mr. and Mrs. Henry J. Dekker, Mr. and Mrs. J. S. Hill, and Mr. Adger S. Johnson to the Virginia Tech Foundation, and by a grant from the College of the Liberal Arts, The Pennsylvania State University. Additional support is provided by the *Review* Association, a group of major universities which support the aims and purposes of the series. Member universities are as follows:

>City College of New York
>Columbia University
>University of Colorado
>Duke University
>University of Minnesota
>University of Virginia

Contents

"The people have set Literature free":   1
The Professionalization of Letters in
Nineteenth-Century England
   by Robert L. Patten
      Review of Nigel Cross, *The Common Writer: Life in
      Nineteenth-Century Grub Street*

George Eliot and the Threats of Story-Telling: 35
The Critic as Raffles or the Critic as Romola?
   by U.C. Knoepflmacher
      Review of Alexander Welsh, *George Eliot and Blackmail;*
      Gillian Beer, *George Eliot*

The Pleasure of Their Company   53
   by Donald Gallup
      Review of Edward Burns, ed., *The Letters of Gertrude
      Stein and Carl Van Vechten 1913–1946;* Timothy
      Materer, ed., *The Letters of Ezra Pound and
      Wyndham Lewis*

L'orbe est sur Joyce   67
   by Morris Beja
      Review of Wolfhard Steppe, with Hans Walter Gabler,
      A Handlist to James Joyce's Ulysses: *A Complete Alphabeti-
      cal Index to the Critical Reading Text;* Patrick Parrinder,
      James Joyce; Sheldon Brivic, *Joyce the Creator;* Cheryl
      Herr, *Joyce's Anatomy of Culture;* Richard Brown, *James
      Joyce and Sexuality*

A Book that Percolates 81
  by Peter L. Shillingsburg
    Review of Jerome J. McGann, ed., *Textual Criticism and Literary Interpretation*

Talking the South 89
  by Michael O'Brien
    Review of Richard Gray, *Writing the South: Ideas of an American Region*

The Politics of Shakespeare's Plays, 95
Then and Now
  by Richard A. Burt
    Review of David Bergeron, *Shakespeare's Romances and the Royal Family*; Michael Bristol, *Carnival and Theater: Plebeian Culture and the Structures of Authority in Renaissance England*; Jonathan Dollimore and Alan Sinfield, eds., *Political Shakespeare: Essays in Cultural Materialism*; John Drakakis, ed., *Alternative Shakespeares*; Patricia Parker and Geoffrey Hartman, eds., *Shakespeare and the Question of Theory*; Leonard Tennenhouse, *Power on Display: The Politics of Shakespeare's Genres*

Teaching the Literature of the Vietnam War 125
  by Arthur D. Casciato
    Review of Jeffrey Walsh, *American War Literature, 1914 to Vietnam*; James C. Wilson, *Vietnam in Prose and Film*; Philip D. Beidler, *American Literature and the Experience of Vietnam*; Timothy J. Lomperis, *"Reading the Wind": The Literature of the Vietnam War*; Lloyd B. Lewis, *The Tainted War: Culture and Identity in Vietnam War Narratives*; John Hellmann, *American Myth and the Legacy of Vietnam*

Franklin Well Served 149
  by A. Owen Aldridge
    Review of J. A. Leo Lemay, *The Canon of Benjamin Franklin, 1722–1776: New Attributions and Reconsidera-*

Contents

tions; J. A. Leo Lemay and P. M. Zall, eds., *Benjamin Franklin's Autobiography*

The Legacy of Ruskin: Two Recent Studies   161
   by Paul L. Sawyer
      Review of Tim Hilton, *John Ruskin: The Early Years, 1819–1859;* Gary Wihl, *Ruskin and the Rhetoric of Infallibility*

A Book about Paintings from Books   175
   by George P. Landow
      Review of Richard D. Altick, *Paintings from Books: Art and Literature in Britain, 1760–1900*

Emerson Bibliography: History and Audience   189
   by Albert J. von Frank
      Review of Robert E. Burkholder and Joel Myerson, *Emerson: An Annotated Secondary Bibliography;* Joel Myerson, *Ralph Waldo Emerson: A Descriptive Bibliography*

W. B. Yeats: Early Letters and His Library   205
   by Richard J. Finneran
      Review of John Kelly, ed., *The Collected Letters of W. B. Yeats: Volume One, 1865–1895;* Edward O'Shea, *A Descriptive Catalog of W. B. Yeats's Library*

Melville's Sexual Politics   215
   by Julian Markels
      Review of Robert K. Martin, *Hero, Captain and Stranger: Male Friendship, Social Critique, and Literary Form in the Sea Novels of Herman Melville*

Strine Literature from Sydney Harbour   231
   by Miriam J. Shillingsburg
      Review of William H. Wilde, Joy Hooten, and Barry Andrews, *The Oxford Companion to Australian Literature*

Contents

Whatever Self He Had: 241
The Canonization of Stevens Continues
  by R. D. Ackerman
    Review of Harold Bloom, ed., *Wallace Stevens;* Albert Gelpi, ed., *Wallace Stevens: The Poetics of Modernism;* Charles Doyle, ed., *Wallace Stevens, The Critical Heritage;* Milton Bates, *Wallace Stevens: A Mythology of Self;* Joan Richardson, *Wallace Stevens: The Early Years, 1879–1923*

On Leslie Stephen and the Art of Biography 265
  by Panthea Reid Broughton
    Review of Noel Annan, *Leslie Stephen: The Godless Victorian*

Chaucer's Debts in *Troilus and Criseyde* 277
  by Colin Wilcockson
    Review of Winthrop Wetherbee, *Chaucer and the Poets: An Essay on* Troilus and Criseyde

Classical Psychoanalytic Criticism 283
  by Andrew Gordon
    Review of Daniel Weiss, *The Critic Agonistes: Psychology, Myth, and the Art of Fiction*, eds. Eric Solomon and Stephen Arkin

The Satirists Swift and Pope Reassessed 295
  by Vincent Carretta
    Review of Allan Ingram, *Intricate Laughter in the Satire of Swift and Pope;* Ellen Pollak, *The Poetics of Sexual Myth: Gender and Ideology in the Verse of Swift and Pope*

Watching Our Language 301
  by David Simpson
    Review of Cleanth Brooks, *The Language of the American South;* Dennis Baron, *Grammar and Gender*

Contents

Providence and Poststructuralism   311
   by Roger B. Henkle
      Review of Barbara Hardy, *Forms of Feeling in Victorian Fiction;* Thomas Vargish, *The Providential Aesthetic in Victorian Fiction*

John Smith Whole   323
   by Everett Emerson
      Review of Philip L. Barbour, ed., *The Complete Works of Captain John Smith*, 3 vols.

New Puzzles over the Editing of   329
Tristram Shandy, A Response
   by Ian Campbell Ross

Correspondence   353

Contributors   355

Editorial Board

Felicia Bonaparte
City College, CUNY

Jerome H. Buckley
Harvard University

Paul Connolly
Yeshiva University

A. S. G. Edwards
University of Victoria

Ian Jack
Cambridge University

Robert Kellogg
University of Virginia

James R. Kincaid
University of Colorado

Cecil Y. Lang
University of Virginia

James B. Meriwether
University of South Carolina

Hershel Parker
University of Delaware

Martin Roth
University of Minnesota

George Stade
Columbia University

John L. Sharpe III
Duke University

G. Thomas Tanselle
John Simon Guggenheim Memorial Foundation

Stanley Weintraub
The Pennsylvania State University

"The people have set Literature free": The Professionalization of Letters in Nineteenth-Century England

Robert L. Patten

Nigel Cross. *The Common Writer: Life in Nineteenth-Century Grub Street.* Cambridge: Cambridge University Press, 1985, vi, 265 pp.

Nigel Cross's book on *The Common Writer* is the best account yet written about the conditions under which journeymen and -women writers in nineteenth-century Britain plied their trade. As his subtitle indicates, Cross, who identifies his occupation as "itinerant journalist" (p. vi), describes the lives of those who never reached the top ranks, artistically or financially.[1] Hitherto, accounts of what critics as diverse as Robert Escarpit, Raymond Williams, Richard Altick, and Diana Laurenson have characterized as the "sociology of authorship" have relied on data obtained from the *Cambridge Bibliography of English Literature* and the *Dictionary of National Biography*.[2] By using the evidence contained in the archive of the Royal Literary Fund, Cross expands that sample from several hundred middle- to upper-rank writers to some 3,000, ranging from famous authors such as Coleridge and Ouida down to Altick's "lowest stratum of hacks" (pp. 3–4). On the basis of the careers summarized in the applications to the Literary Fund for financial assistance, Cross concludes "that the prerequisites for literary success are education, social status, and monied leisure" (p. 5).

A conspectus of Cross's chapters will indicate his focus and concerns. The first narrates the history of the Royal Literary Fund from the time of its founding by David Williams during the last quarter of the eighteenth century to the period of its greatest controversy when, in the 1850s, Charles Dickens, abetted by

John Forster and the proprietor of the *Athenaeum*, Charles Wentworth Dilke, led a prolonged and unsuccessful campaign to reform the Fund's character and administration. The second chapter, "From Prisons to Pensions," identifies principal components of a "safety net" of institutions constituting an "informal welfare state for writers" (p. 6). The third looks at the Bohemian character and reputation which writers in Grub Street assumed and displayed as a kind of protective coloration for their perpetual indigence. The fourth, concentrating on working-class writers, selects a few representatives from "a relatively dismal catalogue" of personal histories blighted by "inadequate and cavalier patronage, groundless optimism and commercial failure" (p. 126). A fifth chapter surveys another literary minority, women writers, who often found that their limited educational and employment opportunities doomed them to scribbling not very remunerative pot-boilers. The narrative of these two chapters is especially influenced by the vitas included in applications to the Literary Fund. In the final chapter, Cross looks at *New Grub Street*—not only Gissing's novel and prototypes of the writers portrayed therein, but also the rapidly changing conditions of authorship brought about by technological innovations, syndication, expanding readership, the rise of the literary agent, and above all the proliferation of journalism. During the last decades of the century writers had more outlets for their work than ever before, but Cross shows that the marketplace had divided into high-brow and middle-brow: "By the mid-1880s an irrevocable schism had occurred in the bourgeois literary world" (p. 216). Thus, he notes, the "great cultural debate" of the nineties was not about manifestations of decadence: "it was about art in the marketplace" (p. 215).

The term "bourgeois literary world" signals Cross's unemphatic, undoctrinaire, but pervasive Marxist/socialist orientation.[3] The writers he surveys fail not because they do not understand their craft or because they are poor writers, but because they are poor. Deficient education, ill health, bankruptcy, disappointment, and alcoholism are constants of life in Grub Street. Cross believes that the cobbler Joseph Blacket never soared above the level of a minor Cowper "because his talents were half-starved through lack of learning, and his health undermined by hard work" (p. 130). Women frequently took up their pens in order to support a ruined husband and a large number of children. Mrs. Parsons, Sempstress in Ordinary to the Royal Household, began composing novels after her husband's business was destroyed by fire in 1782, "and in the course of 12 years," she reported to the Literary Fund in 1803, "have written 65 vols of Novels, under every disadvantage of Sickness, Indigence, never ceasing Anxiety and as many repeated misfortunes as human sufferance could well support" (p. 171).

Given this orientation, Cross's book focuses on the *lives* of writers, not on the technological, commercial, and legal revolutions in publishing, nor on the artistic developments in literature, that provided the conditions of authorship insofar as they were different from the conditions of simply surviving in nineteenth-century England. (Lack of education, poverty, and ill-health must surely have been nearly as handicapping to an aspiring clergyman, attorney, physician, engineer, or politician as to a writer.) In his conclusion, Cross concedes that "lasting literary success requires intense dedication and conviction, as well as talent," but he rather downplays the contribution of what the nineteenth-century would have called "genius" to literary survival. "There are," he maintains, "no good grounds for supposing that a Dickens or a D. H. Lawrence will pull through regardless, that genius will rise above neglect. . . . The bulk of what we call English Literature was written by people whose circumstances were both comfortable and conducive" (p. 240). The phrase "what we call English Literature" articulates Cross's skepticism about a canon defined by class values masquerading as academic standards.

Though it must be evident that I have some trouble with this orientation and its attendant simplifications, I find Cross's study both readable and valuable. He has investigated many sources, and made intelligent use not only of the Literary Fund archives but also of materials about the Guild of Literature and Art, about Civil List pensions, and about other charitable institutions such as the Newspaper Press Fund and the Charterhouse. He has a sure sense of the issues he identifies as important, and thus is able to sculpt his argument into recognizable segments, and to integrate telling quotations. He moves well between statistics that establish contexts and narratives of individual cases that are presented sympathetically but not polemically. He argues persuasively for the achievement of administrators like Octavian Blewitt, secretary of the Royal Literary Fund, and Walter Besant, founder of the Society of Authors. And he champions the works of unappreciated writers like Robert Bell and Robert Brough.

What is missing from this study, and from other accounts of nineteenth-century British writers and publishers, is the larger view of the significance of what John Gross has called "the rise of the man of letters."[4] Harold Perkin, in *The Origins of Modern English Society, 1780–1880*, has called attention to "the general rise in the status of the professional intellectual in society," noting that the "inordinately higher claims . . . made in the early nineteenth century for the importance and influence of authors" represent "a social emancipation of the intellectual and the artist exactly parallel to the birth of class."[5] Whereas in Perkin's formulation the rise of the artist and the rise of class structure parallel one another, for critics as diverse as Ian Watt and Nigel Cross authorship, and especially the writing of novels, comes out of and serves the middle-class. That writing became, in the nineteenth-century, an occupation at which increasing numbers could earn a living is a fact of considerable significance to sociologists, cultural historians, and literary critics alike.[6] But so far we have gathered more details than outlines, more narratives of individual careers and more compilations of statistics than studies of authorship that integrate theory, history, biography, and sociology with an understanding of how a literary text is created, published, and marketed and how its utterance might be shaped by the cultural conditions of its creation.[7]

Two recent books have attempted to provide this larger view, but both sketch out their theses as part of even larger concerns, and neither is fully comprehensive, especially about what difference it might make to see writers as part of a more general expansion and elevation of the class of intellectuals. T. W. Heyck, in *The Transformation of Intellectual Life in Victorian England*, maintains that the very concept of an "intellectual" is late nineteenth-century, and that the concept arose as a result of three overlapping developments: "(1) the rise of natural science; (2) the reform of the universities; and (3) the tradition of culturally-oriented criticism of society."[8] In his chapter on "The World of the Men of Letters, 1830s–1860s," Heyck identifies three conditions that affected all kinds of writers, but especially imaginative writers, during this period: first, dependence on an expanding market created by revolutions in publishing technology, an expanding middle-class with leisure, literacy, and disposable income, declining real costs of obtaining books, and the large sums that could be made by extremely successful writers from public patronage; second, the close relations between writers and their public, a closeness that extended to their professional and even to their personal lives, and that permitted successful authors to reach virtually the whole of the governing elite; and third, the widespread agreement among mid-Victorian writers that literature served what Heyck calls a "preaching function."[9]

Though these observations are sound and useful, none is explored in detail. Heyck is notably vague about the relation between writers and the marketplace. He says that most authors accepted their subordination to the demands of the market, and even gave helpful advice to beginners about self-discipline, hard work, and clean living: "Such middle-class values implictly [sic] rejected the romantics' notion of the artist as a genius seized by an uncontrollable inspiration."[10] Here Heyck seems to be at odds with Perkin: whereas for Perkin romantic claims for genius elevated the status of authors, for Heyck it is the rejection of those claims which gave Victorian writers access to power. Heyck is quick to move from a consideration of the marketplace to the question of class status for writers—their ambiguous inclusion within the shifting category of "gentlemen." He then goes on briefly to consider the controversy over the Guild of Literature and Art; on the mid-century quarrels about the "dignity of literature," Cross supplies a more ample, detailed, and accurate account. So though Heyck offers a valuable overview of the rise of the intellectual in nineteenth-century Britain, and thus relates trends in literature to trends in other spheres of intellectual life, especially in science and the universities, he neither explores the ramifications of this development in all its aspects with regard to literary production, nor considers the implications of this development with regard to the ways in which literature is read.

A second recent book providing an overview of the changing place of letters in nineteenth-century culture is Terry Eagleton's *The Function of Criticism from* The Spectator *to Post-Structuralism*.[11] Using Jürgen Habermas's concept of the "public sphere," Eagleton tracks the shifting relationship between it and criticism. He proposes that, in the eighteenth century, criticism arose in opposition to the absolutist state; critics, speaking to and from within an emerging bourgeois society, used the norms of reason and common sense to articulate the values and projects of that society. In the nineteenth century, criticism addressed public morality; its relationship to the hegemonic culture and the governing elite became more problematical as it became more critical of that culture and that elite, until it was sublimated in the name of disinterestedness into a marginalized (and therefore tolerated) home within, and speaking to, the academies. In the twentieth century, Eagleton concludes, the retreat of criticism from addressing public issues to addressing literary ones has resulted in "a handful of individuals reviewing each other's books," and the abandonment of criticism's older, broadly civilizing function.[12]

Eagleton thus connects the character—especially the economic character—of a society to its literary productions. In the shift from the eighteenth-century patronage system to nineteenth-century commodity capitalism, he discerns two factors that are significantly responsible for the gradual disintegration of the "classical public sphere":

[First], the mutation from literary patronage to the laws of the market marks a shift from conditions in which a writer might plausibly view his work as the product of collaborative intercourse with spiritual equals, to a situation in which the 'public' now looms as an anonymous yet implacable force, the object rather than co-subject of the writer's art. The second reason for the decline of the public sphere is a political one.... [The ruling class could not] withstand ... the inruption into it of social and political interests [e.g. working-class interests] in palpable conflict with its own 'universal' rational norms.[13]

For the Victorian man of letters, survival depended on his staking his intellectual assets on two incompatible grounds: that he was a sage whose synoptic vision could encompass all the phenomena of the age with a transcendental detachment (a version of Perkins' Romantic legacy), and that he was "a *bricoleur*, dilettante, jack-of-all-trades," dependent on the very commercial and self-interested hands that as sage he was sometimes obliged to bite (a version of Heyck's middle-class artisan).[14] Mid-century critics were conscripted into acculturating the growing "mass" of semi-literate readers to the dominant values of the bourgeoisie; but proliferating readership, as Cross also observes, first politically polarized, and then fragmented, the market, so that criticism spoke increasingly with a divided voice to segments of the public. Arnold's solution was to urge criticism to rise above questions of social utility, to enunciate a discipline of life derived from an analysis of past cultures. But that solution Eagleton finds "bogus": "the purity of . . . disinterestedness is the blankness of a cypher; [it proposes that] only by a drastic estrangement from social life can [criticism] hope to engage fruitfully with it."[15] Criticism gradually ceased to perform any kind of effective cultural advocacy, disappearing behind the university walls that Jude, and others who sought the secret for transforming a laborer into a gentleman, found so impenetrable.

Brilliant, abstract, and polemical, Eagleton's book rather oddly offers a Marxist reading in order to advocate a return to an idealized eighteenth-century social and literary contract. Its notions of the relationship between literature as commodity and the market, though formidably sophisticated in theory, are rather simplistic and deterministic in their sweeping generalizations. The very structure of his comparatively brief study (133 pages, covering three centuries of criticism) precludes his dealing with all the individual, personal, social, technological, and cultural factors that impinge on Victorian letters. Important for its overview and argument, *The Function of Criticism* is nonetheless a frankly partisan construction and not a complete account of the relation between professionalization and writing over the past two hundred years.

Regardless of what approach is taken towards redefining the place of the writer in society, it is clear that as the nineteenth century progressed, many British essayists, poets, dramatists, journalists, and novelists became full-time, career-oriented authors. That development took place over a long period of time, and is in itself a very complex story; it is also complexly related to other aspects of the advancement of the intellectual in nineteenth-century Europe. I am particularly interested in exploring one piece of that puzzle, and from a rather untheoretical perspective: what it might mean to understand British literature of this period as the product of a professionalizing cohort, a cohort that was not in all respects middle-class in background, income, or outlook, and that can only partially be identified with the other professions—law, medicine, engineering—that also gained their hegemony at the same time.

What is evident at the outset is that the notion of "professions," and of the writer's place therein, changed substantially between 1800 and 1900. Originally "to profess" meant to make a public declaration of one's faith, that is, to take the vows of a religious order; the earliest "professors" were clerics, and so from the beginning the term connoted an ideal of service to a cause greater than and apart from mere economic self-aggrandizement.[16] Somehow "profession" as a noun expanded in meaning and took on secular implications; by the eighteenth century it had come to mean "the occupation which one professes to be skilled in and to follow," or in Dr. Johnson's broader definition, any "calling, vocation, known employment." The three learned professions were divinity, law, and medicine, also called the "liberal" professions because the essential qualification for entry was not training or expertise but a classic liberal education, the education of a gentleman. Thus added to the ideal of disinterested service—"disinterested" in the sense of not primarily for personal gain, rather than in Matthew Arnold's later interpretation of "non-partisan"—were four further characteristics: (1) a profession was an occupation; (2) such an occupation depended on the acquisition of skill and learning; (3) prerequisite to entering the profession was a liberal education; and (4) professionals acquired through education and socialization, if not through birthright, the status, behavior, and ideology of a gentleman.[17]

In the nineteenth century, the concept ramified. Disinterested service often became a claim to work for the public weal, and from Arnold forward got disentangled from political parties, though not from small "l" liberalism.[18] Occupation implied a full-time job for which one got paid: a professional was "one who follows, by way of profession or business, an occupation generally engaged in as a pastime."[19] Professional knowledge came to be distinguished from that which the general public might acquire, and systems of education and certification were organized to register that expertise. But liberal education, apparently the antithesis of specialized training, remained the preferred initial course of study, and most nineteenth-century British professional associations supported the public school system, especially as reformed by Dr. Arnold and his followers, rather than a State system or university education.[20] Staunch conservatives like A. J. Beresford-Hope, defending their territory against incursions from the professionalizing classes, clung to university qualification: "A University education," he said in 1855, "makes a man."[21]

Professionalism became, in Britain, a way to *earn* admission to the class of gentlemen; it was a peculiarly Anglo-Saxon compromise between relatively stable stratifications of class and privilege based on birth and breeding, on the one hand, and the opportunities for economic and social advancement opened up by industrial bourgeois capitalism on the other. "What the older professions seem to have conceived of themselves as doing," W. J. Reader notes, "when they let in new members, was admitting educated gentlemen to small, self-governing groups of their social equals, to whom they would be personally known and by whom their fitness would be judged."[22]

Part of this "peculiarly Anglo-Saxon compromise" involved a radical shift in valuing service for hire. Whereas earlier centuries had devalued the "hireling" in contrast to the amateur, one who did something out of love and general rather than specific knowledge, Victorians began to respect the professional, one who was paid for his expertise, rather than the less proficient and less single-minded amateur. The growth and codification of Victorian sports contributed to this development; the United States, less dominated by the cult of the gentleman, advanced further along these lines than Britain. Henry Chadwick, editor of the weekly *Ballplayer's Chronicle,* wrote in the first chapter of his book *The Game of Baseball* (1868) that the professional player "not only requires an attentive study of the rules of the game, and of those special applications of them known as 'points,' together with perfect familiarity with each and every rule; but also a regular course of training, to fully develope [sic] the physical powers, in order to ensure the highest degree of skill in each and all of the several departments of the game."

Though professionals offered services for hire, in Britain they tried to construct buffers between practitioners and clients so that the fiscal aspects of the transaction did not seem to subvert the ideal of disinterested service and the conduct of a gentleman. "The specific aims of the professional project" in nineteenth-century England, Magali Larson asserts, were "income security and social responsibility."[23] Professional institutions developed a self-enforced code of ethics that regulated both what the professional could do and what the client could demand, while fees and payments were increasingly handled through an intermediary—the attorney's clerk, for example. At the same time, professionals aspired to control the marketplace through indirect but highly effective means: by claims to a higher standard of ethical conduct, by the appeal of furthering social goals, and especially by limiting entry through standards of qualification, achieved by prescribed courses of study, apprenticeship, and examination that were recognized and ratified by the State.[24] "By 1860," W. J. Reader continues,

> the elements of professional standing were tolerably clear. You needed a professional association to focus opinion, work up a body of knowledge, and insist upon a decent standard of conduct. If possible, and as soon as possible, it should have a Royal Charter as a mark of recogni-

tion. The final step, if you could manage it—it was very difficult—was to persuade Parliament to pass an Act conferring something like monopoly powers on duly qualified practitioners, which meant practitioners who had followed a recognized course of training and passed recognized examinations.[25]

Engineering is a good example of what was once a trade, and which became during the Victorian period a profession claiming to serve the public by means of acquired expertise guaranteed by certification and applied to Benthamite programs in the public interest.

Opportunities for professionals to enhance their social and economic standing were best when the clientele were unorganized, when the individual practitioner, acting as a member of an organized professional association, negotiated with each client acting alone. If the client also belonged to a strong institutional body, room for the professional to maneuver was lessened, and the claim for professional authority and autonomy was diminished.[26] The State, which in the nineteenth century fostered the monopoly powers of the professions, in the twentieth has become a chief client of, and a principal threat to, professional independence.

Romantic writers left no legacy of professionalism. They did not often declare writing to be their occupation, they frequently disclaimed the status of gentleman which might have been theirs by birthright (Byron, Shelley) but which was ideologically inappropriate, their journalism and criticism came to be identified with particular political orientations as expressed in Whig or Tory periodicals, they rarely instituted buffers between themselves and their paymasters (indeed Scott disastrously conflated the roles of writer and publisher), they attacked one another more frequently than they collaborated to articulate the values and aspirations of writers as a group, and they certainly did not organize in order to regulate themselves. Authors parted with their copyrights on comparatively casual terms, and lived, for the most part, in enmity with their publishers. Samuel Rogers, banker by profession and poet by avocation, grumbled that to make literature the business of life was to make it a drudgery.

Coleridge advised, "*never pursue literature as a trade*," and Charles Lamb warned Bernard Barton not to give up his bank job and try to live by his writings alone.[27] Virtually no one could, except Southey. Writers had to have another source of income as parsons, lawyers, civil servants, farmers, or persons of independent means.[28] Lacking such resources, the common writer, and even on occasion the uncommon one, had to turn to the Royal Literary Fund for a handout, and as Southey pointed out in an attack published by John Murray in the September 1812 *Quarterly Review*, the Fund distributed its pittances with patronizing ostentation and self-congratulation.[29]

Just a glance at the list of Victorian authors whose income derived primarily from their writing, editing, and lecturing dramatizes the difference: Douglas Jerrold, Dickens, Ainsworth, Thackeray, Tennyson, Hardy, Wilkie Collins, G. P. R. James, George Augustus Sala, George Eliot, George Henry Lewes, Harriet Martineau, Carlyle—one could go on and on, and with Cross's help, reach down into the lower end of Grub Street for additional, though much less heartening, instances. True, some authors continued to depend on family income—Browning and Ruskin, for example—or another job—Arnold, Trollope, Meredith. Conversely, and for the first time ever in significant numbers, authors could depend on writing as their only job. Women kept themselves and their families on publishers' remittances: Eliza Lynn Linton, Fanny Trollope, Mrs. Oliphant, Mrs. Gore, and Mrs. Norton.[30] Writers still could, and did, starve: Laman Blanchard cut his throat, John Poole shivered in a Parisian garret, Leigh Hunt sponged off his friends, and Theodore Hook ended his days in grinding poverty. Nigel Cross's case-histories of Grub Street Bohemians, working-class poets, and middle-class female novelists add considerably to our knowledge of authorial privation. Dickens, who, though he escaped such toils, knew hardship as a boy and tried to relieve it as a man, observed to his friend the Baroness Burdett Coutts: "Men have been chained to hideous prison walls and other strange anchors 'ere now, but few have known such suffering and bitterness at one time or other, as those who have been bound to Pens."[31]

But, and the point bears repeating, for the first time in Western culture substantial numbers of writers could, and did, make an adequate living at least some of the time, "bound to Pens." The overwhelming profusion of Victorian literature is partly the product of a literary revolution that gave authors a fighting chance to stay solvent through writing. Trollope freely confessed: "I write for money. Of course I do;—as does [the critic] also—It is for money that we all work, lawyers, publishers, authors and the rest of us."[32] (The contradiction between Trollope's frank avowal of mercenary motives for authorship and his fictional ideal of a gentleman illustrates the difficulty of trying to relate the conditions under which literature was produced to the ideology it expresses.)

The reasons why it became possible, in the mid-nineteenth century in England, to make a living by writing are complex, as Heyck and his predecessors have recognized.[33] Mechanization of book production made larger editions practical and cheap; rising real wages and the spread of literacy encouraged the purchase of books; reliable transportation on land and by sea opened new markets in the provinces and abroad; middle-class leisure had to be filled with some activity; changes in the legal status of authors through the 1842 copyright reforms finally assured some writers who were well-enough off not to sell their copyrights outright a lifetime interest in their works.[34] As Cross shows in several contexts, however, legal provisions making copyright more favorable to authors were of little advantage to the working poor, who sold their manuscripts to obtain bread and pay the rent. "The whole concept of authorship, implying intellectual property, copyright and contractual obligations," Cross notes, "was irrelevant to street literature" (p. 126).

These are fascinating developments, intricately interrelated, and they would repay further study. England became more favorable to the development of authorship than Germany, France, or the United States, in part, John Sutherland believes, because the artificially high price maintained in England on certain kinds of books guaranteed authors £300–£400 per work, a modest but sufficient annual income. Cross's statistics suggest that at the lower range prices per title were considerably less, and the hardships proportionately greater. In America, conversely, democratic ideals and sharp practice combined to produce inexpensive books in large quantities, books often reprinted in newspapers or cheap volume editions from European sources without any royalty payment to the authors.[35] It was difficult in the United States for native authors to compete with European writers whose works were freely available to American publishers.

Thus Victorian authors were professional in the sense that they were paid, not amateurs scribbling for the love of writer's cramp. The number of British citizens recorded in the decennial censuses as following the "Professional Occupation" of "Author" (authors, editors, shorthand writers, and journalists) rose from 167 in 1841 to 3,434 in 1881 and to 13,786 in 1911—the dramatic increase being attributable substantially to the growth of journalism.[36] Of those, Cross estimates that twenty percent were female (p. 167). But the more interesting development is writers' self-conscious promulgation of themselves *as* professionals. The phrase "author by profession" seems to have gained currency towards the middle of the eighteenth century. Certain writers of the period, because of their devotion to their calling and the proportion of their income derived from writing, have been called "professional"—Pope, Fielding, and Johnson in particular.[37] But few writers *thought* of themselves as professionals before the second quarter of the nineteenth century.

What they meant by the term, however, is unclear. Whether one inclines to the definitions of "profession" offered by members of the "traits" school of analysis, or opts for a "functional" or "structural" approach, many of the features prominent in the older professions of ministry, law, and medicine, and emerging in the newer professions of military service, engineering, and teaching, simply are inapplicable to writers. There was no educational qualification for entrance, nor any system of certification. Cross insists that a lack of education hindered working-class writers and women. But exceptional talent—a qualification that Cross slights—could override the differences between the Cambridge education of Thackeray and the few years of schooling Dickens received, or between the formidable self-education

George Eliot managed to obtain and the restricted curriculum Charlotte Brontë studied.[38] Nor was apprenticeship in Grub Street any guarantee of eventually entering into the ranks of the masters: it could lead to respectability and fame, to a life of hand-to-mouth journalism and editing, or to collapse from overwork and underpay. And neither the number of practitioners, nor the size or character of the market, could very effectively be controlled by a single writer, or even by a single editor.[39]

On the other hand, some of the behavior exhibited by many Victorian writers does seem to emulate that of their professional brethren. Senior writers could and did, in a variety of ways, help their juniors into prominence: Dickens and Mark Lemon, the editor of *Punch*, are representative if exceptionally successful examples. In collaboration with publishers and wholesale book dealers such as W. H. Smith, George Routledge, and Mudie, authors did try to define and expand the marketplace and to control some aspects of distribution. "The organizations by men of letters which *were* effective," Heyck notes, "were conventional trade associations aimed at improving the position of authors within the market systems—organizations with friendly publishers to break the price-setting monopoly of the London booksellers, and the Society of Authors (established in 1883), which worked mainly on copyright law."[40] He might have added that authors were instrumental, especially through their social contacts with M.P.s, in obtaining the passage of the 1842 Copyright Act as well.

However, the "service orientation" and "ethical standards" of professionals were often for writers—as sometimes for others—compromised by financial exigency, by overriding claims for artistic integrity, and by unorthodox life-styles and values. By the 1880s some writers had by their public conduct and moral teachings established their claims to be spokespersons for the middle-class and respectability, but others were still stigmatized by the designation "artist"—a fact which Oscar Wilde enjoyed turning against the stigmatizers. As T. H. S. Escott, press historian and editor of the *Fortnightly Review*, put it: "The keen-scented, eminently decorous British public perceives a certain aroma of social and moral laxity in the atmosphere of the studio, a kind of blended perfume of periodical impecuniosity and much tobacco-smoke."[41]

Perhaps, as Burton J. Bledstein argues, professionalization was just another vehicle for moving into the middle class.[42] But some Victorian writers when they struggled to articulate and enact their values seem to have meant more than that. Bernard Barber's functional analysis of traits has been criticized for its ahistoricism, for its uncritical acceptance of the professionals' rationalizations of their status, and for its refusal to acknowledge, as Terence Johnson puts it, that "a profession is not . . . an occupation, but a means of controlling an occupation."[43] Nonetheless, the four attributes of a profession that Barber identifies provide a framework for comparing authors' *views of their status* to those promulgated by the more established professionals. These attributes, or traits, are:

(1) a high degree of generalized and systematic *knowledge*;
(2) a primary orientation to the *community interest* rather than to individual self-interest;
(3) a high degree of self-control of behavior through *codes of ethics*;
(4) a system of rewards that includes honors as well as money and that establishes a set of symbols for work achievement; what I would call *peer recognition*.[44]

Loosely applied, each of these conceptions—knowledge, community interest, codes of ethics, and peer recognition—illuminates aspects of what Victorian writers were trying to do for themselves.

It is clear, to take the first trait, that writers express *generalized* knowledge, but not nearly so clear that at any time they possessed or disseminated *systematic* knowledge. But with the post-Enlightenment collapse of hegemonic Christian ontology and epistemology, writers began constructing their own systems of belief: Blake, Wordsworth, Coleridge, Shelley, and Keats come immediately to mind. The next generations of British writers—Carlyle, Ruskin, Tennyson, Arnold, George Eliot, George Meredith—continued, amplified, and extended the claims of their predecessors to possess a special *kind* of knowledge, a specialized knowledge *of particular things*, and a mastery over the *craft* of writing. The special *kind* of knowledge, deriving from German idealist philosophy, Goethe, and Coleridge, was articulated by Carlyle, who asserted that the writer might possess a penetrating and resonant vision which made him a Vates, a seer or prophet, one through whom divine purposes were transmitted and whose insight could interpret the spirit of the age: ten silent centuries found their tongue in Dante and Shakespeare.[45] Scholars and critics have long emphasized the visionary character of Victorian literature. Jerome Hamilton Buckley stresses Tennyson's mystic vision, and E. D. H. Johnson explores the *Alien Vision of Victorian Poetry*, that private, often unorthodox set of beliefs and values which came into conflict with public duties. John Holloway has characterized the prophetic voices employed by the Victorian sages.[46] Ruskin translocates the vatic power from utterance to vision: "To see clearly is poetry, prophecy, and religion,—all in one."[47] But however it is expressed, the Victorian assertion that the artist is gifted with a special and privileged kind of knowledge reinforces and canonizes the Romantic claims for elevating the status of art which Harold Perkin sees as one of the factors promoting the emancipation of the artist in the nineteenth century.

What have been less often stressed are two other dimensions of Victorian writers' knowledge: their learning on the one hand, and their craftsmanship on the other. Victorian writers swotted up the most arcane knowledge: Browning's *Yellow Book*, Arnold's Persian epics, Charles Reade's scrapbooks filled with the most extraordinary miscellaneous information, George Eliot's notebooks for *Middlemarch* and research for *Romola*, Swinburne's unmatched knowledge of Greek poetry and Jacobean drama. This drive to master specialized bodies of knowledge differs in some ways from the efforts of earlier authors who, while prodigiously learned, worked within a tradition of knowledge common to philosophers, theologians, politicians, painters, *and* poets. The corpus of Renaissance humanism that informed Erasmus and More, the corpus of Christian teaching that informed Chaucer and Spenser and Donne and Swift, was a universal culture, common at least among the educated. Victorian writers, like Victorians in other fields, claimed *specialized* knowledge: not only visionary glimmerings but also expertise in diverse subjects, periods, and languages.

The other thing many Victorian authors claimed was a knowledge of their craft. Tennyson, it is said, knew the quantity of every English word except *scissors*; Gerard Manley Hopkins reviewed the history of poetic meters; Dickens boasted that he understood the peculiar requirements of serial publication better than anyone else. Artists before 1850 had defended their craftsmanship: Shakespeare and Pope implicitly, Johnson and Fielding explicitly. But the chorus of Victorian voices saying to one auditor or another, in prefaces, letters, speeches, essays, and reviews, that they know how to make a literary artifact, how to compose it and shape it to an audience, even how to market it, swells until it culminates in such divergent but representative utterances as George Henry Lewes's *The Principles of Success in Literature* (1865), George Bainton's *The Art of Authorship* (1890), and Henry James's Prefaces to the New York Edition (1907–09).

Barber's second trait, a concern for the public weal, is one that many commentators have selected to discriminate naked self-interest from that more mixed set of motives distinguished by the term "professional." We can hardly overemphasize the earnestness with which some Victorian writers cautioned and enjoined their society. Carlyle, Mill, Dickens, George Eliot, Ruskin and others felt it their duty to address the public on the issues of the day, to speak, not only or even primarily from the impulse of private vision, but also and especially for the public good. Many Victorian writers, especially novelists, journalists, and editors, justified their activity by appeals to furthering the public welfare at least as often as they appealed to personal inspiration or partisan political causes.

Authors also began to organize around common interests and to free themselves from dependence on patrons, aspects of Barber's third trait characterizing professionals. Preternaturally sensitive about patronage, Dickens expressed himself with characteristic gusto about the liberation Victorian writers had experienced:

From the shame of the purchased dedication, from the scurrilous and dirty work of Grub Street, from the dependent seat on sufferance at my Lord Duke's table today, and from the sponging-house and Marshalsea tomorrow, from that venality which, by a fine moral retribution, has degraded statesmen even to a greater extent than authors, because the statesman entertained a low belief in the universality of corruption, while the author yielded only to the dire necessity of his calling,—from all such evils the people have set Literature free.[48]

What Dickens did not say in this 1853 talk, what he may not even have foreseen, was the eventual segmentation of the market and its imprisoning effect on writers: one kind of public demanding one kind of book, such as escapist fiction for the circulating libraries, while another demanded a quite different kind, say high-minded essays and fictions for an academicized intelligentsia. Cross addresses some of the problems growing out of that segmentation of the market in his last chapter, as does Eagleton in his sections on the fate of nineteenth-century criticism.

Victorian authors wanted professional organizations that were self-constituted, self-financed, and self-directed.[49] One such effort commenced in 1843, when Dickens, stung by American response to his call for an international copyright agreement, convened on 25 March the first Society of British Authors. The aims were vague: to secure further copyright protection and the enforcement of existing laws, and to establish a corresponding society. The Prospectus which the Society circulated elicited a good many replies, of which the most favorable came from the redoubtable Harriet Martineau:

I do think a society of authors desirable, and I do see it to be my duty to assist if possible in establishing it.
 The field of beneficent operation . . . seems to me almost boundless. The objects indicated in your prospectus—so various and so important—make one wonder how one can have gone on so long suffering under evils which union might ere this have obviated, and deprived of advantages which union might long ago have secured.[50]

Others were not so confident. Dickens dropped out shortly, "as well convinced of its inevitable hopelessness as if I saw it written by a Celestial Penman in the book of Fate."[51] Walter Besant, who in 1883 founded the Society of Authors, spoke scornfully of its predecessor's failures:

They began, in fact, with an impossible theory: that authorship is a profession as distinct as law or medicine; and that it is possible to unite its members, as those called to the Bar are united, into a guild or company governed by its own laws. At the most, authorship is a collection of professions. . . . There is one thing, and one thing only, for which those who write books and papers which are sold can possibly unite—viz., their material interests.[52]

Between 1843 and 1883 other efforts to organize authors into professional associations that were more than charitable foundations likewise fizzled. The Guild of Literature and Art, for which Dickens and Bulwer-Lytton worked so hard, was eventually incorporated under an Act of Parliament, but when the homes for retired artists were completed on land near Stevenage, no one wanted to occupy them, even rent-free. To the artists of mid-century, charity from more successful practitioners was even less acceptable than charity from the Privy Purse. In his first two chapters Cross traces the history of a number of institutions that tried to provide artists with an alternative to debtors' prison, and he supplies the best account yet, though it is still incomplete, of the mid-century struggles over the charter of the Literary Fund and the mission of the Guild of Literature and Art.

As Besant observed, authors' unions aimed less at promoting the public welfare than at improving the lot of their members, or rather, as Cross's book repeatedly reminds us, the lot of their middle-class members. Often, as in other professionalizing organizations, the rationale of public service concealed more fundamental private interests. These early authors' societies in complex ways also attempted to set standards of ethics and canons of procedure, and thus appear to operate according to Barber's third trait, self-regulation. But authors were more often motivated by efforts to regulate others—and especially the book trade—than themselves. They sought out legal and accounting assistance to arm them in their struggles against rapacious and secretive publishers, who yielded up their ledgers only under duress. In alliance with some publishers, writers successfully opposed the net book agreement, which prohibited retailers from discounting books. Systems of arbitration for disputed accounts became common features of contracts by the 1870s. And a number of laws and judicial decisions covering copyright through the Victorian period clarified doubtful points of conduct, made statutory declarations of rights, and materially assisted the continuing endeavor to enable authors to earn a living from their pens. Before mid-century, John Forster was acting as unofficial agent for Dickens, interposing between the author and his publishers in a largely successful effort to wrest more favorable terms on the one hand, while on the other distancing Dickens from the crass commercial bargaining. George Henry Lewes came to function in analogous ways for George Eliot. By the end of the century A. P. Watt, William Morris Colles, J. Eveleigh Nash, and James Brand Pinker had set up businesses as full-time authors' agents.[53]

Though the progressive regulation of conduct within the publishing world had largely to do with securing better market terms, the professionalization of letters also led to changes in writers' attitudes toward their own conduct. Artistic license gave way, in many instances, to bourgeois respectability; the poet's eye in a fine frenzy rolling to the dignity and honor of the literary profession. Dickens chided Thackeray for satirizing his fellow authors, rather complacently urging his own example by contrast: "In all my social doings I am mindful of this honour and dignity and always try to do something towards the quiet assertion of their [writers'] right place. I am always possessed with the hope of leaving the position of literary men in England, something better and more independent than I found it."[54] The three quarrels in which Dickens participated in 1858—with the Literary Fund, at the Garrick Club, and with his publishers Bradbury and Evans—were all the direct result of the assertion by some of a new status and code of behavior for authors, a professional behavior marked by self-restraint, dignity, and unimpeachable public ethics.[55]

There was a certain amount of humbug and hypocrisy in

Dickens' professionalism. His defenses of his authorial integrity sometimes masked self-interest, and often stemmed from his sensitivity to his lower-class background and his desire to be accepted into the middle-classes. Trollope exposed the commercial motives in his satire on Dickens as Mr. Popular Sentiment in *The Warden* (1855), and in his *Autobiography* implicitly rebuked the sometimes self-serving rhetoric of professional service and conduct. There were other authors who reacted to mid-century efforts to establish the dignity and honor of letters: on the one side, the Bohemians of Fleet and Grub Street, radicals and arrivistes, people like Douglas Jerrold and George Augustus Sala, and on the other, people like A. J. Beresford-Hope and Fitzjames Stephen, cultural and political conservatives who wrote for the *Saturday Review* and who, as Cross characterizes them, "wished to preserve the amateur, gentlemanly and classical status of English literature" (p. 97).

Finally, to take Barber's fourth point, Victorian writers developed an extensive range of peer recognitions to complement their new wealth. Writers became patrons in their own right, and sat on boards of charitable organizations; they were elected to membership in committees and academies and clubs; they were invited to country-house weekends and asked to run for Parliament; they were presented to the Queen, decorated, ennobled. They became celebrities, and used that celebrity to make further money by lecturing, though John Forster grumbled that it was beneath the dignity of an author to show himself in public as a performing mountebank.[56]

An important part of this alternate rewards system was reviews. Earlier generations of writers, who did not depend greatly on public sales for their income, were seldom made or broken by reviews. Good notices, especially from patrons, helped of course; but not until the *Edinburgh* and the *Quarterly* began in the first quarter of the nineteenth century did writers depend on reviews. If the public set Literature free, it also in new ways bound writers to their pens. Keats may not have been killed by a review, nor Tennyson silenced; but reviews made some difference, both to sales and to that bubble reputation. And Victorian writers were not always so armed with cynicism as Jaques.

Unmistakably, the character of reviewing changed during the century. The magisterial, partisan, vituperative, and dogmatic evaluations served up in the first decades continued in the *Westminster Review* and the *Saturday Review*, but not all notices were so weighty. Grub Street was sustained by hacks who "got up" a factitious familiarity with any subject, and slashed or lauded depending on their editor's instructions. To appropriate Eagleton's notion of the hybrid critic, the sage frequently hacked his adversaries, and the hack borrowed the robes and authority of the sage. In *Illusions Perdues* (1837–43) Balzac chronicles the interrelationship between reviewing, politics, notoriety, and literature in Paris of the 1820s; Thackeray depicts the Bohemian reviewers at work and hard-drinking play in *Pendennis* (1848–50); and Trollope shows in Lady Carbury of *The Way We Live Now* (1874–75) a writer who solicits favorable commentary by exercising her personal charms and her social connections. It is hard to comprehend the force and relevance of Arnold's standard of "disinterestedness" without knowing how polemical, irresponsible, vicious, and inconsequential mid-century reviews could be. The unwritten canons of ethics that middle-class writers often observed also extended by the end of the century to the most influential reviewers; expertise rather than amateurism became a qualification, and if the resulting assessment damned rather than praised, it often did so with the authority of a George Eliot or a Housman.

Not all authors aspired to all these aspects of professionalization. There are exceptions among the majors, the Brontë sisters and Robert Browning and Matthew Arnold, and there is a whole secessionist movement from the Pre-Raphaelites through William Morris. The lower end of Grub Street persisted in its disreputable, expedient way, while working-class writers, though perhaps enjoying some additional advantages from the general rise in the status, opportunities, and rewards of a career in letters, rarely had the chance to adopt a professional style or code of conduct. The eponymous heroes of Charles Kingsley's *Alton Locke* and of Robert Brough's *Marston Lynch* exemplify, as Cross points out, representative histories of working-class and Bohemian writers, respectively: Locke goes to prison for his Chartist activities, and Lynch fails as an editor because of his self-destructive attacks on thin-skinned fellow authors. Neither is ever elected to a committee, presented to the Queen, or insulated from direct participation in the market-place by a literary agent. As J. W. Saunders puts it, "The literary profession of the nineteenth century embraced, side by side, idealists and frauds, honest professionals and dishonest amateurs, men of unquestionable genius and men of the most questionable ingenuity, a complex scene which became even more complicated as the mass market evolved."[57]

Professionalism, then, does not so much describe the emerging status of Victorian authors as it identifies an interlocking set of principles and practices which some authors, for various reasons, adopted at some times. If we understand that professionalism was neither monolithic nor mandated among writers at any period during the century—if we see the adoption or rejection of an identity as a professional as one chosen or enforced by circumstance, personality, and chance—then the melange of attitudes towards the vocation of letters becomes more comprehensible as a range of options, not a uniform set of conditions or codes. It is the absence of such choices, Cross believes, that plagues impecunious authors, while in *New Grub Street* Gissing anatomizes the social, moral, and economic consequences of those choices.

Why should students of literature care whether authors chose to adopt professional attitudes, principles, and practices? Does it matter to the interpretation of Meredith's lyrics that he spent his life as a reader for Chapman and Hall? Do we understand Dickens better or differently because he helped to found the Guild of Literature and Art? Does Tennyson's support for the Society of Authors affect his persona as Poet Laureate? Are Hardy's opportunities to earn a living as a writer enlarged or constricted by the conditions of authorship and publication emerging in the 1880s and 1890s?

In at least four ways the professionalization of letters impinges on the study of Victorian literature: it alters authors' relationships to their texts, it helps to define their sense of themselves in society, it shapes the voice through which they address that society, and it affects the choice of subjects and role models portrayed in their works.

Authors' professional concerns extended first and foremost to their own writings. Whereas earlier generations had sold copyright outright for a pittance, after 1842 writers could, and sometimes did, part only with a lease on their literary property, and thus could control their publications for as long as forty-two years. This control made a difference to their income, which in later years might be cushioned by back sales and reprint editions. It also made a difference to their attitude toward their texts. John Sutherland demonstrates that "many of the great novels of the period which appear to be the unaided product of creative genius were often . . . the outcome of collaboration, compromise or commission [by publishers]."[58] The converse is equally true. Victorian writers took an unprecedented interest in every aspect of the publication and distribution of their works: they advised about format, the color of endpapers and wrappers, the price, the reprints, overseas licenses, dramatic adaptations; they made extensive changes in galley and page proof, had trial editions printed (Tennyson kept his poems in this stage for months), inserted stop-press corrections and required stereotypes to be altered, commissioned and canceled illustrations, published not only novels but also poems serially, and revised their texts in new editions for domestic and foreign markets.

We are just beginning to explore the implications of this kind of professionalism. Notions of copy-text based on Elizabethan models and Platonic ideals of a single version that best represents authorial intention do not easily apply to texts altered by their authors over several decades.[59] Thackeray, for reasons that have yet to be adduced, altered words, phrases, and paragraphs, and even canceled an illustration, after *Vanity Fair* was cast in stereotype.[60] Dickens did not decide on the number of chapters in *Oliver Twist* until 1846, nine years and four editions after the novel's serial run.[61] *In Memoriam* got more stanzas and an altered order in later printings; and the *Idylls of the King* was developed and expanded from 1859, when the first four idylls were issued, to the year before Tennyson's death, 1891.[62] The texts of Meredith's, Hardy's, and James's early novels were so extensively revised for later editions that it is almost impossible now to produce one authoritative reading. We need to be much more aware than we have been of the extent to which Victorians, knowledgeable about their craft and professional in their approach to publishing, devoted themselves to the most minute aspects of their text and its transmission.

Second, writers who aspired to professional status often adopted the customs and pursuits, if not all the ideology, of the middle-class. They bought large homes and put their sons down for places in public schools. Some amassed large fortunes, hoping thereby to ensure that the next generation could live like gentlemen. Trollope bought his son a share in Chapman and Hall, so that he might enjoy dividends earned largely on the continuing sale of Dickens's novels. George Eliot provides an example of a writer who, while violating some aspects of the dominant social code, otherwise lived a life of such rectitude, and endorsed in most of her fictions such an unexceptionable morality, that in the end she was venerated by a major segment of the bourgeoisie. Thomas Hardy, Rudyard Kipling, and Bernard Shaw in their transformations from itinerant hack journalists of no fixed address to country squires and grand old men, trace a curve characteristic of many successful professional authors, especially towards the close of the century, when journalism was less a dead-end, hand-to-mouth occupation than it had been. What looks like Dickens's snobbery, or Kipling's opportunistic jingoism, from the perspective of Romantic ideals of integrity, or even like unadulterated materialism, takes on additional implications when seen in the light of general professional aspirations. At the very least a fuller acquaintance with the conditions of authorship and the nature of Victorian professionalism would correct such simplistic formulations as the recent observation that Dickens hated the "foremost representatives and furthering agents [of capitalism], the men who live for personal aggrandizement and profit," and took for granted "the benign possibilities of capitalism."[63] The ambivalent critique of the economic foundations of Victorian culture embedded in much Victorian literature was inscribed by writers who earned their way into a class which was both a part of and apart from the mainstream. The ambiguities of professionalism are embodied both in the lives and in the works of those authors.

Third, Victorian writers addressed their society as professionals, wrapping the mantle of *secular sanctity* around their pronouncements. Not all of them, not all the time, of course: the notion is equally inapplicable to *Three Men in a Boat* and "The Higher Pantheism in a Nutshell." But major authors, in major works, speak not only with a vatic voice, but also with a professional one. There is a claim to knowing one's business, to working for the public good, to being a person of integrity, common sense, wisdom, and compassion. "Secular sanctity" is an apposite term, and applies to Tennyson, Browning, and Arnold as well as to Dickens, Thackeray, George Eliot, Meredith, and Hardy. One has more trouble with the playwrights: Douglas Jerrold, Tom Taylor, and Dion Boucicault belong in part to an earlier conception of authorship—slap-dash, fun-loving, irrepressible if not irresponsible, passionate but not necessarily persuasive. But Reade, with his attacks on such evils as the prison system, and Robertson with *Caste,* prepare the way for the theater of Ibsen and Shaw, and the mockeries of Gilbert and Wilde, which could not have existed had there not been by the 1880s a solid tradition of earnest reform-minded Victorian drama.

Further explorations of the collective persona adopted by nineteenth-century writers speaking as professionals might supply useful amendments to our current notions about the prophetic voice. These authors sound as much like lawyers, doctors, and ministers as they do like Isaiah or St. Paul. Thackeray compares his calling to a preacher's. To Coral Lansbury, Trollope sounds like a lawyer, and to Juliet McMaster, like a professor:

> Trollope reminds one often of an accommodating lecturer, a personal presence responding to the needs of a present audience, humorous often, and patient and engagingly concerned with his students' full understanding of the subject in hand. Are you with me? Am I going too fast? Shall I explain that again? Don't hesitate to ask a question. Such is the tone behind the narration.[64]

As criticism of Victorian fiction turns to examining the problematics of narrative voice, its oscillation between distanced objectivity and sympathetic subjectivity, an understanding of the voice employed by professional clergymen, doctors, and lawyers during the era—at least as they are portrayed in the literature—may provide illuminating analogies to authorial strategies of utterance.

Finally, the professionalization of letters had important consequences for the kinds of subjects and figures treated in Victorian literature. Is the absence of working-class subjects, even from authors born into the working-class, complexly related to professional aspirations? George Gissing and Arthur Morrison would be interesting instances to study. Is the changed focus of Victorian art also related? Romantic poets, as recent critics may have overemphasized, are ontological; Victorians are sociological. Mythic constructs are replaced by epics of a culture. And where Romantic novels were ethical and political, Victorian three-deckers are vocational. Victorian authors, assimilating some of the authority of their fellow professionals, become the diagnosticians of society, interpret society's laws, and preach conversion.

Their images of themselves within these texts may not always be *as* artists. It is Arthur the Statesman, not Merlin the Magician, who is Tennyson's "ideal manhood closed in real man." Browning's Pope, not the professional legal rhetoricians, best addresses the moral and epistemological issues in *The Ring and the Book*. Lydgate the doctor, and Dinah Morris the preacher, adumbrate, however fallibly, callings which can save mankind. The obsessional energy with which Dickens satirizes ministers, lawyers, and doctors reflects his sense that these professions had a special mission: in a diseased state, the Allen Woodcourts are our only hope. For Dickens such conventional artists as Miss La Creevy and Henry Gowan have no potential to reform their world. The models he offers in the late novels are variations on the figure of Daniel Doyce, an engineer who has harnessed his vision to practice, who works steadily and ethically for the benefit of others:

The ingenious [Doyce] was a man of great modesty and good sense; and, though a plain man, had been too much accustomed to combine what was original and daring in conception with what was patient and minute in execution, to be by any means an ordinary man.[65]

It is Doyce's misfortune, as Dickens perceived it to be to a degree his own, to have become, as one who is "original and daring in conception" and "patient and minute in execution," a public offender—not by being guilty, as accused, of "murder, manslaughter, arson, forgery, swindling, housebreaking, highway robbery, larceny, conspiracy, [or] fraud," but by "trying to turn his ingenuity to his country's service."[66]

It may be to such characters and such passages that we should turn for an image of the artist working in and for society in Victorian literature. James Kincaid disagrees: "Doyce is not only too limited to represent the creative mind; he is, in many ways, its antithesis. He is merely clear; he is not joyous, resilient, imaginative, or, in any real sense, creative."[67] But Kincaid appears to harbor Romantic notions about the defining characteristics of the artist, ideas about creativity and its limitless energy and vision more appropriate to Blake, Coleridge, and Shelley than to George Eliot or Hardy. The truth may be that authors like Dickens married the earlier claims to status based on "genius" to the Carlylean virtue of hard work, and projected as an ideal in their writing a portrait of the artist as professional.

By concentrating more on how Victorian writers saw themselves as professionals, how they conducted their affairs, insisted on the relevancy and accuracy of their knowledge, cooperated with their colleagues, sought self-regulation and honors, and wrested control of their own works, we can better identify and explain those models of conduct that are proposed within the literature. We might also be better able to define and enjoy that ideal of the knowledgeable, sympathetic, sensible, wise, and ethical voice by which, at their best, Victorian authors spoke to their age, and to ours.[68]

Notes

1. Only references to Cross will be identified parenthetically within my text.
2. Robert Escarpit, *Sociology of Literature*, trans. Ernest Pick (Painesville, Ohio: Lake Erie College Studies, Vol. IV [1958], 1965); Raymond Williams, *The Long Revolution* (New York: Columbia Univ. Press, 1961); Richard D. Altick, "The Sociology of Authorship," *BNYPL*, 66 (1962), 389–404; Diana F. Laurenson, "A Sociological Study of Authorship," *British Journal of Sociology*, 20 (September 1969), 311–25, and with Alan Swingewood, *The Sociology of Literature* (London: MacGibbon and Kee, 1972).
3. I have tried to employ terminology consistent with nineteenth-century usage and with the range of implications discussed by Raymond Williams in *Keywords: A Vocabulary of Culture and Society* (New York: Oxford Univ. Press, 1976).
4. John Gross, *The Rise and Fall of the Man of Letters: Aspects of English Literary Life since 1800* (London: Weidenfeld and Nicolson, 1969). Gross's book is more anecdotal than analytic.
5. (London: Routledge & Kegan Paul; Toronto: Univ. of Toronto Press, 1969), pp. 255–56.
6. The bibliography is immense, but in addition to those works already cited, I would mention A. S. Collins, *The Profession of Letters: A Study of the Relation of Author to Patron, Publisher, and Public, 1780–1832* (London: Routledge, 1928); Richard D. Altick, *The English Common Reader: A Social History of the Mass Reading Public, 1800–1900* (Chicago: Univ. of Chicago Press, 1957); J. W. Saunders, *The Profession of English Letters*, in Studies in Social History, ed. Harold Perkin (London: Routledge & Kegan Paul; Toronto: Univ. of Toronto Press, 1964); W. J. Reader, *Professional Men: The Rise of the Professional Classes in Nineteenth-Century England* (New York: Basic Books, 1966); Martha Vicinus, *The Industrial Muse: A Study of Nineteenth Century British Working-Class Literature* (London: Croom Helm, 1974); John Sutherland, *Victorian Novelists and Publishers* (London: Athlone Press, 1976); Elaine Showalter, *A Literature of Their Own: British Women Novelists from Bronte to Lessing* (Princeton: Princeton Univ. Press, 1977); and Victor Bonham-Carter, *Authors by Profession*, vol. 1 (London: Society of Authors, 1978). Sociological studies will be cited hereafter.
7. N. N. Feltes, *Modes of Production of Victorian Novels* (Chicago and London: Univ. of Chicago Press, 1986) "studies . . . the production of five English novels" between 1836 and 1910, taking a Marxist approach. It arrived too late to be incorporated into this review.
8. (New York: St. Martin's Press, 1982), p. 9.
9. Heyck, p. 41.
10. Heyck, p. 30.
11. (London: Verso, 1984).
12. Eagleton, p. 107.
13. Eagleton, pp. 34–35.

14. Eagleton, p. 45.
15. Eagleton, p. 41, p. 61.
16. OED; see also the historical survey by Everett C. Hughes, "Professions," in *The Professions in America*, ed. Kenneth S. Lynn, reprt. from *Daedalus*, 1963 (Boston: Houghton Mifflin, 1965), pp. 1–14.
17. Reader, pp. 9–10.
18. Magali Sarfatti Larson, in *The Rise of Professionalism: A Sociological Analysis* (Berkeley: Univ. of California Press, 1977), p. 59, doubts that the "service ideal" is more widespread or more intense among professionals than among other workers.
19. The contrast between professional vocation and leisured avocation structures Alfred North Whitehead's definition too: "The antithesis to a profession is an avocation based upon customary activities and modified by the trial and error of individual practice" (*Adventures of Ideas* [New York: Macmillan, 1933], p. 73).
20. Reader, pp. 114–16.
21. Quoted in Cross, p. 98, from a speech on behalf of "the Universities" delivered at a Royal Literary Fund dinner.
22. Reader, p. 47.
23. Larson, p. 81.
24. Larson, p. 63: "Anti-market and anti-capitalist principles were incorporated in the professions' task of organizing for a market because they were elements which supported social credit and the public's belief in professional ethicality. Thus, at the core of the professional project, we find the fusion of antithetical ideological structures and a potential for permanent tension between 'civilizing function' and market-orientation, between the 'protection of society' and the securing of a market, between intrinsic and extrinsic values of work."
25. Reader, p. 71. The monopolistic tendencies of professionalization are analyzed by Larson, and aspirations to social control by William J. Goode, "Community within a Community: the Professions," *American Sociological Review*, 22 (April 1957), 194–200.
26. Wilbert E. Moore, *The Professions: Roles and Rules* (New York: Russell Sage Foundation, 1970), and Terence J. Johnson, *Professions and Power* (London: Macmillan, Studies in Sociology, 1972) are particularly concerned with questions of professional autonomy.
27. Examples from Collins, pp. 10–12.
28. Writers' other occupations have been surveyed by Saunders and by Bonham-Carter.
29. Southey's attack on the Literary Fund is discussed by Cross, pp. 22–23.
30. I am indebted to Patrick Leary, not only for his unpublished B.A. thesis, "An Essay in Search of the Professional Novelist, 1840–1890," which in part analyzes and categorizes the sources of income for 109 novelists during the mid-Victorian era, but also for valuable help at all stages of the composition of this review.

31. Charles Dickens, *Letters,* vol. 3, ed. Madeline House, Graham Storey, and Kathleen Tillotson (Oxford: Clarendon Press, 1974), p. 500. The letter is dated 2 June 1843.

32. Anthony Trollope, *Letters,* ed. Bradford Allen Booth (London: Oxford Univ. Press, 1951), no. 159; to Frederic Chapman, 1 January 1862.

33. For additional studies of the relations between authorship, publishing, and the marketplace, see Marjorie Plant, *The English Book Trade: An Economic History of the Making and Sale of Books* (New York: R. R. Bowker, 1939); Royal A. Gettmann, *A Victorian Publisher: A Study of the Bentley Papers* (Cambridge: Cambridge Univ. Press, 1960); James J. Barnes, *Free Trade in Books: A Study of the London Book Trade since 1800* (Oxford: Clarendon Press, 1964), and *Authors, Publishers, and Politicians: The Quest for an Anglo-American Copyright Agreement, 1815–1854* (Columbus: Ohio State Univ. Press, 1974); Guinevere L. Griest, *Mudie's Circulating Library and the Victorian Novel* (Bloomington and London: Indiana Univ. Press, 1970); Robert L. Patten, *Charles Dickens and His Publishers* (Oxford: Clarendon Press, 1978); and the archives of and monographs about individual publishing houses.

34. On the mechanization of printing, see S. H. Steinberg, *Five Hundred Years of Printing* (London: Penguin, 1961), and Michael Twyman, *Printing 1770– 1970: An Illustrated History of Its Uses and Development in England* (London: Eyre and Spottiswoode, 1970). On copyright, see Sir Frank Mackinnon, "Notes on the History of English Copyright," in *The Oxford Companion to English Literature,* ed. Sir Paul Harvey, 4th edn. (Oxford: Clarendon Press, 1967), pp. 921–31; and Simon Nowell-Smith, *International Copyright Law and the Publisher in the Reign of Queen Victoria* (Oxford: Clarendon Press, 1968).

35. To ensure first crack at a new work, American publishers began offering British writers payment for the transmission of early proofs or stereotypes; they would then advertise the work as forthcoming and, when "trade courtesy" was observed, no other publisher would bring out an edition of that work, at least immediately.

36. Reader, Appendix I, pp. 208–11.

37. Collins, *The Profession of Letters,* pp. 17–18; Collins instances Pope and Johnson: see his *Authorship in the Days of Johnson: Being a Study of the Relations between Author, Patron, Publisher and Public, 1726–1780* (London: Robert Holden, 1927). Alan Dugald McKillop calls Fielding a "true author": "He is never the amateur in letters; . . . his genius and his education qualified him for discriminating compliance with the current demand for moral and professional responsibility, a demand which crossed class lines" (*The Early Masters of English Fiction* [Lawrence, Kansas: Univ. of Kansas Press, 1956], p. 98).

38. However, forty-five percent of the novelists in Leary's sample went to university.

39. Leary maintains in a forthcoming paper that overproduction in the 1870s and 1880s was cited repeatedly by journals as the cause of declining standards: too many people were writing, and good works were overwhelmed by a Gresham's law of surplusage.

40. Heyck, pp. 32–33.
41. Quoted by Reader, pp. 150–51, from T. H. S. Escott, *England: Its People, Polity and Pursuits*, rev. edn. (London: Chapman and Hall, 1885), pp. 332ff.
42. Burton J. Bledstein, *The Culture of Professionalism: The Middle Class and the Development of Higher Education in America* (New York: W. W. Norton, 1976).
43. Bernard Barber, "Some Problems in the Sociology of the Professions," in Lynn, pp. 15–34; criticized by Johnson, *op. cit.* and p. 45.
44. I paraphrase Barber, p. 18, adding my own italics.
45. Thomas Carlyle, *On Heroes, Hero-Worship, and the Heroic in History*, esp. Lecture III, "The Hero as Poet," first delivered 12 May 1840. Eagleton says that Carlyle's effort to elevate "the man of letters to heroic stature" is a "gesture which can only seem to us profoundly bathetic" (p. 46).
46. Jerome Hamilton Buckley, *Tennyson: The Growth of a Poet* (Cambridge: Harvard Univ. Press, 1960); E. D. H. Johnson, *The Alien Vision of Victorian Poetry*, Princeton Studies in English, no. 34 (Princeton: Princeton Univ. Press, 1952); John Holloway, *The Victorian Sage: Studies in Argument* (London: Macmillan, 1953).
47. John Ruskin, *Modern Painters*, Vol. III, Part 4, chap. 16, quoted from *The Genius of John Ruskin*, ed. John D. Rosenberg (Boston: Houghton Mifflin, 1963), p. 91.
48. Charles Dickens, *Speeches*, ed. K. J. Fielding (Oxford: Clarendon Press, 1960), p. 157; talk delivered in Birmingham, 6 January 1853.
49. Bonham-Carter, chapter 4.
50. Quoted by Bonham-Carter, p. 87, from papers acquired by Walter Besant, now lost; letter of 25 April 1843.
51. Dickens, *Letters*, vol. 3, 477–78; to Charles Babbage, 27 April 1843.
52. Quoted by Bonham-Carter, pp. 82–83.
53. James Hepburn, *The Author's Empty Purse and the Rise of the Literary Agent* (Oxford: Oxford Univ. Press, 1968).
54. Dickens, *Letters*, vol. 5, 227; 9 January 1848.
55. Michael Shelden provided an unsympathetic assessment of Dickens's battle with the Literary Fund in a paper, "Dickens and the Royal Literary Fund," delivered at the Victorians Institute conference on "The Author as Professional," 8–9 October 1982.
56. Paul Schlicke maintains that Dickens's public readings were not so much a desperate psychological and financial gambit as the acting out of the values Dickens located in earlier forms of popular entertainment that waned with the advent of large-scale commercialized amusements. The readings were therefore an enactment of his artistic credo, and though amateur as regards the qualifications of the performer, thoroughly professional as regards the "public service" standards of the writer (*Dickens and Popular Entertainment* [London: Allen & Unwin, 1985]).
57. Saunders, p. 246; there were of course women of genius and ingenuity too, whom Vicinus and Showalter consider in their books cited in note 6.
58. Sutherland, p. 6.

59. A point made frequently by scholars working on diverse machine-printed materials; see, for example, Robert Darnton, "A Bibliographic Imbroglio: Hidden Editions of the 'Encyclopedie,'" *Cinq Siècles d'Imprimerie Génévoise* (Geneva: Sociète d'histoire et d'archéologie, 1981), pp. 71–101, and Philip Gaskell, *From Writer to Reader: Studies in Editorial Method* (Oxford: Clarendon Press, 1978).

60. Peter L. Shillingsburg, "The Printing, Proof-reading, and Publishing of Thackeray's *Vanity Fair*: The First Edition," *SB*, 34 (1981), 118–45.

61. Charles Dickens, *Oliver Twist*, ed. Kathleen Tillotson (Oxford: Clarendon Press, 1966).

62. Alfred, Lord Tennyson, *Idylls of the King*, ed. J. M. Gray (New Haven and London: Yale Univ. Press, 1983).

63. John McVeagh, *Tradefull Merchants: The Portrayal of the Capitalist in Literature* (London: Routledge & Kegan Paul, 1982), pp. 134–38.

64. Coral Lansbury, *The Reasonable Man: Trollope's Legal Fiction* (Princeton: Princeton Univ. Press, 1981); Juliet McMaster, *Trollope's Pallister Novels: Theme and Pattern* (New York: Oxford Univ. Press, 1978), p. 208.

65. Charles Dickens, *Little Dorrit*, ed. Harvey Peter Sucksmith (Oxford: Clarendon Press, 1979), p. 184 (Part V, Book 1, chap. 16).

66. Ibid., p. 113 (Part III, Book 1, chap. 10).

67. James R. Kincaid, *Dickens and the Rhetoric of Laughter* (Oxford: Clarendon Press, 1971), p. 199.

68. An early version of portions of this paper was given at the University of Alberta, Edmonton, on 1 October 1979; revised and expanded, it was delivered at the Victorians Institute Conference, held at Virginia Polytechnic Institute and State University, Blacksburg, on 8–9 October 1982. The publication of Cross's book, and the kindness of the editors of *Review*, have allowed me to develop the arguments further in this format. I am grateful to those who responded with suggestions about earlier versions, to my Rice colleagues Thomas Haskell and Martin Wiener of the History Department, and to Harold Perkin, Jerome Hamilton Buckley, Donald J. Gray, and Patrick Brantlinger, for their guidance on historical, sociological, and theoretical issues.

George Eliot and the Threats of Story-Telling: The Critic as Raffles or the Critic as Romola?

U. C. Knoepflmacher

Alexander Welsh. *George Eliot and Blackmail.* Cambridge: Harvard University Press, 1985. xii, 388 pp.

Gillian Beer. *George Eliot.* Bloomington: Indiana University Press, 1986. xii, 246 pp.

On 10 February 1874 George Eliot wrote to Sara Sophia Hennell to express her repugnance at the "venomous as well as harassing" attacks that had been levelled in recent periodicals at the ideas of her onetime friend Herbert Spencer. "Such are the delights of philosophical celebrity," she acidly noted. But then, in an abrupt and unexpected shift, she turned from the "bitings and snappings" of critics hostile to a living fellow-thinker to the more dangerous indictment made possible by the release of the private thoughts of a dead fellow-novelist: "[delights]—of a better sort however than those of poor Dickens, as they are painfully revealed in this third and last volume of his life."[1] She had been reading Forster's *Life of Dickens*.

The tonal shift in this letter resembles that which takes place in Chapter 29 of *Middlemarch*. There, the narrator turns from a satirical account of Mr. Casaubon's belittlement by rival critics (those "leading minds of Brasenose" are given the names of piscatory snappers, Carp, Pike, and Tench) to an expression of sympathy with an author's own sense of his demerits. External rivals, George Eliot seems to suggest in both of these instances, may pose less of a threat than the anxieties that can beset us when we ourselves expose our inner weaknesses. Our private self may fear betrayal by those "poor little eyes" that peep out "behind the big mask" we wear in public. Forster's *Life,* which first publicized the childhood trauma which Dickens had zealously concealed during his lifetime, apparently so disturbed George Eliot that ten days after writing to Sara Hennell she returned to the subject of invaded privacy in a letter to John Blackwood, her publisher: "Is it not odious," she asked, "that as soon as a man is dead his desk is raked, and every insignificant memorandum which he never meant for the public, is printed for the gossiping amusement of people too idle to re-read his books?" Such acts of exhumation seemed intolerable to her: "It is something like the uncovering of the dead Byron's club foot."[2]

Mindful of her own hard-attained public persona and of her tenuous status as "Mrs. Lewes," Mary Ann Evans here clearly pleads in her own behalf. Her remarks seem to be primarily aimed at future literary biographers: "Something should be done by dispassionate criticism towards the reform of our national habits in the matter of literary biography," she insists in the same letter to Blackwood. And, to ensure that criticism would indeed be "dispassionate" in its treatment of her, she soon burned many a diary and memorandum. And yet, as George Eliot undoubtedly understood, her remarks not only applied to the incriminations contained in such private documents but also to materials imbedded in published novels and stories. For authorship itself constituted a potential threat. Like Dickens, George Eliot knew all too well that her fictions were, like his, rooted in personal anxieties and conflicts that the act of story-telling tried to master and objectify. Since Edmund Wilson's pioneering essay on Dickens, critics and biographers of George Eliot's great rival have made much of the blacking warehouse incident that Forster first exposed in 1874. Did George Eliot, too, possess—or feel that she did—a similar secret? And might the discovery of such a secret furnish our own critical establishment with a coveted key to all her mythologies?

Until the publication of Alexander Welsh's fascinating and rich study, *George Eliot and Blackmail,* such questions seemed to be moot. Protected by John Cross, who allowed the novelist to tell her own story in his 1885 biography, George Eliot fared almost as well with her twentieth-century biographers and critics. Quoting a passage from *The Dead Secret,* a sensation novel which Wilkie Collins published in Dickens's *Household Words* in 1857, Welsh shows how Victorian female secrets, "often sexual in nature," threatened "the social standing and peace of mind" of figures such as Collins's young lady, who expects a "vague Something" to "rise visibly before her," "sound audibly behind her," and "touch her on a sudden from above" (p. 25). Yet when, at the very center of his book, Welsh provides a two-chapter section tantalizing entitled, "Part III. The Secret of George Eliot," the vague Something that might have contributed to George Eliot's hidden dread seems to be screened behind an unlifted veil. Like Gillian Beer, who at least mentions in her *George Eliot* the "amatory attention" (p. 32) shown by John Chapman towards the Miss Evans who came to live in his house in 1851, Professor Welsh is no vulgar Raffles. For all his multiple insights into the widespread ramifications of what he calls the Pathology and the Psychopathology of Information, despite his extraordinarily valuable analysis of both the nineteenth-century phenomenon of blackmail and the intricate blackmail plots that became so prominent in George Eliot's later novels, he avoids the author's psychopathology. In this he proves himself to be as scrupulous as the late Gordon Haight was in 1940, when, in *George Eliot and John Chapman,* he refused to sensationalize the "secret" he had decoded in Chapman's diary.

What, then, *is* for Alexander Welsh, "The Secret of George Eliot"? And why should such a secret have led the novelist to inject, with ever-increasing complexity, blackmail plots into the fictions she wrote after *The Mill on the Floss*? In a formulation that seems unimpeachable in its reasonableness (and safety), Welsh attributes George Eliot's discomforts with the intrusion of privacy to the "discontinuity" between her secure, past provincial self and the two new identities she secretly and uneasily adopted when she became first "Mrs. Lewes" and then the pseudonymous author of *Scenes of Clerical Life* and *Adam Bede.* Welsh is careful to distinguish between Mary Ann Evans's handling of her two secrets: whereas she and Lewes "were frank and assertive" about their liaison with those persons "whose opinion mattered to them," the "secret of the authorship" of her fictions "was another matter" (pp. 124–25). Only when the imposter Joseph Liggins encouraged people to believe that he was George Eliot, could the Leweses no longer invoke the precedent of Sir Walter Scott, who had patently lied in order to conceal his authorship of the Waverley novels. By the time of *The Mill on the Floss,* the incognito had to be dropped and, with it, the male gender that had masked the identity of a writer whom the Victorians might well now pronounce to be a "fallen woman." The private and the public could no longer be kept apart. Hereafter, the fiction of a writer calling himself "George Eliot" would be perilously coupled to the fiction of a woman calling herself "Mrs. Lewes."

It is this thesis which Welsh enlists to license his examination of George Eliot's later works, from "Brother Jacob" to *Daniel Deronda.* The "discontinuity" he stresses, a discontinuity which forever severed George Eliot from the safe identity of her provincial past, is also enlisted to account for the gap between her early writings and those later works. According to Welsh, the public exposure of her two secrets caused the novelist to turn away from the pastoralism of her first books to fictions that now dramatized "the divorce between public and private life" (p. 129) through their obsessive concern with secrets, shame, and blackmail.

Though cogent in outline, this formulation strikes me as somewhat imprecise. For it raises several unanswered questions. Would not the secret author of *Adam Bede,* fearful of losing her audience if her identity were to be revealed, be far more insecure about her authority and authorship than the writer of *Romola* or *Middlemarch,* whose reputation as a major Victorian sage had become so fully established? And is it really true that the "discontinuity" between her past and present selves shapes her later novels far more markedly than the early ones? Why did the earlier fictions dramatize the secrets of women compromised by males (Tina Sarti, Hetty Sorrel, Maggie Tulliver), while the later ones, though written by an acknowledged woman author, turned to males fearing exposure by another male (Godfrey and his brother Dunstan, Edward Freely and his brother Jacob, Tito and his father Baldassarre, Bulstrode and his associate Raffles)?

In trying to separate the "pastoralism" of the earlier books from the later fictions of "discontinuity," Welsh tends to exaggerate the presumed calmness of novels such as *Adam Bede*. Even if one accepts his contention that Hetty Sorrel "is treated somewhat like Amos Barton, as too limited to be morally responsible" (p. 137), the guardedness with which George Eliot handles the girl sinner "who had lost her miserable consciousness" (ch. 36) should at least arouse some suspicion. For George Eliot's distancing from Hetty's "dread of discovery" and "flight from shame" does not mean that the book ends quite as "tidily" as Welsh asserts (p. 140). Hetty's secret irrevocably alters the patriarchal order of Loamshire. The patriarchal mode may be reasserted at the end when Hetty dies outside its confines and Dinah is forced to "submit" to Adam. Yet this reassertion involves disturbing inequalities acknowledged by an ending which relentlessly dwells on the male silencing of a woman preacher's powerful voice.

Protected by his male identity, the narrator of *Adam Bede* could cleverly conceal a female point of view that George Eliot had just as successfully masked, still as Mary Ann Evans, in *Westminster* essays such as the notable "Silly Novels by Lady Novelists." Vulnerable female eyes could thus safely peep out behind the big mask she still managed to wear with impunity. But with the revelation of her gender, the protection that a father can no longer provide for Maggie in *The Mill on the Floss* was similarly denied to that novel's author. The woman who had based Adam Bede on her artisan father and who later professed always to have preferred males to females felt secure in the very patriarchal world she had so subtly criticized from within. Late in his book, and only when he comes to consider the "substitution of ideology for fathers in *Daniel Deronda*" (p. 328), Welsh remembers Mary Ann Evans's oft-quoted outcry, back in 1849, upon her father's death: "What shall I be without my Father? It will seem as if a part of my moral nature were gone. I had a horrid vision of myself last night becoming earthly and sensual and devilish for want of that purifying restraining influence."[3]

In that anguished outcry, so often quoted yet still not fully enlisted by George Eliot's critics, lies a clue to her later "secret." Throughout her fictions, early as well as late, the novelist tried to exorcise the unrestraint of the earthly and sensual and devilish self she detected within. Her strategies were manifold: she could divide her female protagonists into altruists and egotists, as Barbara Hardy first noted, or she could displace her fears of female aggression and sexuality unto male figures, as I have elsewhere argued.[4] The concealments her novels so repeatedly dramatize are almost always sexual in nature: Tina's infatuation with a seducer she will try to murder prevents her from surviving as Mr. Gilfil's legally wedded wife; Hetty's affair and pregnancy subvert the hierarchy of her stable community; Maggie's illicit meetings with Philip and her elopement with Stephen result in her ostracism from what Welsh calls the "shame-culture" of her narrow provincial world (p. 143). The same pattern obtains in the later works. Molly Farren, whom Godfrey Cass has secretly married and impregnated, threatens the young squire's near-bigamous involvement with Nancy Lammeter by exposing "an ugly story of low passion, delusion, and waking from delusion" (*Silas Marner*, ch. 3). Tito weds Romola as well as a Tessa who gives birth to his illegitimate children; the adulterous Mrs. Transome passes off Harold as her husband's child rather than that of her power-hungry lover; Bulstrode seduces his employer's widow and Rosamond almost seduces Ladislaw; Gwendolen sells herself to Grandcourt yet refuses to identify herself with the Mrs. Glasher who lost her reputation by bearing Grandcourt's children.

Conversely, in a pattern that has offended several feminist critics, George Eliot's females yield to the "restraining influence" of males: Dinah "submits" to both Adam and to the Methodist Conference that forbids women to preach; Maggie can be redeemed only through the death-embrace of her humbled brother; Eppie, though marrying Aaron Winthrop, refuses to desert her "father" Marner's home; Esther and Mirah find a "perfect" lot in revering men they regard as masculine heroes. Even Romola, who profits from the deaths of all the male figures in her life, continues to revere the memory of her flawed spiritual father, Savonarola, just as Janet Dempster had revered the memory of the saintly Reverend Mr. Tryan. Only in "The Lifted Veil," written at the height of George Eliot's despair about the impossibility of returning to the patriarchal world of her intransigent brother, is such a fusion of male and female modalities totally denied. The male narrator's powers of omniscience fail him when he tries to fathom the secret thoughts of the devilish Bertha Grant, named, as Sandra Gilbert and Susan Gubar remarked, after the sexual demon chained in Rochester's attic.[5]

If, as Welsh at one point contends, George Eliot's fictions can be read as an attempt to "make up for her sexual transgressions" (p. 126), those transgressions were hardly perceived by her, as Welsh would have it, as the burden of her healthy relation with George Henry Lewes. What was at stake when her identity became known was her fear that this relation might be misconstrued, that her matured self would be falsely equated with the imprudent, Maggie-like younger woman who had allowed herself to become entangled in unsatisfactory involvements in which she had been exploited by men such as Robert Brabant and John Chapman. Welsh quotes from a letter in which the author of the first *Scenes of Clerical Life* tried to describe her domestic happiness with Lewes to a Mary Sibree who had recently become Mrs. John Cash:

I am very happy—happy in the highest blessing life can give us, the perfect love and sympathy of a nature that stimulates my own to healthful activity. I feel, too, that all the terrible pain I have gone through in past years partly from defects of my own nature, partly from outward things, has probably been a preparation for some special work that I may do before I die.[6]

The words could easily have been penned by a Dorothea Brooke Casaubon Ladislaw to a Mary Garth Vincy, were not the "special work" awaiting George Eliot destined to become infinitely more rewarding than the "hidden life" Dorothea must spend with Will. Yet in his gloss of the passage Welsh rather hastily asserts that the "immediate reference to 'the past' . . . is to the past two years with Lewes." Pressing his case further, he insists that George Eliot's "future protestations of sensitivity—'I am subject to depression about authorship'—may derive in part from 'the terrible pain' of her affair with Lewes" (p. 127).

Perhaps so. The isolation produced by her decision to live with a married man certainly exacerbated, for George Eliot, some of the acute pains she had felt earlier, on the occasions of her break with her father on the issue of religion, of the loss of his "restraining influence" upon his death, and of the alienation from her brother.[7] But what the exposure of her gender unleashed, in 1860, was the fear that her liaison with Lewes would be wrongly equated with the sad misfortunes that followed her imprudent behavior with married men such as Brabant and Chapman. Though innocent, she would, like Maggie Tulliver, be indicted for her past impulsiveness. And, what is more, her novels, stories of "passion, delusion, and waking from delusion," based, as they were, on her need to master that earlier, unruly, demonic self, might be falsely adduced as testimonies against her by those who might remember the literal origins of what she had fictively recast and transmuted. As Welsh shrewdly notes, George Eliot had herself invaded the privacy of a living being when she based the figure of Amos Barton on a Reverend John Gwyther, who politely complained about his presentation as a caricature (p. 132). Might not other readers go to her works and find in them private incrustations of events in which she had herself played an original part? It was some such fear, I would submit, that continued to plague the novelist who nonetheless reworked her understanding of earlier infatuations in the ironic stories of Dorothea's worship of the Dr. Brabant called Mr. Casaubon or of Romola's entanglement with a Tito who exploits her far more cruelly than Chapman had ever exploited Mary Ann Evans.

Dr. Brabant is never mentioned in *George Eliot and Blackmail*. And Chapman is cited only as the recipient of a letter in which the novelist reproves him, significantly enough, for speaking "carelessly of rumours concerning a supposed authorship of mine" (p. 125). Was she not worried, too, that the man she had once over-idealized might "speak idly" on other matters that could now produce an even more "serious injury" to her reputation? By deftly reversing the scenario of victim and victimizer (a pattern which, by the way, Welsh elsewhere shows to be a common feature of blackmail), George Eliot hints at the end of the fragment that survives of her original letter that if Chapman were to be put in her position he might become just as vulnerable to an exposure of secrets he should prefer to keep concealed:

Should you like to have unfounded reports of that kind circulated concerning yourself, still more should you like an old friend to speak idly of the merest hearsay on matters which you yourself had exhibited extreme aversion to disclosure?[8]

The reversal of roles is as significant here as the fact that the reports were, in this case at least, hardly "unfounded." Chapman is asked to respect a fiction. In exchange, George Eliot seems to imply, she will preserve the fiction of his authorship of pieces she had actually helped him to write as well as the fiction of his founding editorship of a journal she had almost single-handedly brought into being. And both, she also implies, should maintain an equal silence on other matters which, if disclosed, might prove injurious to each. Victorian circumspection ought to prevail.

If here and elsewhere Professor Welsh misses some possible twists and turns of "The Secret of George Eliot," his own circumspection is hardly damaging to his critical enterprise. For even in this central, and, for me, the weakest portion of his fine book, he produces significant insights. His analysis of the rhetorical strategies George Eliot employed to protect herself from the intrusion of her readers is deliciously astute. He questions her repeated protestations of diffidence by remarking:

The striking thing about such letters is not so much the tortured modesty, but the overt statements about sensitivity. The repeated formula is itself a publicizing act, a way of coping with the intrusion of publicity by reversing its direction, almost by celebrating it. [p. 115]

Similarly, Welsh has important things to say about George Eliot's ambivalence towards the literary culture she both embraced and distrusted. He notes how book-learning could itself produce an alienating sense of "discontinuity" for those who, like herself or like Maggie, were still tied to the anti-verbal energies of rustics to whom print remained a "mystery." His recreation of the debate between young Maggie, whom he calls "a little member of the Society for the Diffusion of Useful Knowledge," and the mill-hand Luke thus nicely captures George Eliot's partial resistance to the very erudition she could so impressively display (p. 118).

It is in the other four sections of his book, however, that Welsh displays his own range and erudition to much better advantage. The first part, which yokes Hitchcock's 1929 film, *Blackmail*, to Mary Elizabeth Braddon's 1862 pot-boiler, *Lady Audley's Secret*, is a brilliant *tour-de-force* that intelligently lays the groundwork for the later anatomies, not just of George Eliot's fiction (considered in Part Four, the longest of the book), but also of the writings of Hawthorne and Freud (linked to each other and to her works in the fifth and final part). Part Two, a densely packed, three-chapter examination of the cultural and socio-economic ramifications of the "disturbances" caused by the explosion of knowledge in the nineteenth century, can almost be read in its own right as an autonomous eighty-page monograph. Solidly anchored in primary texts of the Victorian era as well as in the writings of contemporary social historians and of thinkers such as Foucault, this section deftly weaves together the seemingly disparate activities of Victorian mathematicians, lawyers, postal reformers, scientists, the Metropolitan Police, and sociologists in order to create a panoramic overview that might allow us to locate "sources of anxiety in quantifiable aspects of social change" (p. 58). It is in this informative section that Welsh comes closest to realizing his avowed ambition to write a book that is itself "about information" (p. ix). As he admits in his preface, these wide-ranging chapters "make almost no use of George Eliot; they are about the general conditions of blackmail" (p. vi).

It is not surprising, therefore, that even when Welsh does return to George Eliot's later novels in the fourth and bulkiest portion of the book, he should still continue to be far more interested in finding out what their "management of discontinuous lives" can "teach us about the culture of information" than in what they reveal either about their author's psychology or about her art. What he calls "a book about the later novels of George Eliot and the culture of information" (p. v) thus turns out to be a book about the culture of information in which those later novels play an important, but decidedly secondary role. Welsh's true emphasis is conveyed by some of the chapter-titles in Part Four:

"Knowledge in *Middlemarch*" or "Ideology in *Daniel Deronda*." As he candidly acknowledges at one point, his choice of George Eliot was almost arbitrary: Dickens, whose obsession with secrets, guilt, and blackmail is profitably introduced at pertinent points in this book, or even Trollope, might have served him just as well as an exemplum. Thus, despite his sensitive reading of individual novels, his steady perception of connecting threads among them, and his skillful highlighting of salient scenes, Welsh's intention to write a study of George Eliot's later "mental phases" is, if not at odds with, still subordinated to his prime aim of using them as ancillary documents for a book about the culture of information. In this sense, George Eliot's intersection with so many spheres of Victorian knowledge makes her a better choice than Dickens or Trollope, and allows Welsh to display, as I have said, syncretic abilities that approach the novelist's own. Welsh never deforms the fictions he tries to keep in the foreground. He respects the texts he intimately knows and ably analyzes. And he enlists, just as ably, what modern literary critics have said about them.

And yet, in its attempted amalgamation of competing aims, *George Eliot and Blackmail* is a book without a center. The brave, but ineffectual attempts to make "George Eliot's Secret" a central kernel out of which the other portions of the book could presumably radiate call attention to an irreparable fissure in Welsh's ambitious design. The macrostructure that investigates the "relation between knowledge and accountability" tends to crowd out the novelist who made that relation her arch-theme. Although this suggestive study is a major work of scholarship, it should be read as a philosophic inquiry such as that which Sissela Bok conducted in her 1983 *Secrets: On the Ethics of Concealment and Revelation* (an analogue which goes strangely unmentioned here) rather than as a sequel to the two book-length studies of George Eliot's early fictions which Welsh, in his preface, claims to be eager to "complement" (p. vii).

If Welsh's efforts to press together competing aims and materials result in a bounteous mix, Gillian Beer's modestly elegant *George Eliot* is much more smoothly honed. Beer's own ability to create a vaster "web of affinities" was effectively demonstrated in her 1983 *Darwin's Plots*, a book which Welsh respectfully cites. There, she profitably placed George Eliot's novels against the models of analogy, variation, and individuation furnished to them by evolutionary science. Her more recent book, written to fit the specifications of a series on "Key Women Writers," is shaped, as she explains in her opening chapter, by very different assumptions: "I have seen my task here as being the study of the novels in light of their being produced by a woman" (p. 1). This task, which Beer discharges with an almost olympian poise, might easily veer into special pleading: a female critic writes for a female audience to validate the "specific value as sister" of a female writer who became a target for female critics in the 1970s because, in the words of the late Ellen Moers, she "was no feminist" (pp. 6, 5).

Although Beer is far too sophisticated a critic to engage in one-sided polemics, she nonetheless regards her job as one of rescue and rehabilitation. Clearly worried about those who still might be disposed to question George Eliot's "immense worth to other women" (p. 1), she sets out to convert those unconverted. The reader she addresses (as a "you" sometimes, in emulation of George Eliot) is always a female. And, when she slips (also in emulation of the novelist) into a "we" or an "our," that communal plural is (as George Eliot's is not) gender-exclusive. Thus, when she asserts that "*we* should be wary of the imprimatur of *our* generative organs as a sufficient description of creativity" (p. 16, italics added), those organs hardly belong to a phallocentric order. "Leave the room, sir!," the lawyer Jermyn was told in a memorable scene in *Felix Holt* (ch. 47). Male readers (and reviewers) of Beer's book may experience some of Jermyn's discomfort. If Wordsworth's ideal poet was a man speaking to men, Beer's ideal critic here is a woman speaking to women. Though a handful of male critics are admitted (usually to reenforce some point about this or that text), Beer brings in a veritable chorus of female critics and feminist theoreticians to help her persuade any recusant reader how foolish it would be to dissociate George Eliot's "achievement" from "our needs as women and her powers as a woman" (p. 3). These female voices are by no means left undiscriminated. Quite to the contrary, Beer is determined to correct sisterly misreadings of George Eliot. Gilbert and Gubar are invoked only to be quietly reproved (pp. 38, 42, 51, 55), as is, less frequently, Showalter (pp. 43, 88). Beer is impatient with Redinger's retention of masculinized oppositions (pp. 36, 44) and with Sadoff's retention of a phallocratic Freudianism (pp. 53–54). Her most vehement reaction, however, is against the "energetic perversity" of judgment of Millett, Basch, and Moers (p. 5).

Given the rich dividends this book yields, the exclusivity of its approach should hardly be held against it. The filter through which Beer examines George Eliot allows her to pinpoint much that escaped previous critics, both male and female. She deftly explores the writer's relation to foremothers and female contemporaries: Barrett Browning, Austen, Fuller, Martineau, Gaskell, George Sand, Charlotte Brontë, Mme. de Sablé. She reinterprets the emblematic value that figures like Sophocles' Antigone or Titian's Madonna held for George Eliot. And, in an extremely valuable section, she examines the relevance for the novelist's development of the fictions by Geraldine Jewsbury and Frederika Bremer (pp. 45–49), rightly noting the "creative importance of writers who are no longer much read" (p. 45). The point could have been extended to those half-forgotten eighteenth-century female predecessors whose ideological and stylistic impact on George Eliot was first shown by Margaret Anne Doody in an important essay Beer never cites.[9]

Female creativity has for too long "been conceptualized on the basis of masculine parameters," as Luce Irigaray (another female voice that goes unheard in Beer's book) has so convincingly shown.[10] Beer's attempts to wrest George Eliot free from those masculine parameters should be respected. Yet what are we to make of a book which, as a result, never examines the novelist's relation to literary fathers and brothers? George Eliot's "dearly beloved" Scott, her favorite Wordsworth, Milton, Shelley, Johnson, Goethe, Samuel Daniel, Fielding, Richardson, Keats, are never once mentioned in this study. And neither are the male contemporaries who were so important for her self-definition: Hawthorne, Browning, Spencer, Arnold, Tennyson, Mueller, as well as a good many male "writers who are no longer much read."

Even the allusions to figures such as Thackeray or T. H. Huxley are sparse and perfunctory. It is on occasions such as these that we remember that Jermyn, the excluded male, was actually debarred by another male, Sir Maximus Debarry, who had insisted: "This is a meeting of gentlemen" (ch. 47).

Given Beer's wonderfully incisive discussion of the gender-inclusiveness of George Eliot's universal "we" (p. 28), one must wonder whether she is not, in effect, contravening, by her own gender-exclusivity, what remains the central thesis of her book. Again and again, Beer wisely insists that George Eliot set out to collapse the marked gender distinctions so prominent in Victorian culture. Challenging "essentialism" by "inclusion" (p. 29), George Eliot's female-in-male and male-in-female imagination tried to erode the polarities on which that culture rested. This is why, as Beer rightly insists, George Eliot ends *Middlemarch*, her greatest effort in the art of inclusion, by forcing us "still to recognise exclusion, false consciousness and atomism as part of daily experience for women, and for men and women in their relations with each other" (p. 199). And this is why, too, Beer reserves her greatest indignation for those feminist critics who would prefer George Eliot to have written either a novel which might have mimetically allowed Dorothea the triumphs her creator enjoyed or at least a book with demarcations as clear-cut as Jewsbury's *Constance Herbert,* in which Mary Ann Evans, still safely anonymous and hence also safely bi-gendered, professed herself unable to find a single male character "who is not either weak, perfidious, or rascally," or any female who was not a model of "magnanimity and devotedness" (p. 46).

Why, then, given her profound understanding of George Eliot's attempts to break down "the ghetto of gender" (p. 25), does Beer ghetto-ize her own discourse? Does she feel that she must lecture as a woman speaking to women because male readers of George Eliot's novels do not, paradoxically enough, find the writer's gyno-androus fusions as disturbing as some of their female counterparts? Whatever the reasons behind her own choice of persona, the result is a less complete George Eliot than we might otherwise have obtained. Beer astutely handles some of the same questions raised by Welsh's book, such as the complica-

George Eliot and the Threats of Story-Telling

tions that arose when, in the early fictions, the pseudonymous writer could put on a "man's apparel"; her reading of Hetty's role in *Adam Bede* is better attuned to these complications than is Welsh's. Whereas he sees the presentation of Hetty as not dissimilar from that of an Amos Barton, she shows how that presentation constitutes "a radical challenge to stereotypical portrayals of virgins and fallen women" and of innocent sinners such as those depicted by Elizabeth Stone and Elizabeth Gaskell (pp. 69–70). What is more, she recognizes, in ways that Welsh does not, how not only Hetty but also Dinah "disturbed" the male narrator forced to sacrifice both of these female personations (p. 73).

Like Welsh, however, Beer does not do enough with George Eliot's retention of the masculine components of her imagination in the later works she, too, privileges. Why did the writer who as early as 1846, in "The Notebook of an Eccentric," had adopted a male persona choose to return to the masculine "I" in her final publication, *The Impressions of Theophrastus Such* (1879)? Beer, though willing to consider the portrait of a failed female singer in "Armgart," a poem she relates to the character of Gwendolen Harleth (pp. 206–09), seems totally uninterested in the characterization of the jaundiced male speaker George Eliot devised for the *Impressions,* a book written because there were "some things in it which I want to get said."[11] Beer lumps the work together with "The Notebook of an Eccentric" and "The Lifted Veil" as a male I-narrative, but then forgets to return to it after she contends that the 1859 horror story was George Eliot's "farewell to masculine voice" (p. 79).

If Beer is somewhat over-eager to silence the "masculine voice" that George Eliot resurrected in 1879 (and, I would argue, had continued to modulate in her entire *oeuvre* even after her identity as a woman became known), she also denies a hearing to those who have tried to explain why George Eliot could never quite bring herself to embrace a wholly matriarchal or gynocentric ethos. The psychoanalytic explanations proffered by critics such as Ruby Redinger and Dianne Sadoff (whom Welsh genially entertains) are rebuffed as displaying a preoccupation with "origins," an "obsession which Freud" shared with male predecessors like Darwin and which George Eliot increasingly "satirised and evaded" in her later books (p. 54). But why did the writer so preoccupied with secrets discourage such a burrowing into origins? One of the finest portions of Redinger's often clumsily Freudian biography involves a very cogent reconstruction of George Eliot's relation to her mother and father. George Eliot's evasion of the mother in her writings, very briefly noted and then dismissed by Beer, would, one might have thought, have deserved more attention in a book devoted to the novelist as woman. "Amos Barton," her first work of fiction, kills a mother and allows a daughter to take her place. Despite her subsequent efforts "to leave behind the father/daughter seduction" (p. 54), George Eliot continued to be hampered by her enmity towards the neglectful mother who had driven her to over-identify with male modalities for her self-definition. Twice does Beer comment on the implications of George Eliot's "allusion to Erinna," the legendary young Greek poet who died "chained by her mother to the spinning-wheel" (pp. 23, 207). She dwells, as one might expect, on the woman singer's cry for "freedom" (p. 208); but she remains conspicuously silent on the issue of the culpability of the mother who thwarted Erinna's art.

Romola, a book that turns out to be as important to Beer as it is to Welsh, was first conceived when George Eliot recognized herself in the figure of Savonarola, a flawed father. It is a novel in which she tried to exorcise her ties to patriarchalism through the fictive figure of Romola, a figure given primacy, at the end, over her imaginary and miniscule community of women. Yet even in this, her most decidedly female romance, gender-exclusiveness remains an impossibility. The novel begins with the puzzled shade of a departed male Florentine; it ends with Romola's tribute to the puzzling shade of the departed Savonarola. Fathers, brothers, husbands, uncles, male mentors have all been eliminated in the course of the book. And yet, in its epilogue, a Romola who acts as George Eliot's surrogate winds up instructing a boy in the nobility of men to prepare him for his impending manhood. The delusions of a power-hungry Savonarola are forgotten and forgiven by the narrator who demands sympathy for his Maggie-like martyrdom in Chapter 71 and by a Romola who continues to extol his memory in the very last sentence of the epilogue. A historical self—a self with an antecedent, verifiable history—becomes erased, taken over by idealized romance; a male identity can be internalized by an idealized Madonna we perceive from without. Thus enveloped, Savonarola's secret life—and George Eliot's profound empathy with it—remains safe.

Alexander Welsh and Gillian Beer stand in the same relation to George Eliot's inner self as Romola stands in relation to Savonarola's. Their discourse protects and envelops, rather than penetrates, George Eliot's Secret. They are compelled to view from without what she always views from within: the hungry, shivering self of a Savonarola or of a Bulstrode stems from George Eliot's ability to burrow into male identities without ever allowing us a similar privilege into the roots of her own Shakespearean powers of empathy. This is what she wanted, and it became the hall-mark of her mature art of self-protection. In her brilliant "Secret Performances: George Eliot and the Art of Acting," Nina Auerbach concludes that "George Eliot experienced and wrote about the ways in which prescribed modes of female self-concealment could be transmuted into irresistible vehicles of self-revelation."[12] The formulation, however, is also reversible: fictions that acted for George Eliot as her prime vehicles of self-revelation and self-understanding inevitably relied on constructs of female self-concealment, ever-beckoning yet ever-enigmatic.

Welsh and Beer (like this reviewer) always prefer to use George Eliot's full pseudonym because, as Beer explains, it was the "name she chose for herself" and hence cannot be converted "back again into a pseudo-patronymic, 'Eliot'" (p. 24). Yet that full pseudonym also has the effect of discouraging the kind of familiarity with which the blackmailer Raffles can strip Bulstrode down to a monosyllabic "Nick." George Eliot retains the mask that she forces Bulstrode to drop. Teased by the success of Raffles, eager to emulate a writer so capable of exposing the darkest recesses of male and female minds, the critic as would-be Raffles will be perennially thwarted by a self-protecting novelist, safely sequestered through her intricate art. Whereas the Dickens who confided his secret to Forster wanted to be discovered in his novels of self-inscription, George Eliot dramatizes the process of discovery only to distinguish it from an uncovering that she profoundly resists. She will not permit her reader-critics to assume Raffles's role. Yet she also explains why privacy must be maintained in a celebrated passage in Chapter 20 of *Middlemarch*. Our "frames," the narrator assures us, could hardly bear too deep a penetration into another's inward life:

If we had a keen vision and feeling of all ordinary human life, it would be like hearing the grass grow and the squirrel's heart beat, and we should die of the roar which lies on the other side of silence. As it is, the quickest of us walk about well wadded with stupidity.

Until that apocalyptic roar is heard, readers of George Eliot's novels should be grateful for the books, well wadded with a more than usual intelligence, by fine critics such as Welsh and Beer.

Notes

1. To Sara Sophia Hennell, 10 February 1874, *The George Eliot Letters*, ed. Gordon S. Haight (New Haven: Yale Univ. Press, 1954–1955, 1978), VI, 15.

2. To John Blackwood, 20 February 1874, *Letters*, VI, 23.

3. To Mr. and Mrs. Charles Bray, 30 May 1849, *Letters*, I, 284.

4. Barbara Hardy, *The Novels of George Eliot* (London: Athlone Press, 1959), pp. 78–114; U. C. Knoepflmacher, "Unveiling Men: Power and Masculinity in George Eliot's Fiction," in *Men by Women*, ed. Janet Todd (New York and London: Holmes and Meier, 1981), *Women and Literature*, II, 130–45.

5. Sandra M. Gilbert and Susan Gubar, *The Madwoman in the Attic: The Woman Writer and the Nineteenth-Century Literary Imagination* (New Haven: Yale Univ. Press, 1979), pp. 462–63.

6. To Mrs. John Cash, 6 June 1857, *Letters*, II, 343.

7. A fuller account of the relation between these events and the dynamics of George Eliot's creative interaction with Lewes can be found in my "On Exile and Fiction: The Leweses and the Shelleys," *Mothering the Mind*, ed. Ruth Perry and Martine Watson Brownley (New York and London: Holmes and Meier, 1984), pp. 102–21.

8. To John Chapman, 5 November 1858, *Letters*, II, 494.

9. Margaret Anne Doody, "George Eliot and the Eighteenth-Century Novel," *Nineteenth-Century Fiction*, 35 (December 1980), 260–91.

10. Luce Irigaray, *This Sex Which Is Not One*, transl. Catherine Porter (Ithaca: Cornell Univ. Press, 1985), p. 23

11. To John Blackwood, 5 April 1879, *Letters*, VII, 126.

12. Nina Auerbach, *Romantic Imprisonment: Women and Other Glorified Outcasts* (New York: Columbia Univ. Press, 1985), p. 267.

The Pleasure of Their Company

Donald Gallup

Edward Burns, ed. *The Letters of Gertrude Stein and Carl Van Vechten 1913–1946.* New York: Columbia University Press, 1986. 2 vols. xv, 901 pp.

Timothy Materer, ed. *The Correspondence of Ezra Pound: Pound/Lewis: The Letters of Ezra Pound and Wyndham Lewis.* New York: New Directions, 1985. xxii, 346 pp.

During her lifetime, Gertrude Stein seemed destined to be remembered primarily for her personality and for what she considered to be her less important writing. Her thirst for fame and financial success had led her to abandon her earlier abstract method to write *The Autobiography of Alice B. Toklas* (1933) and *Everybody's Autobiography* (1937), capitalizing in the latter on the publicity generated by the Stein-Virgil Thomson opera *Four Saints in Three Acts* (1934) and by her American lecture tour of 1934–35. The lectures themselves and the bulk of her work from the mid-1930s were, for a large public, accessible in a way that the earlier writing, after the first short stories, *Three Lives* (1909), had not been. Her book about her old friend Picasso, first published in French in 1938, reflected the growing recognition that he was the greatest artist of their century; *Paris France* (1940) was a loving portrait of her adopted city and country; *Wars I Have Seen* (1945), the play of the French resistance *Yes Is for a Very Young Man* (1946), and her book about her beloved GIs, *Brewsie and Willie* (1946), dramatized World War II and the immediate postwar years; while the final Stein-Thomson opera, *The Mother of Us All* (1947), provided in the glorification of Susan B. Anthony both a rallying point for feminists and a commemoration of Stein's own "long life."

But since her death, her reputation and influence, especially among younger experimental writers, have grown surprisingly. The unpublished manuscript that she had been most eager to have printed, *Four in America* (written in 1932–33), was issued in 1947 by Yale University Press. In it she allowed her trained philosophic mind to play with fascinating possibilities concerning George Washington, Ulysses S. Grant, Henry James, and Wilbur Wright. Thornton Wilder handsomely fulfilled his promise to her to introduce this book by writing what is still the best short essay on her work. It was Stein's own bequest that supported the publication, also by Yale, between 1951 and 1958, of the bulk of her unpublished and mostly abstract writings in eight substantial volumes. Her previously uncollected and, again, mostly abstract work, edited by Robert Bartlett Haas, was issued in two volumes in 1973 and 1974 by Black Sparrow Press. An excellent Stein bibliography, compiled by Robert A. Wilson, appeared in 1974.

Carl Van Vechten has not fared so well. His pioneering criticism of music and ballet, remembered with respect by the experts, is generally unknown, although a collection entitled *Dance Writings,* edited by Paul Padgette, was published by Dance Horizons in 1974, ten years after his death. His seven novels, bestsellers in their day, are perhaps too closely identified in the public mind with the period of the 1920s that produced them and have not yet gained the status of important sociological documents. It is as photographer and as publicist for the Harlem Renaissance and advocate of closer relations between whites and blacks that Van Vechten is now most often remembered. Two collections of his photographs have appeared, and fifty of his studies of black men and women have been superbly reproduced in hand gravure by Richard Benson in a portfolio, *'O, Write My Name,' American Portraits, Harlem Heroes,* issued in 1983 by the Eakins Press and exhibited under such distinguished auspices as those of the Ford Foundation, the National Portrait Gallery, and the New York Public Library. The James Weldon Johnson Memorial Collection of Negro Arts and Letters that Van Vechten established at Yale in 1941 ranks with the Schomburg Collection of the New York Public Library in providing the most extensive documentation of the achievement of blacks in the United States

The Pleasure of Their Company

in the twentieth century in the fields of the fine arts. Van Vechten's *Selected Writings . . . about Black Arts and Letters,* edited by Bruce Kellner, author of the most extensive biography, was published in 1979 by Greenwood Press. The same firm issued Kellner's exhaustive *Bibliography of the Work of Carl Van Vechten* in 1980. A collection of the letters, edited by Kellner, is scheduled for publication in 1987 by Yale University Press.

When, in 1941, Van Vechten arranged and annotated the first 392 of his letters from Gertrude Stein before placing them in the Yale Library, sealed until the deaths of both writers, he wrote Miss Stein that he hoped she would eventually give Yale his letters to her, and commented: "What a volume they will all make some day. Terrific!" Their correspondence, which began in 1913 and continued without a break until Stein died in 1946, finally totalled some 886 letters, postcards, and telegrams. She did give the Van Vechten letters to Yale, and he added those she wrote him after 1941. The complete exchange, along with a few letters to and from Alice B. Toklas and Mrs. Van Vechten (the actress Fania Marinoff), has now been printed with detailed annotations by Edward Burns (whose selection of Alice B. Toklas's letters appeared, under the title *Staying on Alone,* in 1973), and it makes not one but two volumes. Prepared initially as a dissertation at Columbia, the edition won the 1983 Ellen Knowles Harcourt Award in Biography and Memoirs, thus insuring its present publication by Columbia University Press. Finely printed in good-sized type on excellent, opaque paper, with plenty of open space, both the letters and the accompanying commentary are easy to read. Each volume contains a frontispiece and sixteen other illustrations, the latter placed in the text as closely as possible to the pertinent passages. Such a luxurious presentation would doubtless have been impracticable as a purely commercial venture. Even at seventy-five dollars, the set is a good buy in these days of high-priced books; it ought certainly to be purchased by most libraries as well as by collectors and students of American culture.

Gertrude Stein and Carl Van Vechten are both vividly present in their correspondence. (Each published an account of their first chance encounter—at the second performance of Stravinsky's *Le Sacre du Printemps* in Paris on 2 June 1913. Both versions, as Burns demonstrates in an appendix, depart strikingly from the actual facts.) Since the two writers did not meet at all between 1913 and 1928, it was through letters that their friendship developed. Van Vechten, six years younger than Stein, was quite willing to serve her. He sincerely admired the portion of her work that he could appreciate (it included her monumental "history" of her own family, *The Making of Americans*, written 1903–11, published 1925), and was willing to accept her own high valuation of the part that he did not understand. He was knowledgeable in the world of publishers and literary critics and, in New York, was useful in getting things printed. It was through him that the very first volume of her abstract writing, *Tender Buttons*, was published in 1914. His enthusiastic support was invaluable to her all through her life, and in her will she made him responsible for overseeing the publication of her unpublished work.

Although their friendship may have begun on the basis of Van Vechten's usefulness, it soon became much more than that. Van Vechten was witty and entertaining; he and Stein were interested in the same things and, although deadly serious about their writing, were quite willing to savor life as they lived it. Neither one was a great letter-writer, in the tradition of Horace Walpole, William Cowper, and John Keats. Their letters are mostly short, and Stein's later ones are filled with promises to tell Van Vechten "all about it" when she next sees him. Her laziness is reflected in her handwriting, as may be seen in the six-page letter that is produced as an illustration, where a wiggle of the pen may stand for any of various combinations of m and n. She often seems in her letters to be reserving her energies for her more serious writing. Van Vechten's letters too are those of a writer almost always caught up in many other pressing activities.

But the personalities of both writers come through and make their letters highly entertaining. They delight in simple things— shell boxes and pottery pigs, cats and dogs, nut stores and Burma-Shave jingles, birthdays and Christmases. They are passionately interested in people and introduce a large cast of subsidiary characters, the lowly along with the exalted: houseboys, maids, and pastry cooks mingle in these pages with the famous. Van Vechten sends Stein "amusing" people, among them the black singers Paul Robeson and Nora Holt, and she dispatches such acquaintances as the Duchess of Clermont-Tonnerre and the artist Giorgio de Chirico for him to photograph and show New York. Although both enjoyed gossip, there is little of it here; what there is chiefly concerns their mutual friend Mabel Dodge Luhan, who being herself addicted to gossip tended to inspire it in others. Their affection, reinforced by relatively few meetings, grows with the years and is so obviously genuine that the reader comes to accept their eventual vocabulary of endearment, excessive by conventional standards, as, for them, a natural form of expression.

Like Gertrude Stein, Ezra Pound has gained in reputation since his death in 1972. Controversy still rages about him and seems destined to continue to do so, for the old charges of anti-Semitism and treason have been neither forgotten nor forgiven. His economic theories, regarded as crackpot by most, are generally either ignored or deplored as having had a pejorative influence on his poetry. But his stature as one of the literary giants of our century becomes ever more solidly established. The proliferating treatises on his major work, the unfinished *Cantos*, supply additional grounds for its acceptance as a flawed but still mighty monument; while Carroll F. Terrell's two-volume *Companion to the Cantos*, published 1980–84 by University of California Press, provides for those willing to make the effort the basis for an enlightened appreciation of that extraordinary "epic." The shorter poems, especially *Mauberley* and *Propertius*, and the translations are increasingly seen to warrant the high praise that T. S. Eliot and others were giving them more than a half century ago. An updated edition of the present reviewer's bibliography of Pound's work, first published in 1963, was issued in 1983 by University Press of Virginia.

As Carl Van Vechten tried to be useful to Gertrude Stein, so Ezra Pound made continued attempts to help Wyndham Lewis after their first meeting in 1909, and succeeded notably during the first decade of their friendship. Then, and especially during the period 1916–19 when Lewis was on active duty with a battery of the Royal Artillery in France, Pound acted as unpaid agent for the promotion and sale of his art, chiefly to John Quinn, the American lawyer-patron-collector. Pound agreed to act as Lewis's literary executor, placed his writing in the *Little Review*, the *Egoist*, and other magazines, and played a part in facilitating the publication of his first book, *Tarr*—all at a time when he himself was hard-pressed to find adequate leisure for his own work.

But Lewis was an odd character, very definitely his own man. Although he was responsible for the support of two illegitimate children and had no steady income, he enlisted and seemed even to enjoy being under fire, writing with great vividness of life at the front in his letters of 1916–18. Having gained that experience, he was glad to have Pound and other friends use their influence to get him into less hazardous and more congenial duties—but not until his battery was safely out of its immediately dangerous position. It is not surprising that, after the war, Lewis came to resent some of Pound's efforts in his behalf as an attempt to run his life. In July 1922, he turned down an exhibition in Italy for which Pound had paved the way. In spite of the near break in their relationship that resulted, Pound was soon offering to Lewis funds that he could ill spare, and Lewis was accepting them. When Pound in 1925 wrote ten pages to the Guggenheim Foundation urging its support for Lewis, his friend again reacted angrily, telling Pound to "consult me in advance in future." The correspondence dwindles off as Lewis grows blind and Pound, in St. Elizabeths Hospital for the Criminally Insane, writes letters that are idiosyncratic, cryptic, often unintelligible. But even under such circumstances he still prepares detailed commentaries on Lewis's books in an attempt to be useful to his old friend, and his confidence never wavers in the quality of Lewis's achievement.

The campaign to establish Lewis as both a great artist and a great writer has been joined by an active group of English and American supporters. A retrospective exhibition of his work at the Tate Gallery in London in 1956, the year before he died, and Walter Michel's definitive catalogue of the paintings and drawings, published in 1971, have confirmed his importance as an artist; while two separate bibliographies, both in the same year, 1978, have chronicled in detail his literary achievement. Writings still unpublished when he died have been appearing over the years, and several of his out-of-print books have been issued in new editions.

Both collections under review aim to print *all* letters, published and unpublished, between their correspondents, and print them complete. This is surely the ideal way in which such exchanges should be presented. Now that even letters of startling intimacy are accepted for publication as a matter of course in our ever more permissive society, it seems at least more decorous that they should appear in the comparative privacy of a single exchange: the feeling of reading someone else's personal letters becomes less intrusive. When only two people are involved, the reader can follow a single relationship chronologically, without interruptions. Properly annotated, such editions give as well a sense of the period in which the two correspondents lived. Of course some of the letters are bound to be of negligible significance, and such all-inclusive publication will tend to be exceptional given the present economic state of the industry and the general lack of enthusiasm of most publishers for volumes of letters. The potential audience for such books is small (unless the content is in some way sensational—as that of these volumes is not), and hard to establish. When publishers do consent to issue collections of letters, most of them opt for a selection of the best letters written to many correspondents. Such books are seldom read straight through, like novels, except by reviewers. Most often they are used as reference books, to document the life or particular interests of an author, and they are consequently purchased chiefly by libraries.

An obvious way to increase the appeal of books of correspondence between only two writers is to add their writings about each other, when they are not too bulky. These were included in the most extensive collection of Stein letters previously published, the Gertrude Stein/Sherwood Anderson correspondence, edited by Ray Lewis White and issued in 1972 by University of North Carolina Press. The only other publication of a complete Stein correspondence, that to Samuel M. Steward,

Dear Sammy: Letters from Gertrude Stein & Alice B. Toklas (1977), included his extensive memoir, filling in the background. Although the Stein/Van Vechten volumes do not contain Van Vechten's numerous writings about Stein, they do include his notes on the correspondence, made in 1941 and 1947, as well as transcripts of occasional manuscripts that she happened to draft on the versos of his letters. An appendix prints for the first time a third Stein "portrait" of Van Vechten. None of the Stein letters has previously been published, except for brief excerpts in the *Yale University Library Gazette*. Twenty-five of the Van Vechten letters were included in a book of letters to Stein, *The Flowers of Friendship*, originally published by Alfred Knopf in 1953 and reissued in 1979 by Octagon Books.

Ever since a selection of his correspondence, edited by D. D. Paige, appeared in 1950, Ezra Pound has been recognized as the writer of some of the liveliest letters of our century. *Pound/Lewis* is the fourth book in a series being published by New Directions in this country and by Faber and Faber in England. *Pound/Joyce* (1967), edited by Forrest Read, included only a few letters and excerpts from Joyce, his letters having already been published in three large volumes, but it did print all of Pound's letters as well as all of his writings about Joyce. *Pound/[Ford Madox] Ford* (1982), edited by Brita Lindberg-Seyersted, included all of their letters and all of their writings about each other. *Ezra Pound and Dorothy Shakespear: Their Letters: 1909–1914* (1985) printed, with minor omissions, the letters exchanged by the couple before their marriage, along with related writings by Ezra Pound. The editing of that volume, by Omar Pound and A. Walton Litz, was exemplary, setting a standard for other editors to follow.

Pound/Lewis contains some 252 letters, but the only formal writing of one author about the other is a hitherto unpublished statement prepared by Pound for, but not used in, the selection of Lewis's letters made by W. K. Rose in 1963. Although the book is expensive ($37.50), it has no illustrations beyond the well-known Lewis portrait of Pound—in black-and-white—on the dust-jacket, and contains none of the numerous drawings by Lewis of Pound and none of the graphic works referred to in the text. Ten letters from Pound to Lewis are reprinted from Paige's edition of Pound's *Letters,* and twenty-three of those from Lewis to Pound from the Lewis *Letters.* Six long "communiqués" addressed by Pound to Lewis on his "intellectual autobiography," *Rude Assignment* (1950), are not printed here, although they were included as letters in an appendix to a new edition of Lewis's book published in 1984 by Black Sparrow Press. Two similar communications from Pound to Lewis on his *The Hitler Cult* (1939) have appeared only in the third issue of *Blast.* The New Directions series is scheduled to continue, with books of Pound's letters to his parents and of selected correspondence between him and Louis Zukofsky, William Carlos Williams, and Marianne Moore in active preparation.

Other collections of Pound's letters have appeared under the auspices of other publishers. Those to Louis Untermeyer were published as *EP to LU* (1963) by the Lilly Library at Indiana University, and those to Louis Dudek as *Dk/Some Letters* (1975) by DC Books in Montreal. His letters to Joseph Darling Ibbotson, his old professor at Hamilton College, were printed in 1979 by the National Poetry Association. Those to John Theobald, a teacher of English in California, with most of Theobald's replies, were issued in 1984 under the imprint of Black Swan Books. That same firm has announced the forthcoming publication of Pound's correspondences with Thomas H. Carter, one of the editors of *Shenandoah,* and Senator William E. Borah of Idaho, along with *Ezra Pound and Japan,* a book that will include more than a hundred of his letters to Japanese correspondents. Some of his letters in Italian to correspondents in Italy were included in an Italian translation of his selected letters published in 1980 by Feltrinelli in Milan.

Besides all these, Pound's letters to a number of other correspondents, *e.g.*, Eustace Mullins, Julien Cornell, and Harry M. Meacham, have been incorporated in their books about him. Such extensive publication of his correspondence has had much to do with the growth, already commented upon, of Pound's reputation. The *Letters,* in 1950, already documented the extent of his self-denying efforts on behalf of other writers and artists, especially in the difficult years when they were attempting to establish themselves. These included not only individuals, like

Eliot and Joyce, who became famous, but a great many others, like Iris Barry and Mary Barnard, who never became widely known. The effect of the appearance of the various two-sided correspondences has been generally to provide additional examples of Pound's remarkable generosity, his absolute dedication to the highest ideals in literature and art, and his all too stubborn insistence on following courses of action in which he believed despite disastrous consequences for himself. *"Ars longa, vita brevis est"* could well have been his motto.

The method of annotation differs markedly in the two books under review. In the Stein/Van Vechten volumes the editor's introduction is general and brief, and the notes supply the necessary background information. These are keyed by the usual superscript numerals and appear at the end of each letter. They are copious and, if anything, tend now and then to give rather more information than is absolutely necessary. In *Pound/Lewis*, the letters are arranged by period in four groups, each with a long introduction and with an occasional special prefatory note to a particular letter or sub-group. Supplementary explanatory notes, without superscripts in the text, follow each letter, but persons frequently mentioned are identified only in a "Glossarial Index" at the back of the book. This arrangement is cumbersome: the lack of reference numbers in the texts of the letters makes it difficult to have pertinent information when one actually needs it, as one reads, and it is even more awkward to be obliged to turn to the final pages to discover the identities of persons referred to. In the glossarial index, works by Lewis, grouped as "Fiction," "Paintings and Drawings," and "General Works," are listed only under his name. It thus becomes necessary to know that *Tarr*, for example, is a novel in order to be able to find it readily under "Lewis, Wyndham. Fiction." Pound's writings are treated in the same way, grouped as "Poetry," "Translations," and "General Works." The use of the index is thus complicated for the reader not intimately acquainted with the two authors' work.

Pound's letters present special problems for an editor largely because of the way in which most of them are typed. His spacing, indentation, paragraphing; his use of exclamation points, diagonals, asterisks, and, occasionally, red ribbon; the multiplicity of his typing errors and his correction of some of them by restrikes or in manuscript, all help make the products of his typewriter unique. They have to be seen to be believed, and some editors provide facsimiles of the letters, in addition to transcribing them—a method used in several of the editions cited. In *Pound/ Lewis*, although there are no facsimiles, an attempt is made to reproduce the appearance of the typed letter by following as closely as possible the spacing and underlining, with the result that the printed page has a distinctly unconventional look about it.

Pound's intentions, especially in his late letters, are not always easy to determine. His deliberate misspellings, at first almost invariably humorous and to the point, become increasingly quirky, as, for example, "opHinYum" (p. 193) for "opinion," "KittyLug" (p. 297) for "catalogue," and "pipper" (p. 303) for "paper." Even Lewis sometimes had difficulty in grasping Pound's meaning—as he complains on a number of occasions— and it is of course unreasonable to expect an editor to explain a reference that may well have escaped the correspondent. Lewis himself was probably puzzled, as is the reader, by his friend's reference to George Santayana "weepin over coral insects" thirty years ago (p. 248) and his mention of "Port[eus]'s friend the son of the char lady" (p. 254). Materer sheds no light. Indeed he does not always offer as much help as he might: "devMo" (p. 206) could have been explained as (Italian) "devotissimo"; in Pound's "occid[ental]/ 1/2" (p. 258), "1/2" might have been interpreted as standing for "hemisphere"; " 'lesinait' " (p. 272) could have been translated for the average reader who may not remember that the French verb "lésiner" means "to be stingy," etc. "Revista M" has a questioned identification with *Rassegna Monetaria* which could easily have been made definite by checking the reference's citation of *Count Your Dead* "in the June issue."

Alyse Gregory, a former editor of the *Dial* and the widow of Llewellyn Powys, once assumed, in correspondence with me, the role of *advocata diaboli,* arguing that all letters ought to be destroyed because if even one of the correspondents could occasionally mistake the meaning, readers after the passing of years can certainly not be expected fully to appreciate their actual intention. Even in the Stein/Van Vechten letters there is an example of this kind of problem. Van Vechten writes to Miss Stein from Rome on 8 June 1934 about plans for their approaching meeting: "I suggest that we have lunch somewhere in Chambéry . . . & visit the house where John Paul Dunbar & Madame Walker carried on." It is quite possible that he intended deliberately to puzzle her by this reference, planning to explain it when they met. It is one of the rare instances that have partially defeated the editor. Burns presumes, correctly, that Van Vechten is referring to Madame C. J. Walker, explaining in a note that she won fame and fortune by perfecting a process for the straightening of kinky hair. But that is all he can offer, beyond some gratuitous information about A'Leila Walker, who used her mother's money to become a well-known Harlem hostess. The explanation is that Van Vechten was referring here to Les Charmettes, the country villa where Jean Jacques Rousseau lived for several years in the 1730s as the protégé of Madame de Warens. Arthur Spingarn, chairman of the NAACP's legal committee, once told Van Vechten that the Negro regiment with which he was affiliated in World War I had visited this villa. One of Spingarn's jobs was censoring the enlisted men's mail, and he later came across this statement in a soldier's letter: "Yesterday we visited the spot where Paul Laurence Dunbar messed around with Mme Walker." In recalling the story in his letter to Stein, Van Vechten made things even more difficult for his present-day editor by giving to the black poet Dunbar an Anglicized version of the French philosopher's first name.

Granted that private correspondences may contain passages that we fail fully to appreciate, still such publications as the two under review afford us a privileged opportunity to share vicariously in significant relationships as they began, developed, and matured. Much is of course lacking, especially the conversations, the social intercourse, but the letters help us to know these people more intimately and perhaps thus gain a deeper understanding of their published work.

Writers and artists, especially after they have enjoyed a certain amount of success and attendant popular adulation, almost inevitably develop public personae, become at times Great Panjandrums. Stein, Van Vechten, Pound, and, I daresay, Lewis, though I cannot speak of him from personal acquaintance, all had their moments approaching pontificality. Certainly there is no mistaking the seriousness of the concern of all four for literature and art, and yet in their letters they are ever willing to indulge in a spirit of play. It is especially this playfulness *cum* seriousness that makes almost all of their letters a pleasure to read. Although there may be grounds at times for reservations about the later Wyndham Lewis, in his cantankerousness, we become convinced that these correspondents, besides being highly significant figures in the world of art and letters, were interesting, entertaining, and sincere human beings who cared passionately about the things they believed in. In these letters that they exchanged over exceptionally long periods, we see the young rebels gradually become established and respected, and find their human qualities starting out from almost every page.

L'orbe est sur Joyce

Morris Beja

Wolfhard Steppe, with Hans Walter Gabler, compilers. *A Handlist to James Joyce's* Ulysses: *A Complete Alphabetical Index to the Critical Reading Text.* New York: Garland, 1986. x, 300 pp.

Patrick Parrinder. *James Joyce.* Cambridge: Cambridge University Press, 1984. x, 262 pp.

Sheldon Brivic. *Joyce the Creator.* Madison: University of Wisconsin Press, 1985. xiii, 177 pp.

Cheryl Herr. *Joyce's Anatomy of Culture.* Urbana and Chicago: University of Illinois Press, 1986. xiii, 314 pp.

Richard Brown. *James Joyce and Sexuality.* Cambridge: Cambridge University Press, 1985. viii, 216 pp.

> At the end of an enumeration of Joyce's achievements, Lucan exclaimed, *"L'orbe est sur Joyce"* ("the world is about Joyce").
> Sheldon Brivic, *Joyce the Creator* (p. 9)

Wolfhard Steppe and Hans Walter Gabler stress, quite accurately, that their "handlist" for *Ulysses* is not a "word list" as such, but a list of all symbols, numbers, graphic units, and "language tokens" appearing in the novel. For most users, however, such subtlety will not affect their view that what the *Handlist* primarily provides is a complete list of all the words in *Ulysses*.

The words are terrific, no doubt about that: they are extraordinarily well chosen. Still, as Joyce knew (and said), the real trick is putting them together right. This word- (and graphic-unit-, and language-token-, etc.) list has been put together by the computer that was used to prepare Gabler's *Ulysses: A Critical and Synoptic Edition.* One wonders what might result were such a computer, or some vastly more sophisticated model, to be fed all these words, graphic units, etc., and instructed to come up with a novel—the rules being that all the words would have to be used, and in precisely the same frequency as they are in the Gabler edition: 12,615 instances of "the," 1,026 of "The," 166 of *"the,"* only one of *"demiurgos,"* and so on. (Would the computer be well-read enough to be thrown off by the instance of the term *"Goldfinger,"* and thereby attempt to write a novel of a certain genre?)

Such are some of the conjectures suggested as one peruses this immensely useful reference tool. It is not an "edited" compilation: what you see (in *Ulysses*) is what you get (here). We find out under each entry how many instances of a given word (or whatever) there may be: "Midlothian," for example, appears only once; and we find out the episode and line number, not the page, of each appearance (for "Midlothian," episode 17, line 1651); the line numbers are of course provided in the Gabler edition.

One can think of reservations in regard to such a "mechanical" method, but the introduction to this compilation disarmingly raises most of the problems that might occur to most readers—and some that, surely, few of the rest of us would have thought of. Above all, what the computer lacks are, well, brilliance, shrewdness, and imagination: the qualities displayed in Clive Hart's *A Concordance to* Finnegans Wake, with its list of "syllabifications" (such as *"abound"* when the word as it appears in the *Wake* is actually *"meditabound"*), and its compilation of "overtones" (so that the reader looking up "neighbour" will be helpfully sent to page 5, line 21, and discover "nabir").

I do not have to dwell, however, on the usefulness of what we *do* have here. The reader who wishes to look up all instances of "jew" and its variations (none of them "Jew," by the way) is vastly helped, although he or she will have to remember to try the synonyms as well (and will find no "kike," no "yid"). Sometimes, one will find corroborations of what one would have expected, but that experience can be enlightening: so, for example, one discovers that "yes" occurs much more frequently in the last chapter than in any other, although "Yes" is *less* frequent, appearing only at the very start and the very end. Or consider the fact that the word "theory" appears six times in the Scylla and Charybdis chapter, and only three times in all the rest of the

L'orbe est sur Joyce

novel. Some variations are not easy to explain: why does Davy Byrne's yawn appear in Lestrygonians as "Iiiiiichaaaaaaach" and in Circe as "Iiiiiiiiiaaaaaaach"? Such are some of the imponderables of Joyce studies.

The word "American" appears in *Ulysses* only six times, compared to seventeen instances of "British" and 103 of "Irish." Yet for decades it was a commonplace (and sometimes an accurate one) that almost all the exciting or even interesting work done on James Joyce was being done by Americans. In recent years, however, that trend has been reversed, and there has been a great deal of activity in all of Europe in Joyce studies; the *Handlist* and the edition upon which it is based were both produced in West Germany ("German": four instances in *Ulysses*), and a number of French critics and theorists have been doing especially interesting work. But the Irish and, even more, the British have also produced criticism and scholarship at an impressive rate, and of impressive quality.

Witness Patrick Parrinder and Richard Brown, both of them British. Parrinder's *James Joyce* is an introductory book, and it is a very successful one, which I believe would be useful to an intelligent reader who has a desire to know more about work he or she has (preferaby) already read, or is setting out to read—or, let's face it, has been assigned to read. It is also true, surely, that the best such introductions are achievements that somehow also manage to enlighten and challenge the reader who has read a great deal of both Joyce and Joyce criticism. On that score too Parrinder does well, although one's enthusiasm here must become more tempered.

One of the chief strengths of Parrinder's book is that, while on the one hand he never loses sight of Joyce's work, and on the other he is familiar with current trends in theoretical approaches to literary study, he is also fully aware of the literary and cultural background that both Joyce and his readers have brought to his canon. (Parrinder's historical interests become intriguing in a brief and underdeveloped comment that the rebellious behavior of Francis Skeffington—the counterpart to McCann in *A Portrait of the Artist*—"became so notorious that members of the English branch of the Skeffingtons, including some of my own relatives, changed their names" [p. 20].) From the world of literature he brings in Dickens, Wilde and Ibsen, but does not do so needlessly or pedantically. And the following evocation of the relationship between the art of *Dubliners* and that of the most exciting contemporary painting of the time is exemplary:

> The subjects of the impressionists were 'found' *en plein air* rather than being elaborately designed and reconstructed in the studio. Established rules of pictorial composition were ignored and the paintings were executed deftly and rapidly, so as to capture the 'impression' before it was lost. The literary equivalent of the impressionists' concern with capturing the moment was the so-called 'slice of life' story which attempted to recreate a particular emotional 'atmosphere.' [p. 43]

But it is "the art of the grotesque"—the art of the *Book of Kells*—that Parrinder finds particularly relevant to Joyce, especially in *Ulysses* and, understandably, above all in *Finnegans Wake*. Parrinder's sense of the grotesque is particularly influenced by Bakhtin's view of Rabelais, and he has little patience with those—including Joyce himself, at some misleading moments—who associate his art with classicism; for surely Parrinder is correct in arguing that "classical proportion and classical decorum are alien to most (though not quite all)" of Joyce's writing (p. 8).

As his use of Bakhtin suggests, Parrinder knows about narrative theory and can bring it in, although he does not do so very often—no doubt feeling that it could hardly play a major role in a volume meant to be "introductory." Yet he is perhaps too reluctant, especially given his willingness in other ways to discuss the work of many previous critics. In such confrontations he is not always just, I might add: he quotes a quite reasonable warning by Marvin Magalaner—to the effect that we should not assume that Stanislaus Joyce's relationship with his brother means that he can provide the "last word" on various topics relating to James Joyce's fiction—as a "gem of scholarly self-importance" (p. 51). Nor does Parrinder discuss all the critics he might. One of his chapters is entitled "The Styles of *Ulysses*," yet he never mentions Karen Lawrence's fine study of 1981, *The Odyssey of Style in Ulysses*.

The handling of *Finnegans Wake* is especially problematic. Parrinder's discussion is quite derivative (depending a great deal upon James Atherton, Bernard Benstock, Roland McHugh, and Margot Norris), and that obviously limits its interest to those who need no introduction to that book (assuming, I suppose, there are such people). Yet his procedure throughout this discussion is rambling and confusing—even more confusing, that is, than is necessary in any treatment of the *Wake*—and will therefore, I think, not be all that useful for beginners either.

Earlier, too, there are moments at least of carelessness. He mistakes Stephen's recollection of an encounter with his father, Simon, for a supposed meeting during his mother's last illness with Bloom (p. 140). Worse, he shows occasional confusion between various characters and Joyce himself: as when he somehow feels that Stephen is prevaricating in the *Portrait* when he claims that he has written down a series of questions in regard to aesthetics, since it turns out that Joyce himself did not set down similar notations until later in his own life (p. 102); generally, in fact, Parrinder's impatience with Stephen clearly leads him—as it has unfortunately led others before him—to feel uncomfortable with the *Portrait* as well. He claims that "the book is uncertainly poised between mature reservation and an almost intoxicating sympathy with Stephen's experience" (p. 72). Why "uncertainly"? Isn't the novel quite *clearly* and forcefully so poised?

In other ways too Parrinder seems unable fully to respond to indeterminacy, or to acknowledge its presence or power. When Bloom scrawls "I. . . . AM. A." on the sand, Parrinder assumes—surely too readily—that Bloom "cannot bring himself to write the word cuckold" (p. 174). For Sheldon Brivic (in *Joyce the Creator*) the words refer to "I am Alpha and Omega . . ." (p. 95). The truth (in any case *a* truth) seems to be that we do not know what the scrawl means, or might be leading to, if anything; that, one imagines, is much of the point. Like Brivic, Parrinder occasionally makes easy cosmic generalizations about Bloom, who, he says, cannot "face" history "because for him it represents "personal failure" and "racial impotence"—whatever that last phrase might possibly mean (p. 149).

Still, as I hope I have made clear, there is much of value in this book; and as we read we frequently come upon enlightening insights or phrases, as when—discussing the role of repression in *Dubliners*—Parrinder remarks that Eveline is victimized and "stopped, not by external restraints, but because she has learnt a self-restraint which cuts off her capacity for action and wipes out the adult personality she was struggling to establish" (p. 59). More essentially, Parrinder constantly reminds the reader of Joyce's comedy—and of the humaneness of Joyce's life's work.

The word "Creator" appears five times in *Ulysses*, and "creator" only twice; even more one-sidedly, "God" occurs 194 times, and "god" only fifteen (and "Goooooooooood" just once). I do not have similar word-counts for Sheldon Brivic's *Joyce the Creator*.

Brivic's challenging and often intriguing study comes at Joyce through what he calls the "multimind": "as the Joycean mind grows through the canon to include more parts and levels of personality, this developing conception comes to unite a group of minds in one multimind without a single center," and "the multimind of Joyce's work continued to express his mind even while it included those of his characters, narrators, and readers" (p. 4). In connecting this concept with the mind and multimind of God, Brivic is extensively influenced by his reading of Julian Jaynes's *The Origin of Consciousness in the Breakdown of the Bicameral Mind*.

Brivic's thesis depends on the argument that Joyce is a "presence" in all his work in a very special way—in the special way that God is present in His creation. The notion of the artist as the God of creation is an old one, of course, even a commonplace, but Brivic takes it beyond the realm of metaphor (which is presumably why he mentions only once, in passing, that it was from Flaubert that Joyce "got the idea of the novelist as God" [p. 47]):

Joyce continually played the role of a god in the world he created. Though he played the role comically as often as seriously, his presentation of himself as a parody of the Deity was partly a reaction to his sense of the awful responsibility involved in the position he filled. . . . No artist has represented himself through images of godhood more systematically or intrusively. [p. 8]

When Brivic makes arguments for Joyce that go beyond the comparisons that can be made between God and any mortal creator, any artist, the possible theological implications of his thesis are foregrounded, and the argument itself becomes almost semi-mystical and hard to prove, though also hard to refute.

One difficulty that he never quite overcomes entails Joyce's own attitude, ambivalent at best, toward religion—and, specifically, its "truth." Even Brivic has to acknowledge that "Joyce had difficulty accepting one consequence of Stephen's view of the artist as deity—that Joyce's characters lived in a world in which God exists" (p. 9); actually, Brivic does not really show that Joyce had all that much difficulty in that respect, though it is clearly a problem for Brivic himself. So he resorts to providing "evidence" of Joyce's belief by citing other critics—such as Hugh Kenner's early statement that "Joyce never doubted the existence of God" (p. 13).

To his credit, in my opinion, Brivic is fully aware that to some contemporary theorists his approach—his insistence, for example, on finding *meaning* of all things in Joyce's work—will seem "naive and old-fashioned" (p. 45). In fact, however, he frequently shows an intimate familiarity with contemporary theory—with Lacan and Derrida, notably—and uses it for his own purposes in sometimes fascinating discussions, as when he argues that "Joyce uses deconstructive techniques constructively to generate spiritual content" (p. 75).

Cheryl Herr's Joyce is a much less spiritual and more material artist, forging his handiwork out of the matter of the earth—and, especially, out of the world of popular culture. But it is also a world with deep troubles and repressive ideologies. The word "censor" occurs only once in *Ulysses,* and no cognates ever appear at all, but it and similar terms abound in *Joyce's Anatomy of Culture.* Her first chapter is entitled "Culture as Censor," and, according to her, "for Joyce culture is largely constituted by the censoring efforts (that is, the conventionalizing, stereotyping, and hegemonic maneuvers) of institutions" (p. 34). The cultural world she concentrates on is that of journalism, the theatre, and the Church of Joyce's own day. Yoking together the world of the daily Dublin newspaper, the pantomime and music hall, and the

Catholic sermon, and their role within (and as) "popular" culture, is a brilliant coup. Herr realizes that no one can "escape" his or her culture, Joyce not excepted:

> Joyce did not speak beyond the terms laid out for him by his culture; there was a firm limit to the novelty of what he could say. But this limitation was not so much because of censorship but because even with conditions of suppression being pervasive in Anglo-Irish life, what was suppressed was always insuppressible. What Joyce courted exile to announce had already been said.
> On the other hand, Joyce's steady and various undermining of the absolute opposition of those binarisms (male/female, saved/damned, upper class/lower class, and good/evil) on which Western cultural mores are built engineers in his text what we might call a liberating vision of culture. [pp. 284–85]

As such a passage reveals, Herr comes to Joyce—as everyone does—with an "ideology." (She would presumably quite readily agree that her own writing is like "the daily newspaper, the popular play, and the sermon" she examines, for they too are "signs for the institutions whose ideological practices they embody and articulate" [p. 4]). The central point is that she does so with full awareness and a keen intelligence, combined with an impressive amount of scholarly research; not everyone does that. Her approach is, I think it fair to say, that of a new historicism which is basically Marxist, as influenced by such figures as Fredric Jameson, Michel Foucault, and Edward Said. A mere decade or so ago, a book starting out as this one must have would probably have ended up being a "straight" historical and scholarly study of "allusions" and "cultural background." Herr, however, is much more interested in making theoretical arguments, for example, than in coming up with identifications of allusions—though she is quite adept at the latter in any case.

I hope I have not in any way given the impression that Herr's book is merely trendy; actually, it goes against widely current theoretical trends and even movements, such as those that—oddly like the old New Criticism, as she realizes—"cut off the literary work from the social forces which are in some sense responsible for its production" (p. 282). Among the most refreshing of the results of Herr's approach is a blurring of the distinction between high art—and in some minds no writer of the twentieth century seems more an elitist taste than Joyce—and popular culture; few serious writers have so elaborately and consistently blended esoteric allusion, complex techniques, and references to mass media, thereby creating, as Herr puts it, "the avant-garde out of the demotic" (p. 15). She considers what Joyce wrote and the "texts" of sermons, newspapers, and the evidence we have from the world of the popular theatre of his time, all as "parallel" texts; sometimes, one must admit, *Joyce's* texts seem in danger of being lost in the process, but that is not a persistent problem here, and when she does get to the texts that will inevitably be of primary interest to anyone coming to read her book in the first place, Herr is consistently enlightening. She is especially so when she brings together on the one hand her demonstration of "the ideological practices" which the popular play, the daily newspaper, and the sermon "embody and articulate," and on the other hand her echo of the call by Sidney Feshbach for critics to go "beyond the definition of Joyce's beliefs to articulate the ideology of his works" (pp. 4, 8).

Other references to Joyce critics are, however, sometimes oddly cryptic—as when she cites a "recent very fine book" which nevertheless "carries overtones" of a view she dislikes, and quotes several lines from the book, but never identifies it (pp. 26–27). Similarly, she writes that "the *Irish Times* for 16 June 1982 records the events surrounding the centenary celebration in Dublin of Joyce's birth but not the most interesting parts of what Richard Ellmann really said on that occasion" (p. 49). I was there too, but I am not at all certain to which of Ellmann's remarks Herr may be referring.

But there are excellent discussions here, of the backgrounds and of the Joycean texts: for example of Rudy as "the most obvious example in *Ulysses* of a character constructed, as all are, from cultural discourses" (p. 175); of Gerty, in some brief but telling references to how both she and Bloom measure themselves against "the stereotypes offered in the [music] halls of men, women, love, marriage, family relations, and the working life" (p. 195); and of "Grace," in a long discussion within a chapter on "The Sermon as 'Massproduct.'"

One of the intriguing things revealed in the *Handlist* is that words like "sex" and its variations do not really occur very frequently in *Ulysses:* "sex" itself appears only fourteen times, and "Sex" twice; "sexual" occurs three times, and "sexuality" not at all. Ah, but "sin" or its variations appear thirty-three times. But don't be depressed: "love" and its variations occur in 156 instances.

I mention those figures because, on that whole subject, one is tempted—upon picking up Richard Brown's *James Joyce and Sexuality*—to observe that someone has finally gotten it up. That is, I mean of course, someone has finally erected an entire scholarly volume on one of the most central aspects of Joyce's work: sexuality. I say "finally" because, although there have been many particular discussions of limited aspects of the topic, they have almost always been partial in scope: that is true, for example, even of such earlier full-length studies as those by Margaret Solomon and Mark Shechner; and while numerous essays on the fascinating topic may be individually penetrating, they are invariably arruginated keys to an unstable puzzle. Moreover, Richard Brown is correct in asserting that early critics seemed to feel that they had to legitimize Joyce studies by not dwelling on what was creating notoriety and causing censorship problems, while in some more recent quarters *all* discussions of "subject matter"— Brown's term—have seemed to be regarded as naive and misguided, as if subject matter can have no role in the "text."

But to be, well, up front, I might as well confess at the outset that Brown's approach is not what I myself would have desired. The stress is clearly and emphatically on Joyce-the-person, or Joyce-the-author (or, as I shall show, on Joyce-the-reader), rather than on Joyce-the-works: in that sense, the text gets the short end of the stick. Sometimes the autobiographical stress goes so far as to create confusion: "It is," Brown writes, "the semi-autobiographical Stephen who delights in heresy, from the fascination with the 'heresiarchs of initiation' in the early *Portrait* essay to the 'wave of speech' which introduces them to the young lady in *Giacomo Joyce*" (p. 161). With whom is Stephen Dedalus conflated in that passage? Joyce? The protagonist of the early "Portrait of the Artist"? The narrator of *Giacomo Joyce?* Its protagonist? The answer is in any case complex in ways in which

Brown's flaccid approach itself too often fails to recognize. In any case, his book leaves itself wide open to the intrusive charge that it is more about sexuality in Joyce's life and thought than about its presence in his fiction, and more about its presence in his reading than either.

Like Herr's, Brown's book is in some ways a study in intertextuality, although almost all the other texts he brings in are little-known philosophical, medical, psychological, or otherwise scientific or pseudo-scientific studies from the late nineteenth and early twentieth centuries. Brown starts off with some relevant references to recent theoretical defenses of such interests in (Harold) Bloom, Barthes, and Genette, and later brings in Riffaterre as well, but despite that sort of tease the truth is that his appeal is old-fashioned, for better as well as for worse; for this is a receptive scholarly account of Joyce's wide reading on sexuality and connected themes and topics, with extended commentaries on what he read. The commentaries indeed are perhaps more analytical as well as more extended in regard to those works than they are in respect to Joyce's.

So, typically, Brown wonders about the "source" of Joyce's "feminism," and, also typically, decides that it is "to be found in his reading"—in this case "of Ibsen at university" (p. 94). And when Brown complains that Fritz Senn's discussion of "inversions" in *Finnegans Wake* tells us "relatively little about the attitude the fictions take to homosexuality itself," his solution is automatically and immediately to inform us that "Joyce's library contained some material on the question," thereby leading us into Huysmans' *A Rebours* and Gide's *L'Immoraliste,* as well as Burton's *The Book of the Thousand Nights and a Night* (p. 79). The result is often to leave one frustrated, longing for more.

The naked truth is that this book has a central topic, but not what one might truly regard as a central argument with a forceful thrust. We have in effect a collection of essays on various aspects of sexuality and gender in Joyce, rather than a book which embodies an overall thesis on that topic. Appropriately, the understanding of what is covered by "sexuality" is very broad: some of the major areas included—such as feminism, or common attitudes toward "sexual dimorphism" (the "belief in dimorphism of secondary sexual characteristics" [p. 96])—make one wonder if the title of the book may not be a bit misleading. (If so, perhaps it could have been called *James Joyce and Gender*. One way out of it.)

Without beating around the bush, I should stress that, given his general approach, Brown's book is helpful and contains excellent discussions that arouse our excitement. Among the most titilating are those that concentrate on works we would not expect to be given so much emphasis; *Exiles*, notably, looms quite large in the study, compared to the space devoted to analyses of the major works.

Brown's chapter on "Women" is interesting, and certainly much more alert than one might expect from its opening sentence, which tells us that "Joyce's writing has played little part in the upsurge of interest in feminism and feminist literary criticism that has taken place since the 1960s" (p. 89). That remark is clearly out of date, and was presumably so when Brown wrote it—although it may not have been so emphatically inaccurate when he began the original dissertation upon which the book is based. In any case, he does not do justice to—or, in truth, pay much attention to—the major and fascinating studies of Joyce by many feminist critics in recent years.

On the other hand, among his most seminal discussions is that of Bloom's masturbation in Nausicaa, for Brown stresses an aspect of it that I do not recall being given anywhere else the full attention it deserves. As he says, "one of the most remarkable features of Bloom's onanism, though no one has cared to make anything of it, is that this act is pointedly performed with another person. In this sense it is not just as a masturbatory act that we need think of it but as what [Paul] Garnier calls an '*onanisme a deux*.'" Here Brown's ability to connect what is going on within *Ulysses* with the cultural thinking of the time pays off, as he connects the view he has suggested with Freud's distinction between "the endorsed reproductive act and all others," a distinction which makes all non-reproductive sexuality "onanistic inasmuch as its goal is gratificatory not reproductive"; in such a conception, "there seems to be an important similarity between the act performed by Bloom and Gerty and that performed simultaneously by Molly and Boylan at 7 Eccles Street." Brown even goes so far as to suggest that we have in Nausicaa a "shared gratificatory act" performed by the Blooms "on a huge geographical scale" (pp. 61–62). One need not be willing to go all the way with Brown to be grateful to him for organizing the pleasurable experience of a different perspective on the events of that chapter.

Yet even that discussion is probably less tumescent than it might have been, and other assumptions—also about *Ulysses*, notably—need some elaboration or defense. Of Molly, for example, Brown says that "few of her so-called lovers are intimate enough with her . . . to deserve that title" (p. 21). Are *any*, besides Boylan? Brown acknowledges that Molly's "adulterous past" is frequently regarded as "one of the deliberate modernist uncertainties of the book" (p. 21). But such a seemingly grudging offhand remark is not what is demanded in regard to so climactic a point within a study of sexuality in Joyce's major works: the issue calls for a major confrontation, not a mere assumption, and should not be treated as a casual affair.

Similarly, when Brown alludes to Bloom's thoughts about how "when we left Lombard street west something changed. Could never like it again after Rudy," he does point out that the pronoun "it" may refer to sex, or having children, or even their home in Lombard Street, but he oddly assumes that the subject of the verb "could" is quite definitely plural: that is, that it refers to "they," the Blooms, rather than—as it might, after all—solely to Bloom, or to Molly. An argument might demonstrate that the reference is plural, but as an assumption it is quite illicit. In the same paragraph, he also states that the reference in Ithaca to "incomplete" carnal intercourse, "without ejaculation of semen within the natural female organ," is—we may be assured—"an 'Ithacan' way of describing a contraceptive sexual relationship rather than sexual abstinence" (p. 67). Again, he may be right, but he needs to demonstrate that rightness and not merely assume that the reader will be seduced into going along with him.

Sometimes, a good, solid, learned, and intelligent book can nevertheless be a bit of a disappointment. In this case, I am personally grateful for all the scholarship that has gone into this study, and indeed for the thought that has been devoted to all that Brown has found. Yet I am also (no doubt perversely) regretful about the missed chance: about all that might have been done with about as promising and—truly, if surprisingly— as insufficiently examined an aspect of Joyce's work as there is. I would have longed for him to probe deeper.

For all my bones of contention with this or that discussion in one or another of each of these studies, they are all interesting and valuable, and I think you would enjoy exposing yourself to them. If you were to do so, I would be curious to know, afterward, if the experience had been good for you, too.

A Book that Percolates

Peter L. Shillingsburg

Textual Criticism and Literary Interpretation. Ed. Jerome J. McGann. Chicago: University of Chicago Press, 1985. xii, 240 pp.

This collection of essays represents most of the papers delivered in a March 1982 conference at the California Institute of Technology exploring the relationships, or perhaps, more accurately, allowing a variety of textual critics to express their views of the relationships, between textual criticism and literary interpretation. On the whole the essays reveal consciousness of a rift in contemporary academe between these two activities: textual criticism seen as the province of experts in bibliography, paleography and related "sciences" and literary interpretation seen as the main concern of persons who leave textual criticism to the experts. On the whole, the essays record concern over this apparent rift, exploring various ways in which the work of textual criticism either cannot proceed without literary interpretation or suffers for lack of it and, likewise, ways in which literary interpretation is dependent on or enriched by textual criticism.

The conference pre-dates by two years the publication of McGann's *A Critique of Modern Textual Criticism* (1984), but one can see that book percolating in this one. In some ways this is a more important book, however, because some issues are raised in thought-provoking ways here which McGann tries, unsuccessfully I think, to settle in the 1984 book. For example, there is a sense in several of the articles in this book that textual criticism has settled too comfortably into its role as arbiter of the established text. Hints arise that works of literary art are more complex and more problematical, as products of creative composition, than can be adequately represented in a single standard text. Questions worth pondering are asked about the roles played by literary advisers, editors, and the production staffs of publishing establishments in shaping the "final" work of art. By 1984, McGann seems to have shifted his position from asking questions to offering solutions that seem as rigidly authoritarian as those he is seeking to discredit. While he articulates some of these issues more clearly in *A Critique,* there is a freshness in the essays of the present book that inspires more thoughtful consideration.

Unfortunately not all the essays are of consistently high calibre or openminded inquiry, nor do they all raise the provocative questions that should grip both editor and critic and compel a reassessment of how editions are produced and used. Those questions do arise in this book, and they are why its contents are of primary importance to textual criticism and literary interpretation. McGann is right when he says that there is something fundamentally wrong with editorial procedures and goals conducted and reached before the exercise of literary interpretation, and that there is something fundamentally lacking in interpretation that starts only after textual criticism has been completed. While I don't think the solutions McGann offers in *A Critique* are as universally applicable as he seems to suggest there, he is right also in his fear that modern textual criticism, by which he means usually the Bowers school of textual bibliography (whatever that is), has a tendency to breed a technocratic approach to editing, professing to eschew critical interpretation in favor of "objective" criteria for editorial decision making. Perhaps it says something about my own critical stance to say I share McGann's fear of modern literary criticism, by which he usually means interpretation unaffected by historical contexts, for its tendency to ignore the influence on meaning, not only of histories of composition and publication that produce variant readings, but of place, method, and melior of publication even when no variants survive, displaying a naive belief in the text undisturbed by question of its origin, accuracy, or indeterminateness.

The range of texts discussed in this volume is such that I cannot judge the accuracy or comprehensiveness of the scholarship represented. I suppose that students of Shakespeare, *Piers Plowman,* Chaucer, Byron, and Tom Stoppard may find the

A Book that Percolates

results of significant original research here, but that is not why I think the volume is valuable. The range of literary examples, the range of scholarly points of view within the relatively narrow confines of the discipline of textual criticism, and the variety of arguments brought to bear on the following questions, make the book a breeding ground of inquiry. The central questions are: (1) What is a literary work of art, what is the act of authorship, what is the relevance of revision, what is the role of editorial advice to authors, what is the role of the publisher's production staff in relation to "the work of art itself," and is literary art a determinable and determinate "end product"? (2) What is the goal of scholarly editing, what interpretational acts are involved in editorial procedures, what interpretational consequences result from editorial decisions, what sorts of apparatus are necessary or desirable in an adequate representation of the work of art? and (3) Of what use is textual criticism to literary interpretation, how should critics use scholarly editions, what responsibility does the literary critic have to the indeterminate elements of a text, what does the presence of revision and alternate versions require of critics?

The first question explores our concept of the work of art, its nature, its makeup, its status as an art object and as an extant identity. The second question explores our concept of the editorial responsibility vis-à-vis the art object, the extent to which it can be identified, objectified, cleaned, restored, and made accessible as text or texts. The third question explores our concept of the interpretational responsibility vis-à-vis the art object, the pertinence to criticism of variant forms of a text and of the contexts from which it arose and through which it has travelled.

The authors represented in *Textual Criticism and Literary Interpretation* hold a variety of opinions on these questions, a variety deriving in large part, I think, from the textual situations most familiar to them. Ernest A. J. Honigmann, Michael J. Warren, and Lee Patterson are the writers most keenly aware of the fundamentally indeterminate nature of works of art and of the interpretational element of editorial choices. Patterson and Derek Pearsall both confront squarely what Pearsall calls the "universal and so urgent . . . demand by readers and critics for unambiguous editorial assertion . . . whose need of an unequivocal text, whether out of apathy, exhaustion, innocence, or complacency, is imperative" (pp. 92–93). He points to the facts of given cases which make conclusive editorial decisions possible only by distorting evidence. The indeterminate order of Chaucer's *Tales* dictated, or rather left undictated, by the manuscript evidence would, says Pearsall, "not make studies of the structure and design of the *Tales* impossible or illicit; it would merely ensure that such studies were conducted in a proper context of understanding" (p. 97). What better could one ask?

Peter J. Manning's study of unauthorized editions of Byron contributes little to these issues, though in its own way it is interesting and sound in its research. It functions, however, by its emphasis on unauthorized publishing procedures in the "life" of the work of art, to soften up the audience for the remaining contributors, most of whom seem to assume that works of art may be edited so as to be satisfactorily represented in one reading text. To be fair, Philip Gaskell's study of Stoppard is a model compositional study and is, in its details, perhaps the most complex and interesting of the explorations of variant texts, but since Gaskell uses the evidence to support the authority of non-authorial intervention in the creative process and because he sees the author's and his collaborators' efforts as part of an extended reaching for a final form, his editorial conclusions do not exhibit the sense of textual ambiguity arising from formal multiplicity evidenced in the early essays. My understanding of Gaskell's argument is that editing may be complex and difficult, but it *can* be done right.

Donald Pizer's essay is, unfortunately, quite negligible. Pizer unself-consciously clings to the notion that editing is the process of establishing the text that *should* be regarded as the work of art. The word 'should' is often used in this essay. Pizer's world has apparently been shaken by editions that attempt to replace generally received texts with texts representing the author's early intentions. The essay's one reasonable point is that these texts are versions of the work, not replacement texts, but his argument is frequently marred by reliance on colorful rhetoric rather than close attention to evidence. He "supports" his preference for texts reflecting final intentions and published polish by labeling early versions as "discarded"; he mocks dissenting opinion with exaggeration and oversimplification: "Within this now almost religious allegory of the journey of the text, the editor becomes something of a priest. Confronting the inevitably corrupt thing that is the published text, he cleans it of its worldliness and restores it to its original purity" (p. 147). His definition of self-censorship is vague and slippery; his four tests for the presence of self-censorship are all highly subjective, depending for answers on the critical stance of the editor and, therefore, are no tests at all. He is willing to argue conclusively from the absence of evidence about the really real *Red Badge of Courage*. When confronted with the kind of essential ambiguity earlier handled so well by Honigmann and Warren, Pizer abandons textual ground, seeking refuge for his one-text theory in the long established life of published texts: "The more problematical question for textual scholars is whether efforts of this kind, whatever their interest as literary criticism, are sufficient to overthrow [notice the rhetorical weight of the verb] a text that has been established in the canon for some eighty years" (p. 153). Oh well, never mind the evidence then. Just give us a good, familiar, comfortable text.

It is impossible to read Honigmann's essays on Shakespeare and Chaucer and Warren's on Shakespeare and still desire an edition established by an expert editor who has settled once and for all, in a responsible, scholarly, disciplined way, what is the really real text of a Shakespearean or Chaucerian work. Honigmann argues engagingly and "impartially" in favor of the belief that Shakespeare revised his plays. His examples are interesting, and his development of the argument of "serial revision" to refute the idea of accidental alteration seems convincing to one as unfamiliar with the evidence as I. But he uses such apparently trivial details to raise such a powerful issue that, whether one agrees or disagrees with the conclusion that Shakespeare did revise, the uncertainty can only be addressed by an edition that does not settle the issue one way or another. Honigmann points to the critic's responsibility toward indifferent variants in a work known to be revised; their indifference makes any editorial choice between alternatives interpretive—their possible authority makes every responsible interpretation dependent on contemplation of the alternatives. For those who would rather not trouble themselves with that effort, Honigmann says, "All we can safely say is that the variants in a revised play are just as likely to be Shakespeare's as the readings in a single-text play . . ." (p. 15)—a thought not calculated to inspire complacent confidence. "Once we see that Shakespeare sometimes revised and tinkered with his texts," he goes on, "we must reexamine all the high-quality variants in the canon and ask ourselves whether other rejected readings might not be authorial" (p. 20). If the critic is to exercise his responsibility to the text, the editor must not prevent him from doing so by adopting as his own responsibility the establishment of the text.

Michael Warren demonstrates ways in which editorial decisions, even in such apparently ancillary matters as stage directions, restrict the potentialities of original texts by making some interpretations more likely than others. Uncertainty of interpretation is not sufficiently acknowledged by editors, he contends, when they make emendations or gloss cruxes. The mad editorial pursuit of an established text may be slowed, if not stopped, by calm logic and patient contemplation of the facts demonstrated here. Warren proposes an editorial format that confronts the reader with unedited texts and with commentary designed to force the critic to deal with the potentialities of the text rather than to lull him into a false sense of security about the authority of a standard established text.

In some ways Lee Patterson's essay is both the densest and most thought-provoking in the collection. In the course of reexamining the Kane-Donaldson edition of *Piers Plowman*, Patterson explores the foundation for distinctions between internal and external evidence. He mounts a persuasive argument for the idea that external evidence is no more "objective" than internal evidence, and that internal evidence is just as "objective" as external. No evidence is functional in an editorial argument until interpreted. He concludes that an appeal to documentary evidence is no more authoritative than an appeal to lectional evidence: "Every editorial decision is a function of precisely the same process: the application of the interpretive capacities of the observer to a set of facts." To claim certainty for "objective" or documentary principles of editing is to "take comfort in a set of dangerously unexamined assumptions" (p. 67). If these propositions tend to undermine the critics' firm ground in an established text, that is precisely the point. The condition of editing from the evidence, rather than editing by the rules, is the condition of uncertainty. Patterson's arguments are scarely represented by this commentary.

If *Textual Criticism and Literary Interpretation* consisted only of the first five essays, it would still be well worth the price. The inescapable, though never explicitly stated, conclusion of those essays is that textual criticism *is* literary interpretation and that therefore editing *is* literary criticism. The rest of the essays cling, it seems to me, to the view that textual criticism and literary interpretation are two different activities that touch each other in significant ways. Those essays reflect the notion that works of art are textually determinate, though sometimes the complexities require an expert editor to produce the right edition. Much has been made in recent years of the debate in editorial circles that seems to have polarized in America around Fredson Bowers (the text is that which reflects the author's final intention), Hershel Parker (the text is that which reflects the author's most concentrated creative effort), and Jerome McGann (the text is that which reflects the social contract between author and book producer). All of those views, here oversimplified, have two fundamental elements in common: the text of a literary work is normally one determinate final form of the work, and the editor's task is to comprehend what that form is and produce it. The essays by Honigmann, Warren, Patterson and Pearsall in *Textual Criticism and Literary Interpretation* urge a very different point of view: the text of a literary work is normally indeterminate, and the task of the editor is to assemble and clarify the relevant facts concerning the making, remaking, and preserving of the work, being especially careful not to give the reading public a determined text. A determined or single established text can be produced only by an editor who interprets the evidence for all of us and restricts the interpretational possibilities by selecting emendations for THE edited text. Honigmann, Warren, Patterson, and Pearsall appear to reject such editing and to say instead that the critic should confront all the interpretational possibilities equally.

Talking the South

Michael O'Brien

Richard Gray. *Writing the South: Ideas of an American Region*. Cambridge: Cambridge University Press, 1986. xiv, 333 pp.

Richard Gray published *The Literature of Memory: Modern Writers of the American South* in 1977. It was a good book, thoughtful and independent. Having these virtues, it was dismissed by an anonymous hand in the *Sewanee Review* as "cavalier, idiosyncratic, and self-indulgent," presumably from a preference for the roundhead, the imitative, and the self-denying. One hopes that this second book will fare better, even though it has the same virtues and invites the same repudiation.

Writing the South: Ideas of an American Region is really a book of essays. The preface speaks modestly of the volume being no survey or synthesis, but offering "a series of notes towards a definition of the Southern idea" (p. xii), with each chapter incrementally sketching the historical circumstances of thought, before moving to a scrutiny of texts that offer "a preliminary chart" of regional ideology (p. xiii). The analysis is firmly based in the (now more common) premise that the South is "primarily a concept, a matter of knowing even more than of being," and that "Southerners have . . . been engaged not so much in writing about the South as in writing the South" (p. xii). These defining notes concentrate on Southern literature since the Civil War, though there is a preliminary chapter on early Virginia and another on the Old South. But the meat of the book, and its best passages, comes after 1865.

It will be charitable to skip lightly over the first two chapters, which are often mistaken. Gray's strength as a literary critic is a willingness to consider historical and social evidence, to ponder the necessary gap between 'reality' and perception, and closely to scrutinize literary texts. His pages are full of sensible references to the necessity and function of myth, and slightly less beguiling quotations from Roland Barthes, which do at least have the merit of adding spice at a Southern literary criticism that has been doggedly stodgy in its theories of knowing. The richer and more abundant his texts, the more absorbed Gray is, the less inclined to wander around in the historical context. The weaker and more scattered his texts, the more he is pushed out into that context, where his touch is far from sure. Earlier Southern thought, being strong on political and social philosophy and weak in belles lettres, tempts him with unhappy results. It is not that he does not read those sources away from the novel and poetry. His early chapters freely cite the likes of William Byrd, the Hakluyts, Francis Bacon, and Robert Beverley. But he does not seem to have read much recent historiography. In the first two chapters, the endnotes cite just three historical (excluding literary historical) works published after 1969, Eugene Genovese's *Roll, Jordan, Roll*, Daniel J. Singal's *The War Within*, and a textbook on Southern history. For the rest, Gray relies on an antediluvian collection of historians, including Philip A. Bruce and Thomas J. Wertenbaker, whose shades must be pleased at a mention after the lapse of so many decades. The consequence is not so much error (though there are errors) as redundancy. For the argument of Chapter 1, "Virginia and the arguments for the South," is that the pastoral and utopian vein of seventeenth-century English thought informed early ideas about Virginia, and that an equivocal vision of a society both robustly yeoman and planter patriarchal was a legacy of English ideology, obliged to bend to colonial social realities. Unfortunately this is a commonplace standpoint for a host of historians, including Bernard Bailyn and Rhys Isaac. Again, in the second chapter, "Holding the line in the Old South," Gray makes much of the Old South's being a fief of great planters, whose ideologists were mired in gentlemanly delusion and unable to grasp the "fluid and amorphous" character of antebellum society (p. 43). This vision has been cast into grave doubt by the writings of such as Mills Thornton, David Goldfield, and Lacy Ford on the score of planter and agrarian dominance, and by the work of Drew Gilpin Faust and (it is best to confess the partisanship) myself on the matter of intellectual eclecticism among antebellum intellectuals. None of these names seems to have brushed Gray's thoughts. Now it is perfectly possible to write distinguished criticism by sticking to original sources and abjuring the merely secondary and fashionable (it may indeed be easier), but these chapters offer mixed encouragement. On Simms and the Southwestern humorists, Gray is illuminating, but his discussion of Calhoun is a disaster, mostly because Gray insists on regarding Calhoun as representative of the South, ideologically as well as politically, when the South Carolinian was decidedly not so and the pathos of his political career resided precisely in his inability to make himself representative. It is the more improbable to see Calhoun as aristocratic, when his power in South Carolina was firmly rooted in the democracy that Gray mistakenly persists in seeing as an unfulfilled dream in Southern political culture.

But things begin to pick up in the third chapter, "The New South, the lost cause, and the recovered dream." A discussion of the plantation romance is conventional, but a scrutiny of Sidney Lanier is better, and there is the best attempt I have seen to construe Mark Twain as a Southern writer, more convincing than, though in places echoing, Louis Rubin's reading of *A Connecticut Yankee in King Arthur's Court* as an attack on the New South. Instead Gray argues that Twain was best as an autobiographer of childhood, one imbedded in antebellum culture. The analysis is the more persuasive for being skeptical of Twain's achievement, aware of its unevenness, so that praise, when bestowed, is telling. There is none of that crashing of gears, so common in literary criticism, when the critic moves from the uncanonical to the canonical, from a sneer to a rosary.

The fourth chapter, "A climate of fear: the South between the wars and the Nashville Agrarians," may be the book's best. Its first half, though not especially original, is an efficient discussion of the nuances of emphasis among the Agrarians. It is perhaps too much in thrall to Allen Tate's own analysis of the historical position of himself and the South. But the second half, subtitled "Speech and Silence: 'I'll Take My Stand' and the Defence of the

South" is a valuable contribution to Southern intellectual history in that it offers a detailed scrutiny of the parallels between the *Proslavery Argument* of 1852 and the symposium of 1930. The venture proves extremely worthwhile, and oddly alone, considering how much has been made of the place of the Agrarians in the Southern tradition. But the paradox is readily explained, when one recalls that, however much the Agrarians talked about continuity with their Southern forebears, they were much more entranced with their own originality and always better informed about Eliot and Baudelaire than Calhoun and Fitzhugh. Gray carefully shows apparent continuities: organic historicism, pastoralism, an awareness of human sin, a disinclination to abstraction, an enthusiasm for inequality, a rejection of the idea of progress and the reality of capitalism, a fondness for the paternalist ethic, a mistrust of experimentalism. Nothing in this list would surprise Richard Weaver, but the detailed exegesis by Gray is arresting, even as it leaves unexplained how or whether the continuity was transmitted within the confines of the region's local intellectual history.

There is a chapter on William Faulkner. Literary critics would reduce the world's tedium if they suppressed the urge to write chapters on William Faulkner. Failing that, reviewers can help by withholding comment on such chapters.

The final chapter, "The Southerner as amphibian: the region since the war," is discursive and delicately ambivalent about the death of the South. Gray briskly deploys the usual statistics about the pace of industrial and urban change to argue that the old themes of Southern thought and literature are moribund, obliging the Southerner to be amphibious: "Alterations in the material fabric of society are not necessarily or immediately accompanied by alterations in the consciousness of its members. So the cultural lag persists, even if in weakened form; and the war between the old codes and the new continues, with the new slowly but steadily gaining ground. The Southerner, in effect, still belongs in two worlds, two moral territories, even if he is turning back ever less easily or frequently to one of these; in terms of his mind or imagination at least, he remains an amphibious creature" (pp. 230–31). To demonstrate this, Gray briefly examines William Styron and Barry Hannah, before moving to an admirably sensible and detailed consideration of Eudora Welty and Walker Percy. Welty, naturally, stands for the survival of the old, Percy for the arrival of the new, though it is unclear which of these amphibians is still mainly at sea, which primarily on land. The new is postmodernist, in Richard Gilman's definition: "open-ended, provisional, characterized by suspended judgements, by a disbelief in hierarchies, by mistrust of solutions, denouements and completions, by self-consciousness issuing in tremendous earnestness but also in far-ranging mockery" (p. 236). Hence in Percy is an epitaph for the South.

Or so, in the manner of Lewis P. Simpson, Gray believes, knowing that this is not a matter for firm opinions, being a judgement of a very fluid present and a dubious future. My own unfirm opinion is that Southerners have been intellectual amphibians since the beginning of the South, and we are witnessing only the most recent phase of a continual process. The death of the South is a very old tradition, one to which Walker Percy greatly belongs. His writing, after all, insistently refers to that death and, by that reiteration, the tradition lives.

Fragments of the social history of the region have, of course, really died. Slavery was once indispensable to Southern imagery, but is no longer so. Poverty plays a small part now, when once it loomed large. Politics was central to antebellum writing, but modern Southern literature is apolitical. Content dies, but the necessity for form lives. Gray's point that there are modern writers to whom the South is uninteresting is true, but a little beside the point. There have always been writers indifferent to 'writing the South': these were and are outside the discourse. Yet there are still many to whom the South is a usable tradition. The South will only be dead when these cease to exist. Put more schematically, the South will die when Romanticism, the premise of the discourse, dies. Postmodernism offers little prospect of that, and seems indeed something of a return to the old traditions of Romantic irony. There is little in Gilman's definition with which Friedrich von Schlegel would have been uncomfortable or unfamiliar.

So this too is a good book, with much of substance and insight, much with which to disagree. Gray, in his preface, seems aware that the volume is a little ramshackle. An author who characterizes his venture as "notes towards a definition of . . ." is confessedly bashful. But Gray writes well, conversationally, like a rather earnest and intellectual guest, sherry glass in hand before dinner, talking engagingly on some books he has just finished. ("Ah, but would you not say that Barthes has shown us that . . . yes, thank you, a little more. I had the dry.") The conversational style, like conversation, runs the danger of redundancy, repetition, murkiness of thought. Gray does not always evade these difficulties, and a certain slackness now and then creeps in. Parentheses abound, sometimes as many as three to a sentence. Speculations are hazarded, only to be retracted a paragraph later in the musing monologue. He seems to have half an eye on the skepticism of his listener; much is tentative that need not be. More rarely there is dogmatism to overbear the unconvinced. But at least Gray has a voice, which is more than can be said for most authors.

The Politics of Shakespeare's Plays, Then and Now

Richard A. Burt

David Bergeron. *Shakespeare's Romances and the Royal Family*. Lawrence: University of Kansas Press, 1985. xiii, 257 pp.

Michael Bristol. *Carnival and Theater: Plebeian Culture and the Structures of Authority in Renaissance England*. New York: Methuen, 1985. x, 287 pp.

Jonathan Dollimore and Alan Sinfield, eds. *Political Shakespeare: Essays in Cultural Materialism*. Ithaca: Cornell University Press, 1985. vii, 244 pp.

John Drakakis, ed. *Alternative Shakespeares*. New York: Methuen, 1985. xii, 260 pp.

Patricia Parker and Geoffrey Hartman, eds. *Shakespeare and the Question of Theory*. New York: Methuen, 1985. xiv, 335 pp.

Leonard Tennenhouse. *Power on Display: The Politics of Shakespeare's Genres*. New York: Methuen, 1986. ix, 201 pp.

It is perhaps more than coincidental that the topic of Shakespeare's politics should receive renewed attention at roughly the same moment broad questions about the literary canon and about the role of the profession have become widespread topics of critical debate. As traditional humanist justifications for the study of literature have entered what is regularly termed a state of crisis, the celebration of Shakespeare's plays as classics, sacred texts not of an age but for all time, has come under scrutiny by critics who seek to displace the traditional celebration of literature with alternative constructions of its cultural and sexual politics drawn from a variety of disciplines. Criticism conceived as the critical appreciation of literary monuments and of the artistic geniuses who built them largely gives way, in the books and collections under review here, to polemical inquiry into the way Shakespeare's plays were and are inscribed, encoded, and embedded in historically specific cultural practices and institutions. Most of these critics are as concerned with the way Shakespeare's plays might be said to reinforce or resist the dominant ideologies of the English Renaissance as they are with the politics of teaching and producing Shakespeare in the present.

Underlying much of this criticism is a central opposition between what may be termed "essentialism" and "constructivism": the former regards literature (or gender) ahistorically; conversely, the latter regards literature and identity as a social construction. The central thrust of much current criticism is first to reveal the limitations of an essentialist account of literature and then to put some version of a constructivist account in its place. The works considered here reveal both the undoubted importance of this move and also its limitations.

Before considering its limitations, however, it is best to understand fully its value. This is perhaps best shown in the most widely studied aspect of Shakespeare's politics, namely, the sexual. Feminist criticism of the plays has tended by and large to be ahistorical, preferring the general term *patriarchy*. One of the most important books yet written on gender and Shakespeare is Peter Erickson's *Patriarchal Structures in Shakespeare's Drama*. Like much earlier feminist criticism, Erickson's book raises a series of ethical questions about the sexual politics of each play: "Does the range of options for male and female roles in a given play promote mutuality and equality, or does it foster a disparity that favors one sex at the expense of another?" (p. ix) Yet the book is at the same time a pointed and polemical critique of previous liberal feminist readings of gender and genre, particularly those of Marilyn French and Linda Bamber.[2] Rather than distinguish gender and genre in terms of strict antitheses, men and women lining up with comedy and tragedy respectively, Erickson wants to account for what the comedies and tragedies have in common. More specifically, he implicitly challenges the argument widely made by a number of psychoanalytic feminists that comedy is an "anti-patriarchal" norm from which "patriarchal" tragedy departs. Erickson makes a central (if unfortunately ahistorical) distinction between "crude" and "benign" patriarchy, a distinction he keeps collapsing: "Benevolent patriarchy, despite its merits, is not without its problematic side; it cannot be mistaken for the attainment of fully independent female characters" (pp. 12–13). Erickson sees the plays as essentially patriarchal, even if the forms of patriarchy have been modified, and this argument is made through skeptical, deidealizing readings of the plays; in this respect, the book nicely complements David Sundelson's similarly hardnosed account of Shakespeare's investment in his own partriarchal culture.[3]

Erickson's book contains more fine readings than can be summarized here, but even one will I think suggest the quality of the readings as a whole. In a chapter comparing *Love's Labor's Lost* and *As You Like It*, Erickson argues that male bonding is an impediment to heterosexual relations in both plays. Yet Erickson does not draw a neat contrast between them and argue that male bonds block a happy ending in the earlier unsuccessful comedy while in the later comedy fuller heterosexual bonding enables a happy ending. Instead, he argues that *As You Like It*, through Rosalind and Celia's transvestism, succeeds in doing precisely what *Love's Labor's Lost* tried and failed to do, namely, secure male bonds at the expense of heterosexual bonds. *As You Like It* achieves this conservative political end chiefly by "phasing out" the independent Rosalind in order to reduce a fear of powerful women (whose power is maternal): closure comfortably occurs first by having her submit to husband and father, then by displacing her as a source of magic with Hymen; as if that were not reassurance enough, Rosalind reminds us in the epilogue that she is only a boy actor after all. Erickson concludes that "Fear of women can be encountered in the relatively safe environment of the theater, acted out, controlled . . . and overcome" (p. 34).

Erickson offers similarly deidealizing readings that other feminists have celebrated for being progressive, particularly those of *Antony and Cleopatra* and *The Winter's Tale*. He shows convincingly that neither play is as "wholly positive" as we might wish to believe. At the end of *Antony and Cleopatra*, "We are left at the end with a painfully divided response, for which there is no resolution" (p. 145). Similarly, *The Winter's Tale* fails to move beyond patriarchy, no matter how benign a form patriarchy takes in the play. Hermione is largely diminished: she never recovers the kind of wit we see in evidence in the second scene of the play. It is precisely through this reduction of independent women, including Paulina (who is married to Camillo by Leontes), Erickson argues, that the play can end as a romance at all.

Focused on major plays from all four genres, Erickson's book stands as an important and necessary corrective to a number of recent liberal feminist studies which tend to save Shakespeare as a feminist, and the enviable elegance and clarity of Erickson's prose will earn his book an honored place at the top of current feminist studies of Shakespeare. Despite the real virtues of this book, however, the force of Erickson's critique of Shakespeare's conservatism is radically limited by his ahistorical commitment to the very values his book explicitly challenges. Like Coppelia Kahn's study of male identity in Shakespeare, Erickson's attempts to link a psychoanalytic framework with social history, and thus to begin to historicize both patriarchy and the formation and engendering of identity.[4] Yet like Kahn, Erickson does not really break with the fundamental assumptions of liberal feminism, as his rhetoric of "growth," psychic "wholeness" and "fruitfulness" implies. Here is a sample: "Male wholeness depends on an integrated view of women. This rigid separation of masculine and feminine and the systematic suppression of the latter, held to be essential to a secure male identity, are counterproductive. The separation prevents fruitful coordination of masculine and feminine elements, thereby blocking psychic wholeness in the male" (p. 95). The difference between Erickson's account and earlier accounts of the extent to which Shakespeare's plays are patriarchal is not in the assumptions about feminism but in whether Shakespeare holds those assumptions. More crucially, Erickson's notion of sexual politics is itself ahistorical. Why did Shakespeare have to modify patriarchy from crude to benign forms? What is the "power of women" to which Erickson, like other psychoanalytic critics, so often refers? What

The Politics of Shakespeare's Plays

is the "fear of women"? The generalizing of both "fear" and of "women" here is clearly a function of an ahistorical psychological framework. Similar questions could be raised about the way Erickson ahistorically (and inaccurately) gives social practices like feasting or the dispensation of bounty a gendered inflection. (He refers to bounty as specifically "maternal.") Feasting and bounty were in fact very much culturally and historically specific. It was the duty of the (male) gentry to show hospitality to their tenants, as a number of proclamations during the period make clear; similarly, James I published in 1610 a *Book of Bounty* regulating the dispensation of patents and gifts from the court.[5] Erickson claims that he is not importing "patriarchy" into the plays, but he doesn't bother to historicize the notion of patriarchy at all. (He merely footnotes Lawrence Stone's *Sex, Marriage, and the Family in England: 1500–1800* and Louis Monstrose's essay on Shakespeare's theater.)

The way to resolve these problems, a number of other critics suggest, is to see gender not in terms of essential eternal human essences but as a social construction both in Shakespeare's culture and in ours. To put it another way, gender has to be historicized, located in specific discursive practices. Issues such as androgyny and transvestism are not evidence of a specifically Shakespearean imagination so much as they resemble a much wider cultural and political way of imagining and perhaps resolving gender and power.[6] One historicizing study of the family is David Bergeron's *Shakespeare's Romances and the Royal Family*. Bergeron rightly criticizes Peter Erickson's account of patriarchy on the grounds that it is ahistorical, and tries at the same time to move past "old" historicist accounts of the romance as allegories of contemporary politics, the sort of argument advanced by Glynne Wickham, among others. Instead, Bergeron sees the royal family as the point of crucial political connection. Like so many critics who have taken up the issue of the family in Shakespeare, Bergeron draws on Lawrence Stone's *The Family, Sex, and Marriage*. More particularly, his first chapter on the royal family is deeply indebted to Jonathan Goldberg's recent study of the Jacobean family (*James I and the Politics of Literature: Shakespeare,*

Jonson, Donne, and their Contemporaries) to link Shakespeare's romances with celebrations and festivities such as those held for the wedding of Princess Elizabeth and the Elector Palatine in 1614.

Bergeron draws on a post-structuralist and anthropological metaphor, namely the text, to make this link: "James's family becomes a prototext for the Romances where the reunion of royal families signals feasts, marriages, and other public displays. Shakespeare, standing in London's streets for James's royal entry in 1604, must have been impressed with the royal family as family and its concomitant expression of the language of power. With his own power of language he creates royal families in the Romances, families susceptible to suffering and separation yet ultimately able to triumph in ways possible in fiction but sometimes alien to actual experience" (p. 72). Despite Bergeron's typically "new historicist" chiastic formulation—the language of power/the power of language—his account of the relation between the text of the royal family and the texts of Shakespeare's plays remains essentially an old historicist one, with a clear distinction between historical documents and literary texts. The book's structure reinforces the conceptual opposition. After a brief introduction, a chapter follows on the royal family. The remainder of the book discusses plays: after the chapter "Sex, Family, and Marriage in Jacobean City Comedy," Bergeron proceeds to discuss all of the romances, including *Henry VIII*, in the accepted chronological order. Thus, the readings of the plays stand apart from the reading of the culture. Not to put too fine a point on it, the readings are conventional thematic readings of the plays awkwardly dressed up in "new" historicist garb. Consequently, crucial questions about the plays' political effects are simply never raised or explored. Instead, like Gary Schmidgall's similarly problematic but still far superior study of *The Tempest*, Bergeron's book tacitly holds the romances to be idealizing celebrations of the royal family.[7] Unlike Schmidgall, however, Bergeron never connects the question of courtly authority to Shakespeare's representation of that authority.

Much more forceful and original critiques of humanist feminism are offered by Kathleen McCluskie in an essay entitled "The Partriarchal Bard" in *Political Shakespeare* and by Jonathan

The Politics of Shakespeare's Plays

Goldberg in an essay entitled "Voicings of Power" in *Shakespeare and the Question of Theory*. Both McCluskie and Goldberg address the kind of ahistorical feminism practiced by critics like Linda Bamber and argue that gender has to be historicized. Goldberg observes that Bamber's conceptual categories are anachronistic: Shakespeare's world "excludes most of the conceptual categories (e.g., autonomy and growth) that she projects on from her modern, liberal vantage point upon his world. This means that we must give up notions of character as self-same, owned, capable of autonomy and change; that biological difference is an a priori fact, and to return to Simone de Beauvoir's essential insight in *The Second Sex* that woman is a cultural construct and category and therefore not the same then as now. Ironically, feminists like Bamber reimpose the prescriptions they mean to erase by restating the oppressive categories that must be sent through and must be read beyond for a genuine feminist discourse to arise" (p. 118). Similarly, McCluskie criticizes what she calls the "essentialism" rather than historicism of feminists like French and Bamber. McCluskie believes "liberal feminism" is to be faulted for viewing "feminist struggle as concerned with reordering the values ascribed to men and women without fundamentally changing the material circumstances in which their relationships function. It presents feminism as a set of attitudes rather than as a project for fundamental social change." By contrast, McCluskie suggests that "A more complex discussion of the case would acknowledge that the issues of sex, sexuality, sexual relations and sexual division were areas of conflict of which the contradictions of writing about women were only one manifestation alongside the complexity of legislation and other forms of social control of sex and family" (p. 91). As a critical method, historicizing is thus a necessary and (welcome) relief to the kind of attitudinizing that so often substitutes for critical analysis of Shakespeare's plays.

In both essays, McCluskie and Goldberg offer alternative readings of several plays. McCluskie offers readings of sexuality in *Measure for Measure* and *King Lear*, and Goldberg talks about the importance of "voicing," of attending, that is, to who speaks, for whom, and under what circumstances. Still these readings seem a bit abstract and thin; Goldberg's readings are not exactly compelling, and McCluskie's reading of *Measure for Measure* seems retrogressive. If you like the play, if you see it as a comedy, she argues, then you read it as a sexist male. If you see the comedy as undermined, then you're a feminist.

If ahistorical modes of feminism are to be effectively displaced, what seems needed are more closely historicized accounts of Renaissance constructions of gender and sexuality and of the ways Shakespeare's plays participate in and resist those constructions. By far the most interesting reading along these lines comes out of an explicitly Foucauldian account and history of sexuality as a discursive practice in Jonathan Dollimore's brilliant and penetrating essay in *Political Shakespeare*. Entitled "Transgression and Surveillance in *Measure for Measure*," Dollimore's essay rejects a Bakhtinian model of transgression as a form of liberation and subversion and argues that in *Measure for Measure* the transgressors "signify neither the unregeneracy of the flesh, nor the ludic, subversive carnivalesque. Rather, as the specter of unregulated sexual desire, they are exploited to legitimate an exercise in authoritarian repression. At the same time, in this period, in its laws, statutes, proclamations, and moralistic tracts, the marginalized and the deviant, as it were, endlessly react in a complex ideological process whereby authority is ever relegitimating itself" (p. 84). The play's concern with sexual behavior as potentially subversive and criminal, something to be detected, punished, and perhaps pardoned by authority, registers a similar concern in the period to regulate sexual behavior. I can only refer the reader to this essay where he can see how originally and forcefully Dollimore combines a Foucauldian model of theater as an instrument of power and social history to produce an extraordinarily discerning account of the interpenetration of Shakespeare's play and Shakespeare's culture.

Dollimore's reading of sexuality as a force which authority regulates continues a much larger inquiry into the politics of Shakespearean drama, focused on the relation between the theater and authority, which he began in his book, *Radical Tragedy: Shakespeare and His Contemporaries*.[8] To what extent was the theater subversive of authority? In his introduction to *Political Shakespeare*, Dollimore pursues these questions in order to make possible what he and others have termed "oppositional criticism." In the first section, entitled "History Versus the Human Condition," Dollimore criticizes the Tillyardian sense of the Elizabethan period as consolidating, that is, "socially cohesive in the positive sense of transcending sectional interests and articulating a genuinely shared culture and cosmology, characterised by harmony, stability and unity" (p. 10). Dollimore goes on to discuss "The Politics of Renaissance Theater" and offers "Consolidation, Subversion, and Containment" as the terms in which those politics should be thought about. (The terms are of course borrowed from Stephen Greenblatt's remarkable essay, "Invisible Bullets: Renaissance Authority and Its Subversion," at the front of this collection.)

Though his essay, like Greenblatt's, is indebted to Foucault, Dollimore advances not a Foucauldian theory of power but a cultural materialist theory of ideology, one indebted to Gramsci and to Raymond Williams. Dollimore argues that "Cultural domination is not a static, unalterable thing; it is rather a process, one always having to be renewed" (p. 13). Crucial to this account of ideology is the concept of "appropriation," a concept which signals that meaning is the site of political contestation, not something intrinsic to a literary text: "Instead of monolithic power, power is made up of different, often competing elements, and these not merely producing culture but producing it through appropriations. . . . Although subversion may indeed buy authority for its own purposes, once installed it can be used against authority as well as used by it" (p. 12). Dollimore does not explicitly oppose Foucauldian and materialist theories, but he implicitly differentiates between them on the grounds that cultural materialism leaves open the possibility of resistance and opposition both in literary texts and in our own critical practice.[8]

In the Drakasis collection, *Alternative Shakespeares*, Dollimore and Alan Sinfield develop this theory of ideology in a related essay on *Henry V*. They criticize both Tillyard and Lily Campbell for using a simple reflection theory of literature and history; similarly they criticize Jan Kott for simply inverting the world picture they construct—instead of order, Kott sees chaos and fragmentation. "Perhaps the most fundamental error in all these accounts of the role of ideology," they conclude, "is to unify history and/or the individual human subject." (And, they might have added, the literary text.)

> Our concern for a materialist criticism is with the history of . . . resistance, with the attempt to recover the voices and cultures of the repressed and marginalized in history and writing. Morever, ideology is stablized not only from below but by antagonisms within and among the class or class fraction (high, as opposed to popular, literature will often manifest this kind of destablization.) Whereas idealist literary criticism has tended to emphasize the transcendence of conflict and contradiction, materialist criticism seeks to stay with them, wanting to understand them better. [p. 214]

Despite their desire to find resistance and opposition, both Sinfield and Dollimore are aware of the difficulty of doing so. Dollimore says that it would be a mistake to underestimate the capacity of power to contain possible threats: "Arguably, an oppositional criticism will always be deficient, always liable to collapse, if it underestimates the extent, strategies and flexible complexity of domination" (p. 14). Thus, any critic looking for evidence of opposition and resistance must be prepared to ask whether he has only uncovered evidence of ideological containment, containment which depends on the licensed production of subversion.

Dollimore announces at the beginning of his essay on *Measure for Measure* that he hopes it is not too late to forestall a Bakhtinian account of Shakespeare's problem comedy:

> With the considerable attention recently devoted to Mikhail Bakhtin and his truly important analysis of the subversive carnivalesque, the time is right for a radical reading of *Measure for Measure*, one that insists on the oppressiveness of the Viennese State and which interprets low-life transgression as *positively* anarchic, ludic, carnivalesque—a subversion from below of a repressive official ideology of order. What follows aims (if it is not too late) to forestall such a reading as scarcely less appropriate than that which privileged true authority over anarchic desire. Indeed, such a reading, if executed within the parameters of some recent appropriations of Bakhtin, would simply remain within

the problematic, only reversing the polarities of the binary opposition which structures it (order/chaos). [p. 74]

Dollimore's warning is certainly worth heeding. It came too late, however, for Michael Bristol, who takes up precisely a Bakhtinian account of carnival to argue in his book, *Carnival and Theater: Renaissance England and the Structures of Authority*, that the theater and popular culture continually subverted Renaissance authority. Bristol's book is highly speculative and opens fruitful areas of inquiry and research on the relation between the theater and the drama to carnival. Bristol begins with useful if somewhat redundant surveys of current "new" historicist accounts of the theater and of anthropological theories of carnival from Durkeheim to Barber. Mikhail Bakhtin's theory of carnival is heralded by Bristol as the authoritative way to construct a relation between the structures of authority and the theater.

It is precisely the way Bakhtin is used that makes Bristol's book both interesting and ultimately unconvincing. Bristol derives from Bakhtin a set of critical oppositions which he applies to the English Renaissance theater and drama: the ephemeral, incomplete, and unfinished are to be privileged over the permanent, complete, and finished. These conceptual categories are identified with a political opposition between the ruling elite and the plebeians. The theater is dialogic and heteroglot, while elite authority is just the opposite. This account of the theater's social subversiveness also traces a historical transition: the theater is essentially continuous with the plebeian life of the market square.

Though Bristol admits that carnival can have a conservative social function, he stresses what he calls the element of "class struggle" and focuses on the ways "ruling class" authority is resisted through plebeian culture: "The forms of festive life are always available for appropriation to particular social and political purposes. In early modern Europe such appropriation is by no means exclusively confined to the dominant culture. Carnival is put into operation as resistance to any tendency to absolutize authority, and to the disruptive radicalizations of social life proposed and implemented by powerful elites. This resistance is purposeful, and proceeds in accordance with the ethical imperatives of plebeian culture" (p. 39). Bristol's thesis thus complements Robert Weimann's argument that Shakespeare used the popular tradition to criticize the elite social and political codes. Bristol goes even further than Weimann, however, in giving carnival a subversive potential: certain forms of popular culture enable the lower sort to resist and struggle against early exploitative forms of capitalism.

The links between carnival and the theater and between culture and authority are certainly important and interesting, and attention to the theater as a social institution is certainly worthwhile. Perhaps the major strength of the book is that it opens up important new areas of research as well as new ways of conducting that research: Bristol devotes a fascinating chapter to the Battle of Lent between Fishmongers and Butchers, for example, while raising anew questions about the politics of transferring traditional pastimes to the professional theater.

Despite his book's real virtues, however, Bristol never proves his thesis that the theater was essentially subversive. One might be convinced by this argument were it based on either historical research or on close historicizing readings of texts (either literary or non-literary). Instead of doing research based on primary sources which might ground his theory in the Renaissance, Bristol relies on the theories of Bakhtin and on work done on carnival in France by historians like Emmanuel Le Roy Ladurie. Bristol ignores the controversy over the *Book of Sports*, issued in 1617 and in 1633, as well as the assimilation of carnival into the court masque by Jonson, Davenant, and others.[10] *Bartholomew Fair* is left undiscussed. (The induction is mentioned briefly.) Bristol never demonstrates how carnival was used on behalf of plebeian interests; moreover, he neglects all the evidence which shows how carnival was appropriated by the monarchy and patricians to form an alliance with plebeians against the bourgeoning middle groupings that ultimately suppressed both the monarchy and carnival.[11] Were it not for more conservative elites who patronized rural pastimes, the games would have been suppressed entirely by the early seventeenth century. Nor does Bristol mention the effects of commerce on plebeian culture.[12]

Most crucially, Bristol's essentialist conceptual and political oppositions are by definition ahistorical. The opposition between plebeian culture and established authority as opposed does not really hold up. Recent research by leading historians has shown that the elites were as divided as were plebeians about the status of traditional forms of culture.[13] Moreover, popular and official cultural practices often overlapped.[14]

Bristol's readings of texts that are now part of the literary canon do little better to convince one that plebeian culture was essentially subversive. Nashe's *Summer's Last Will and Testament* gets about three sentences, and that is typical of what counts as a reading of a text. Shakespeare's plays also suffer short shrift. We don't get an account of the carnivalesque in these texts and how it operates so much as we get citations of one or two passages of texts to which carnival is relevant; moreover, the readings are both predictable and forced: moments of subversion are identified with moments which are not finished or closed. Thus, *A Midsummer Night's Dream* is said to be subversive of social order: Bottom and the rude mechanicals "oppose" the Athenian aristocracy. Even the range of Bristol's readings—from More to Erasmus, to Shakespeare, to Nashe—which links literature to carnival—would seem to call his Bakhtinian opposition between "high" and "low" culture into question.

For a book concerned with excess and plenitude associated with carnival, this one is disappointingly penurious. The book exhibits none of Weimann's breadth of scholarship or his thematic focus on the way popular tradition is adapted in the Renaissance and by Shakespeare. This study could have offered an important dialetical exploration of the problems with Bakhtin's account of popular culture, particularly the way it opposes high and low culture. The tensions between English culture and Bakhtin's theory might have produced an interesting new theory of the theater and authority. (Precisely this kind of critical use of Bakhtin has been put to powerful use by Jean-Christophe Agnew in his recent study, *Worlds Apart: The Theater and the Market in Anglo-American Thought, 1550–1750* [Cambridge University Press, 1986].) But Bristol chose to pursue no such exploration, and the problems with his book can be traced, I think, precisely to the way he uncritically makes the English Renaissance match Bakhtin's theory.

In contrast with Bristol's attention to the subversiveness of the theater, Leonard Tennenhouse advances a much stronger account of the way the theater *authorized* the state both in an essay on Shakespeare's history plays in *Political Shakespeare* and in his *Power on Display: the Politics of Shakespeare's Genres*. (The essay has been incorporated into the book.) Tennenhouse's extremely important and provocative book complements works by Goldberg, Dollimore, and others. It may also be said to rank above them in its scope and in the originality and daring of its formulations. Tennenhouse draws on Foucault and Bakhtin as well as on semiotics and cultural history to construct an altogether original and compelling case for viewing Shakespeare as "a servant of the state." The book is clearly written and intelligible, but its complexity and its remarkable scope prevent similarly clear exposition within the space alloted a reviewer.

Tennenhouse's account of the ideology of the plays is essentially regiocentric. He argues that Shakespeare's plays revise and adapt Elizabethan and Jacobean strategies of state. This account of the plays as culturally determined means that we must conduct our readings of the texts differently. Instead of attending to imagery, language, theme, character, and structure, taking them to be evidence of Shakespeare's artistic mastery, Tennenhouse reads the form of the plays, particularly genre, "semiotically." This means showing how the way cultural icons and materials are "staged" is at the same time an ideological strategy. It is this operation that Tennenhouse repeatedly discloses in his readings of particular plays, an operation he finds to be a mutual authorization of theater and the state.

Tennenhouse views the theater not as a reflection of other cultural practices but as analogous to those of the court: drama was similar to entertainments at court, progresses, etc.—displays on state. Of crucial significance for Tennenhouse is what he calls, following Foucault, the theater of punishment; similarly, Tennenhouse draws on the work of Roy Strong and others to examine what he terms the iconography of state. Shakespeare affirms the legitimacy of the state by appropriating its symbolic forms

The Politics of Shakespeare's Plays

and developing them. While monarchs shift, the theater remains a means of idealizing power. The book is organized alone generic lines. It opens with a chapter on the comedies entitled "Staging Carnival and the Politics of the Aristocratic Body," proceeds to a chapter on the histories entitled "Rituals of State: History and Elizabethan Strategies of Power," then moves to a chapter on the tragedies, "The Theater of Punishment: Jacobean Tragedy and the Politics of Misogyny," and ends with a chapter on the romances, "Family Rites: City Comedy, Romance, and the Strategies of Patriarchalism." The differences between Elizabethan and Jacobean strategies of representation are carefully mapped out in Shakespeare's plays.

In the chapter on the comedies Tennenhouse begins by outlining the way that Elizabeth herself shaped the sexual lives of her court and then shows how Shakespeare's comedies indirectly reinforce Elizabeth's authority. In contrast with modern critics who want to discuss the theme of romantic love in the comedies without talking about politics, Tennenhouse argues that love was always political in the Renaissance, as was the way that love was imagined. The Elizabethan court gave rise to a specific discourse on love, namely Petrarchanism and romance. This discourse was formulated by courtiers, such as Sidney. But this aristocratic discourse was used differently in the theater by Shakespeare. While Sidney separates aristocrats and the commoners along lines of blood, Shakespeare does something altogether different. He often parodies aristocrats and aristocratic love; moreover, he manages through the figure of the aristocratic woman and through the use of carnival forms of license to purify the common people, thereby making them worthy of participation in the life of the court. Thus, carnival or the Bakhtinian opposition between the mass body and the body does not subvert the state but serves the state.

This argument is made initially in the context of Shakespeare's festive comedies:

Rather than dissolving the boundaries which authorized aristocratic power, the inclusion of the parodic—the mechanicals play about aristocratic love—within the official festivities of the state offers perhaps the most perfect manifestation of the political fantasy driving romantic comedy and lending it its characteristic form. By this, I mean to suggest that comedy takes shape as it marshalls all manner of cultural materials to produce a specific cultural formation. . . . A romantic comedy is not a romantic comedy in other words, without the banquet scene, marriage ceremony, processional, or dance which incorporates the whole range of the social order within a celebration of power. *A Midsummer Night's Dream* is the most forthright of the romantic comedies in declaring the power of theater to create the illusion of a totalizing community out of the contradictory bodies of power. . . . The grotesque body has been included within the social order without overthrowing it, indeed with the effect of reinvigorating that order, as the entire community appears on stage, reconciled and joyful, all its elements reinscribed within a traditional hierarchy. [p. 44]

Tennenhouse shows in convincing and original readings that other comedies such as *The Taming of the Shrew*, *The Merchant of Venice*, and *Twelfth Night* work similarly. Tennenhouse buttresses his argument about the ideological effect of Shakespeare's plays with an original argument about Shakespeare's social position and his desire for advancement. Shakespeare resembled the courtier in that both sought advancement; moreover, both were on the outside looking in at the center of power. Ironically, however, Shakespeare was in a better position to advance the interests of his theater and the interests of the monarchy that licensed it:

While for Sidney the act of writing set him in a marginal position in relation to the court, Shakespeare was in a very real sense writing for the Queen by writing to the public. He demonstrated that he was capable of making a world he called into being through wit and disguise. Though his world existed only on the stage, it could announce itself as occupying a more central political role in Elizabethan life than the writing of courtiers. Shakespeare obviously recognized he was forging a more inclusive form of nationalism, one that both employed the signs and symbols of the state and revitalized them in the service of the Queen. Thus he regularly displayed his own importance as a playwright within his plays in authorizing her power as a monarch. [p. 44]

The Politics of Shakespeare's Plays

Tennenhouse develops this argument brilliantly, attending to more plays than can be adequately summarized here. Broadly speaking, however, it may be safely said that Tennenhouse's thesis about the interconnection between the plays and the culture depends on a sharp contrast between the Elizabethan and the Jacobean Shakespeare. (The organization of the book neatly reinforces this thesis: the first two chapters focus on Elizabeth I and the last two focus on James I.) Tennenhouse argues that Shakespeare effectively revises the conventions of Elizabethan comedy in order to authorize the power of James I. Shakespeare's "later drama remodeled his Elizabethan materials for purposes of the Jacobean theater. To this end, I will try to describe the form of Shakespeare's Jacobean tragedies as the revision of the cultural strategies upon which his Elizabethan genres depended. He takes the materials of those earlier genres apart according to a later strategy for authorizing political power ... which makes them represent what we might call a more conservative form of patriarchy" (p. 123). The strategies of Shakespeare's plays are homologous with the strategies of the Jacobean state in that both imagine a resemblance between husband and wife and king and subject and in that both use the theater to punish transgressors.

This homology leads Tennenhouse to discuss the mutilation and murder of women in Jacobean tragedy and, more narrowly, the way the desiring female of Shakespeare's comedies becomes threatening in the tragedies: "Tamyra, the Duchess of Malfi, Desdemona, Cleopatra, Vittoria Corrombona, and others obscure within themselves the boundary differentiating what belongs to the body politic from what belongs outside. The breakdown of gender differences within the Jacobean tragedy represents the loss of political boundaries. Purifying the female body of its male sexuality resolves this dilemma, symbolically subordinates the female body to male authority, and thus renews the symbolic power of the sexual body to authorize patriarchy" (p. 121). This subordination takes place through extravagant theaters of punishment.

Tennenhouse reinforces his thesis in a final chapter on the

romances, a genre that flourished under James I. Tennenhouse reads the romances in a light that sets up an opposition between paternalism and patriarchy. Paternalism constitutes a Puritan attempt to reduce the king's authority: The King is only the head of another household and thus does not exercise authority within the subject's household. Patriarchy contrarily enhances the monarch's power by drawing a distinction between king and husband as heads of households. Both city comedy, particularly the disguised ruler plays, and Shakespeare's romances show the necessity of patriarchy. The plays depend on an initial overinvestment in the natural family at the expense of the patriarchal family, on which the continuation of the state depends. The natural family becomes monstrous, represented by a Cloten or Caliban. The romances typically end with "tropes of resurrection" which both support the state and authorize Shakespeare's art: "We might regard this [the trope of resurrection] as the ultimate revelation of the strategy of the work of art in all the romances—a perfect collaboration of art and ideology" (p. 185). By the same token, the romances might be said to stand for Tennenhouse's Shakespeare in the sophisticated and complex ways they idealize the state.

Tennenhouse's thesis is sure to be controversial. One might want to challenge both the causal connection Tennenhouse implicitly makes between the monarchy and the theater and the way this causal determinism produces allegorical readings of the play: Left out of this account is the possibility of resistance or opposition within the theater. But the broader controversy will certainly be the way that Tennenhouse makes Shakespeare thoroughly political. No doubt some will find this argument objectionable, especially those who do not like their literature or their criticism to be "ideological." Such readers are likely to want more detailed, "close readings" of the plays themselves. Certainly, Tennenhouse does advance significantly new readings of the plays. Yet at the same time, the "pay-off" of this book is not so much that it generates "new" readings as it is the way it advances altogether new ways of conducting readings. Tennenhouse's book is not a "new refutation of Shakespeare," to use Richard Levin's phrase, but an examination of the way

The Politics of Shakespeare's Plays

that an artist, even of Shakespeare's caliber, never has priority over larger cultural forms and forces.[15] Tennenhouse's emphasis on genre has interesting implications for criticism of Shakespeare (especially psychoanalytic criticism) that focuses on Shakespeare's development or on a specifically Shakespearean imagination. This approach, according to Tennenhouse, leaves unexamined the fact that other dramatists of the period wrote romantic comedies at the same time Shakespeare did; when Shakespeare turned to tragedy, so too did everyone else. (Indeed, one of the many virtues of this book is the way Tennenhouse includes, as so much Shakespeare criticism does not, an examination of drama and poetry by Shakespeare's Elizabethan and Jacobean contemporaries, ranging from Sidney's *Arcadia* to Jacobean city comedy to Jacobean revenge tragedy.) Tennenhouse concludes that changes within the Shakespearean canon do not reflect an artistic development independent of ideology so much as they reveal the fact that every English Renaissance dramatist (including Shakespeare) responded to the "cultural" imperatives of Elizabethan and Jacobean power. What will make this reading of Shakespeare controversial is not the readings of the plays so much as Tennenhouse's critique of the still predominant liberal humanist construction of Shakespeare's works as timeless and eternal works of artistic genius. The book is a full-scale critique both of liberal, post-enlightenment humanism and of the modes of appreciative criticism which continue to shore up that ideology.

If critics interested in politicizing Shakespeare share an interest in criticizing humanism, they differ over the status of Shakespeare's politics. Tennenhouse implicitly suggests that all resistance to power is contained within Shakespeare's plays, while revenge tragedy, city comedy, and the history plays all serve the state. The theater is not a space of opposition but instead establishes a mutually authorizing relation between playwrights and power. In contrast with this Foucauldian account of power, Dollimore and Sinfield advance a Gramscian theory of hegemony derived from Raymond Williams; culture is for them always a site of contestation between dominant, residual, and emergent cultures. Whatever the disagreement about the status of power, these critics share in common a welcome intellectual sophistication.

For Dollimore and Sinfield, however, the intellectual discussion about theory should not be conducted in isolation from concerns about current critical practice; rather, the need for theory arises not only out of a desire to account for the plays but also out of a desire to have a political effect in the present through criticism that can be called oppositional. Dollimore implicitly equates the position of the theater in relation to Renaissance authority with our position as critics in relation to the authority of the state. This equation is made, currently at least, specifically by English critics, and it has much broader implications for criticism than this local comparison between Dollimore and Sinfield and Tennenhouse might suggest. Both *Political Shakespeare* and *Alternative Shakespeares* explicitly connect Renaissance politics to contemporary politics. The second half of *Political Shakespeare* addresses the way that contemporary institutions such as the university, the BBC, and the theater appropriate Shakespeare for particular political purposes. In an introduction to the second half of *Political Shakespeare*, Sinfield connects the two sections of the anthology in this way: "If Shakespeare can be appropriated by . . . conservative standpoints, there is scope for intervention also for an oppositional criticism, and that is the project of this book. The essays in the first part of this book may be discussed in terms of a materialist analysis; the second part considers how they are being handled in the principal institutions through which they are produced in modern times—education, theatre, film and television. We assess both the tendencies toward conservative reproduction and the conditions and modes of radical intervention" (p. 132).

Similarly, in his introduction to *Alternative Shakespeares*, John Drakakis wastes no time in making explicit his desire to "displace the conservative tradition of history within which Shakespeare's texts have so often been inscribed" (p. 17). This anthology also importantly foregrounds the way that reading itself has a political function: "What follows firmly resists those strategies habitually mobilized by liberal humanism to draw into its historical aegis an infinite variety of interpretations generated by individ-

The Politics of Shakespeare's Plays

ual sensibilities, which it then permits to circulate around a stable and unchanging text.... What is proposed in a number of very different ways is a series of explorations of the ways in which historically specific readings are generated and which acknowledge the existence of structures within the text as devices of exclusion and repression" (pp. 23–24). The criticism in this volume is specifically critical of the way that humanism has appropriated Shakespeare: "The objective common to all these essays is the demystification of the myth of Shakespeare" (p. 24). This means that criticism must break with "admiration of Shakespeare's poetry and characterization" (p. 4). Through poststructuralism and recent developments in Marxism, this collection "threatens to break the dominant paradigm of English studies" and "accelerate the break with established canons of Shakespeare criticism" (p. 23). Stephen Greenblatt and other "new" historicists are faulted because they have not explicitly tried to displace "the conservative tradition of history within which Shakespeare's texts have been inscribed" (p. 17).

By contrast, the American anthology *Shakespeare and the Question of Theory*, edited by Patricia Parker and Geoffrey Hartman, leaves the contemporary political effects of theory untouched. This contrast between American and English anthologies, despite the fact that critics like Greenblatt and Terence Hawkes contribute to anthologies of both nationalities, is significant. As Louis Montrose has observed,

Among American practitioners [of new historicism], the emphasis has been almost exclusively on refiguring of the sociocultural field in which Renaissance texts were originally produced—although not without an awareness of the role of the present in remaking the past. In Britain— where class barriers remain more clearly articulated than in the United States; where, too, radical politics and radical discourses enjoy strong traditions; and where the coercive pressure of the state upon the educational institutions and practices is now conspicuously direct and intense—there has been a relatively greater emphasis upon the uses to which the present has put its versions of the past. In Britain, for obvious reasons, the field of English studies more readily becomes the site of a struggle over the definition of national problems and priorities, a struggle to shape national consciousness.[16]

Montrose's observation holds true for the anthologies under review here. Perhaps one of the major limitations of the Parker and Hartman volume is precisely that the "question of theory" is never raised as such. The essays are generally extremely good, but they often have little to do with theory. Two fine essays, one on dilation and delation in *Othello* by Patricia Parker, the other on *The Rape of Lucrece* by Nancy Vickers, offer only a brief closing note on the theoretical implications of their readings. Only Terence Hawkes' stimulating and provocative essay on *Hamlet*, "Telmah," examines the politics of the modern reception of Shakespeare's tragedy.

In his historicizing essay, "Shakespeare and the Exorcists,"[17] the best in any of the collections reviewed here, Stephen Greenblatt announces that his essay is "written against theory, if theory inevitably involves the desire to escape from contingency into a higher realm, a realm in which signs are purified of the slime of history, then this paper is written against theory" (p. 163). The absence of theory does not prove to be an impediment to historicizing *Lear*, as Greenblatt's brilliant and original essay evidences. (Indeed, terms such as 'brilliant' and 'original' do not begin to do the essay justice.) Yet in attempting to account for the fact that we continue to celebrate a text even though we have little in common with Shakespeare's audiences, the absence of a theory of reception is perhaps more problematic. Attention to the historical differences between audiences drops out of Greenblatt's discussion:

The force of *King Lear* is to make us love the theater, to seek out its satisfactions, to serve its interests, to confer upon it a place of its own, to grant it a life by permitting it to reproduce itself over generations. Shakespeare's theater has outlived the institutions to which it paid homage, has lived to pay homage to other, competing institutions which in turn seem to represent and empty out. The complex, limited institutional independence, this marginal and impure autonomy, arises not out of an inherent, formal self-reflexiveness but out of the ideological matrix in which Shakespeare's theater is created and recreated. [p. 183]

Greenblatt goes on to ask why we pay homage to *Lear* now:

> Why has our culture embraced *King Lear*'s massive display of mimed suffering and fraudulent exorcism? Because the judicial torture and expulsion of evil have for centuries been bound up with the display of power at the center of society. Because we no longer believe in the magical ceremonies through which devils once were made to speak and were driven out of the bodies of the possessed. Because the play recuperates and intensifies our need for these ceremonies, even though we do not believe in them, and performs them, carefully marked out for us as frauds, for our continued consumption. Because, with our full complicity, Shakespeare's company and companies that followed have catered profitably to our desire for spectacular impostures. . . . Shakespeare's center empties out the center that it represents, and in its cruelty—Edmund, Goneril, Regan, Cornwall, Gloucester, Cordelia, Lear: all dead as earth—paradoxically creates in us the intimation of a fullness that we can only savor in the conviction of its irremediable loss:
> "We that are young
> Shall never see so much, nor live so long" (5.2). [pp. 183–84]

Despite the brilliance of Greenblatt's analysis of the play and the originality of his historical line of questioning, one might nevertheless wish to view critically Greenblatt's use of the rhetorical "we." For rather than undertake historical inquiry into the reception of Shakespeare's plays, into their transformation as literature, Greenblatt seems to close such inquiry down by collapsing Shakespeare's audience and later audiences into one; all audiences become the same "us."

If the lack of a theory of ideology poses a problem for Greenblatt's attempt to historicize the reception of Shakespeare's plays, the lack of any explicit position on theory in *Shakespeare and the Question of Theory* leaves it with the crucial limitation of being an exercise in pluralism. Critics indirectly disagree. In his essay, "Shakespeare's Poetical Character in *Twelfth Night*," Geoffrey Hartman takes a slap at "today's ideological critics" who "would probably purge" the plays of "everything but Shakespeare's representation of power relations and hierarchy" (p. 38). By the same token, Hartman's attempt to read the language of *Twelfth*

Night ahistorically would presumably be objectionable to contributors such as Jonathan Goldberg. According to Parker, the collection wants to develop a sense of the differences among contributors: "Together the essays raise for debate a whole range of central issues, both in the criticism of Shakespeare and in the larger field of thinking and theorizing about literature itself— from its formal and linguistic structures to its relation with power, politics, gender, and history. And no more clearly than when they differ sharply from one another" (p. xi). But the differences Parker notes are never debated openly. The possible political and intellectual conflicts between various theoretical positions are left unraised. And because Parker never bothers to say what the question of theory is, the significance of these differences is difficult to determine. However many of the contributors might challenge pluralistic accounts of Shakespeare's texts, the fact that theory is never raised as a question leaves us with the rather conventional position that different theoretical perspectives have equal validity because they address only partially an essentially stable Shakespearean text.

By contrast, both English anthologies seek precisely to call a pluralist account of the Shakespearean text into question by actively pursuing theoretical inquiry into the reception of and institutionalization of Shakespeare. In two fine essays in the second half of *Political Shakespeare*, Alan Sinfield critically exposes the way the English education system and the Royal Shakespeare Company both preserve an essential Shakespeare forever relevant to humanity as a way of preserving a class society. This kind of analysis ought to be extended to American English departments and theaters.

Nevertheless, there are a number of problems with equating radical political opposition and radical intellectual opposition, problems that are unfortunately in evidence in the most polemical collection examined here, *Alternative Shakespeares*. Will, as Drakakis insists, changing one's way of reading change one's politics? It seems doubtful that such a narrow correlation can in fact be made. If historicizing and politicizing the activity of "reading" Shakespeare seems a laudable aim, too often this collection shows how those activities do not produce a radical break

The Politics of Shakespeare's Plays

with conservative practices. Instead, liberal humanism is made into a monolithic Other which is then scapegoated; far from being rigorously historical, the essays dehistoricize criticism, making every critic from Johnson to Leavis the same. This trend is especially evident in Christopher Norris' essay, "Post-structuralist Shakespeare: Text and Ideology," the focus of which is the Leavis/Bradley debate over *Othello*. Norris ends with the assertion, "Johnson stands near the beginning, Leavis near the end of a certain dominant cultural formation in the history of Shakespeare studies. It is an effort of ideological containment, an attempt to harness the unruly energies of the text to a stable order of significance. . . . Shakespeare's meaning can no more be reduced to the currency of liberal humanist faith than his text to the wished for condition of pristine, uncorrupt authority" (p. 66). Even if Norris' assertion were true, he has no positive alternative; indeed, politics gets reduced here to the assertion that Shakespeare's text has "unruly energies." If that is indeed the case, one could ask a theoretical and a practical question: isn't that assertion ahistorical? And how are we to liberate or release the energies?

Norris' failure to open up an alternative to liberal humanist readings is generally true of the essays in this collection. One alternative is the location of gender and identity in "discourse" and "language" (post-structuralist versions of it). In a very good essay (I believe it is one of the two best in the collection) "Sexuality in the Reading of Shakespeare: *Hamlet* and *Measure for Measure*," Jaqueline Rose argues that there is a convergence between male characters like Hamlet or the Duke and Angelo and modern critics like Eliot and Ernest Jones, all of whom focus on woman's sexuality as excessive, the cause of immorality and aesthetic disharmony. Just as the male characters want to regulate sexuality, so too the male critics want to regulate aesthetic form. The moral and aesthetic problem of the plays stem from the specific excess of female sexuality and female speech. Like the males of the plays, modern critics, especially Freudian critics like Ernest Jones, end up scapegoating female sexuality. By contrast, Rose argues, "The problem of subjectivity, of the Oedipal drama and the ordering of language and literary form—the necessity of that regulation and its constant difficulty or failing—is not, to put it at its most simple, the woman's fault. . . . Failing in a woman, whether aesthetic or moral, is always easier to point to than a failure of integration within language and subjectivity itself. If we try to read Shakespeare in terms of the second, however, it might be possible to lift the onus off the woman, who had for so long been expected to take the responsibility, and to bear the excessive weight" (pp. 116, 118). Rose's critique of Shakespeare's characters and his critics is marvelous, but her notion of language doesn't seem to get us very far. Are we to blame it instead of men? Does blame need to be fixed? What would a reading of sexuality in *Hamlet* or *Measure for Measure* based on language be?

Other essays lack even the virtues of Rose's critique, especially those by Catherine Belsey and James Kavanagh. In "Disrupting Sexual Difference: Meaning and Gender in the Comedies," Catherine Belsey argues that the comedies are radical in that they call into question the notion that gender is something natural: "Even while it reaffirms patriarchy, the tradition of female transvestism challenges it precisely by unsettling the categories which legitimate it" (p. 180). Belsey argues that the comedies constitute a "radical challenge to patriarchal values by disrupting sexual difference itself. Of course the male disguise of these heroines allows for plenty of ironies and double meanings, and thus offers the audience the pleasure of a knowingness that depends on a knowledge of sexual difference. But it can also be read as undermining that knowledge from time to time, calling it in question . . ." (p. 180). She urges that we "disrupt difference." But to what end? One would like a far less abstract, less strident alternative here. After hunting unconvincingly for evidence of subversion in *A Midsummer Night's Dream* and *King Lear*, James Kavanagh ends his essay with the assertion that "Shapespeare is, as he always was, in ideology" (p. 165), as if that were an especially startling conclusion.

While the history and theory of reception are extremely important, and while this anthology is to be lauded for opening up such inquiry, it does not make available useful ways of conducting it. Instead of essentializing Shakespeare, these critics essentialize his reception. One finds no investigation of the history of editions of Shakespeare (certainly one way to trace constructions of sexuality in Shakespeare); of adaptations by later dramatists in England or abroad (the attention to appropriations is provincially centered in England); of the history of canonization (the apochrypha; the rise and defeat of disintegrationism; the process by which the authority of one of several texts or cruxes is established; and so on). Instead of historically specific analysis of the reception of Shakespeare's plays, which might show that the effect of constructing a category of texts called literature was not always conservative, the essays in this anthology tend to give us sweeping generalizations.

And here we come to what is perhaps the central limitation of opposing essentialism to some alternative form of anti-essentialism. To what extent in the Renaissance and in the present does control of signifying and symbolic practices equal political control? Does essentialism carry within itself a specific political effect? Will it always be politically conservative? Has it indeed always been so? And will drawing attention to Shakespeare's plays as political constructions necessarily have a politically progressive effect? Put another way, does it follow that because literature may have served somewhat conservative interests in the past that it will always do so? I find it hard to answer these questions affirmatively. To do so would seem to displace one kind of essentialism with another. Clearly, literature could be revised as a category in which it would serve the interests of the left. It is still very clearly a privileged kind of text for study even among the most radical of cultural critics. To be able to put literature to alternative uses, however, one must first be willing to look critically at the opposition between essentialism and constructivism.

Notes

1. See, for example, *Re-Reading English*, ed. Peter Widdowson (New York: Methuen, 1982). See also Derek Longhurst's essay in the same volume, "'Not for all time, but for an Age': An Approach to Shakespeare Studies," pp. 150–63,

which is particularly noteworthy in terms of its attention to Shakespeare in this regard.

2. David Sundelson, *Shakespeare's Restoration of the Father* (New Brunswick, N.J.: Rutgers Univ. Press, 1981). See also the special issue of *Women's Studies*, 9 (Fall 1981) devoted to feminist criticism of Shakespeare.

3. Coppelia Kahn, *Man's Estate: Male Identity in Shakespeare* (Berkeley and Los Angeles: Univ. of California Press, 1982).

4. See *Stuart Royal Proclamations: James I*, ed. Philip Larkin and Paul Hughes, (Oxford: Oxford Univ. Press, 1973), pp. 21, 44, 323, 356, 369. For the *Book of Bounty*, see *The Commons Debates*, ed. Wallace Notestein, et al., 7 volumes (New Haven: Yale Univ. Press, 1935), 7, 491–95.

5. See, for example, Leah Marcus's remarkable essay, "Shakespeare's Comic Heroines, Elizabeth I, and the Politics of Androgyny," in *Women in the Middle Ages and the Renaissance*, ed. Mary Beth Rose (Syracuse: Syracuse Univ. Press: 1986), pp. 135–54.

6. Gary Schmidgall. *Shakespeare and the Courtly Aesthetic* (Berkeley and Los Angeles: Univ. of California Press, 1981).

8. Jonathan Dollimore, *Radical Tragedy: Religion, Ideology and Power in the Drama of Shakespeare and his Contemporaries* (Chicago: Chicago Univ. Press, 1983). For related arguments about the theater, see Margot Heinemann, *Puritanism and Theatre: Thomas Middleton and Opposition Drama under the Stuarts* (Chicago: Chicago Univ. Press, 1980); Franco Moretti, "The Great Eclipse: Tragic Form as the Deconsecration of Tragedy," in *Signs Taken for Wonders: Essays in the Sociology of Literary Forms* (London: New Left Books, 1983); Martin Butler, *Theatre and Crisis: 1632–1642* (Cambridge: Cambridge Univ. Press, 1984).

9. Alan Sinfield has criticized Greenblatt's theory of power explicitly in his essay, "Power and Ideology: An Outline Theory on Sidney's *Arcadia*" (ELH, 52 (1985): 259–79.

10. Robert Weimann, *Shakespeare and the Popular Tradition in the Theater*, trans. Robert Schwartz (Baltimore: Johns Hopkins Univ. Press, 1979).

11. Leah Marcus has written numerous essays on this subject, and her book length study, *The Politics of Mirth*, is forthcoming from the University of Chicago Press. See also David Underdown, *Revel, Riot, and Rebellion: Popular Politics and Culture, 1603–1660* (Oxford: Clarendon Press, 1985), esp. pp. 44–72. On James's issue of the *Book of Sports* in 1617 and in 1618, see J.R. Tanner, ed., *Constitutional Documents of the Reign of James I, 1603–1625 with an Historical Commentary* (Cambridge: Cambridge Univ. Press, 1960), pp. 54–55. For a discussion of the circumstances leading up to the *Book of Sports*, see James Tait, "The Declaration of the *Book of Sports*, 1617," *English Historical Review*, 32 (1917), 561–68; L.A. Govett, *The King's Book of Sports* (London, 1890); and Christopher Hill, "The Uses of Sabbatarianism," *Society and Puritanism in Pre-Revolutionary England* (1964; rpt. New York: Schocken Books, 1972), pp. 145–218. For the 1633 *Book of Sports*, see *The Constitutional Documents of the Puritan Revolution 1625–1660*, ed. Samuel R. Gardiner, 3rd ed. (Oxford, 1906), 99–

103. See also Thomas G. Barnes, "County Politics and a Puritan Cause Célèbre: Somerset Church Ales, 1633," *Transactions of the Royal Historical Society*, 5th Ser., 9 (1959), 103–22.

12. On the commercialization of popular culture, see Robert Ashton, "Popular Entertainment and Social Control in Later Elizabethan and Early Stuart England," *The London Journal*, 9 (1983), pp. 3–27. See also Peter Burke, "Popular Culture in Seventeenth-Century London," *The London Journal*, 3 (1977): 143–62, rpt. in *Popular Culture in Seventeenth-Century England*, ed. Barry Reay (New York: St. Martin's Press, 1985), 31–90.

13. See David Underdown, *Revel, Riot, and Rebellion*, pp. 44–73.

14. See Martin Ingram, "Ridings, Rough Music, and the 'Reform of Popular Culture,'" *Past and Present*, 105 (1984), 105.

15. Richard Levin, "The New Refutation of Shakespeare," *Modern Philology*, 83 (1985), 289–302.

16. Louis Montrose, "Renaissance Literary Studies and the Subject of History," *ELR*, 16 (1986), 7. In a paper on "The Politics of Intertextuality," presented to the Shakespeare Division at its meeting at the 1985 MLA convention, Don Wayne also reflected on the difference between American and English historicisms. See also Jean E. Howard, "The New Historicism in Renaissance Studies," *ELR*, 16 (1986), 13–43.

17. See also Greenblatt's related essays, "Samuel Harsnett and the Devil Fiction," in *Genre*, 15 (1982), 239–44; "Exorcism into Art," *Representations*, 12 (1985), 15–23; and "Loudon and London," *Critical Inquiry*, 12 (1986), 326–46.

Teaching the Literature of the Vietnam War

Arthur D. Casciato

Jeffrey Walsh. *American War Literature, 1914 to Vietnam*. New York: St. Martin's Press, 1982, xii, 218 pp.

James C. Wilson. *Vietnam in Prose and Film*. Jefferson, N.C.: McFarland & Company, 1982. x, 130 pp.

Philip D. Beidler. *American Literature and the Experience of Vietnam*. Athens: University of Georgia Press, 1982. xiv, 220 pp.

Timothy J. Lomperis. *"Reading the Wind": The Literature of the Vietnam War*. Bibliographic Commentary by John Clark Pratt. Durham: Duke University Press, 1987. xii, 174 pp.

Lloyd B. Lewis. *The Tainted War: Culture and Identity in Vietnam War Narratives*. Westport, Conn.: Greenwood Press, 1985. xvi, 193 pp.

John Hellmann. *American Myth and the Legacy of Vietnam*. New York: Columbia University Press, 1987. xiv, 241 pp.

"I don't think we ought to focus on the past. I want to focus on the future. I want to put history behind me."[1]

The words are Ronald Reagan's, but the specific history to which the President refers is not the Vietnam War but the Holocaust. At Bitburg he deliberately confused Waffen SS with the inmates of Bergen-Belsen in order to fit a recalcitrant past to the needs (by his lights) of a political present. His attempt is not so much to revise as to ignore—a flight, as Michael Wallace has pointed out, from history into myth.[2] Reagan the historian inhabits a cinemagraphic never-never land in which the "truth" must always conform to a certain ideological (read anti-Communist) perspective. Here he goes again, this time on the Vietnam War:

> And there wasn't anything surreptitious about it, but when Ho Chi Minh refused to participate in such an election and there was provision that the peoples of both countries could cross the border and live in the other country if they wanted to, and when they began leaving by the thousands and thousands from North Vietnam to live in South Vietnam, Ho Chi Minh closed the border and again violated that part of the agreement.[3]

Never mind that it was not Ho Chi Minh but Ngo Dinh Diem, president of *South* Vietnam, who refused to participate in the elections. Or that American officials supported Diem's maneuver. "Will it play in Peoria?" seems to be Reagan's only historiographic imperative. His is a sanitized Vietnam, a history without ears, with X-rated scenes edited out and a PG (Patriotic Gore?) rating secured at the expense of the facts.

Rambo and Ronbo notwithstanding, the history of the Vietnam War is not easily left on the cutting-room floor. It is indeed "the war that won't go away,"[4] and its terrible memory lingers in many quarters, from the floor of the Congress where *Contra* aid is debated, to the classrooms of our universities where more and more courses are devoted to the Vietnam experience each academic year. For those of us who teach literature, the challenge of the Vietnam War is especially keen. Our most basic question, what texts should we teach, is confounded by an astounding outpouring of books, as if every veteran—every grunt, pilot, nurse, and journalist—must write his or her way out of "the Nam." In the twelve years since the evacuation of Saigon, well over two hundred novels about the Vietnam War have been published, but only a handful or so can appear on a semester's syllabus. And this does not even begin to account for the hundreds and hundreds of poems and short stories or the films, dramas, and personal memoirs or works that defy traditional genres or those whose manifest subject is not Vietnam but whose imaginative landscapes are nevertheless haunted by it.

No canon of the literature of the Vietnam War has yet been established (or, put another way, no comprehensive anthology of the literature of the Vietnam War has been published).[5] We should not mourn this fact, however, since the question of what texts we should teach is inextricably bound to another more difficult question: How should we teach them? And behind those two logistical questions, according to Robert Scholes, lurk two theoretical ones: "*What* we are trying to teach here and *why* are we trying to teach it."[6] Only after a rigorously self-critical examination of the connection between our pedagogy and our politics can we begin to construct a meaningful course on the literature of the Vietnam War, one that illuminates for our students the shadowy terrain not only of Vietnam itself but also of our nation's problematic relationship to its longest war. So far the best guides to this significant project are the so-called "secondary" works listed at the head of this essay. We should be careful, however, not to view them merely as criticism; as much as the texts they discuss, these books tell "war stories," narratives that attempt to contain the physical danger and moral chaos of history *in extremis*.

Published in 1982, Jeffrey Walsh's *American War Literature, 1914 to Vietnam* offers, in its final chapter, one of the first critical treatments of the literature of the Vietnam War.[7] Neither synthesizing nor inclusive, Walsh's chapter aims instead to "establish parameters" (p. ix), a modesty of ambition and scope reflected nicely in its title, "Toward Vietnam." Although he mentions such works as Mary McCarthy's memoir *Vietnam*, Megan Terry's play *Viet Rock*, John Balaban's *Vietnam Poems*, and Robert Litell's *Sweet Reason* (one of the rare naval novels of Vietnam), Walsh discusses at length only four texts: Joseph Heller's *Catch-22*, Kurt Vonnegut's *Slaughterhouse-Five*, Michael Herr's *Dispatches*, and Philip Caputo's *A Rumor of War*.

The juxtaposition of Heller's and Vonnegut's books, both novels of World War II, with Herr's and Caputo's Vietnam narratives mirrors Walsh's strategy throughout the earlier chapters of his study: "to suggest historical development and to analyze through formal exegesis the internal complexities of the literary text" (p. ix). In terms of the evolution of the American war novel, Walsh argues that Vietnam occasioned a return to a "more accessible public form" rather than a continuation of the "oblique post-modernist mode" (p. 7) represented by Heller's and Vonnegut's 1960s novels. True enough for *A Rumor of War*, less so for *Dispatches*, but had Walsh examined, say, John Sack's *M* or Asa Baber's *The Land of a Million Elephants*, he would have discovered works about Vietnam that try to outdo *Catch-22* at its own game. Walsh, of course, never claimed to survey the field, but it is exactly this lack of breadth that often attenuates his generalizations.

Walsh's double vision of literature as "a cultural product which retains a relative autonomy" (p. 191) is admirable but difficult to maintain, and too frequently he lapses into a monocular view of texts as self-contained artifacts. This one-sightedness produces a too literary "Vietnam," one for which the historical, cultural, and political particularities fade as Walsh luxuriates in "the internal complexities of the literary text." Related to this New Critical bias in his effort to establish *Dispatches* and *A Rumor of War* as Vietnam "classics" (p. 199). He may be right, but he never questions the notion of a "classic" or the literary values that inform such judgments, content instead to measure his choices against *Catch-22* and *Slaughterhouse-Five*, supposed "classics" from an earlier war. This kind of "natural" critical behavior is unfortunate, especially since scrutiny of one's own practice is at least, in part, a legacy of the Vietnam era. Well-intentioned but too brief, promising more than it delivers, Walsh's chapter is a start but not much more.

In *Vietnam in Prose and Film*, James C. Wilson replaces Walsh's aesthetic criteria for determining the "literature" of the Vietnam War with utilitarian ones. Wilson announces from the start that he is not interested in "purely formalistic analysis" but rather only in books and films that "clarify important historical, moral, and political questions" (p. 7). Such a high standard is hard to attain; according to Wilson, most Vietnam narratives fall short. Still Wilson manages to locate enough texts to flesh out a semester's reading and viewing list. His "syllabus" would include three personal memoirs (*Dispatches*, *A Rumor of War*, and Ron Kovic's *Born on the Fourth of July*), six novels (Robert Stone's *Dog Soldiers*,

Tim O'Brien's *Going After Cacciato*, Charles Durden's *No Bugles, No Drums*, David Halberstam's *One Very Hot Day*, Victor Kolpacoff's *The Prisoners of Quai Dong*, and William Eastlake's *The Bamboo Bed*), and two films (Francis Ford Coppola's *Apocalypse Now* and Peter Davis' *Hearts and Minds*).

Wilson's inclusion of Caputo and Herr, unlike Walsh's, does not signal their books as exemplary Vietnam texts; he attacks both of them, in fact, as "literary evasions" (p. 6) which distort as much as they reveal. *A Rumor of War* constitutes for Wilson a denial of "the very possibility of moral responsibility" in Vietnam (p. 63); *Dispatches* is for him the primary example of "the dope and dementia theory" through which Vietnam is seen as "insane" and ultimately "incomprehensible" (p. 44). Such judgments, harsh and reductive, characterize Wilson's critical demeanor throughout, and although few of the works he examines escape unscathed, his treatment of *Dispatches* seems especially mean-spirited. Granting Herr's "stylistic brilliance," Wilson condemns him for his supposed lack of "a consistent moral stance" and for his failure "to go beyond a surface description" of the Vietnam War (pp. 45–47). These shortcomings, however, do not keep Wilson from drawing upon Herr's text again and again—for his epigraphs, for his half-titles, and, most consistently, for quotations meant to clinch his own arguments. It would be hard to imagine a more obvious case of biting the hand that feeds you, and Wilson's over-reliance on others' language weakens his study in general. Far too often *Vietnam in Prose and Film* is merely a pastiche of plot summary and second-hand insights.

For Wilson, the *locus classicus* of the literature of the Vietnam War remains Graham Greene's 1955 novel *The Quiet American*, a book that, unlike subsequent American attempts, succeeds in "not only recording but illuminating history" (p. 9). Narrated by Thomas Fowler, a cynical British journalist, Greene's novel is indeed remarkable for its prescience. It reveals, through Alden Pyle, the "quiet American" of the title, what Wilson takes to be at the heart of America's future involvement in Vietnam: "the failure to imaginatively and sympathetically identify with others" (p. 12). Pyle's (and America's) "absence of moral vision" (p. 12) is assessed correctly as imperialistic and racist, but once again

Wilson's tendency to schematize the works he discusses betrays him. By ignoring Phuong, the most prominent Vietnamese character (she is mentioned here only as Fowler's "obedient mistress"), Wilson is guilty of the same racism (and sexism) as Pyle.

Wilson's chapter on Hollywood is even less supple. He argues that commercial films about Vietnam sell us "a simplistic, soap opera version" of the War and thus "derealize" their subject more than the literature (p. 80). Although he grudgingly praises Coppola's *Apocalypse Now*, the only movie to pass Wilson's rigorous muster is Peter Davis' *Hearts and Minds*. Davis' film appeals to Wilson for its political directness and clarity: through its juxtaposition of domestic and combat footage, *Hearts and Minds* exposes America as "an insensitive, militaristic culture" (p. 95) and, at the same time, fosters the kind of sympathetic identification with the other that Wilson finds wanting in most Americans. By valorizing Davis' film and Greene's book, one a documentary, the other a realistic novel, Wilson reveals his not-so-hidden agenda in *Vietnam in Prose and Film*. Fresh from a reading of Gerald Graff's *Literature Against Itself* and Christopher Lasch's *The Culture of Narcissism*, Wilson fashions a study whose subject is not so much the literature of the Vietnam War as the moral and political impoverishment of postmodernist texts, all of which are assumed to be narcissistic, nihilistic, and willfully obscure. Vietnam, Wilson seems to say, is too serious a subject, our need to wrestle with it too urgent, to be refracted through the playful (and, I would add, equally serious) prism of postmodernism. Finally, then, Wilson is more concerned with formal matters than he admits. For him, certain rich texts—Steven Wright's *Meditations in Green* springs to mind—are beyond the pale simply because they are experimental and fragmented.

In *American Literature and the Experience of Vietnam*, Philip D. Beidler gives us the comprehensive introduction that Walsh and Wilson fail to supply. Beidler's range of reference is more than broad enough to instill confidence in his judgment about which books will endure. To Wilson's reading list he adds, among others, Gloria Emerson's *Winners and Losers* and Frances Fitzgerald's *Fire in the Lake*, works whose documentary status reveal Beidler's flexible and inclusive view of what constitutes the "literature" of the Vietnam War. Orthodox literary forms that Walsh and Wilson slighted or ignored are also represented fully here—poetry by Michael Casey's *Obscenities*, D. C. Berry's *saigon cemetery*, John Balaban's *After Our War*, and Bruce Weigl's *A Romance*; drama by Arthur Kopit's *Indians* and David Rabe's trilogy *The Basic Training of Pavlo Hummel*, *Sticks and Bones*, and *Streamers*; the short story by Ronald J. Glasser's *365 Days* and Tom Mayer's *The Weary Falcon*. Beidler is especially alive to the great variety of responses that the Vietnam War has inspired, from traditional combat novels like Josiah Bunting's *The Lionheads* to surreal fantasies like William Eastlake's *The Bamboo Bed*; from those texts, like Al Santoli's *Everything We Had*, that situate themselves (and the reader) "in-country," to those, like Robert Stone's *Dog Soldiers*, that bring the War, in all its absurdity and violence, back home to America. (One could easily abstract from *American Literature and the Experience of Vietnam* an undergraduate seminar organized around genre, mode, theme, or viewpoint, so various is Beidler's treatment of his subject.) According to Beidler, the most significant books about Vietnam, despite their differences, are bound together by their commitment to "an unstinting concreteness" and their engagement in "a primary process of sense-making" (p. xiii). Put another way, the best works all exhume the mean facts in order to make those facts mean.

Beidler's volume is much more than a general introduction. Using the Vietnam War as a "case study," he examines "the larger process of cultural myth-making" (p. xi), how Americans generate, sustain, and re-invent their collective visions. His model for such an inquiry is Paul Fussell's *The Great War and Modern Memory*, and in much of what he writes about Vietnam, Beidler is indebted to Fussell's central insight—that the "reality" of World War I is determined as much by our "cultural imagining" (p. 27), before, during, and after the fact, as by combat experience itself. This crucial tension between fact and fiction, experience and imagination, which supplies the interpretive lens through which Beidler observes the literature of the Vietnam War, is felt most strongly in his first two chapters. In "Situation Report" Beidler portrays the War as essentially fluid and opaque, hermetically sealed from an outsider's perception; in "Prophecy and Context" he argues, paradoxically, that Vietnam was prepared for and even predicted by American culture high and low, the experience of the War located somewhere between Melville's *Billy Budd* and the Saturday-morning cartoons. These two chapters are a *tour de force* not to be missed; they suggest, too, just how intensely personal Beidler's study is. *American Literature and the Experience of Vietnam* is, as much as anything else, Beidler's attempt to reconcile his own "experience," first as a combat veteran of the Vietnam War, later as a professor of English at the University of Alabama. Beidler's struggle can be sensed most dramatically in his eschewal of the usual academic discourse in favor of a more personal voice that navigates between then and now, past and present, subjective memory and professional objectivity, a kind of subdued version of the rock-and-roll diction that Michael Herr employs in *Dispatches*. In allowing himself to step forward as artist (and thereby allowing his passion to show), Beidler fights the good fight and should be applauded.

Unlike Walsh, who treats Vietnam as an aesthetic abstraction to be placed in the tradition of the American war novel, or Wilson, who reduces it to a moral, cultural, and political problem to be solved by literary expression, Beidler approaches the War as "experience" and thus must allow for its heterogeneity, its shifting contours over the course of time. Accordingly, he divides Vietnam literature into discrete periods: the early writing of 1958–1970, the middle range of 1970–1975, and the new literature of 1975 to the present. In the first he finds what might be called a "generic imperative," almost an obsession with discovering the appropriate form for depicting the War. To represent the spectrum of narrative possibility, from artifice to actuality, Beidler chooses three novels: Eastlake's *The Bamboo Bed*, James Crumley's *One Count to Cadence*, and Halberstam's *One Very Hot Day*. At one extreme Eastlake attempts, through his relentless inventiveness, to produce a fiction truer than fact; at the other Halberstam tries, through a mountainous accretion of quotidian detail, to reveal the nightmarish intensity of the ordinary; and striking a graceful balance between, Crumley locates the single theme that resonates through all the works of this period, what Beidler terms the "creative mutuality" (p. 34) of the literal and the literary. At the heart of the experience of Vietnam, claims Beidler, is the realization of what Fussell calls "the curious reciprocity of art and life."[8] Not only does art imitate life, as is usual, but life returns the favor.

Attention to the process of sense-making, how Vietnam might be made to signify, was the great legacy of these early writers to their successors who wrote in the years when, as Beidler puts it, "large-scale American involvement had ceased while the war itself ground brutally on" (p. 87). Some of these middle-range writers were more self-conscious, more aggressive in their experimentation within the matrix of memory and imagination. According to Beidler, this period saw the War's first full-blooded metafiction, James Park Sloan's *War Games*, a book preoccupied not with Vietnam itself but with the writer's predicament in making sense of it. And there was a spate of conventional naturalistic war "epics" during this period, like Robert Roth's *Sand in the Wind*, which exploited unabashedly the received literary strategies of Hemingway, Jones, and Mailer. Most writers, however, avoided these extremes and, like Crumley before them, worked hard to heal the split between experience and artifice. For Beidler, the exemplary text of the middle range is Tim O'Brien's *If I Die in a Combat Zone*. Here O'Brien achieves what earlier writers could not—an organic or "mediating perspective" (p. 78), the ground of which is consciousness itself. Throughout his memoir O'Brien problematizes the idea of "courage" in the field in order to suggest a more profound bravery: the veteran-writer's ongoing attempt, inevitably doomed, to force experiential memory to surrender at last some provisional or tentative meaning. It is this struggle, what Beidler calls, memorably, "the heroism of consciousness itself" (p. 103), that will serve as a model for later writing about the Vietnam War, most notably for Herr's *Dispatches* and, I would argue, for Beidler's own writing.

Enlarging upon these accomplishments, post-Vietnam writing is characterized by what Beidler calls the composite or "optative" mode (p. 137), a phrase meant to suggest its radical eclecticism. Combining the qualities of the various literary genres with those of such mass media as film, newspaper journalism, and television, these works self-consciously blur the boundaries between "fact" and "fiction." Nowhere is the breakdown of traditional categories more evident than in Herr's *Dispatches*. A work of "orphic suggestiveness" (p. 147), *Dispatches* manages to inscribe "a genuine architecture of consciousness within which experiential memory persistently undergoes imaginative assimilation into newer and more complex patterns of achieved meaning" (p. 146). Similarly distinguished, according to Beidler, are C. D. B. Bryan's *Friendly Fire*, Caputo's *A Rumor of War*, Kovic's *Born on the Fourth of July*, Gustav Hasford's *The Short-Timers*, Rabe's *Streamers*, and Weigl's *A Romance*. All of these "war stories," instead of describing the familiar journey from innocence to experience, chart a common trajectory from the personal to the public, in which the "odyssey of consciousness" (p. 158) of the author is coupled with a search for significant context, "an attempt to connect the experience of the war with some idea of a representative American consciousness" (p. 154). The operative phrase is "attempt to connect," for, as Beidler concludes, no commanding perspective has yet been achieved. Only time, and a continued "heroism of consciousness" such as Beidler's own, will accomplish that.

For Beidler, the essence of the veteran-writer's dilemma is how to transcend his or her personal experience. Speaking on 9 May 1985, fifteen years to the day after he returned home from Vietnam where he had served for a year as a reconnaissance platoon leader in an armored calvary troop, Beidler offered this advice:

We truly can be transformed, and even possibly be redeemed by electing to write of times, of what happened—but also of what might have happened, what could have happened, what should have happened, and maybe also what can be kept from happening or what can be made to happen. . . . Words are all we have. In the hands of brave and true artists such as those we have heard here, they may yet preserve us against the darkness. [Lomperis, p. 87]

Beidler's remarks were part of a panel on "The Role of Literature in Understanding the War," and the "brave and true artists" in attendance included Balaban, Bryan, Kovic, O'Brien, and Weigl, among others, all of whom had assembled on 7 May to participate in a three-day conference on "The Vietnam Experience and American Literature." Sponsored by the Asia Society, a nonpartisan educational organization, the conference brought together some seventy writers, educators, and publishers, the majority of whom either had served in Vietnam or had traveled there during the War. Besides Beidler's, the panels on which they spoke focused on such topics as "Combat Literature," "Fact and Fiction in Literature," "Literature on the Veteran Experience," "The Impact on Those at Home," and, most significantly, "Images of Asia and Asians in the Literature." In *"Reading the Wind": The Literature of the Vietnam War*, Timothy J. Lomperis not only summarizes but interprets and critiques the proceedings of the Asia Society conference.

Only someone who has attempted such a summary can appreciate the difficulty of Lomperis' primary editorial task. Too much transcription of the speeches and responses would bloat and paralyze his narrative, too little and the texture and feel of the conference would be lost. Happily, Lomperis manages this delicate balance as ably as anyone could hope. Though I suspect that the most stimulating and profitable exchanges took place, as at most conferences, in hallways and hotel rooms, Lomperis' account of the official proceedings is both readable and worth reading. Following roughly the chronology of the conference, he organizes his summary around what he calls "lightning bolts" (p. 6)—speeches by James Webb, Ron Kovic, and Al Santoli. These he renders more or less fully, then follows them with telescopic versions of the passionate responses they provoked.

In his keynote address Webb, a highly-decorated Marine captain during the War, introduced the issue that would polarize the participants repeatedly: "the separability of art and politics" (p. 13). Webb's speech was, in sum, a polemic meant to justify American military policy in Vietnam in terms of the situation in Southeast Asia today and, as such, is best answered by quoting the poet and editor W. D. Ehrhart, himself a Marine combat veteran: "What I saw and did in Asia in thirteen months was unspeakably evil and immoral. What is happening there now does not change that" (p. 20). Delivered on the afternoon of the conference's second day, Kovic's speech, too, was an impassioned riposte aimed at Webb. Left paralyzed from the chest down by a bullet that severed his spinal cord on 20 January 1968 at the Ashau Valley, Kovic told Webb that his words the previous evening had wounded him again: "This man, in a very insensitive and callous fashion, was trying to negate my suffering, and the suffering of thousands and thousands of Americans and Vietnamese" (p. 26). However, the most vociferous interchanges did not occur until the conference's final day when Al Santoli, like Webb, defended American intervention in Vietnam in the light of subsequent Communist oppression in Indochina. Whether one agrees with Ehrhart and Kovic, or Webb and Santoli, what is clear here is just how contested and contestable the memory of Vietnam remains for most Americans. Much of the credit for the effectiveness of this powerful example must go to Lomperis for his sensitive handling of this often unwieldy, always emotionally explosive material.

Unfortunately, Lomperis' "interpretive critique" is not nearly as adept as his editorial efforts. His commentary, it must be said, had to address not only the conference itself but also the contribution of "creative literature" to our understanding of the Vietnam War. This last objective must have been particularly challenging to Lomperis, a political scientist (and veteran) whose own study, *The War Everybody Lost—and Won: America's Intervention in Vietnam's Twin Struggles*, is decidedly non-literary. Breaking out of the narrow bounds of disciplinary expertise, of course, opens up at least the possibility of a fresh perspective. But when Lomperis finally summons himself to comment on the Vietnam War literature, he falls back upon a tired, simplistic formula for "good" writing that would make even the most unreconstructed New Critic blush: "But the point is, there need to be more allusions in our literature. . . . Where indeed would such literary giants as Shakespeare and Milton be without their rich allusions and metaphors drawn from the Bible and Greek mythology?" (p. 98). By arguing for works "anchored . . . with references and allusions to other great pieces" (p. 98), Lomperis endorses a literature that hovers above the fray somewhere in the "timeless" realm of art, a literature that never becomes "too overtly political" (p. 100). To buttress his argument, Lomperis imagines a "future poem" about a Vietnam "lifer" in which anti-war demonstrators are referred to as "jackals," thereby alluding to *Kangaroo*, D. H. Lawrence's 1923 novel about World War I: "At home stayed all the jackals. . . . And they bit us all" (p. 98). To think that such arcane references as this one would necessarily enrich our literature is naive; to suggest, however aesthetically, that anti-war protestors are jackals is something more dangerous.

It would be unfair to claim that the tail wags the dog in this book, but the thirty-seven page bibliographic commentary that follows Lomperis' much longer "interpretive critique" is by far the most valuable section of *"Reading the Wind."* Written by John Clark Pratt, an Air Force fighter pilot in Laos and the author of the novel *The Laotian Fragments*, this "bibliographic commentary" glosses nearly 140 works of history, fiction, poetry, and drama as well as most of the major criticism (including doctoral dissertations). Pratt's research is based on the Vietnam War Literature Collection, an ongoing project begun in 1975 at Colorado State University at Fort Collins, where Pratt is presently a professor of English. The collection includes all published literary work, and many of the books Pratt discusses escaped the notice of earlier commentators. For instance, to the list of significant poets one could cull from Beidler's study, Pratt appends the names W. D. Ehrhart (*A Generation of Peace* and *To Those Who Have Gone Home Tired*) and Walter McDonald (*Burning the Fence* and *Caliban in Blue*). Likewise, Emilio de Grazio (*Enemy Country*) and Amil Gray (*How I Got That Story*)—writers who have produced outstanding examples of the short story and drama respectively. Pratt, however, quite properly devotes the bulk of his essay to the Vietnam novel.

What distinguishes Pratt's bibliography from previous scholarship is not so much its virtual completeness or the wisdom of his comments but the good sense with which he arranges his material.[9] He insists that readers (and, by implication, teachers) approach Vietnam fiction mindful of a double temporal frame of reference, "not only of the time periods in which they are set but also of the times in which they were written" (p. 124). Thus, the seventy-seven novels he reviews follow a chronology more strictly historical than even Beidler's was in *American Literature and the Experience of Vietnam*. Viewing the War as a kind of "Shakespearean tragedy" (p. 124), complete with five acts, prologue, and epilogue, Pratt divides the fiction according to key historical moments (Act III, for example, covers the period from the Tet Offensive in January 1968 to the invasion of Cambodia and the deaths at Kent State in May 1970). Whatever else it affords, such a shrewd structuring of his bibliography allows Pratt to suggest both that Vietnam has generated the most time-bound and political of literatures and that its study must always be "contextual" in the crucial double sense he outlined.

Pratt's bibliography amounts to an anatomy of Vietnam fiction in which he traces, from novel to novel, themes and characters that predominate at certain points in history. By the end of 1965, for instance, when the number of American servicemen in Vietnam had increased by 161,000 in ten months, the subject that pervades the fiction is the relationship between "the new draftee" and "the experienced but war-wise 'lifer' NCO" (p. 135), whose main lesson for the "fresh meat" was that the real business of Vietnam was not winning the War but merely surviving it. In *The Tainted War: Culture and Identity in Vietnam War Narratives*, Lloyd B. Lewis arrives at the same conclusion, though by much different means. Lewis' is an interdisciplinary approach that borrows freely (and expertly) from psychology, sociology, anthropology, and American Studies in an attempt to recover no less than "the subjective reality" of the Vietnam War (p. xii). The result of such "opportunistic eclecticism" (p. 9) is sometimes impenetrable, often jargon-ridden, but still the most theoretically sophisticated handling of the literature of the Vietnam War we have to date. Any frustration with Lewis' abstract dissertationese ("Objectivations give spatio-temporal substance to subjective meanings") is outweighed by the many insights such discourse produces.

The specific "subjective reality" that Lewis pursues is that constructed in the minds of the combat troops themselves, how the enlisted personnel and NCOs who did the actual ground fighting perceived the experience of Vietnam. To capture such inaccessible terrain, Lewis draws upon all manner of personal narratives, ranging from novels and autobiographies to latrine graffiti and "barely articulate offhand remarks" of troops fresh from combat (p. 11). Unlike Pratt, Lomperis, Beidler, and the rest, Lewis resists the seemingly "natural" temptation to privilege literary texts over non-literary ones, or to distinguish among traditional literary genres, or even to rank such utterances according to aesthetic properties supposedly inherent in literary texts. In fact, for the traditional "English teacher," the main challenge of *The Tainted War* is its implied attack on an essentialist notion of "literature" as created by inspired geniuses who transcend their socio-historical environment. By bracketing out the usual questions of literary merit and genre, Lewis insists on the social "constructedness" of all interpretations of reality, whether fictional or factual (p. 12). One practical consequence of such a view is that Lewis never valorizes the author; for him, he or she is just another "informant" whose literary discourse supplies more data with which to reckon.

The theoretical underpinning of Lewis' socio-cultural interpretation of Vietnam War narratives is provided by the "sociology of knowledge" school founded by the German Alfred Schutz and developed in America by Peter L. Berger. Originating in the fundamentally Marxist assumption that man's consciousness is socially determined, Berger's model denies any essential or self-evident "human nature" and argues instead that man produces himself through a dialectical interchange between "social structures (institutions) and culture (symbolic universes)" (p. 10). Applying this general insight to the specific instance of the American infantryman in Vietnam, Lewis attempts to answer two questions: "What do members of a particular social world believe? And why do they hold such beliefs?" (p. 9). Lewis organizes his inquiry into three main chapters that correspond roughly to Berger's "production, maintenance, and modification" of symbolic universes (p. 6). In the first he examines how "American males learn[ed] war in the 1950s"; in the second how they "practic[ed] it in Asia in the 1960s"; and in the third how they "suffer[ed] its aftermath in the 1970s and 1980s" (p. 10).

According to Lewis, Vietnam War narratives identify three major institutions or agencies of enculturation: the media, the family, and the military. It was at these sites that future American combat veterans were initiated into a "war-consciousness" (p. 20) wholly inappropriate to the Vietnam conflict. The images of warfare transmitted to them were based upon the cultural mythology of World War II, so that "the Vietnam War conbatants' most pressing business upon arrival in the war zone was shedding the cultural knowledge they had accumulated about war" (p. 21). From the media (especially films) adolescent American males learned, among other things, what Michael Herr calls the "John Wayne Wet Dream," a conception of heroism as "displaying aggression under dangerous conditions" (p. 26). From their families (mainly the fathers, themselves typically veterans of WWII) American sons internalized a romantic ideal of war as "duty" to the past as well as an opportunity to prove one's manhood. In the military (especially during basic training) American draftees were taught to pray for war and to view the enemy as inferior. When these culturally constructed meanings of combat inevitably collapsed under the weight of a war that constantly denied their validity, the disillusioned "grunt" fell back into an instinctual state where, Lewis claims, personal survival was the only meaning.

This process of "reality disconfirmation" (p. 67), what Lewis refers to as "a retreat from meaning," was given impetus by the formlessness of the Vietnam War. "It was no orderly campaign, as in Europe," wrote Philip Caputo in *A Rumor of War*, "but a war waged in a wilderness without rules or laws." The only rhythm of Vietnam combat was supplied by the "firefight" and the "search-and-destroy mission," both of which offered few if any occasions for traditional "World War II" heroism and none for the death-defying charges popularized by John Wayne in such movies as *The Sands of Iwo Jima*. Similarly, the nature of guerrilla fighting made it difficult for American GIs, raised on images of conventional warfare, to distinguish between the enemy and the civilian populace. Such confusion, according to Lewis, resulted in frustration and fear and ultimately in the kind of atrocity associated with the name My Lai. Morality, then, was one of the first casualties of a military action in which success was measured not by ground taken or enemies captured, but by body counts and kill ratios. The ruthlessness with which the ground war was waged indicates again that the old ideals of honor and patriotism had been replaced by a more palpable self-preservation.

Lewis' most impressive chapter attempts to explain why those infantrymen who did manage to survive often see themselves as "walking wounded" (p. 122). Drawing heavily upon role theory in social psychology, he demonstrates convincingly that the "Vietnam world view" brought home by the combat veteran was incompatible with the world to which he returned (p. 133). "I went from a free-fire zone to the twilight zone," reported one returnee in Mark Baker's oral history, *Nam*. The vets' disorientation and alienation was exacerbated by an American public that failed to recognize their sacrifice and instead treated them as "social outcasts to be ignored or reviled" (p. 151). Unlike their fathers, on whose World War II war stories they were nurtured, Vietnam combatants were "sentenced to silence" (p. 153) by family, friends, and neighbors. "Coming back to America," said another grunt in *Nam*, "I was shocked, not by the fact that no one cared, but that no one even talked about it." Much worse than the "silent treatment," however, was the veterans' identification in the popular imagination as "butchers" or "baby-killers." By locating these two forms of the vets' continued estrangement from American society, Lewis means to change the perception of "Post-Vietnam Stress Syndrome" from a clinical condition to a sociological one, from a private psycho-pathology to a public issue.

Like Beidler, Lewis recognizes that the Vietnam War remains ambiguous to most Americans, even to those who participated (his title, *The Tainted War*, refers to the words of a former Marine sniper who called the War "the big taint—T'aint reality, and t'aint a dream"). In his final pages Lewis challenges us to go beyond such uncertainty, to confront our lack of a collective memory of the War. His concern is shared by John Hellmann, for whom Vietnam remains "an unexplained national nightmare" (p. 222). "No nation can survive without a myth," writes Hellmann in *American Myth and the Legacy of Vietnam*, "no nation profits from holding onto a myth that cannot plausibly include recent historical experience" (p. 222). Hellmann's study is an attempt to suggest how the story of American failure in Vietnam can usefully be incorporated into our national myth.

Hellmann's approach, like Lewis', is interdisciplinary, but his volume more closely resembles such seminal American Studies texts as R. W. B. Lewis' *The American Adam* and Henry Nash Smith's *Virgin Land*. The reading and viewing list one might extract from *American Myth and the Legacy of Vietnam* mixes together "best sellers, popular articles, memoirs, serious novels, and films" (p. x). Potboiling successes like William Lederer and Eugene Burdick's *The Ugly American* receive the same careful scrutiny as Stone's *Dog Soldiers*, Herr's *Dispatches*, and O'Brien's *Going After Cacciato*; George Lucas' *Star Wars* trilogy joins Coppola's *Apocalypse Now* and Cimino's *The Deer Hunter* as important Vietnam narratives. Hellmann's principle of inclusion is akin to Jane Tompkins' and Philip Fisher's in two recent critical studies of American literature.[10] Like them, Hellmann values texts not for their unity, subtlety, or complexity but instead for the kind of "cultural work" they accomplish.[11] *The Ugly American*, for instance, is treated as a significant cultural document because it "stands beside *Uncle Tom's Cabin* (1852) and *The Jungle* (1906) as a work of fiction catalyzing American political debate" (p. 15).

According to Hellmann, however, the most powerful Vietnam storyteller is neither a novelist nor a filmmaker. Rather, it is John Fitzgerald Kennedy, whose myth of the New Frontier galvanized our misadventure in Vietnam. Heeding Lederer and Burdick's warning that Americans had grown fat, stupid, and loud, JFK constructed a domestic and foreign policy aimed at revitalizing America's sense of national mission. Such programs as the Peace Corps and the Council for Physical Fitness were largely symbolic, "offering Americans participation in a ritualistic return to the hardiness, self-sacrifice, and purposefulness of the true American character" (p. 44). Kennedy's championing of the Army's Special Forces was, Hellmann believes, the crucial move in rededicating Americans to "the virtues and imperatives of America's frontier mythos" (p. 38). The Green Beret symbolized a return to the Western hero, a kind of latter-day Natty Bumppo armed this time around not only with rifle and Indian knife but also with the technological know-how of twentieth-century civilization. Using Robin Moore's best-selling novel *The Green Berets*, Hellmann exposes the dark side of the Kennedy myth, revealing the "unashamed fascination with violence" (p. 57) lurking just beneath its frontier ideals.

After Kennedy's assassination, his depiction of Vietnam as a symbolic landscape in which America could manifest its true destiny as saviour gave way to an image of the War as "cold technological aggression against an agrarian society" (p. 67). LBJ's escalation of air and ground warfare was opposed by the New Left, whose counter-cultural myth Hellmann chronicles in three texts: Mary McCarthy's *Hanoi*, Susan Sontag's *Trip to Hanoi*, and Norman Mailer's *Why Are We in Vietnam?* Each of these writers employs the language and imagery of the traditional American frontier myth in order to subvert it. For McCarthy and Sontag, North Vietnam becomes ironically "the America that no longer exists" (p. 85), a kind of ideal self-concept "usurped in their own land by a technological and decadent society" (p. 84). This identification with the enemy is also evident in such films as Arthur Penn's *Little Big Man* and Ralph Nelson's *Soldier Blue*, antiwesterns that invert traditional frontier values. Hellmann does well, however, when he warns his readers that most Americans, however disillusioned, did not desire American defeat in Vietnam. Whatever one's politics, Vietnam undoubtedly represented a "disruption of our story" (p. x.) which more and more of us, especially after the 1968 spring Tet offensive, were unprepared to counter. We were left, in Hellmann's particular sense, "mythless"—an untenable position from which we have yet to emerge.

The second half of *American Myth and the Legacy of Vietnam* concerns our country's subsequent search for a usable past in its experience of Southeast Asia. "Vietnam," writes Hellmann, "was now a landscape in the American consciousness that would have to be journeyed through many times over, self-consciously experienced through narrative art as myth and symbol, if Americans were to begin to understand what had happened to their story and to their idea of themselves" (p. 95). Rather than putting the War "behind them," as now President Ford wished, Americans found themselves on a second journey to Vietnam, this time through the agency of memoirs and novels written by veterans, who refused "to forget the distance they traveled, the identity they lost, or the expectations with which they had set out" (p. 102). The most important of these works, according to Hellmann, are Kovic's, Caputo's, and O'Brien's literary memoirs as well as William Turner Huggett's *Body Count*, James Webb's *Fields of Fire*, Roth's *Sand in the Wind*, and John M. Del Vecchio's *The 13th Valley*, realistic novels that attempt to elevate naturalistic details into meaningful cultural symbols. Common to all these texts is "an ironic antimyth in which an archetypal warrior-representative of the culture embarks on a quest that dissolves into an utter chaos of dark revelation" (p. 102). What each protagonist discovers in Vietnam is a "nightmarish wilderness" (p. 111) that frustrates his expectations of personal (and national) destiny.

These later chapters, however, are slightly more traditional and thus less interesting than previous ones. Instead of moving skillfully back and forth from text to context as he had done earlier, Hellmann often offers extended "close-readings" in which the relationship between the word and the world is obscure. Still, his ambitious analyses hold their own pleasures and rewards. He discusses brilliantly the exploitation of the hard-boiled detective "thriller" and the classic western in Stone's *Dog Soldiers*, Herr's *Dispatches*, O'Brien's *Going After Cacciato*, and Coppola's *Apocalypse Now*. Equally impressive in his attempt to recuperate Cimino's *The Deer Hunter*, a film that until now seemed beyond saving. The highpoint of Hellmann's own myth-making occurs in his penultimate chapter, "Toward New Myth." Here he interprets *Star Wars*, *The Empire Strikes Back*, and *Return of the Jedi* as a self-conscious reconceptualization of our old collective beliefs into a new mythic vision. Some will doubtless resist Hellmann's treatment of Lucas' mythological fantasy as a Vietnam text, tracing America's move forward "from traumatic self-discovery to energizing triumph" (p. 217),

Teaching the Literature of the Vietnam War

but it is exactly this sort of imaginative cultural reading, here and elsewhere, that makes *American Myth and the Legacy of Vietnam* the best book on the literature (in the broadest sense) of the Vietnam War that we have so far.

Others have taken up and extended Hellmann's "cultural studies" tack. The new journal *Cultural Critique* devoted an entire number to "American Representations of Vietnam," and one of its editors, John Carlos Rowe, is currently completing a volume entitled "The Americanization of Vietnam: Representations of an Undeclared War."[12] Also noteworthy is Charles L. Griswold's essay on the Vietnam Veterans Memorial, which appeared recently in *Critical Inquiry*.[13] At this point, it is a time-honored strategy to turn from what has already been written to new directions that future criticism of the literature of the Vietnam War might follow. Instead, I would like to mention several primary works unnoticed in the books reviewed above. My choices are based less on some supposedly inherent "literary" excellence than on the pedagogical opportunities these texts afford. Larry Lee's *American Eagle* is an autobiographical novel that details the struggle of a Native American veteran to readjust to his indigenous culture.[14] Gerald Rosen's *The Carmen Miranda Memorial Flagpole*, also a post-Vietnam work, is a rare comic novel, the manic equivalent of Stone's *Dog Soldiers*.[15] Jayne Anne Phillips' well-known book *Machine Dreams*, though not specifically about the War, focuses on the father-son theme and thus represents Vietnam in the context of the mythology of World War II.[16] Finally, I know of no poem that better captures the plight of the Vietnam vet than C. K. Williams' "From My Window."[17] These texts alone, however, cannot guarantee successful teaching. This can only be achieved through an empowering pedagogy that is participatory rather than authoritarian, dialogic rather than monologic. "In courses on Vietnam," writes William Alexander, "where murderous and illicit actions by high authority are revealed and studied, there must also be a pedagogical style that abolishes unthinking obedience, quiescence, alienation, hostility, powerlessness, and the propensity not to know and not to know how to know the existence of painful and unjust events."[18]

Only when we have transformed our classrooms in this way shall we be able to teach our students the real lessons of the Vietnam War.

Notes

1. *New York Times*, 22 March 1985; quoted in Alvin H. Rosenfeld, "Another Revisionism: Popular Culture and the Changing Image of the Holocaust," *Bitburg in Moral and Political Perspective*, ed. Geoffrey H. Hartman (Bloomington: Indiana Univ. Press, 1986), p. 93.
2. Michael Wallace, "Ronald Reagan and the Politics of History," *Tikkun*, 2 (1987), 16.
3. Presidential News Conference, 18 February 1982; quoted in *Quotations from President Ron* (London: Father/Daughter Ventures, 1986), p. 15.
4. John Gregory Dunne, "The War that Won't Go Away," *New York Review of Books*, 25 September 1986, pp. 25–29.
5. There are, however, several useful anthologies collected according to genre. For poetry, see especially *A Poetry Reading Against the Vietnam War*, ed. Robert Bly and David Ray (Madison, Minnesota: Sixties Press, 1966); *Winning Hearts and Minds*, ed. Larry Rottmann, Jan Barry, and Basil T. Paquet (Brooklyn: 1st Casualty Press, 1972); *Demilitarized Zones*, ed. Jan Barry and W. D. Ehrhart (Perkasie, Pennsylvania: East River Anthology, 1976); and *Carrying the Darkness: American Indochina: The Poetry of the Vietnam War*, ed. W. D. Ehrhart (New York: Avon Books, 1985). For short fiction, see *Between Two Fires*, ed. Ly Qui Chung (New York: Praeger Publishers, 1970); *Free Fire Zone*, ed. Wayne Karlin, Basil T. Paquet, and Larry Rottmann (Coventry, Conn.: 1st Casualty Press, 1973); and *Writing Under Fire*, ed. Jerome Klinkowitz and John Somers (New York: Delta Books, 1978). For drama, see *Coming to Terms: American Plays and the Vietnam War*, ed. James Reston, Jr. (New York: Theatre Communications Group, Inc., 1985). Most recently, an anthology of science-fiction stories set in or about Vietnam has been published: see *In the Field of Fire*, ed. Jeanne Van Buren Dann and Jack Dann (New York: St. Martin's Press, 1987). Also important are *Ca Dao Vietnam* (Greensboro, N.C.: Unicorn Press, 1980), John Balaban's translations of Vietnamese folk poetry, and *Vietnam Voices: Perspectives on the War Years, 1941–1982*, comp. John Clark Pratt (New York: Viking, 1984).
6. *Textual Power: Literary Theory and the Teaching of English* (New Haven: Yale Univ. Press, 1985), pp. 19–20.
7. The earliest scholarship is Wayne Miller's 1972 unpublished Modern Language Association paper, "Southeast Asia: the War in Fiction." Other significant early essays include, among others, John Hellmann, "The New Journalism and Vietnam: Memory and Structure in Michael Herr's *Dispatches*,"

South Atlantic Quarterly, 79 (Spring 1980), 141–51; Gordon O. Taylor, "American Personal Narrative of the War in Vietnam," *American Literature*, 52 (May 1980), 294–308; and Peter McInery, "'Straight' and 'Secret' History in Vietnam War Literature," *Contemporary Literature*, 22 (Spring 1981), 187–204.

8. *The Great War and Modern Memory* (New York: Oxford Univ. Press, 1975), p. ix.

9. The earliest enumerative bibliography is Tom Colonnese and Jerry Hogan, "Vietnam War Literature, 1958–1979: A First Checklist," *Bulletin of Bibliography*, 38 (January–March 1981), 26–31, 51; the first annotated list is John Newman, *Vietnam War Literature* (Metuchen, N.J.: Scarecrow Press, 1982); see also Christopher L. Sugnet and John T. Hickey, *Vietnam War Bibliography* (Lexington, Mass.: Lexington Books, 1983).

10. Jane Tompkins, *Sensational Designs: The Cultural Work of American Fiction 1790–1860* (New York: Oxford Univ. Press, 1985); Philip Fisher, *Hard Facts: Setting and Form in the American Novel* (New York: Oxford Univ. Press, 1985).

11. Tompkins, pp. xv, 38, 200; Fisher, pp. 3–21.

12. Special issue of *Cultural Critique*, ed. Richard Berg and John Carlos Rowe, 3 (Spring 1986).

13. "The Vietnam Veterans Memorial and the Washington Mall: Philosophical Thoughts on Political Iconography," *Critical Inquiry*, 12 (Summer 1986), 688–719.

14. *American Eagle* (Cambridge, Idaho: Packrat Press, 1981). Lee has published poems and short fiction under the name Larry Rottmann.

15. *The Carmen Miranda Memorial Flagpole* (New York: Avon Books, 1979).

16. *Machine Dreams* (New York: E. P. Dutton/Seymour Lawrence, 1984).

17. In *Tar* (New York: Vintage Books, 1983), pp. 3–5.

18. William Alexander, "Vietnam: An Appropriate Pedagogy," an unpublished paper presented at the 1981 Modern Language Association Convention, p. 4.

Franklin Well Served

A. Owen Aldridge

J. A. Leo Lemay. *The Canon of Benjamin Franklin, 1722–1776: New Attributions and Reconsiderations.* Newark: University of Delaware Press, 1986. 162 pp.

J. A. Leo Lemay and P. M. Zall, eds. *Benjamin Franklin's Autobiography.* Norton Critical Edition. New York: W. W. Norton and Co., 1986. xxiv, 392 pp.

In a sense J. A. Leo Lemay has presented the literary world with the archetype of a new literary genre in the first of these books; so far as I know, no previous author has written a book-length survey and critique of an on-going edition of the papers of a major literary or historical figure. The edition which Lemay examines is the *Papers of Benjamin Franklin,* published by Yale University Press, the first volume of which appeared in 1959 and the last considered by Lemay in 1984. The latter volume covers the year 1777, and the series is expected to continue through the year of Franklin's death, 1790. Obviously the editors of the complete works of any personality should print every piece that he is known to have written. There would be no problem if the editors had available a signed manuscript version of each of the author's works. Unfortunately for many authors, including Franklin, these basic manuscript materials must be supplemented by attributions of printed works which originally appeared anonymously or pseudonomously. Lemay ranks attributions to Franklin under five categories: those made by scholars before the publication of the *Papers* and not treated therein; those made by scholars other than the editors after the publication of the relevant volumes of the *Papers*; those incorrectly made by the editors of the *Papers*; those classified by the editors as tentative; and those made by Lemay himself in the present book for the first time. In his discussion of 96 attributions, Lemay concludes that

74 of them refer to works actually by Franklin and should, therefore, be included in the canon, and that two pieces already printed in the *Papers* as Franklin's are not his and should be dropped from the canon. Most of these 96 writings appeared as anonymous or pseudonymous contributions to literary periodicals, and only a scholar with Lemay's encyclopaedic knowledge of the history, esthetic values, and rhetorical practices of Franklin's milieu would be capable of determining which are the genuine products of his pen. As evidence for his attributions, Lemay used Franklin's own manuscripts (the editors actually rejected one piece in Franklin's hand and overlooked another), Franklin's references to his own authorship, the testimony of his contemporaries, information from biographical relationships, and, finally, internal content and style. The latter criteria, as Lemay remarks, are "notoriously tricky," and only a highly-trained professional is capable of discerning such internal indications. Lemay relies extensively on the repetition of exact words and phrases in similar contexts and on colloquial expressions, specialized vocabularies, and patterns of burlesque and irony. When particular subject matter associated with Franklin is combined with these stylistic techniques, it is appropriate to attribute such a piece to Franklin. Those purists who might be inclined completely to rule out the use of internal evidence should consider Lemay's observation that for most periodical pieces already accepted as Franklin's in the *Papers,* "no positive external evidence of his authorship exists, only the necessarily doubtful internal evidence, supplemented by circumstantial external evidence such as the time and place of publication" (p. 21).

In regard to incorrect attributions found in the *Papers* and in standard editions of other writers, Lemay makes a valid point concerning the value of reviews and the need for the scholarly world to pay more attention to them than is now customary. He observes that a review of the first volume of the *Papers* revealed that a significant piece in the volume was not Franklin's, "but subsequent scholars who have published books on Franklin have generally overlooked this information, perhaps because hundreds of reviews of various volumes of the *Papers* have appeared, and few reviews make any scholarly contribution" (p. 18). I can attest from my own experience with Thomas Paine that once a work is attributed to an author in an edition of his works, he long continues to be regarded as the legitimate parent, no matter how much contrary evidence is adduced. As far back as 1930, Frank Smith definitely proved in an article in *American Literature* that "An Occasional Letter on the Female Sex" is not by Paine. Even though a subsequent biography of Paine repeated this information in 1959, three later biographies and a mass-market printing of *Common Sense* have persisted in considering Paine as the author. The editors of Franklin's *Papers* have announced a policy of considering in later volumes new information which has been brought to light about Franklin's writing in the periods covered by those already in print. It will be instructive to see what use they make of Lemay's repertory.

Lemay concludes that his book demonstrates "that Franklin wrote more than we knew before—and more, no doubt, than we know now" (p. 136). It is perhaps significant that out of the 96 pieces considered in his book, 88 cover the years 1722–1750, and of the remaining eight only four are Franklin's. There may be more than one explanation. He worked as a printer and journalist during his early years and thus had more reason then to write anonymous and pseudonymous pieces than in later periods. During the later years he was actively engaged in politics and was required to devote most of his writing to signed documents. He never abandoned literary work, but in his later years either signed his writings for the press or circulated his manuscripts among readers who were acquainted with their provenance. The periods when Franklin was associated with newspapers, particularly during his youth and his middle years in Boston and Philadelphia, are the periods when he was likely to conceal his authorship.

That an entire book can be written on the omissions in a critical edition of a major author's writings does not speak well for that edition. Lemay refers politely to "the ongoing publication of that greatest edition of Franklin's writings" at Yale (p. 24), and in the interests of diplomatic relationships I presume he could do no less. The editors, past and present, have had vast resources at their disposal; their intentions are honorable; they are undeniably performing a valid service. But it would be closer to reality to refer to the Yale edition as "the greatest of Franklin editions so far published" rather than as actually a "great" one. In this instance the superlative means less than the positive.

In the edition of Franklin's autobiography, Lemay and Zall more realistically refer to the *Papers* as a "splendid series" and acknowledge merely that "its documents and annotations are the essential source where all Franklin scholarship must now begin" (p. xi). It might perhaps be said in defense of the Yale editors that with one exception all have been trained as general historians rather than literary historians. This, however, serves to explain rather than to excuse. One can only regret that, in the more than twenty years during which the Yale edition has been in progress, not a single editor has been appointed with training in American literature, not to speak of scholarly expertise and experience comparable to that of Lemay. I hasten to exempt from these comments one of the editors of the *Papers*, Claude-Anne Lopez, who has been trained in European rather than American literature, and whose knowledge has been applied mainly to documents dealing with Franklin's continental period.

Nearly all of the attributions which Lemay makes are based on the painstaking and exhaustive study of eighteenth-century periodicals, particularly Franklin's *Pennsylvania Gazette*. The discerning of authorship in newspapers and other periodicals through the intensive study of ideas, themes, and rhetorical similarities has become almost a lost art. This is a historical reality worth bringing to the attention of the entire modern language industry. In the 1940s and 1950s the study of literary periodicals was considered a major key to the culture and esthetic achievements of historical periods, and many valuable studies of magazines and newspapers were carried out in various literatures, not only in English and American ones. Since approximately 1960, however, the analysis of literary periodicals along with similar intensive studies in the history of ideas has been to a large degree replaced by criticism and literary theory. As a result, investigative textual study designed to identify previously unnoticed works by major authors has been neglected and even denigrated. Although subservience to the text—that is, to the text already identified or edited—has been elevated almost to a religious rite, few attributions of the kind reported by Lemay have been registered in recent scholarship. Fortunately for literary studies a few scholars such as Lemay have refused to follow contemporary fads and have devoted their persistence and intellectual rigor to the discovery rather than to the exploitation of a major author's works.

Contemporary historians in recent years have been no more assiduous than literary scholars in exploring literary periodicals. In the years just after World War II, Verner W. Crane made a notable contribution to the Franklin canon with his authoritative study of Franklin's letters to the English press, but no recent historians have to my knowledge attempted to carry on his labor.

My praise of the work done by Crane, a professional historian, in identifying newspaper texts may seem to be inconsistent with my criticism of the powers behind the Franklin *Papers* for not including in the project an editor with training in American literature. This I admit, and I acknowledge in addition that ordinarily a skilled historian is able to handle literary texts just as competently as a skilled literary scholar is able to deal with historical ones. It is relevant to mention, nevertheless, that most of the material brought to light by Crane is political in nature; whereas the seventy-odd new items considered by Lemay are primarily literary.

It is perhaps even more important for scholars to remove from an author's canon works attributed to him with insufficient evidence than it is to add new ones. I am awaiting with interest the volume of the *Papers* dealing with the year 1784 to see what the Yale editors will do with an essay (attributed to Franklin in the Smyth edition of his writings) entitled *A Letter from China*, dated 5 May 1784. This fascinating venture into Sinology, comparable to the best pages on the China theme in the works of Defoe, Rousseau, and Voltaire, has little relationship to other works by Franklin, and I have no idea why it should ever have been attributed to him. But this is a problem for Lemay and the Yale editors to deal with in the future.

Only scholars of Benjamin Franklin and other professional students of early American culture and history will concern themselves closely with Lemay's revision of the Franklin canon, but his and P. M. Zall's splendid edition of Franklin's memoirs will have a wide readership of both students and scholars. In principle, it is true, as they indicate, that Franklin's story of his life is "the only enduring best-seller written in America before the nineteenth century" as well as "the most popular autobiography ever written" (p. xiii). If this statement were amended to read "best-seller written by an American," it would be entirely true, but it is not literally accurate to say that Franklin wrote his memoirs "in America," for over half of the work (the first and most interesting two parts out of four) was composed in England and France. Although the entire life was printed in a condensed and fragmentary fashion in Philadelphia periodicals in 1790, Part I was first printed in book form in French translations in Paris in the following year, and four other editions appeared in London or Paris before the first American edition in 1808–18. The first edition to include all four parts in English was the historically significant one issued by John Bigelow in 1887–88.

The text of the present edition is based on a previous work by Lemay and Zall, *The Autobiography of Benjamin Franklin: A Genetic Text* (Knoxville: University of Tennessee Press, 1981), which prints with meticulous care a diplomatic transcription of the holograph manuscript in the possession of the Henry E. Huntington Library. The great contribution of this earlier edition is not in the printing of the manuscript (it is transcribed also, although less accurately, in the Franklin *Papers* and in an earlier edition by Max Farrand), but in the historical record it contains of the early printed editions of Franklin's memoirs. Before the Lemay-Zall *Genetic Text*, the main controversy among Franklin scholars concerned the revisions of the original manuscript made by his grandson William Temple Franklin in a London edition of the *Memoirs* in 1817–18. It was generally believed that these changes had been dictated by Franklin himself, and scholars were constantly being forced to decide, when the versions differed, between the style of the holograph version (vivid and blunt) and that of Franklin's supposedly corrected version (refined and literary). Scholars were at a loss to choose between Franklin's original language and his presumed refinement of it. Lemay and Zall prove conclusively, however, that Franklin him-

Franklin Well Served

self had nothing to do with the William Temple Franklin version and that his grandson's revisions were based entirely on "his own literary judgment" (p. liii). The only authoritative text, therefore, is that of the holograph, the one reproduced in *A Genetic Text*. In this review and elsewhere, I have had difficulty selecting a proper title for the record of Franklin's life written by himself. The word *autobiography*, which is now in general use, is anachronistic since the word itself did not exist until the nineteenth century. The earliest forerunner of Franklin's life history was entitled "Authentic Memoir" (p. 208), and later anticipatory publications were entitled "History of the Life and Character" and "Memoirs." The first French printing in book form bore the title *Mémoires de la vie privée*, and some form of this phrasing was used by all early editions. Sparks in 1840 used the title *autobiography*, but I am not sure whether he was the first to do so. In this review, I shall refer to the work as memoirs, in lower case.

For Franklin scholars as well as for the general reader, the text of Lemay and Zall's *Benjamin Franklin's Autobiography* will be vastly more useful than that of their *Genetic Text*. The content is the same, but the presentation differs. In the *Genetic Text*, the editors reproduce the text (with the aid of sigla) essentially as it appears in manuscript, with all editions, cancellations, and emendations made at a later time included on a line-by-line basis. In the later printing, the editors give only Franklin's final choice, correct his slips of pen, and normalize his spelling. But they list all changes and variants in textual notes at the end. The result is both a readable and an accurate text, the only such in print. Indeed it is as close to definitive as we are likely to come unless other manuscripts are someday discovered. To illustrate the difference between the *Genetic Text* and that of the Norton edition, I shall transcribe the first two sentences of a typical paragraph.

About ↑ this time ↓ I met with an odd Volume of the Spectator ↑ ⟨a⟩ ↓ . ⟨It was the third.⟩ ↑ ⟨I ha⟩ ↓ I had never before seen any of them. [*Genetic*, p. 13]

About this time I met with an odd Volume of the Spectator. I had never before seen any of them. [*Norton*, p. 11]

In the *Genetic Text*, the editors make no comparisons with the text reproduced by the editors of the *Papers,* but in the Norton edition they affirm that they have "discovered over six hundred discrepancies in Farrand's and Labaree's editions, including more than fifty substantive passages" (p. xvii).

Although Lemay and Zall recognize the division of Franklin's memoirs in four parts, they affirm that this division is a "modern practice" (p. 161), suggesting that it is artificial as well. "The trouble with dividing the book into parts," they argue, "is that this denies its unity, for, as the outline shows, it was planned as a whole in 1771" (p. 161). There is nothing modern or artificial about this division, which is structurally inherent and based on chronology. Franklin wrote the first part in England in 1771; the second in France in 1784; the third in Philadelphia in 1788; and the fourth (consisting of only seven paragraphs) in 1789–1790. One of the major topics that Franklin scholars have debated extensively is whether his memoirs have the literary quality of unity. Lemay and Zell argue that they have, and on this point I disagree. Although Franklin may have had an outline before him when writing all four parts, he did not follow it with the same degree of attention in all four. The second part diverges most radically. Of the three topics it covers, only one, Franklin's activities in establishing a public library in Philadelphia, is indicated in the outline. Since Franklin, when writing this part, did not have a copy of the first part in his possession, he had forgotten that he had already treated the Philadelphia library, and the relevant material in the second part is essentially a repetition. The other topics consist of his personal religious creed and his scheme for attaining moral excellence. The religious creed is repeated almost verbatim in the third part. These repetitions certainly do not contribute to unity. Lemay and Zall do not exaggerate the significance of Franklin's unity or lack of it, but they present only one side of the argument. The main obstacle to unity in Franklin's memoirs is tone rather than content. In Part I, Franklin indicates that he is writing for purely personal reasons, not for publication. He speaks of the pleasure of reliving his life through reminiscences, of following the natural inclination of old age to talk of one's past activities, and even of indulging his vanity. He also suggests that his son, to whom the work is formally addressed, might find it agreeable to know some of the circumstances of his life. He adds that his "Posterity" (presumably descendants other than his son, who was then forty years of age) might like to know some of the means he had used to rise from poverty and obscurity to affluence and high reputation. After a few pages, he interrupts his discourse to apologize for his "rambling Digressions" and attributes them to his old age. He then remarks that he "us'd to write more methodically. But one does not dress for private Company as for a public Ball. 'Tis perhaps only Negligence" (p. 8). This is not an example of contrived inattention, common in the period, but of natural informality appropriate for diaries or intimate letters to friends or family members. Part I concludes with the Memo: "Thus far was written with the Intention express'd in the Beginning and therefore contains several little family Anecdotes of no Importance to others. What follows was written many Years after in compliance with the Advice . . . [of two of his friends] and accordingly intended for the Public. The Affairs of the Revolution occasion'd the Interruption" (p. 57). One of the two friends referred to had seen Part I and had written a letter urging Franklin to complete his biography and publish it in order "to promote a greater Spirit of Industry and early Attention to Business, Frugality and Temperance with the American Youth" (p. 58). The other friend, after seeing this letter, had written one of his own, exhorting Franklin to publish his memoirs and to add to them the condensation of a plan for achieving personal virtue (p. 59). Both friends envisioned the continuation as a "noble rule and example of *self-education*." It is clear that Franklin intended Part I as merely personal reminiscences and that he changed his design in Part II to inculcate moral concepts and to write for publication. Just before beginning Part III, he wrote to a friend that "what is to follow will be of more important Transactions" (Smyth ed., *Writings*, IX, 665), referring to his exploits in science, politics, and international diplomacy. As a result, he adopted a tone of historical objectivity. Part III does not carry his activities beyond 1757, and most of the colonial affairs he does discuss are matter-of-fact in comparison with the lively anecdotes and personal reflections in the earlier parts. William Dean Howells percipiently affirmed in comparing Franklin's autobiography to Goethe's that "if either had gone farther, the record might have come to things of less real value to the reader, to impersonal things, to the things that history is made of" (quoted, p. 278). Part III already goes too far in this direction. Indeed I agree with Thomas A. Couser that this section is "increasingly dull and drained of individuality" (quoted, p. 373). So much for unity of tone. Lemay suggests in an excerpt from a previous publication that the unity is thematic and that the most obvious theme is that of the American dream (p. 358). Certainly this notion is present along with more than a dozen other major ones, but these themes are disparate and frequently occasional. The only unity of Franklin's memoirs is that of the autobiography and of the picaresque novel as literary genres—that is, the character and personality of the protagonist.

Lemay and Zall indicate that Franklin "intended at one time to include six supporting documents" in his memoirs, including the two letters from friends mentioned above. They state with apparent satisfaction that they print all six, whereas no previous edition has offered more than three (p. xix). I wonder whether Franklin did not actually intend to include one other document, for he records in his outline "At Albany. Plan of Union of the Colonies. Copy of it" (p. 171). I do not know how else to interpret this reference. This historical material, if included, would further detract from the unity of the whole, however much it would contribute to the aura of authenticity, and I believe that both Franklin and his editors were right in leaving it out. Indeed none of the supporting documents adds to the esthetic force of the narrative. (These documents include an advertisement concerning the procuring of wagons for Braddock's army as well as the two letters from Franklin's friends urging him to make his life story public in order to provide a model of self-attained virtue for the youth of the time.)

Some commentators have pictured Franklin as self-serving because he put himself forward as a prototype of moral perfection. Others have suggested that the virtues he proposes are not universally desirable. To counteract such criticisms, the editors have included three pages designed to place in a favorable light

Franklin Well Served

Franklin's Art of Virtue or "project of arriving at moral Perfection." These pages present excerpts from Franklin's other works illustrating the meaning of the word *perfection* in the eighteenth century. It did not mean as it does today "a completed, finished state," but instead an "approach to that condition" (p. 226). In other words, Franklin did not propose to become morally perfect, but merely to approach as close as possible to this ideal. No competent student of Franklin or of the eighteenth-century would hold this goal against him, but in the twentieth century the notion of virtue itself or inquiry into its nature has an anachronistic flavor.

In addition to the superb text of the memoirs, almost perfect in the eighteenth-century sense of the word, the Norton edition provides valuable supplements in the form of biographical notes, anecdotes and other biographical references to Franklin by his contemporaries, excerpts from Franklin's writings on the major themes in his memoirs, and criticisms of Franklin's character and writings. The biographical references are not only the most nearly complete to be found anywhere, but they are closely articulated with the text. Franklin refers, for example, to a curmudgeonly citizen of Philadelphia, Samuel Mickle, "an elderly Man" who had given Franklin a gloomy and discouraging prophecy of the economic destiny of the city and who, accordingly, refused for many years to invest in a house. When he eventually did so, he was forced to pay five times more for it. The note indicates that Mickle "was an 'elderly' forty-four in 1728" and "optimistic enough to have built a new stable only eight years earlier." In an essay in the section devoted to twentieth-century criticism, Lemay interprets Franklin's falsifying the facts about Mickle as a means of promoting the moral principle that optimism is better than pessimism (p. 358).

Many of the commentaries on Franklin included in this edition have never before been published or even mentioned in a book about him. Everybody knows that D. H. Lawrence wrote a scathing attack, but even dedicated Franklinists will find something new in the remarks of Edmund Burke, Charles Brockden Brown, John Keats, Leigh Hunt, Frederick Jackson Turner, and William Dean Howells. I regret, however, that the editors limited themselves to writers in English—with the exception of Max Weber. Condorcet in France, Domingo Faustino Sarmiento in Argentina, Tolstoi in Russia, and Yukichi Fukuzawa in Japan, all expressed opinions about Franklin's memoirs. Tolstoi is particularly relevant, since a controversy has been carried on among Slavic scholars for some years as to whether a scheme for attaining virtue which Tolstoi practiced was based on that in Franklin's memoirs. My only reservation about Lemay's concluding essay on Franklin as a reflection of the theme of the American dream is that it unintentionally ignores Franklin's enormous reputation abroad. His memoirs are taught as a required text in many secondary schools in Taiwan and Japan; so far as I know this is no longer true of the United States and never has been of the United Kingdom. The appeal of Franklin's enviable character and his way of life are not limited to America. His virtues embody universal values and stimulate universal admiration. But this is a minor objection. In summary, the splendid edition of Lemay and Zall is almost perfect, in either the eighteenth- or the twentieth-century sense. I do not know how in any major regard it could be better.

The Legacy of Ruskin: Two Recent Studies

Paul L. Sawyer

Tim Hilton. *John Ruskin: The Early Years, 1819–1859*. New Haven: Yale University Press, 1985. xvi, 301 pp.

Gary Wihl. *Ruskin and the Rhetoric of Infallibility*. New Haven: Yale University Press, 1985. xiv, 234 pp.

As a child, John Ruskin began a poem entitled *Eudosia*, an epic on the universe. He quickly abandoned the project, yet in another sense, he continued it all his life: the complete works are themselves a kind of discontinuous epic on things in general, each part ranging restlessly from topic to topic and from digression to digression until nothing seems alien, no subject impertinent, to Ruskin's voracious and all-inclusive intelligence. He produced one of the most extensive written records ever left by anyone. Tim Hilton lists, in addition to the 250 separate titles that make up the nearly forty volumes of the collected works, "more than thirty volumes of diary, around forty volumes of published correspondence, and dozens of thousands of letters which remain unpublished, and will not see print for many a year yet" (p. x). To the list of writings one could add the sketches, watercolors, engravings, and studies of architectural details, as well as the collections of art objects and natural specimens he bequeathed to various museums, all of which in some sense "express" him and belong to his works. He was forever analyzing and propounding, erecting his intuitions on presumedly ordered principles and irrefutable proof; yet so deeply are his doctrines the expression of his total temperament, emotional and intellectual—so suggestive are his structuring metaphors on so many levels—that the books arise before us, at one moment as treatises, at another as poetic structures, most densely significant when they express the conjunction of private feeling with the outlines of what Ruskin saw as the spiritual condition of his age. His books both baffled and excited his contemporaries, even before the 1860s, when the illness that eventually destroyed his mind began to show itself through streams of private allusion, uncontrolled punning, and apocalyptic rages. Soon after his death, the gnarled mausoleum of the complete works fell into neglect; their resurrection in the past decades has formed a minor industry of scholarship and interpretation.

The landmarks of what Elizabeth Helsinger has called the "Ruskin renaissance" are now clearly discernible. John D. Rosenberg's *The Darkening Glass* (1961), a concise and eloquent book, set out for a new generation of readers the essential shape of Ruskin's achievement as both thinker and prose-poet. For the first time since Ruskin's death, Rosenberg also attempted to chart the unread later works, in which Ruskin converted some of his private obsessions into a public diary, at once didactic and confessional. Since Rosenberg, the bulk of Ruskin studies has consisted of ever clearer and more systematic accounts of Ruskin's evolving aesthetic thought.[1]

Biographical studies have also followed a complicated course. As with so many of the great Victorians, the official portrait has undergone substantial revision with the publication of successive volumes of correspondence and other materials; but with Ruskin, the story of recent biographical studies has also been the story of our changing understanding of the first "official" portrait, the great autobiography *Praeterita*. Seeking to account for both the suffering and joy of his life while touching directly only on those things that gave him joy to remember, Ruskin presented his childhood as a charmed space, serene but isolated: there are few friends or companions, and the garden at Herne Hill was like Eden except, as he put it, all the fruit was forbidden. Forever afterward, in Ruskin's account, he felt himself an exile from that ambiguous paradise, forever wayward because of parental overprotection, forever unsatisfied, forever yearning for the lost Wordsworthian felicity and for the image of Adèle Domecq, the love of his adolescence. This portrait convinced modern readers, particularly because of the honesty with which it

The Legacy of Ruskin

treated the elder Ruskins—the mother's religious rigidity, the father's snobbery, their idolatrous love. But with the publication of Van Akin Burd's edition of *The Ruskin Family Letters* (1973), as well as other documents, it became apparent that Ruskin's famous memory was both inaccurate and highly inventive; *Praeterita* is now thought of as a kind of myth of the past, true at most to the "spirit" of what happened, rather than a reliable factual record. I will return to *Praeterita* presently.

The most curious fact about Ruskinian biography, given the enormous volume of information we now have and the ever-growing audience for Ruskinian studies, is that no one has yet begun a modern multi-volume work comparable in detail and comprehensiveness, say, to Leon Edel's life of Henry James. Instead, there have been five one-volume studies since 1949, of which the best is John Dixon Hunt's *The Wider Sea* (1982)—a sensitive and valuable work which is likely to fall into undeserved neglect. Tim Hilton's *John Ruskin: The Early Years*, the first of two volumes, carries its subject to midlife (1859). The whole will still be short—presumably under 600 pages—but the fullest account we have and, if the second half is as good as the first, the most engaging and useful as well.

Hilton is a first-rate narrator: he compresses worlds of fact, statement, and incident into compact, lucid paragraphs that give us an unprecedentedly specific and dense sense of Ruskin's social milieu—his associates and readers, the issues he addressed, the political events surrounding him. There is hardly a superfluous phrase in these lithe, rapid sentences, hardly a fact without its multiple implications. Everyone knows, for example, that Ruskin's parents were strict Scottish Evangelicals and that they sent their son to Christ Church, Oxford; what Hilton points out is that Christ Church was also the most Anglican of all Oxford colleges: "Its undergraduate body is aristocratic: on occasion it is royal. . . . To enter this society was to renounce the nonconformist heritage of the Ruskin family" (p. 43).

The following passage gives a good idea of Hilton's novelistic sense of the telling detail, of his racy economy of style, and above all of the many-sided awareness belied by the unpretentiousness of his style. In an unpublished letter of 1844, Ruskin had written to a friend that "I would not check at praying to the Virgin—I abhor not the invocation of saints—I deny not the authority of the Church—But there are two things that I *do* deny . . . the first—that man can forgive sins—the second—that God can behold iniquity—i.e.—the doctrines of a purchased absolution—and a merited redemption. In these two—& in them only—it seems to me the power & poison of the Papacy rests." Hilton comments: "Those who best understood him, like Acland, knew that he would say something quite different to the next friend. To Ruskin, religious belief was often a matter for argument. Many men in holy orders were to rue his delight in being contentious. If he felt falseness in another man's God, he was capable of arguing with a strange, pitiless gusto" (p. 84). The letter and comment prepare Hilton's reader for an account of Ruskin's momentous first trip alone to Italy, the heart of the Papacy—a visit during which his parents were particularly anxious for their son's religion but which resulted in the discovery of Tintoretto and earlier Italian art that was so influential to the young Pre-Raphaelite Brotherhood. Ruskin's many-sidedness is shown in the fact that despite the letter quoted above, and despite the letter to his mother attacking "the narrowness and inflexibility" of Bunyan's faith, he and his servant nevertheless read and discussed a chapter or two of scripture every day:

> As they drove south, Ruskin approached the papist Continent as though he bore St. George's own banner. That did not prevent him from travelling luxuriously. His coach was a marvel, a *calèche* drawn by two horses, shining black and gilt. . . . Inside were any number of pockets and drawers and little bookcases; a place for his writing-case (the only part of his luggage Ruskin ever packed for himself) and clever leather frames to hold the selection of Turner water-colours he took with him wherever he went. Who could not be happy as the day is long, to travel in a vehicle such as this? [pp. 84–85]

Hilton remains interesting on Ruskin's religious ambivalences; he is if anything even more interesting on Ruskin's complex relations with Turner, with the Pre-Raphaelites and other young artists he reviewed in his *Academy Notes*, and above all with the students and directors of the Working Men's College, where he taught drawing to London mechanics and artisans. Ruskin's writings on what he called the political economy of art remain neglected, yet nothing about his career is more interesting and contradictory than this rich young Tory's attempt to democratize art. In a letter to a Marchioness, he wrote that "there is no real occasion for the gulph of separation between amateur and artist"; yet he eventually grew tired of his classes at the Working Men's College and more and more used it "to recruit his personal labour force"—the engravers and copyists, for example, that he used for his own books. Once, when an enthusiastic young carpenter who was both a student and reader of Ruskin came to Denmark Hill to regale the family with anecdotes he had learned of Turner, Ruskin was displeased: the carpenter "had mistaken his place" (pp. 240–41). And here is Hilton on the little-known *Elements of Drawing*: "*The Elements* is the last [drawing-manual] to have relevance to living fine art, and its terminal position is what confers on it a poignant importance. For there is no such thing as a drawing manual within the avant-garde tradition. . . . Ruskin's book is in fact a witness of how fragile a period style his realism was" (p. 241).

"What purported to be a timeless book turned out to be utterly and inescapably of its day. How could one expect any book of Ruskin's to be anything but individual, or to belong to any time other than the months in which it was written?" (p. 241). This comment, a propos of *The Elements of Drawing*, brilliantly suggests the importance of biography to the student of Ruskin's ideas, and of this biography in particular. *John Ruskin: The Early Years* is a brilliantly sketched-in background for Ruskin's books, but has only incidental commentary on those books themselves; nor do we ever see Hilton's subject wrestling with an unfinished manuscript, corresponding about newly formed ideas, or planning new stages of his career. We learn, interestingly, that it was Effie Ruskin who suggested that she and her husband spend the winter of 1850 in Venice but not why Ruskin had in the meantime decided to enter a deeper study of Venetian architecture—the new interest that became *The Stones of Venice*. We have no new light on why this ultra-Tory anti-Catholic became interested in the exploitation of the industrial worker, the subject of a famous digression in "The Nature of Gothic" (one of those Ruskinian digressions, that forms the nexus of a new development of thought). That essay is profoundly Carlylean, yet Hilton's accounts of the various meetings between Ruskin and Carlyle serve chiefly to show (what is interesting) that the men did not know each other well during these years. I have quoted above from Hilton's delightful account of the Italian tour of 1845; but Hilton does not tell us that Ruskin was at this point stuck in the middle of *Modern Painters* II, at a loss for a theory of beauty in the human form. This repressed young Evangelical, therefore, was not only traveling alone to the country of the Papacy; he was also embarking on the study of the human body in Renaissance art—and heading, perhaps unconsciously, for Venice, the city he had once held sacred to the memory of his love for Adèle Domecq (herself a Catholic).

Some of these connections are psychological. If certain of Hilton's predecessors have veered towards the melodramatic, highlighting the tempestuous, sensational, and psychologically abnormal elements of Ruskin's character and career, this book seems, by comparison, serenely externalized. Its dominant figure is a strong-willed but amiable, enormously energetic young man continually surrounded by parents that dote on him and a growing audience that idolize him. The following comment is typical of Hilton's delicacy: "Ruskin's sexual maladjustment is not an uncommon one. He was a paedophile. He is typical of the condition in a number of ways, for paedophilia generally emerges in his age-group, often follows a period of marital breakdown, and in old age is accompanied by (or is a palliative to) a sense of loneliness and isolation" (p. 253). This tone—it is the language of post-Victorian medical toleration—is in many ways refreshing, but occasionally it is not. For example, some time in the late 1850s, when a woman who had been corresponding with him about art at last declared that she loved him, Ruskin responded, in part: "You little idiot! fancying you understand my books . . . fancying you love me, and writing me letters full of the most ridiculous egotisms and conceits—and disobeying the very first order I give you—namely to keep yourself quiet for a few days. . . . You modern girls are not worth your bread and salt—one might bray a dozen of you in the mortar and not make a stout right-hearted woman out of the whole set. I suppose you have been reading some of the stuff of those American wretches—about rights of women . . ." and so forth, for several pages. The uncontrollable rage, the deep-seated mysogyny veiled by the sentimental girl-worship, the conversion of fear and guilt into self-pity—this is the dark Ruskin that burst so often into his writings but rarely into the surface of the gracious and well-mannered public figure. Hilton blames the woman for her "importunate tactlessness," although conceding that Ruskin enjoyed a sort of "ponderous flirting" in these years, then comments on the letter itself: "There was as much pain as anger in this letter. The extremity of Ruskin's exasperation laid bare a longing of his adolescence" (pp. 268–70). The comments that follow are astute, yet they suffer from a blandness of response to Ruskin that sometimes, as here, can seem obtuse.

Hilton is also perhaps the first modern biographer to like the elder Ruskins. For him they are hard-working, genteel, passionately loyal, delighting in the success of the young genius who was the glory of the family. About the bizarre episode of Mrs. Ruskin's life in Oxford (she took rooms on the High Street for the three years of her son's college career, during which he visited her every day for tea), Hilton writes: "What could more demonstrate the unity of the Ruskin family, and their disregard of other social forms? The naturalness of the Ruskins's dependence on each other was soon accepted by other students. Often enough, young men of the nobility came to the lodgings to meet Margaret Ruskin. There was something so frank and powerful in her, this innkeeper's daughter, that snobbishness was beside the point" (p. 44)—for the young aristocrats, that is, though not for the innkeeper's daughter, who dutifully wrote every night to her husband, answering his anxious inquiries about the number of lords his son was meeting. Earlier biographers, and many contemporary witnesses, saw the elder Ruskins as pathologically possessive, rigidly controlling, yet damagingly over-indulgent—the worst combination of Evangelical piety and bourgeois acquisitiveness. The positive portrayal in Hilton partly emerges from *The Ruskin Family Letters*, where we learn (contrary to *Praeterita*) that there were toys and friends in the household that Ruskin described as hermetically isolated. Young John's letters to his father are particularly buoyant and affectionate, giving all the marks of a happy child; and the parents, conventionally seen as emotionally frigid, exchanged passionately loving letters throughout the years of the father's travels as wine-merchant. Having said all this, one wants to protest, at the last, in favor of at least some of the traditional view: that Ruskin's sexual maladjustment was something other than "not uncommon," that he was in fact a self-divided and disturbed young man, and that not everyone found his parents frank and natural. Hilton offers few new interpretations in this book and uses unpublished sources unsparingly; in the matter of Ruskin and his family, his comments are often surprising, but do not constitute an explicit refutation of earlier treatments. In one area, however, he departs radically: this is his suppression of the strain that developed between Ruskin and his parents, first over Adèle Domecq and then, increasingly and relentlessly, from the 1850s until the father's death in 1864. Ruskin loved his parents and needed them terribly (he was also financially dependent on them); he was at the same time made desperate by their tight possessiveness, their unconscious unwillingness to permit intellectual autonomy to the genius they nurtured and idolized. That conflict tore Ruskin apart. The evidence lies not just in the tortured themes of some of the books and in Ruskin's persistent, though half-hearted, attempts to buy himself a house in the 1850s (one proposed site was the top of a foothill in Chamonix), but directly in letters to friends and in the extraordinary outburst of pain and rage in letters to John James Ruskin just before his death. To recognize this conflict is not necessarily to blame either party: not to recognize it is to distort the most important relationship in Ruskin's life. This is the major shortcoming in a book that is otherwise balanced, delightful, and indispensable, raising high hopes indeed for its sequel. It is not, obviously, an adequate introduction to the study of Ruskin, but could become one if supplemented by a study such as Rosenberg's or Landow's.

So multifaceted is Ruskin's achievement that his modern student may be anything from a semiotician, literary critic, or occasional essayist to an intellectual historian, an art critic (like Hilton), or simply an educated gossip. It is a mark of the range of these studies that the two books under review share virtually no statements in common. Gary Wihl's *Ruskin and the Rhetoric of Infallibility* is a new thing under the sun, to the credit of Yale University Press—a critical study of Ruskin in paperback, handsomely produced, with thirty-one plates in the back. The difference between the two books is already apparent in the acknowledgments: on the one hand, a whole generation of English scholarly researchers that began poring through manuscript collections in the 1960s; on the other hand, a group of Yale critics—Harold Bloom, George Hersey, John Hollander, J. Hillis Miller, Martin Price, and the late Paul de Man (Wihl seems to have left no one out). For Wihl, Ruskin is "arguably the most important epistemological critic in English" (p. 2), and there is no doubt that the issues Ruskin raised throughout his career as a theorist of art are of major interest to contemporary theorists of literature and language. Wihl's book is informed by the writings of de Man, although his exposition of de Man is largely limited to de Man's essay on Proust; in reading Wihl, then, one should be at least touchingly familiar with de Man's influential critique of the referentiality of language, since he partly expounds, partly takes for granted some of de Man's conclusions.[2]

The aim of Wihl's study is to outline the contradictions between Ruskin's "theoretical texts" and his "figurative texts," or between "theory and poetic description, epistemology and figurative language" (p. xii); but he in fact does more than this, and I can only attempt a partial summary of several of his arguments. He begins with a close examination of Ruskin's distinction in *Modern Painters I* between mere imitation and "ideas of truth." "Imitation" is for Ruskin a confusion of sensory stimuli ending in the realization that one has been deceived, whereas truth is a selective set of signs stimulating cognition or conceptualization in the viewer; when one cognizes, the sign disappears as a sign and the "idea of truth" is substituted for the initial sensory stimulus, which is then canceled out. Thus, "the burden of Ruskin's preliminary argument is precisely to free ideation, even when taken in the most pragmatic sense of perception, from the influence of sensation" (p. 18); or as Wihl puts it elsewhere, "The sign is totally eclipsed by the signified." (This is why, at first confusingly, Wihl calls Ruskin "antimimetic.") But Ruskin provides no real theory of composition and so is unable to move from part to whole: "No proper explanation of the structure of signification has been offered. We still seem to move from a simple grasp of a single truth to a blurred 'mysterious' . . . incomprehensibility" (p. 27). Moreover, "The substitutability of the signs of nature increases the likelihood of tropological error" (p. 29); that is, the total arrangement of signs (marks of percepts) has no fixed meaning as a system but may suggest (invite arbitrary substitutions) many readings to viewers of "sensibility" based precisely on that habitual association that Ruskin wants to banish from perception. Ruskin himself, in the famous reading of Turner's *The Slave Ship*, "undoes" his own epistemology by his "use of tropes, which he mistakes for signs" (p. 37); he attempts to allegorize and so falls into error, as Wihl tries to show through his own reading of the same painting. In later chapters Wihl examines first Ruskin's attempt to ground empirical truth in Christian typology in *Modern Painters II* and then the "fictive" nature of allegory as Ruskin defines it in *Modern Painters III*. In this book Ruskin

is no longer concerned with establishing an immediate empirical ground for the cognition of truth. I have been arguing that, in any case, the attempt to ground cognitive truth in the empirical properties of a signifier fails. The simple sign, as soon as it is intuited, becomes a trope. The material properties of the type prove to be 'symbolic' substitutes, or metaphors, for hidden meanings. In giving up his focus on the empirical properties of a signifier, Ruskin seems to escape self-deception. [p. 88]

Unfortunately, Ruskin does not escape self-deception. In the later works Ruskin defends "rude" or "childish" art precisely because the non-correspondence of sign to signified prevents the viewer from "idolizing" it: "Sincerity of worship is in proportion to the disjunction between intense feeling of belief and the perceivable unbelievability of the icon or poetic image" (p. 126); but then Ruskin himself "seems to confuse metaphorical with material aspects of a substance" (p. 151), with the result that his late work is a massive pathetic fallacy or act of idolatry.

These citations should help suggest the subtlety of Wihl's language and the penetration of many of his insights, even as they perform a translation of Ruskin's language into the terms of post-structuralist analysis. It is time now to consider the problems of this approach. Following the usual practice of deconstructive criticism, Wihl sets aside historical questions (the specific occasion of the text, its generic status, its audience) in order to examine the text as a set of assertions, specifically assertions about signs and their referents. For him Ruskin is interesting whenever he asserts or seems to assert the "fictive" character of allegorical constructs and the "substitutive" or non-mimetic character of signs; when Ruskin seems to assert the opposite, Wihl is disappointed. But in Wihl's terms, this gives Ruskin both more and less than his due: Ruskin is never so "antimimetic" as Wihl makes out, and his "self-deception" is often consistently based on religious beliefs Wihl does not take seriously. In arguing against Herbert Read, for example, Wihl writes that "the text on *The Slave Ship* becomes [in Read's account] a central document in the evolution of expressionism—which is not at all what Ruskin intended. For all its internal contradictions, *Modern Painters I* is an attempt at an epistemology of landscape painting" (p. 35). One wishes Wihl had taken expressionism more seriously, instead of disposing of it through Herbert Read, because the issue raises the fundamental question of the extent to which a polemic in favor of Turner's particular style of representation can be interpreted as an epistemology. *Modern Painters I* is an attempt at an epistemology of landscape *and* a central document in the evolution of expressionism: it is an attempt, one might argue further, to use Lockean assumptions to explain how illusion functions in landscape, but also to read "ideas of truth" in painting as expressions, both of the mind and experience of the artist and of the (for Ruskin) "characteristic" modes of being of nature. Ultimately the artist paints the "soul" of nature, and through that action, his own soul as well. From first to last Ruskin attempts to "ground cognitive truth" in allegorical symbols, not indeed in the "empirical properties" of those symbols but in the energies or qualities which, for Ruskin, they represent, even when (as in the case of similes) they take on a different external shape from the object represented. We may very correctly consider this a tropological confusion, yet that is what Ruskin consistently asserted.

Wihl is on firm ground when discussing the incommensurability of certain allegorical meanings by their signs (as in the symbolic grotesque), but here too there are important omissions. For example, in his account of pathetic fallacy, he neglects to mention that for Ruskin, the highest order of seeing is the inspired or prophetical poet, who beholds landscape as living not because he falsely projects his own mood on natural objects (that would be pathetic fallacy) but because he is so overborne by his perception of the divine power in nature that he renders that power in distorted form as animation. Prophetic seeing becomes for Ruskin the origin of myth: Athena, therefore, is (given the universal imperfection of human organs) a "true" manifestation of the vital power informing nature. Ruskin remained a romantic vitalist until his death, which is the reason he so hated and feared the doctrines of scientific materialism (they were also, for him, morally pernicious). Ruskin's study of myth is not, in his own terms, pathetic fallacy, but an attempt to recapture a mode of inspired seeing, an attempt analogous to typological interpretation in the Christian tradition. That attempt in Ruskin shifts elusively from the literal to the fanciful (where it does indeed become pathetic fallacy) and back again, depending partly on the text and partly on the mood. The interest of his mythological studies today cannot, of course, rest on our acceptance of his elusive religious convictions; but neither, I believe, can they be dismissed as epistemological confusions. They serve, rather, as an attempt at a grammar of the Western religious imagination in terms that would be familiar, say, to Wallace Stevens; and we must recognize the nature of that attempt even if we believe Ruskin's vitalism to be mistaken, even if we do not share the psychic need that drove him to fear science and to ground moral values in some presumed objective perception of a sacred otherness of nature.

Although I have offered severe objections to Wihl's approach,

The Legacy of Ruskin

I do not mean to dismiss it: he is often interesting and valuable, probably more so to students of literary theory for whom the referential status of language is a live issue. But every reader should read him in the company of a truly comprehensive and learned survey, such as Helsinger's *Ruskin and the Art of the Beholder*. This is because Wihl's occasional generalizations about Ruskin's career as a whole are, at best, misleading and, at worst, unreliable. On page 122, for example, he writes that after *The Stones of Venice*, "the 'ruder the symbol, the deeper the significance' becomes the motto of his analysis. The *Vierge Dorée* [in *The Bible of Amiens*] is perhaps the last 'tender' fiction that he allows himself to appreciate." If "ruder" is a synonym for "supernatural entities" of a "non-believable form" (previous sentence), then this may be true, but "ruder" is certainly misleading as a description of the angel in the series of St. Ursula, which obsessed Ruskin throughout the 1870s and even after the death of Rose LaTouche; "non-believable" is misleading in reference to Athena, as we have seen; and finally, *The Bible of Amiens* is very late (1880–1885), so it is unclear what is being claimed. On the same page, Wihl italicizes "The Mystery of Life and Its Arts" and calls it a work on architecture—which it is in the paragraph that Wihl cites, but in fact it is an autobiographical lecture. He similarly calls *The Two Paths* a "theoretical work on architecture" (p. 115), but in fact it is a collection of lectures on topics having to do with art and industrial culture; we never get the title of the lecture from which he draws his text, nor what the complete lecture is about. Under the subject of idolatry, he spends considerable time discussing the aesthetics of imperfection in *Aratra Pentelici*, but never mentions the fullest instance of that argument, "The Nature of Gothic." I do not suggest that these vaguenesses or lapses in themselves seriously damage Wihl's argument, only that they do not give one confidence in his grasp of Ruskin's thought in its full range. Thus, although Yale University Press deserves credit for bringing out a theoretical work on Ruskin in a handsome, inexpensive format, it apparently failed to use readers with a first-hand knowledge of Ruskin and so missed the chance to have Wihl strengthen his final chapter.

"How could one expect any book of Ruskin's to be anything but individual, or to belong to any time other than the months in which it was written?" Tim Hilton's question aptly summarizes the formidable challenge posed by Ruskin to the kind of close analysis attempted by Wihl. If Wihl has no space to consider the historical and textual contexts of the passages he examines, Hilton on the other hand has little space to suggest the intellectual powers of the man he so richly describes. Both by their incompleteness and by their substantial achievement, these books testify to the hugeness of Ruskin's legacy—a legacy that may turn out to be the most various of any nonfiction prose writer in our literature.

Notes

1. George P. Landow's *The Aesthetic and Critical Theories of John Ruskin* (1971) and Robert Hewison's *John Ruskin: The Argument of the Eye* (1976) are milestones in our growing understanding of Ruskin's aesthetic thought in its entirety. Landow's more recent *John Ruskin* (1984) is the best overall account of Ruskin's thought, considered as the work of a Victorian prophet—a genre Landow accurately defines as a mixture, among other things, of biblical speech, prophetic stance, and neoclassical satire. Elizabeth Helsinger's *Ruskin and the Art of the Beholder* (1982) treats Ruskin's shift from the romantic or egotistic sublime to a democratic or viewer's sublime arising from the picturesque tradition, a tradition of "excursive" visual movement through a scene that becomes for Ruskin a technique of exegetical "reading." Helsinger's view of the transition from picturesque landscape to a world of allegory is the subtlest and most sensitive treatment of Ruskin's thought to date. In my own work, *Ruskin's Poetic Argument: The Design of the Major Works* (1985), I attempt to see certain texts as both intellectual arguments and poetic structures, with double reference to Ruskin's life and to his interpretation of his culture.

2. Briefly, for de Man any attempt to ground language in a supposed external reality fails, since language is inescapably composed of tropes (the substitution of one term for another term unlike itself). "Figural" language is language that falsely claims literalness. A classic de Manian critique is his deconstruction of the Coleridgean symbol in "The Rhetoric of Temporality (rpt. in *Blindness and Insight* [Minneapolis: Univ. of Minnesota Press, 1983]). For de Man the romantic symbol is the taking of a part to stand synecdochically for the whole it supposedly embodies; but since language is a system of signifiers that refer to other signifiers in a potentially endless chain of substitutions, the romantic symbol is but the expression of an impossible wish, the nostalgia for transcendent union. Wihl argues that Ruskin sometimes participates in this nostalgia and sometimes overcomes it.

A Book about Paintings from Books

George P. Landow

Richard D. Altick. *Paintings from Books: Art and Literature in Britain, 1760–1900*. Columbus, Ohio: Ohio State University Press, 1985. xxvii, 527 pp. 356 illustrations.

An encounter with Richard Altick's study of the rise and decline of English paintings on literary subjects raises important questions about interarts criticism, the history of taste, and scholarly methodology. As one might expect from a work by the author of *The Art of Literary Research* and *The Scholar Adventurers, Paintings from Books* is the product of much solid primary research. In part a listing of paintings by categories and in part a compendium of approaches to these works, this volume has much to offer and yet embodies some fundamental difficulties of writing interarts criticism and the history of taste. Before examining the implications of Altick's history of literary painting, I shall briefly sum up this massive, well-designed volume chapter by chapter in order to suggest the wealth of information that it contains.

Paintings from Books begins with a characteristically clear, concise introduction that presents the nature and limits of its evidence, in particular the fact that "more than ninety percent of the recorded pictures are lost" (p. 4). It then proceeds to a first chapter that discusses eighteenth-century literary pictures, *ut pictura poesis,* and history painting while the next surveys eighteenth-century book illustration and three major illustrative projects: Boydell's Shakespeare Gallery, Macklin's Poet's Gallery, and Fuseli's Milton Gallery. Chapter 3 moves to the next stage of this historical survey by examining what Altick terms "the period of lethargy" in literary painting (1800–1830), during which time notions of the sister arts changed as did the relative importance of history and genre pictures.

Chapter 4 somewhat changes direction (and methods), for it treats the period after the first reform bill primarily in terms of conditions affecting the production and distribution of art. Altick's promised social history of paintings from books perhaps comes closest to fulfillment in this chapter's useful, if impressionistic, discussions of major shifts in patronage from the aristocracy to the middle class. First pointing to the rise of art collecting as a means of speculation among the new rich, particularly among newly wealthy industrialists, Altick then speculates upon the role of paintings as decoration for middle-class homes, after which he points to the importance of books of engravings and of fashionable depictions, particularly engravings, of beautiful women. Perhaps the most important material in this chapter concerns the growth of the Art Unions, organizations whose members won cash with which to purchase inexpensive paintings—a means of art subsidy that had effects upon painting and popular middle-class culture similar to the effect Mudie's circulating library had upon the novel.[1] A fifth chapter, which examines the taste of the new collectors in terms of their preference for moral content over artistic skill, concentrates upon the aesthetic cost of such patronage—its valuation of moral content above artistic execution and its corollary taboos against nudity and politically or socially disturbing subjects; and it shows the tyranny of convention and the effects of standard authors and anthologies of extracts.

Chapter 6, the first of several that concerns themselves with popular subjects in literary painting, lists a wide range of themes, including faerie painting and depictions of witches, magicians, and prophets, dreams and visions, madness, men as amiable humorists, children, maternal piety, horses, dogs, imprisonment, arrival of a letter or news, emotional parting, deathbed scenes, and those of trial and sudden revelation. Chapter 7 examines works that depict events in the lives of writers, especially Shakespeare and Milton, and the following one continues this survey of iconography and investigates adaptations of older art and the rather different matter of the frescoes for the rebuilt Houses of Parliament. The ninth chapter, like the seventh, again examines interarts relations in instances other than that of paintings de-

A Book about Paintings from Books

rived from books, looking at several not very closely related subjects including the use of literary quotations or epigraphs in exhibition catalogues and poems based upon paintings—at works, in other words, that exemplify a relation that is the obverse of the one that provides the main subject of this book. Chapter 10, which concentrates upon Victorian art journalism, examines critical practice and its influence upon contemporary art, while Chapter 11 continues this look at the criteria found in journalistic criticism by examining its use of the terms *theatricality, vulgarity, coarseness, poetry,* and *realism.* A twelfth chapter, the last of this first section, sketches the decline of literary painting in the late nineteenth century.

Altick divides his study into three parts, the first of which contains these twelve chapters. Part 2, "Images from Shakespeare," surveys paintings from the Bard play by play, and Part 3, "The Rest of the Gallery," similarly discusses paintings based upon the works of individual authors from Chaucer through the Pre-Raphaelites. In fact, only 250 of this book's 527 pages are devoted to its stated main subject, for the second and third parts constitute partially illustrated partial lists of the materials they cover. Interesting and often valuable as is the information they contain, these sections, which generally confine themselves to providing names, dates, and occasional brief descriptions of paintings, fall between the stools of an analytic study of such illustrative art on the one hand and a checklist of the works on the other. Since they contain so little analysis of the materials they discuss, the primary usefulness of these sections lies in their listing paintings of, say, *King Lear, The Rape of the Lock,* or "The Eve of St. Agnes," and one therefore wishes that Altick had provided a fuller, more completely illustrated checklist of such works. In its present form, these lists are neither complete enough to serve as an adequate work of reference nor analytic enough to make easy reading.

Paintings from Books is often at its best when discussing the conditions of artistic production and distribution. It reveals, for example, how literary painting was shaped by matters as different as the decline in prestige of history painting, the manner of exhibition at the Royal Academy (and other institutions), investment in art, pricing of cabinet works, middle-class use of pictures for decoration, the role of the Art Union, fashionable novels, engravings of well-known society beauties, an audience for depiction of dogs, and the influence of high-quality illustrated books. Altick makes many specific observations that add to our understanding of the way that artists drew on British literature. He points out, for example, that in general painters confined themselves to relatively few of the many passages suitable for illustration, even in the best-known and most popular authors like Pope and Tennyson, and he also notes that with the obvious exception of Byron, a book's popularity and critical standing "achieved during, or shortly after, the poet's lifetime seems to have little if anything to do with its use, or neglect, by artists" (p. 335). Many of Altick's greatest contributions lie in information that, however selective or impressionistic, nonetheless adds importantly to our understanding of this issue. Goldsmith's *Vicar of Wakefield* turns out to have been the most widely illustrated single work and Shakespeare turns out to have inspired one-fifth of all literary paintings in England. *Paintings from Books* also tells us that many painters began their careers by first exhibiting pictures whose subjects derive from literature and that after 1850 certain kinds of subjects, such as trial scenes, lose popularity and disappear from the repertoire.

This study frequently makes observations that would seem to have important potential to contribute to our understanding of social history but that it does not develop. For example, it points to the common "motif frequently seen in literary paintings ... of a female model at an open window, or sometimes on a balcony, from which she gazes with whatever feelings the painter wished to ascribe to her" (p. 175). Two points about this remark demand notice, the first of which, perhaps, is the author's obvious lack of sympathy with these nineteenth-century representations of the pensive woman, which he clearly finds boring and regards as inept exemplars of artistic bad faith. Second, one remarks the apparent confusion of the model, a part of the painter's means of creating his picture, and the resulting image: Altick in fact discusses pictures not of female models, but of women standing at windows.

This apparently minor confusion would seem to indicate fundamental problems in Altick's use of iconographical interpretation. Given his claim that he will concentrate upon those elements in a work bearing upon social history, one expects that he will examine the major implications of such common depictions of the pensive or contemplative woman—images whose very obsessiveness reveals much about Victorian taste, ideology, social life, and conceptions of women. David Sonstroem, Susan P. Casteras, and Virginia M. Allen have all shown how one can carry out such a project, and one is surprised to see neither any mention of their work nor application of methods that have such obvious bearing upon the matters in question.[2] Allen, in particular, discusses paintings within the context of the needs and desires of the Victorian audience and against the background of the Woman's Emancipation Movement and reactions against it. The representations of women cited by Altick emphasize woman's supposedly contemplative nature and present female nature in terms of a culturally approved mode of behavior, one that emphasizes inwardness and nonaction. Can one write a historical sociology of taste without mentioning how and why popular images participate in popular attitudes? This question joins closely to a second: Can one analyze or define the taste of a particular age without also defining the attitudes and ideologies that inform that taste? Altick clearly assumes that one can, and I would like to look at some of the implications of this assumption.

Altick avoids these issues and also avoids those involving iconology, for as the example provided by his treatment of the pensive woman at the window suggests, this study has a curiously ambivalent attitude toward iconography and iconological interpretation, one based upon the assumption that they do not play an essential role in understanding either individual subjects or the taste that judges them. Altick early announces that his volume will not concern itself with iconographical interpretations, but in fact his continual identification of works in terms of their subject and approach constitutes a basic form of iconography. *Paintings from Books* was not intended to be art criticism or "a formal contribution to art history. . . . Instead, it explores a hitherto neglected phenomenon in the historical sociology of English literature, the interaction of middle-class literary culture and popular taste under the auspices of painted art. Paintings are not considered as autonomous objects of art but simply as primary documentation of ... literary and artistic tastes" (p. xxv). Such an approach is entirely justifiable, but can one write a social history of taste without connecting the aesthetic objects examined—here paintings and literary works—to other components of social history? Can one, in other words, write a social history of taste largely in terms of lists of works and their subjects?

Other questions about this book's methodology arise because it follows several unannounced major premises that involve specific conceptions of history and the historiography of culture. *Paintings from Books* embodies the fallacy of genetic valuation, the notion that the origins of a phenomenon have more importance—that is, both more historical significance and more aesthetic value—than do later instances of it. An art or cultural historian concerned with the origins of the Gothic, the Court Style of the thirteenth and fourteenth centuries, or European Realism justifiably pays closest attention to such first examples, since they form his project. In contrast, someone concerned with these movements as a whole or with the finest examples of them *and not simply with their origins* has no reason to place greatest value on origins, on first examples. Historians and critics often identify as most aesthetically successful or historically interesting extremely late examples of, say, French fourteenth-century bas reliefs in ivory or Realist paintings produced after Post-Impressionism had become the dominant fashionable mode. Art historians term such works that appear after the height of a movement or school *retarditaire*, and many excellent works often appear at such scholarly inconvenient times. In fact, many superb examples of English literary painting appear late, some particularly fine ones after Altick's terminal date. They can be found abundantly illustrated in recent art historical works, such as those by Anthony Hobson and Christopher Wood.[3]

Although *Paintings from Books* studies literary painting in Britain from 1760 to the close of the nineteenth century, it clearly has most sympathy for various eighteenth-century origins. For in-

A Book about Paintings from Books 181

stance, when discussing nineteenth-century heirs of Hogarthian satire, symbolic realism, and use of linguistic devices within picture space, it presents Hogarth's Victorian heirs as creating mere repetition without the master's originality. In fact, it takes an attitude toward painting that one would not expect to encounter toward literature. It assumes that allusion, borrowing, and partaking of tradition are necessarily parasitical and indications of trivializing belatedness. Furthermore, although *Paintings from Books* admittedly makes no attempt to survey the complex relations among book illustration, painting, and literary works that provide the "source" of the other two for the entire period, it does devote considerable attention to eighteenth-century examples, but not to Victorian ones that are as aesthetically and historically significant. As it ranges across various topics, this study repeats a disturbing pattern. It begins enthusiastically with the eighteenth-century origins of a theme or approach, turns next to developments in the early years of the next century, and becomes increasingly bored with the Victorian materials and cavalier in its treatment of them. Such an approach is unfortunate because in many cases the latest works of many movements of schools, say, the paintings of Waterhouse, Gotch, and Hunt in the last decades of the nineteenth century, represent magnificent achievements. They also provide counterexamples that contradict many of the casual critical judgments that mark this volume.

One cannot argue with Altick's claim that "innumerable pictures that were nothing more than routine treatments of banal themes were decorated with titles or quotations that related them to a favorite work of literature. Pictures titled *The Rivals* were as likely to be sentimental genre pictures of bucolic suitors competing for one woman, or two women in envious contention, as illustrations of Sheridan's play" (p. 183). True, a large percentage of supposedly interarts allusions are numbingly trivial, but one frequently receives the impression that his project has bored and exhausted Altick to the point that he has little patience or sympathy for the works discussed in his pages. Trapped by an emphasis upon origins, Altick apparently makes novelty or chronological priority a chief criterion. In doing so, he often repeats the attitudes and failures of the Victorian journalistic criticism for which he has such proper lack of respect. A major result of the author's valuation of origins and first instances appears in the weariness that surfaces whenever he discusses matters Victorian—something surely rather odd in the work of one of the great Victorian scholars of our time.

The weariness that marks his treatment of Victorians, which is in part a result of the author's dependence upon chronology and simple listing as an organizational principle, may be responsible for inaccuracies and problems of emphasis and interpretation that mar his discussion of these later artists and their work. Since I have done some of my own art historical work in relation to William Holman Hunt, one of the founding members of the Pre-Raphaelite Brotherhood, he makes a convenient benchmark. To take a small but significant point, the correct title of the work by Hunt that has major historical significance as the first work of ethnographic religious realism is *The Finding of the Saviour in the Temple* and not *Christ in the Temple* (p. 76); Altick has taken the title from a contemporary review. This work, incidentally, also speaks to Altick's claim that "forthright social or political comment was never seen, or at least publicly detected, in nineteenth-century literary paintings, despite the heterodox ideas and subversive tendencies so many English literary works contain" (p. 100).[4] Hunt consciously made Christ a member of the lower classes and a Jew, a member of a despised race, in *The Finding of the Saviour in the Temple* (1854–1860) and *The Shadow of Death* (1869–1873), and abundant evidence demonstrates that both journalistic critics and popular audiences understood his political and social themes. For instance, when in *The Finding* Hunt portrayed Jesus as a member of the lower classes and as the descendant of very non-English stock, *The Illustrated London News* attacked him for daring to present the Saviour as a member of a "degenerate race"—"a Jew-boy in the streets of Jerusalem."[5] And, as both Hunt and contemporary reviewers point out, his depiction of Christ as a workingman was correctly understood as a political statement both by workers, particularly in the industrial North, who purchased engraved reproductions of *The Shad-*

ows of Death, and by members of the upper and middle classes who bitterly disliked Hunt's disturbing emphasis upon the sacrifice and dignity of labor—and upon the fact that Jesus himself was a laborer.[6] Again, Hunt's own statements, those of journalists, and those of his associate F. G. Stephens demonstrate that his earliest purely literary works (such as *The Eve of St. Agnes* (1848) and *Rienzi* (1849)), like independent works that make literary allusions (such as *The Awakening Conscience* (1853)), offer detailed social and political criticisms that include attacks on the upper classes, their taste, and their exploitation of workers. Two factors seem responsible for Altick's reluctance to take account of this aspect of Victorian art—his unwillingness to use iconography to interpret individual works and his related assumption that one can judge the significance of individual works within the context of Victorian taste without deciphering what they meant to contemporaries.

Hunt and his associates, particularly Rossetti and Millais in some of their greatest works, also provide abundant demonstration that painting was not nearly so limited as Altick suggests when he emphasizes that "the inadequacy of paint to represent what was more and more the central concern of literature from the Romantic period onward, its account of the inner life of men and women, became further evident as fiction supplied so many subjects to artists and as the psychological element in older fiction commanded the attention of critics" (p. 242). In fact, as Ruskin and more recent critics have pointed out, Pre-Raphaelite hyper-realism in works like *The Awakening Conscience* serves not to create a cold, photographic effect, but rather an intensity that parallels—and expressionistically re-creates—the psychological turmoil of the main figure, and works like Millais's *Autumn Leaves* and Rossetti's representations of the Fair Lady, many of which are paintings from books, similarly function to communicate other moods.

Altick's working principle that one does not have to define exactly the subjects of individual paintings before using them as the raw materials of a historical sociology of taste also prevents him from observing the brilliant means that literary painters devised to solve some of the fundamental problems of their art. In Chapter 12 the author sets forth these problems in an attack upon the entire ideal of literary painting:

> Paintings from literary sources had additional limitations because of the special nature of literary subject matter. They could deal only with surfaces: with appearances, situations, and actions (but with only an instant of an action). They could not fathom or represent the true depth and complexity of a literary work or even of a moment from that work, except by sacrifice of its content, of its dependence on all that had preceded. They could not represent the special effects of language, formal structure, developing characterization, ongoing narrative. They could not reproduce dialogue. They could not represent ideas, except those that could be simplified and conveyed by a single image or set of images. In short, they could only isolate, from the totality of a literary work's artistic and substantive qualities, those few that could be depicted visually and statically. [pp. 241–42]

Much of what Altick here claims is obvious and necessary to recognize, but it does not necessarily lead to his conclusions about art and communication. To claim that painting only communicates by means of visual images is not accurate because it leaves out the capacity of the visual arts to convey mood and emotion by color, tone, composition, handling of space, and other aspects of purely visual design. In making these points about the limitations of art, Altick apparently reduces it to a means of creating recognizable shapes. Without apparently realizing that he has done so, he writes in a way that reduces the capacities of art to the purely mimetic one of creating recognizable images of what already exists or can be imagined to exist. At the same time, as we have already observed, he chooses not to examine the various literary or linguistic meanings that accrue to images in literary art, and this turning away from a large portion of these works' capacity to signify, to communicate, derives from this same mimetic reduction of art.

Paintings from Books simply does not take seriously the capacity of paintings to function effectively in complex verbal contexts or the possibility of a truly literary art. His repeated criticisms of pictures that use a title to create their literary reference reveal a basic assumption, one characteristic of modern art and art theory. This is the assumption that one cannot join verbal and visual modes in a single art and that to attempt to do so leads to an essentially bastard art. Opera, narrative dance, the art of Hogarth, Gothic architecture, and Victorian literary paintings all provide powerful counterexamples, however.

Although Altick clearly does not place much aesthetic value upon paintings derived from literature, he does propose several important uses to which the kind of data he has assembled might contribute. First, he raises what he terms

the tantalizing, truly unanswerable question of what really happened when a man, woman, or child was brought face to face with a picture that purported to represent a character or scene in a familiar book. Such mentions of exhibited paintings as we find in the letters, memoirs, and recorded conversations of the seasonal habitués of the exhibition rooms, like Victorian readers' private notes of their reaction to newly read books, are so brief and unparticularized as to be almost without value as historical evidence. But we do know that their approach to paintings and engravings with dramatic or narrative content took the recommended form of "reading"—that is, of methodically scrutinizing the details of the design in quest of meaning. [p. 246]

Altick, who points out that under the influence of Lamb, Hazlitt, and Ruskin the practice of explicating paintings in detail became widespread in the nineteenth century, offers an answer to his own question, as one can tell from the example of Hunt. This artist's private comments, elaborate exhibition pamphlets, and critical reception provide a great deal of information for such a phenomenology of audience reception. Furthermore, the works themselves point to how Hunt expects one to experience them. The spectator of *The Finding of the Saviour in the Temple* and *The Lady of Shalott* was meant, first, to encounter the work's massive architectural frame that set the picture apart from normal experience, after which he was expected to move to the various inscriptions and epigraph, then to the main points of the painting and back again in a continuing patterned set of movements of eye and mind. Various sermons on individual works by Hunt and long critical analyses of them suggest that spectators did in fact react as the artist wished.

Another equally interesting project lies in Altick's suggestion that "the evidence of literary art"—by which he means paintings with literary subjects and not the techniques of literature itself— "can also be used to amplify our understanding of an individual work" (p. 250). One would have wished to have seen at least a sample of such a proposed critical history that takes illustration as part of the meaning of the main text. Perhaps a casebook method that concentrated upon individual examples in depth might be necessary for such an endeavor.

In conclusion, I should like to emphasize that although Professor Altick's study prompts these queries, suggestions, and downright disagreements, it makes a solid contribution to our understanding of both the history of changing taste and of relations between visual and verbal arts. The entire survey of literary painting, like his analysis of the many factors that have influenced it, will prove of interest to all who concern themselves with paintings and books.

Notes

1. See Guinevere L. Griest, *Mudie's Circulating Library and the Victorian Novel* (Bloomington: Indiana Univ. Press, 1970).
2. David Sonstroem, *Rossetti and the Fair Lady* (Middletown, Ct.: Wesleyan Univ. Press, 1970); Susan P. Casteras, *The Shadow and the Substance: Images of Victorian Womanhood* (New Haven: Yale Center for British Art, 1982) and "Down the Garden path: Courtship Culture and Its Imagery in Victorian Painting" (Ph.D. dissertation, Yale Univ., 1977); and Virginia M. Allen, "'One Strangling Golden Hair': Dante Gabriel Rossetti's *Lady Lilith*," *Art Bulletin*, 66 (1984), 285–94.
3. See, in particular, Anthony Hobson, *The Art and Life of J. W. Waterhouse RA, 1849–1917* (London: Studio Vista/Christie's, 1980); Frances Spalding, *Magnificent Dreams: Burne-Jones and the Late Victorians* (New York: Dutton, 1978); Christopher Wood, *The Pre-Raphaelites* (New York: Viking, 1981); and [Exhibition catalogue] *Victorian High Renaissance* (Minneapolis: Minneapolis Institute of Arts, 1978).

4. Although one might argue that Hunt's religious paintings cannot be cited as evidence against Altick's conclusions about generally secular literary art, several factors permit one to do so. First, paintings from biblical subjects are paintings from books; second, habits of mind associated with Bible reading were applied to purely secular literature; and, third and perhaps most important in this case, Hunt himself used many of the same devices in his secular and religious works, something apparent in his paintings based on Tennyson (*The Ship* and *The Lady of Shalott*) and Keats (*Isabella or the Pot of Basil*).

5. "Holman Hunt's Picture of 'The Finding of the Saviour in the Temple,'" *Illustrated London News*, 38 (28 April 1860), 411.

6. George P. Landow, "William Holman Hunt's 'The Shadow of Death,'" *Bulletin of the John Rylands University Library of Manchester*, 55 (1972), 220–22, quotes contemporary reviews that note the painting's political point. Hunt's memoirs and his pamphlet contemporaneous with the exhibition of *The Shadow of Death* point out the painter's controversial use of sacred art to advance the cause of the workingman.

Emerson Bibliography: History and Audience

Albert J. von Frank

Robert E. Burkholder and Joel Myerson. *Emerson: An Annotated Secondary Bibliography*. Pittsburgh: University of Pittsburgh Press, 1985. xiv, 842 pp.

Joel Myerson. *Ralph Waldo Emerson: A Descriptive Bibliography*. Pittsburgh: University of Pittsburgh Press, 1982. xviii, 802 pp.

It is hard to imagine how students of Emerson got along all these years without convenient access to the information so expertly organized and handily indexed in these two large volumes. Bibliographies, absent any terrific accidents, always supersede their predecessors to become standard, but such a quantum leap in inclusiveness, thoroughness, and accuracy as these works represent—and in an area of such central importance to the study of American literature and culture—is quite rare indeed.

Certainly for better or worse these bibliographies arrive at a crucial time in the history of such study, and it will be a matter of no little interest to see what uses they are put to. As we move deeper into a period aptly characterized by Sacvan Bercovitch as one of "dissensus," it becomes increasingly apparent that the criticism of Emerson, as of other writers, has all but lost the coherence or commonality of purpose it had as recently as the mid-sixties. Assumptions and methodologies—so much alike from one study to another in the past—have become to a considerable extent problematical under the impact of currently competing critical theories—so much so that one begins to wonder whether a survey of past scholarship such as Burkholder and Myerson have given us will prove at all useful to investigators in full revolt from "the narrow textuality of the New Criticism" and "the naiveté of the old historicism."[1] Secondary bibliographies surely have more than ever the look of a sepulchre of the fathers. Still it is good to know where the ideas came from that we inevitably continue to think with, and, however different our operant assumptions may be from modes that once prevailed, it is both a healthy discipline and a source of new inspiration to keep up our contact with the past—history and historicism being, after all, two different things.

These two Emerson bibliographies are, in a conscious and necessary sense, also works of literary history, giving complementary views of more than a hundred and fifty years of commerce between Emerson and his audience. The uninterpreted history of the critical response is comprised in the 5,659 discrete commentaries on Emerson between 1816 and 1979 that Burkholder and Myerson have identified and annotated. This body of material is also, of course, the best if not the only evidence from which to construct a history of Emerson's reputation, which proves, in turn, to be largely a story of shifting cultural preoccupations. It is more certainly the case with Emerson than with most other writers that cultural prejudice played an important part in the ongoing public determination of his significance. The record shows that at no time did Emerson lack serious and intelligent defenders, though they very rarely succeeded in doing much more than contradicting the popular indictments that provoked their attention; that is to say, the Emerson they portrayed was all too often merely the anti-popular Emerson, a caricature in reverse.

Compared with the Divinity School Address (1838), *Nature* (1836) was the subject of little public comment or controversy, and it is clear that the reason for all the attention on the later occasion was simply that Emerson had already earned a suspicious reputation for heterodoxy as a result of his resignation in 1832 from the Second Church pastorate. The Divinity School Address, unlike *Nature*, fit the pattern of public expectation—dangerously so in the eyes of most onlookers, in whom the power of the religious press resided. This controversy, persisting for several years, affected responses to *Essays* (1841), which, because Emerson continued to be regarded as a religious writer, or at least as a writer interested in taking religious positions, was examined more for its bearing on these matters than for anything else. The impression that Emerson's meanings lay squarely in the realm of theology was considerably dispelled during the lifetime of the *Dial*, not simply because he left such topics alone, but because he came to be associated in the public mind with a specific group of "Transcendentalists," a band of philosophers and litterateurs who seemed less interested in "pantheism" than in German aesthetics and French social theory.

It is interesting to note that the critical response to *Essays: Second Series* (1844) was far more tolerant than for the first collection. One suspects that with the demise of the *Dial* and with Brook Farm in disarray, Emerson seemed to the public less the leader of an odd coterie, and more an independent scholar/artist, the only writer, as was now being hinted, who was doing more or less what the late William Ellery Channing had done so respectably and with such distinction for the moral and intellectual life of New England. *Essays: Second Series*, the reviewers said or implied, was a more eligible expression than Emerson had ever published, and—as though looking for a new kind of Gray Champion—these reviewers of 1845 seemed ready to find in Emerson an independent native voice. For the first time, debate over Emerson's religious orthodoxy took a back seat to the problem of his reliance on Carlyle.

The publication of *Poems* in late December 1846 made it clear that Emerson could not be pigeonholed as a mere "American Carlyle," but it revived with a vengeance the old charges of rhetorical obscurantism and indifference or hostility to Christian truth. Reviews of *Poems* were inordinately hostile or excessively laudatory: in either case, it would seem, the public had been surprised. On the whole, I believe, the American reading public in the mid-nineteenth century preferred surprises, and would only be ultimately disappointed if it were bored. In 1847 Emerson had been a controversial figure for fifteen years: his trip to England in 1848, and the considerable impression he made there, confirmed a celebrity status the effects of which are visible in the reviews of *Nature; Addresses, and Lectures* (1849).

Reading through a selection of the reviews, or even through

the careful synopses provided by Myerson and Burkholder, one gets a clear impression that Emerson's contemporary readers were not on the whole bothered by an impression of sameness in Emerson's work (as some twentieth-century readers have been), but were sharply differentiating his production, volume by volume. While it is true that the range of objections brought against Emerson throughout his career was neither wide nor varied, it is fair to say that each book, as it came out, elicited a very distinctive judgment. *Representative Men* (1850), for example, might have built on the prestige that Emerson had clearly won in the preceding two years, but in fact it was a signal critical failure: reviews stress its passionless objectivity, its obscurity (again), and its faulty religious attitudes. Moreover, the book seemed almost deliberately to revive the question of Emerson's derivative relationship to Carlyle.

A few voices were raised to insist that Emerson was a distinctively American writer (Lowell insisted on the term Yankee), but the impression that Emerson had always made with the generality of reviewers was of an exotic dependence on European thinkers and writers. Since the Miracles Controversy of the late 1830s, when he was paired with Cousin, Emerson was seen as a pale reflection of Coleridge or Carlyle or Friedrich Strauss or any of a dozen others—but of course most regularly of Carlyle, whose works he had publicly sponsored in America. It is obvious that for many reviewers the principal link between these two writers was the reviewer's own inability to understand either one. Desperate admissions of incomprehension were being promoted, in the case of *Representative Men,* to the status of criticism: it remained for Theodore Parker, in a brilliant defensive essay in March 1850 to call a halt to this categorical abuse of Emerson by people who in all innocence confessed their ignorance of his aims or practice.

There are a surprising number of reviews of the 1852 *Memoirs of Margaret Fuller Ossoli,* written by Emerson along with James Freeman Clarke and William Henry Channing. The extent of public interest in Fuller, who had died in a shipwreck in 1850, is further suggested by the five printings of this title in the year of publication, compared with only two for *Representative Men.* Most of the reviews were polite enough, but several managed to imply that Fuller was somehow both a victim and an embodiment of the Transcendental movement, and one begins to hear that the movement itself is dead and that Emerson is its only survivor. The *Memoirs* may have served in other ways to strengthen the public impression that Emerson was an independent writer and no longer to be thought of primarily as the center of an ideological group: either in praise or in blame, most reviewers remarked upon his objectivity, by which they meant his willingness to consider Fuller's faults along with her genius. The public, it would seem, wanted Emerson to appear independent—not, perhaps, because it valued intellectual freedom, but because it still disapproved of "Transcendentalism."

Such was evidently the context of the reception accorded *English Traits* in 1856. In America it was praised for its unusual lucidity, as though Emerson had at last condescended to write a readable (if somewhat disorganized) book in a recognizable genre. Most, indeed, saw that it departed from the usual manner of presenting first-hand impressions of travel, but few disliked it on that account. The general impression was of a mature willingness to communicate rather than challenge. The public were willing, for their part, to accept from Emerson whatever seemed to repudiate past intellectual and artistic deviance—anything, that is, that could be seen as confession or recantation. The public thought that this was just what *English Traits* implied, but, as happened ten years earlier, Emerson's poetry proved the vehicle for disappointing the public's expectations. The founding of the *Atlantic Monthly* in 1857 gave him a journal forum— particularly for his poetry—such as he had not had since the failure of the *Dial*. The first issue included several poems by Emerson, among them "Brahma," which, as a flurry of dazzled comment shows, completely flabbergasted the readership. In the late 1850s, as had not been the case during the *Dial* years, Emerson developed a reputation as a poet that was, from the public's point of view, disturbingly at odds with his reputation as a prose writer, a circumstance of his reception that has endured to the present day. His endorsement of Whitman and *Leaves of Grass* further showed that if he was becoming a relatively tame and pleasant writer of non-fiction, the poet in him was still of an unpredictable and aboriginal wildness.

The Conduct of Life (1860) was Emerson's last controversial book, a fact suggested by a return in many of the reviews to the old charge that he had committed to print a mass of obscure transcendental maunderings. A few reviewers objected especially to the difficulty of the style; a few others to the lack of Christian perspective. Most of the reviews were anonymous, though Lowell publicly defended the book.

The two collections issued during Emerson's years of decline—*Society and Solitude* (1870) and *Letters and Social Aims* (1876)—were met with unmistakable signs of polite respect, partly, it would seem, because they were so much in the familiar vein of Emerson's lectures. Reviewers who perhaps were not expecting much from the aged Mr. Emerson, noticed a lack of originality in thought and expression; they were unsurprised to find that the books contained much old material, revised and edited by the author and his daughter. From 1865 on, a valedictory mood prevailed with respect to Emerson, and it was in this context that his last several books were received by the public. Generalized tributes began to appear—by Moncure Conway, Alcott, and the industrious Frank Sanborn, among others—which gave shape to the growing public consensus that Emerson had after all been a benefaction for New England and for America. Conway along with Thomas Wentworth Higginson and George Willis Cooke wrote favorably about Emerson's last books, as the cast of characters who would champion the name of Emerson through the remainder of the century and beyond began to identify themselves.

The decade of the 1880s was dominated by biographical work, beginning with Cooke's life, published in 1881, the year preceding Emerson's death. A considerable number of obituaries and memorial notices appeared, many of which centered on Emerson's connection with Carlyle, who had died a year earlier. Biographies by Alcott, Conway, and Alexander Ireland appeared during the year, while better-known biographies by Holmes and Cabot were published in 1884 and 1887 respectively. The appearance of Charles Eliot Norton's edition of the

Carlyle-Emerson correspondence in 1883 was a stunning revelation on a subject that had long fascinated Emerson's readers, among whom was a highly appreciative Henry James, Jr.

The published commentary of the period from 1890 to 1920 might aptly be characterized by the title of an otherwise unworthy article of 1907: "Emerson for Everyday Use." Among the items that Burkholder and Myerson list for this period, one finds a relatively large group of lesson plans designed to get Emerson into the schools; explications of poems proliferate, and there are several attempts to establish that Emerson had a sense of humor. A large but not surprisingly great number of reminiscences, in stressing Emerson's personal friendships, must have had the effect if not the intention of humanizing the Olympian philosopher. Brander Matthews, the Columbia University professor, introduced Emerson to the juvenile audience of *St. Nicholas*.

Although interest in Emerson had declined very considerably (a fact to be borne in mind in assessing T. S. Eliot's remark of 1919 that Emerson's essays were "already an encumbrance"), a certain amount of significant work appeared, including of course, the long-standard editions of the works and journals. John Jay Chapman's impassioned essay of 1897 ("Emerson—Sixty Years After"), ultimately canonized in Edmund Wilson's *Shock of Recognition,* is written as if to an audience unacquainted with its subject. W. C. Brownell's essay of 1909, reprinted in his *American Prose Masters,* is as debunkingly conservative as Chapman's is promotionally liberal; unfortunately, it was Brownell, fountainhead of the Humanist movement, and not Chapman, spokesman for a kind of middle-class liberalism that died with Woodrow Wilson, whose influence pervaded the universities until the Second World War. George E. Woodberry's short biography of 1907, accurately characterized as "unsympathetic," seems to reflect the impatience of the period as a whole with Emerson's reputation.

The decade of the twenties was notably a period of transition, as the academic study of American literature was organized. Selected editions of Emerson's works appeared in 1920 and 1921, with introductions by Arthur Hobson Quinn and Stuart P. Sherman respectively. An older generation, represented in the differing concerns of George Woodberry, Bliss Perry, W. S. Kennedy, Denton J. Snider, and John Burroughs, was giving way to a new generation intent on specialized and scholarly approaches. Norman Foerster's work on the significance of nature to Emerson's thought began to appear in 1922, in the first *PMLA* article devoted to Emerson. Arthur Christy's study of Emerson's orientalism, to judge only from the chronology, may have been an impetus to Frederic I. Carpenter's dissertation on a similar subject in 1929, published a year later as *Emerson and Asia*. C. P. Hotson's numerous articles on Emerson and Swedenborgianism laid an important foundation for our understanding of the doctrine of correspondence. By the end of the decade, influential synthesizers such as V. L. Parrington and Van Wyck Brooks could begin to draw on solid and detailed scholarship.

The Depression years were a boom time for Ph.D. and Masters theses on Emerson, most of which were topic studies. Similarly, the important published work of the decade of the 1930s was largely devoted to the clarification of Emerson's ideas: Hotson, continuing his study of Swedenborg's influence, was joined by such scholars as Harry Hayden Clark, Clarence Gohdes, Rollo G. Silver, Clarence Faust, and Townsend Scudder. New approaches were opened up by William Braswell, whose pioneering article on "Melville as a Critic of Emerson" was to influence Matthiessen's presentation in *American Renaissance*; an essay by William Charvat concerning the effect on Emerson of the 1837 financial panic raised the political issue of Emerson's class consciousness; the decade closed with an important essay by Henry Nash Smith on "Emerson's Problem of Vocation," an essay in which, as in Charvat's, one might have foreseen the future development of American Studies as a discipline.

It is interesting to note that Emerson seems not to have been especially repudiated by either end of the political spectrum during the period between the wars. While his views on Brook Farm prompted some suspicion on the left about his relations to early socialist thought, his advocacy of self-reliance instead of collectivist ideals did not prevent Floyd Dell, for example, from finding in Emerson's essays "A Gospel of Revolt," or the entire *Masses* group from accounting Emerson, along with Thoreau and Whitman, an important influence. By the same token, Paul Elmer More and Irving Babbitt found enough that was worthy in Emerson to make up for the excesses of his "Rousseauistic" romanticism. The fact that Emerson was large enough (and perhaps inconsistent enough) to provide sustenance to a variety of ideologies was the principal reason why he could never be entirely neglected; he was constantly being rediscovered as an eloquent spokesman for democratic ideals, for uncompromising personal commitment to one's own ideas, for anti-philistinism, and for conservative economic theories. By and large, however, it would be fair to say that though Emerson suffered little outright rejection in the political and cultural climate of the twenties and thirties, he was hardly a central issue in the literary and ideological battles.

Interest in Emerson, in relative eclipse since the turn of the century, was considerably renewed by the appearance in 1939 of Ralph Rusk's carefully annotated six-volume edition of the *Letters*. In the interval between that publication and the appearance of Rusk's standard biography in 1949, the foundation was laid for a sweeping revaluation of Emerson's significance. Most notable among the revisionist landmarks was F. O. Matthiessen's *American Renaissance* (1941), at once a deliberate counterstatement to Parrington's narrow political conception of American literature, and a compelling demonstration that Emerson's permanent value lay in the quality—often the culturally national quality—of his artistry. The inspirational or catalytic effect of this liberating view is to be seen in the dissertations completed over the next ten years by Stephen Whicher, Vivian Hopkins, Charles Feidelson, Leo Marx, and Sherman Paul, which, when published as books—*Freedom and Fate, Spires of Form, Symbolism in American Literature, The Machine in the Garden,* and *Emerson's Angle of Vision*—cumulatively defined the Emerson whom we reckon with today.

Even the most recent books to appear—those published since the 1979 cutoff date of the Burkholder-Myerson bibliography—struggle anxiously against these works and the post-war consensus they represent—especially and continually against Whicher's *Freedom and Fate,* the earliest of the group. The present generation, needing, as Emerson observed, to write its own books, have made substantial contributions, including Jonathan Bishop's *Emerson on the Soul*, Lawrence Buell's *Literary Transcendentalism*, Philip Nicoloff's *Emerson on Race and History*, Joel Porte's *Representative Man*, and Barbara Packer's *Emerson's Fall*, but none (with the possible exception of Bishop's) are books that quite possess the scope and authority of the earlier studies. A period of "dissensus," so far as it concerns Emerson, would seem to be as inevitably a consequence of the strength still felt in the scholarship of the fifties as of the current collapse of agreement on critical methodologies.

The period of relative critical stalemate during the sixties and seventies saw major advances in the editing of Emerson's texts. The single greatest accomplishment of the period was the publication of the superbly edited and annotated sixteen-volume *Journals and Miscellaneous Notebooks* (1960–1982), which has wholly superseded the selective and partly bowdlerized Centenary Edition of 1909–1914. The three volumes of *Early Lectures* (1959–1972) present important material, not previously available, bearing on Emerson's career from 1834 to 1842. The Harvard University Press edition of the *Collected Works*, which began appearing in 1971, promises to provide for the first time accurate texts of works published during Emerson's lifetime. A new point of departure for the study of Emerson's career as a poet has been established by the *Poetry Notebooks* (1986), which makes available early working drafts and analyzes their composition. These editions will soon be joined by a five-volume supplement to Rusk's *Letters* and a four-volume edition of the complete sermons.

It is remarkable, to say the least, that all this work was done in the absence of competent and reliably thorough bibliographical aids—when, indeed, the standard primary bibliography consisted of the first two hundred pages of a 1908 publication by George Willis Cooke (supplemented, to be sure, by the forty pages devoted to Emerson in Jacob Blanck's avowedly selective *BAL*). Now, however, with the appearance of Joel Myerson's painstakingly thorough 800-page compilation, in which the Emersonian canon has for the first time been adequately defined, it is safe to say that descriptive bibliography has caught up with the editing of Emerson's texts.

Even at 800 pages, Myerson's work is a model of concise and judicious reportage. The physical evidence of a hundred and fifty years of contact between Emerson and his reading public hardly falls of its own accord into neat, easily schematized categories; it is, on the contrary, an almost fantastically complex organism, comprising a great many editions and printings (usually, it is worth noting, of a small number of copies each), including British piracies during Emerson's lifetime, a proliferation of unauthorized compilations after his death, and always, of course, separate publications of the most popular works together with new combinations, selections, and reshufflings of items by Emerson and others both named and unknown. There is scarcely room for the bibliographer who sorts all this out to offer extensive tables of variant readings for each and every title, or to provide very much of the most arcane kinds of bibliographical detail (Myerson thriftily depends on the *Collected Works* edition to present this sort of information, as indeed it has done and will continue to do). But the printing history of Emerson's work is nevertheless fully here, presented without self-indulgence, and with a shrewd sense of what needs to be said and known about it.

The format resembles that of other primary bibliographies in the Pittsburgh series (including those devoted to Margaret Fuller and Emily Dickinson, also by Myerson). Section A, by far the longest at 537 pages, is devoted to "separate publications," in which the successive editions of each title, beginning with the *Letter . . . to the Second Church and Society* and concluding with the Slater edition of the *Correspondence of Emerson and Carlyle*, are traced down through the 1980 cutoff date; Section B describes the "collected editions" of the (more or less) complete works, which are grouped according to the stereotype plates from which each was printed, though individual volumes within the collected editions are fully described, when appropriate, in Section A. Section C, devoted to "miscellaneous collections," takes note of certain pirated editions—those that do not pretend to reproduce a Section A title—birthday books, and cut-and-paste items of the "gems-from-Emerson" sort. Sections D and E record the first appearance of Emerson material in books and magazines respectively. Books edited by Emerson are listed in Section F, and Section G gives an accounting of Emerson materials reprinted in books or pamphlets during his lifetime. Brief sections labeled H and I deal with attributed matter and possible bibliographical ghosts.

Section A entries which correspond to first American and English editions of a title typically give photographic reproductions of bindings, title pages, and copyright pages, an extremely useful feature which, as Myerson himself has said elsewhere, deserves to be standard bibliographical practice.[2] This is followed, when called for, by a notation of multiple states; a full collation; a listing of the contents of the book; comments on typography and paper, with measurements in inches; full descriptions of bindings and binding variants (extending to dust jackets when these are present); and, finally, a discussion of the date and circumstance of publication, including information drawn from a great variety of sources, including letters, journals, account books, contracts, publishers' records and advertisements, as well as deposit and association copies. Locations of examined copies in all states and issues are also provided.

Myerson turns up, as it happens, few of the kinds of discoveries that gave such additional interest to C. E. Frazer Clark's 1978 Hawthorne bibliography—certainly nothing to rival Clark's revelation of unsuspected states and even a hidden edition within the previously assumed first and second American editions of *The Scarlet Letter*. What Myerson does turn up is a great deal of very precise information (thanks largely to the survival of publishers' records) about the size of printing runs, royalty income to Emerson, contractual stipulations, and, in frequent and surprising detail, how long it would take to exhaust a printing. As a consequence of Myerson's work, we are in an infinitely better position than before to gauge Emerson's income from his writings and to study not only the extent of his popularity and influence, but also his activities as a professional in the literary marketplace.

To the extent that checking was possible, it would seem that outright errors in the descriptions are rare. The first edition of *Nature; Addresses, and Lectures* (1849) was printed from standing type; therefore the simultaneously issued second edition of *Nature* could not have been "printed from the plates" of the longer work, as Myerson states, but consisted instead of sheets set aside for that purpose. He correctly, if inconsistently, identifies the retitled *Miscellanies* of 1856 as "the first stereotype printing" of *Nature; Addresses, and Lectures,* but gives no reason for regarding it as the second printing within the first edition rather than as a second edition. The designation could only be justified if the 1856 plates had been made from the old standing type, but there is reason to believe that this was not the case.

More deserving of attention than the very few errors are the necessary "judgment calls" that any bibliographer is required to make. While modern descriptive bibliographies achieve in general a very high degree of accuracy, they differ considerably, one from another, in their ability to balance the requirements of "completeness" and usefulness.[3] Myerson's bibliography of Emerson is a model in this regard for its calculated avoidance of clutter, its refusal to indulge finicky discriminations lacking in practical significance, its attention to the structure and thoroughness of its forty-five-page index, and even its honest, common-sense approach to the question of binding colors (resolved by rejecting the Centroid system, which makes no allowance for wear, fading, or the subjective eye of the bibliographer).

In the context of this pervading good sense, there are some isolated decisions bearing on general principles of bibliography that might have been made differently. Discussion of differences in binding, for example, is often quite pointless where no correlation exists between particular bindings and particular printings, issues, or states. It is clear that the two states of the first edition of *Nature* (1836) were indiscriminately bound in whatever cloth James Munroe could procure at the moment. Myerson lists fifteen cloth styles in five stamping patterns, resulting in at least the twenty-three permutations he was able to document in the fifty-three copies examined (out of an edition of 1,500). I can say confidently that the possibilities have not been exhausted, since my own copy (second state, stamping B) is in an unrecorded sixteenth style of cloth. Apart from disabusing those who like to refer to *Nature* as an "azure colored book," it is difficult to see why it is better to attempt such a census than to handle matters as

Clark did in his Hawthorne bibliography, where the existence of a great variety of bindings for the *Life of Pierce* is referred to in very summary fashion as a mere convenience to the publisher.

Another example of a somewhat different kind of decision involves the claim that there are editions of *Poems* (1847) subsequent to the first English and American editions. The very scarce "Little Classic" *Selected Poems* (1876) is designated the fourth edition of *Poems*, with the notation that all poems not collected here for the first time are reprinted from the 1847 *Poems*. Now while the selection shows Emerson's preference for the early poems, many are actually reprinted from *May-Day* (1867), so that the decision to make this book a pendant to *Poems* and not to *May-Day* seems a tad arbitrary. The fact is that Emerson published two volumes of poetry during his life, from which several collective editions follow more or less equally. Calling the posthumous Riverside and Centenary editions of the collected poetry the sixth and sixteenth editions respectively of the 1847 *Poems* may avoid an untidy proliferation of titles in Section A, but the practice seems as intrinsically odd as calling Frost's *Complete Poetry* the umpteenth edition of *A Boy's Will*.

These are local problems, hardly to be avoided and perhaps not even worth avoiding in a work of such magnitude and complexity. They bring us, however, to a final and more general consideration involving a continuing paradox at the core of the bibliographical enterprise. To compare the present work with the relatively primitive bibliography by G. W. Cooke which it supplants is to see immediately that two distinct audiences with distinct and largely unreconcilable expectations have always controlled the decisions and judgments that shape the bibliographer's product. Cooke's bibliography, with its notation of auction prices, catered more openly to the bookdealer, the collector, and the bibliophile, but in giving also a conflated master-list of the titles of individual books, essays, addresses, and poems, with a brief indication for each of its publication history, it served equally the text-centered interests of the reader of Emerson. It is possible, using the index, to gather the same information in much greater detail from the Myerson bibliography, but the absence of such a listing (and it is current bibliographical practice to omit this once-standard feature) might reasonably be taken as an effect of the reduced emphasis on the reader of Emerson as a consumer of bibliographical information. On the other hand, modern descriptive bibliography, increasingly devoted to the book as artifact, has moved beyond the informational requirements of the mere (i.e., book-centered) collector to generate evidence that is often less pertinent to a particular author than to a general illumination of the mysteries of book production. The two audiences of text-centered and book-centered interests are only typically represented by the reader and the collector: if both (as may be) have disappeared for economic reasons, they reappear in the academic avatars of editors and bibliographers respectively. Not surprisingly, in other words, bibliographical theory has developed in the direction of satisfying students of the book or, rather, students of the history of the book, whereas editors might not unreasonably want to use a bibliography, a work of reference ostensibly concerned with the transmission of an author's text, to learn of the relationship between, say, Emerson's 1837 lecture on "The Head" and his later essay on "Intellect"; such editors might even want to pursue the matter back into journal passages and manuscript sources. If "Intellect" were as permissible a unit of discussion as *Essays: First Series*, the balance would be redressed between the conflicting claims of reader/editors and collector/bibliographers. And yet, considering that the balance cannot be redressed without doubling or tripling both the labor and the length of the book, the question will no doubt remain academic, just as Myerson's bibliography will justifiably remain for many years to come an indispensable companion to those who collect and read Emerson's still surprising, still challenging works.

Notes

1. Sacvan Bercovitch, "Preface," in *Reconstructing American Literary History* (Cambridge: Harvard Univ. Press, 1986), pp. vii–viii.
2. "The Development of Hawthorne Primary Bibliography," *Review*, 3 (1981), 288.
3. See G. Thomas Tanselle, "Some Remarks on Bibliographical Nonproliferation," *Proof*, 1 (1971), 170–79.

W. B. Yeats: Early Letters and His Library

Richard J. Finneran

> John Kelly, ed. *The Collected Letters of W. B. Yeats: Volume One, 1865–1895*. Oxford: Clarendon Press, 1986. xlii, 548 pp.
>
> Edward O'Shea. *A Descriptive Catalog of W. B. Yeats's Library*. New York and London: Garland Publishing, 1985. xxi, 390 pp.

In 1969 John Kelly and Eric Domville were commissioned by the Oxford University Press to prepare a complete edition of Yeats's correspondence, to supersede Allan Wade's *Letters of W. B. Yeats* (1954) and the several shorter collections, such as Ursula Bridge's edition of the letters to T. Sturge Moore. A four-volume edition of about 2,000 letters was projected. Years passed, the number of available extant letters grew, nothing was published. During that time (as will unfortunately remain true for years to come) the project had from one perspective a negative effect on Yeats scholarship: as the Press would not allow the publication of the full text of any new Yeats letters, the editing of what would have been any number of useful collections of the exchange of correspondence with a particular writer—say, Yeats's letters to and from Pound or to and from Gordon Craig—was prevented, and the authors of scholarly books were reduced to paraphrase or selective quotation.[1] Several years ago the *Collected Letters* was reorganized: Kelly to remain as General Editor; Domville leaving the project after volume one (he appears as "Associate Editor" on its title page); other editors, including such established scholars as Mary FitzGerald and Ronald Schuchard, to work with Kelly on individual volumes; at least twelve volumes to be published rather than four. We can now look forward to the completion of the project, if we can trust the dust-jacket blurb, "over the next decade."

The first installment has set a very high standard for the remainder. This is true even though the contents of volume one are, on the whole, familiar or unexciting. Given the date of publication, it was inevitable that Wade's *Letters* would be weighted towards the early years, and so much of the significant correspondence has already appeared in print. Other newly published material was doubtless deliberately excluded by Wade, such as the forgettable opening letter written when Yeats was eleven years old (no, despite the inclusive dates of this volume [*1865– 1895*], Yeats did not exit the womb with pen in hand). It is claimed that "nearly half of the letters . . . are printed for the first time" (p. xli), but by my count the figure is nearer 40% than 50%; and if one judged by length rather than separate documents it would be even lower, as many of the new pieces are short notes. The Oxford University Press has perhaps set a new standard for blurbal hyperbole with the dust-jacket claim that "Without exception they are vividly entertaining letters, full of engrossing detail and humorous or self-deprecating asides; entirely unselfconscious, they yet reflect clearly the sensibility and consciousness of a great poet." Here, for one example among many, is the full text of a letter of 6 October [1893] to J. S. Cotton:

I enclose the review of 'Refractions and Reflections' which I promised some time ago.

[p. 363]

Inevitably, too, the edition cannot hope to be complete. Some correspondence is known to have been destroyed; other material has dropped from sight, including "the letters to Lionel Johnson loaned by his sister to a graduate student in the 1940s" (p. xliii); and new letters continue to surface. Kelly's Addenda gives two letters discovered "too late for inclusion in the main body of the text" (p. 521), and to those one could add an 1892 letter to D. J. O'Donoghue, offered at Sotheby's first on 18 December 1985 and again on 10 July 1986, on the latter occasion fetching £330.[2]

However, as Kelly rightly notes, "the proportion of new material increases in every subsequent volume" (p. xli), and even if *all* of Yeats's letters were in print, one could still admire this volume for its scrupulous editing. In addition to a brief General Introduction, Kelly has provided a detailed chronology covering all of the life; a Biographical and Historical Appendix providing extensive information on some twenty-eight individuals or institutions (e.g., Maud Gonne, John O'Leary, The Order of the Golden Dawn); and full explanatory notes to each letter. In line with most modern editors, Kelly takes little for granted: the identity of the "*Erinnyes*" (p. 151), the source of "fit though few" (p. 416), and the nature of "the sincerest form of flattery" (p. 425) are perhaps the exceptions which prove the rule. When Yeats told Katharine Tynan that "I had nothing to do with the Menzoni & Brent Harte things" (p. 273), Kelly presumably does not annotate because of the context; but although the index offers Bret Harte, it is silent on "Menzoni," doubtless the Italian novelist and poet Alessandro Manzoni (1785–1873). By way of contrast, Kelly's notes occasionally tend toward the excessive. When Yeats writes to O'Leary in [? late July 1894] about "the weather which is horrible like a furnace" (pp. 394–95), the editor informs us that

In the week of 23 July 1894 *The Times* recorded afternoon temperatures in London in the upper 70s F., noting on the 28th that *maxima* temperatures exceeding 75° F. had been recorded the previous day 'over the inland parts of England.' After a long thunderstorm on Sunday, 29 July, the London temperature fell; but it rose again on Tuesday, 31 July, to 77° F., and the atmosphere was 'close, unsettled, the barometer falling slowly.'

It may be that the weather reports are being cited to defend Kelly's dating of the letter, Wade having previously suggested [? autumn 1894]; but does any reader need them? Why not, "the last week of July 1894 was unusually warm"? Anyone who wants the details could find a microfilm of *The Times* easily to hand. I for one would have traded the meteorological information for an explanation of the astrological signs in the horoscope offered at 422n1.

Outright errors in the volume are few indeed. In the biographical sketch of Florence Farr, Kelly claims that "they met and became friends, although there is no evidence of an affair between them" (p. 485). One can agree with that analysis but still protest that in 1941 Mrs. Yeats recalled Yeats's own words to suggest otherwise.[3] But aside from a very few additional slips cited in the Addenda below, the only other shortcoming in the *Collected Letters* is the index. It is claimed that "italic page-references indicate passages where the subject is particularly discussed" (p. 525), but that policy has been implemented only haphazardly at best: for instance, italics are lacking in the entries for Ernest Radford ("367–8"), Father Russell ("52n"), and Olivia Shakespear ("396–7" and "511"). More importantly, a spot-check of the entries for *John Sherman and Dhoya* disclosed three omissions: p. 50 ("Papa wants me to write a romance"), p. 100 ("my story which I am once more at work on"), and, a well-known reference, pp.121–22: "In my story I make one of the characters when ever he is in trouble long to go away and live on that island—an old day dream of my own." Kelly does give forty-three citations for *John Sherman and Dhoya,* so fewer than ten pecent have been overlooked; but in a volume which is read cover-to-cover only by reviewers and insomniacs, the index is crucial. I can only hope that my spot-check is not representative, but my fears have not been allayed by the random discovery of a missing entry for *The Countess Cathleen*: "I am starting a new drama founded on an Irish Folk-tale. The best plot I ever worked on" (p. 50).

On balance, though, the editing of volume one of the *Collected Letters* has been extremely thorough. The only controversial decision has been to reproduce Yeats's spelling. Yeats was, to put it simply, a terrible speller (dyslexia is a strong possibility). Some of the misspellings are what Kelly calls "unintentional felicities" (p. xxvi), including—to add to his "woeman" for "woman" and "write on" for "right on"—"Miss Gone" (p. 134 and elsewhere) for Maud Gonne, a lady more often absent than present. But most of the mistakes are simply that, and there are good reasons both for and against regularization. I myself, having argued elsewhere against the regularization of the poetry by Mrs. Yeats and Thomas Mark (Yeats's editor at Macmillan), agree with Kelly's decision. At the same time, though, I can sympathize with someone who wants to quote from this edition in a critical study and does not want to have Yeats arguing that "The really great writers of fiction make their readers' minds like spunges" (p. 108) or recommending the use of Irish material because "It helps origonality and makes one's verses sincere, and gives one less numerous compeditors" (p. 131). Perhaps all Yeatsians and the Oxford University Press should agree to a Treaty of Regularization, allowing the correction of obvious errors when quoting from the *Collected Letters*?

Like the Kelly volume, Edward O'Shea's *A Descriptive Catalog of W. B. Yeats's Library* was long in the making, having been begun in 1971 by the late Glenn O'Malley. This listing of the collection held by Anne Yeats in Dalkey, Ireland, cites well over 2,500 volumes. The items of greatest interest are doubtless those volumes with extensive annotations: to cite just three examples, Bertrand Russell's *An Outline of Philosophy* (1927; item #1798); Swedenborg's *Arcana Coelestia* (1891; #2037); and Wordsworth's *Poetical Works* (1892; #2292). The library also contains numerous copies of Yeats's own works revised for later editions and is thus an essential resource for the study of his texts. Further, to some extent the collection offers a guide to Yeats's reading, though one must exercise restraint in so using it. First, Yeats obviously did not have the funds to buy many books in the early years, and thus the absence of what we know to be seminal works (such as Standish O'Grady's two-volume *History of Ireland* [1878–80]) should come as no surprise. Secondly, the presence of an unannotated volume is not necessarily significant, as the library was clearly enlarged by marriage with George Yeats; and who among us has read every book in his library? It is also true that books once in the library are no longer there (more on this shortly). But if Yeats suffered from unreturned loans, he also profited, his library including such volumes as Katharine Tynan's copy of *The Poems of William Blake* (1887; #207), AE's copy of *The Tibetan Book of the Dead* (1927; #2243), and, rather pathetically, a copy of Charles Erskine Scott's privately printed (by himself) *Circe* (1919; #2290), inscribed by the author as follows: "Loaned to my friend Kathleen O'Brennan with full leave to lend freely but in the trust that it will eventually be returned to me at 1601 Taylor St. San Francisco. . . . Marginal criticisms invited." As O'Shea notes of the anticipated marginalia, "but none here."

Beyond its obvious uses, O'Shea's *Catalog* discloses many curiosities and interesting bits of information. We now know, for example, what Yeats received for Christmas in 1873 from his mother—*Ivanhoe* (1871; #1859), a gift perhaps more welcome than his grandmother's Christmas present in 1886: *Selections of American Humour in Prose and Verse* (1883?; #831). We know, too, what the Godolphin School offered as its prize in History ca. 1877–81: William H. Prescott's *History of the Reign of Philip the Second, King of Spain* (1872?; #1638). But why, we must wonder, did Yeats have a copy of Sir Henry Heathcote's *Treatise on Stay-Sails, for the purpose of intercepting wind between the square-sails of ships and other square-rigged vessels* (1824; #866)—inherited from his nautical relatives, or research for *The Shadowy Waters*?

The library also offers some fascinating information on Yeats's literary relationships. In June 1912, for example, Thomas Hardy inscribed to Yeats a copy of *The Dynasts* (1910; #834); O'Shea's annotation "almost entirely uncut" is a commentary in itself. Likewise, much can be learned about the Yeats/Joyce relationship—as well as about Joyce's contemporary reputation—by the label on the back cover of Yeats's copy of *Dubliners* (1914; #1041), the first edition of June 1914: "The Bargain Floor Library at Harrods Ltd., London, S.W. [stamped beside this:] 2 July 1914." Finally, one can only wish that during the controversy over *The Silver Tassie* O'Casey had recalled his inscription in *Two Plays* (1925; #1472): "a Remembrance of a merciless criticism of a bad play that provoked the Author to a passionate resolve to write a good one."

Unfortunately, this useful volume has some shortcomings. Outright errors are happily few: for instance, P. S. O'Hegarty's copy of *The Countess Cathleen* (n.d.; #2333) is not in Dalkey but rather at the University of Kansas, which purchased his library some years ago; "T. March" (#2381c) should be "Mark"; and Yeats could hardly have inscribed a copy of *The Tower* (1928; #2430f) to his wife in "Sept 1913." More importantly, O'Shea's ability to accurately transcribe Yeats's handwriting or to discriminate between it and that of Mrs. Yeats—both difficult tasks—is open to question. In his review of *A Descriptive Catalog*, George Bornstein has already noted several errors in citing Yeats's annotations to *The Works of Edmund Spenser* (1862; #1978).[4] I would extend that list by expressing my disbelief that Yeats could have mis-inscribed one of his volumes "An aimless job is a pure job" (#2335b), rather than "joy," when the line from "Tom O'Roughley" was one of his standard inscriptions. Moreover, in at least two instances (#1827, #2323b) material which is ascribed to Yeats seems clearly the work of his wife.

It is of course true that a scholar engaged in an extended critical study or textual edition will want to check *anyone's* transcriptions, and the nature of the handwriting will always preclude final agreement on every individual word or mark. But a more fundamental problem with this volume is that of completeness. First, aside from a few exceptions, O'Shea has not listed the volumes in the collection of Michael Yeats. These include on the one hand several volumes inscribed to Yeats, such as AE's *Ireland and the Empire at the Court of Conscience* (1921), John Masefield's *My Faith in Woman Suffrage* (1910), and James Stephens's *Green Branches* (1916); and, on the other hand, several of his own volumes with corrections, including a copy of the *Collected Poems* (1933) with more extensive revision than any of the copies held by Anne Yeats. Secondly, O'Shea does not list an extensive collection of Cuala Press volumes formerly held by Michael Yeats but dispersed at Sotheby's on 23 May 1980. O'Shea claims that "none were revision copies" (p. xxi), but the Sale Catalogue proves otherwise.[5] Included in the collection was *Responsibilities* (1914) with "two major autograph revisions to text and other annotations by the author for a later edition" (#470); *Two Plays for Dancers* (1919) with "a few autograph corrections and a revision by the author in ink" (#478); and *A Packet for Ezra Pound* (1929) with an "addition on one page by the author in ink, and extensive revisions to the text in pencil for a later edition" (#493)—surely a "revision copy" in anyone's terms. Other unique material included the copy of *Last Poems and Two Plays* (1939) which contained Yeats's draft table of contents for the volume (#511), calling for an arrangement of the poems which was violated in the posthumous printing and not restored until *The Poems: A New Edition* (1983).

But transcending these presumably accidental omissions is the deliberate exclusion from *A Descriptive Catalog* of some 521 volumes known to have been in the library as of the early 1920s. O'Shea explains as follows:

> An asterisk (*) before an item number indicates that it appears in an anonymously compiled catalog of Yeats's books done sometime in the early 1920s. For reasons of space, that entire listing (which recorded only basic bibliographical information) is not included here, but there are some 500 items in that catalog which are not found in the library today, and their location is unknown. [p. ix]

This may well have been the decision of Garland Publishing rather than of O'Shea; but when published elsewhere a year later, the list (including a headnote) took up all of twelve pages[6]; so one would have thought that a publisher asking fifty-six dollars for a volume inelegantly produced from camera-ready copy could have thrown in the additional material. As O'Shea notes in his introduction to the later list, it "fills obvious gaps: the Dalkey library contains no books by John Ruskin or Sigmund Freud and only one by Tennyson. The 1920s catalogue records multiple titles by all three." Other authors "but sparsely represented or missing altogether in the library are Strindberg, Schopenhauer, and Jessie Weston" (pp. 279–80). Thus, to put it in the simplest terms, *A Descriptive Catalog* as published is fundamentally incomplete: what is needed is a revised edition which would incorporate the 1920s list as well as the volumes now or formerly in the collection of Michael Yeats. Such a revision could also attempt to list the location of volumes given away by Mrs. Yeats, including a copy of Milton owned by Richard Ellmann which includes a draft of part of "News for the Delphic Oracle."[7]

These two works take their place in the extensive editorial activity which has dominated Yeats scholarship for some time and which will continue at least through the end of the century. The *Descriptive Catalog* is a useful but flawed research tool which will inevitably lead to new avenues of investigation. The first installment of the *Collected Letters* is a superbly edited work (*pace*

W. B. Yeats: Early Letters and His Library

its index) which codifies our understanding of the early years and foreshadows the significant new materials to appear in the later volumes. With John Kelly and his co-editors working alongside the contributors to the Cornell Yeats and the Macmillan Collected Edition of the Works, and with Roy Foster engaged on the authorized biography, the continued flourishing of the "Yeats industry" seems assured.

Addenda for *The Collected Letters*

16.13	Add note number 10 after "empty man."
21n4	The text of "The Protestants' Leap" is reprinted in Kelly's "Aesthete among the Athletes: Yeats's Contributions to *The Gael*," *Yeats*, 2 (1984), 75–143.
31n4	The 1884 edition of *Reliques of Irish Poetry* is a 2nd ed., as correctly cited at p. 116n5.
33n7	*Irish Book Lover*, not *Booklover*. The proper title appears in the index (p. 530), but the citation is incorrectly given as p. 34n.
66n4	Delete the accent on "see."
75n1	In his forthcoming edition of the manuscripts of *The Island of Statues* and *Mosada*, George Bornstein has found it is quite unlikely that Frazer helped with the revisions to *The Island of Statues*.
126n5	For "*Oisin*," read "*Oisin*."
137n2	A line space after "MG asked him" should be added.
164n4	In *A Colder Eye* (New York: Knopf, 1983), p. 162n, Hugh Kenner has noted that Blake's Irish ancestry was attested to in the 1854 edition of the *Encyclopaedia Britannica*, 4:153.
217n3	A line space after "in 1890," should be added.
249.20	What is the date of "John Wilson catalogue no. 3"?
345n1	The last sentence is apparently incomplete.
375n1	For "to WBY" read "from WBY".
411n1	"Who Goes with Fergus?" was not published as a separate lyric in the 1895 *Poems*; it first appeared as such in the 6th ed of 1912.
488.5	Yeats also issued *A Postscript to Essay Called "Is the Order of R.R. & A.C. to remain a Magical Order?"*

488.26   For "membership of" read "membership in".
510.15   For "for. Ireland" read "for Ireland".
521n1   For "W. T. Rolleston" read "T. W. Rolleston".

Notes

1. For instance, in George Mills Harper's *W. B. Yeats and W. T. Horton: The Record of an Occult Friendship* (London: Macmillan, 1980), the section of "Correspondence" includes the full texts of Horton's letters but only summaries of Yeats's, obviously making the "Record" less than complete.

2. See Sotheby's Sale Catalogue for 18 December 1985 (item 206) and for 10–11 July 1986 (item 249), which offer an identical description of the letter. Yeats was asking O'Donoghue to place "a note on Miss Gonne" in a newspaper and also to announce some forthcoming publications.

3. See her "A Foreword to the Letters of W. B. Yeats" in *Florence Farr, Bernard Shaw and W. B. Yeats*, ed. Clifford Bax (Dublin: Cuala Press, 1941), p. 43: "WBY once said to me 'She was the only person to whom I could tell *everything*.' He thought her career as an actress had given her a solitary, perhaps unhappy, personal life and quoted a phrase of hers, 'When a man begins to make love to me I instantly see it as a stage performance.' Their brief love affair came to an end because 'she got bored.'" One might question the exact meaning of "love affair," but Mrs. Yeats was surely the source of Richard Ellmann's statement in *The Man and the Masks* (New York: Macmillan, 1948), p. 179, that Yeats had an affair with Farr in 1903. Ellmann repeats his assertion in the preface to the 1979 edition of *The Man and the Masks* (New York: Norton), p. xxiv.

4. *Yeats*, 4 (1986), 219–21.

5. *Catalogue of Nineteenth Century and Modern First Editions and Presentation Copies*. London: Sotheby Parke Bernet, 22–23 May 1980.

6. O'Shea, "The 1920s Catalogue of W. B. Yeats's Library," *Yeats Annual No. 4* (1986), 279–90.

7. See Daniel Albright, *The Myth Against Myth: A Study of Yeats's Imagination in Old Age* (London: Oxford Univ. Press, 1972), p. 121.

Melville's Sexual Politics

Julian Markels

Robert K. Martin. *Hero, Captain and Stranger: Male Friendship, Social Critique, and Literary Form in the Sea Novels of Herman Melville.* Chapel Hill: University of North Carolina Press, 1986. xvi, 144 pp.

This original and courageous book must be forgiven its flaws for the sake of its indispensable accomplishment in deepening our grasp of Melville's art and thought. In five Melville novels spanning the forty-odd years from *Typee* to *Billy Budd*, and including *Redburn*, *White Jacket*, and *Moby-Dick*, Martin argues for a common structural pattern that "can be expressed most simply as the encounter of, and conflict among, three fundamental characters: the Hero, the Dark Stranger, and the Captain" (p. 3). This encounter involves a sexual politics in which the Dark Stranger represents "a democratic eros . . . finding its highest expression in male friendship and manifested in a masturbatory sexuality reflecting the celebration of a generalized seminal power not directed toward control or production." The Captain represents "a hierarchical eros expressed in social forms of male power as different as whaling, factory owning, military conquest, and heterosexual marriage as it was largely practiced in the nineteenth century, all of which indicate the transformation of primal, unformed (oceanic) sexuality into a world of pure copulation" (p. 4). The Hero is attracted to and caught between these two forms of eros, and the novels "are structured around the possibility of the Hero's discovery of his own capacity for love, through love of the Dark Stranger, and the consequent discovery of the strength to oppose the rule of the Captain" (p. 6).

Martin's focus on the dynamics of narrative structure enables him to address the still vexed question of Melville's homosexuality in freshly compelling terms. Not only are his data the novels themselves, but the novels as integral wholes; the analysis requires neither a privileged biographical assumption about Melville's lifelong reaction to his parents nor a privileged textual status for individual passages imbued with homosexual connotations. On the other hand, it does entail a capacious conception of homosexuality as primarily a form of identity, both psychosexual and political, irrespective of its genital manifestations. Martin claims at the outset: "My subject is not . . . homosexuality in itself, but the way in which sexually charged relationships between men are employed as part of a critique of power in the society that Melville depicted" (p. 4), and also that Melville "quite rightly distinguished between homosexual practices and what we might call homosexual being" (p. 7). Despite some lapses when I think his subject does become homosexuality in itself, I also think Martin's essential analysis justifies these claims. He distinguishes early between the shipboard buggery familiar to Melville from his sailor years and the social institution of male friendship that he also became aware of in the Polynesian Typees and the American Indians. He proceeds to distinguish between such cultures' matriarchal phallicism, which he associates with the Stranger and the myth of the Golden Land, and the West's patriarchal phallicism, which he associates with the Captain and the Faustian myth of knowledge and power. From these controlling distinctions Martin then argues for Melvillean correlations among masturbation, revery, and love between equals on the one hand, and on the other among copulation, action, and exploitation between unequals. Above all, he recognizes and explains why male friendship is appropriately idealized in Melville, and why the "sacred marriage" between men toward which the structure of the novels impels their heroes, a marriage consummated only between Ishmael and Queequeg in all of Melville's writing, cannot be imagined as actual in the society of which he wrote.

The naive reader is bound to feel in Melville's fables the latent pressure of his homosexuality thus conceived, and I think Martin's schema is unprecedented in encouraging us to view that pressure as part of Melville's unfolding dialectic of form and theme rather than as predictable evasion or repression either in

Melville or ourselves. In distinguishing his approach from that of Edwin Haviland Miller in his superciliously clinical biography (*Melville* [New York: Braziller, 1975]), Martin observes that Miller "assumes that all the works are but coded transcriptions of the life and that the life corresponds to a series of crises, all of which have already been described in the psychoanalytic literature" (p. 14). Here too I think Martin's own analysis is marred on occasion by similarly coded assumptions, for example about the basis for Melville's attraction to Hawthorne; even so, the basic success of Martin's appeal to the evidence of the fiction ultimately justifies his criticism of Miller. Martin was evidently unaware of Charles Haberstroh, Jr.'s, *Melville and Male Identity* (London and Toronto: Associated University Presses, 1980), a far more useful book than Miller's in its alternative version of sexual politics in Melville's fiction, but also a book that assumes *a priori* a psychological life crisis shaping the fiction. From the contrast between Melville's father's worldly failure and early death and the worldly success of first his Gansevoort and then his Shaw male relatives, Haberstroh extrapolates for Melville an agenda both personal and literary, the achievement of a patriarchal male identity conventional to his social class. In the light of that agenda he finds Melville's fiction "riddled [with] ambivalences caused by the tension between his hopeless and introverted sense of himself as a lost boy, and his desire to fulfill the extroverted traditions of male status, success, and assertiveness with which he grew up" (p. 29). Haberstroh's biographical assumption (like Miller's) often leads him too easily to ignore what is inconvenient and find what he is looking for, irrespective of its structural or thematic importance, and finally limits the explanatory power of his analysis as compared with Martin's. Even so, Haberstroh's key evidence is often comprehended by Martin's analysis too, so that Haberstroh's alternative version of Melville's sexual politics can provide a fruitful test of "falsification" for Martin's, as we shall see.

But of course Martin's decisive forerunner and counterpart is Leslie Fiedler's *Love and Death in the American Novel,* the influence of which he acknowledges immediately. Fiedler's provocative analysis of *Moby-Dick,* if not his precise terminology, virtually anticipates Martin's schema, first, in proposing Queequeg and Fedallah in effect as Dark Stranger doubles attracting respectively Ishmael (the Hero) to Golden Land life and Ahab (the Captain) to Faustian death; then, in associating masturbation with Ishmael's openness to friendship first with Queequeg and eventually, in "A Squeeze of the Hand," the entire crew; and finally, in describing the life-redeeming relationship of Ishmael and Queequeg, which Martin calls a "sacred marriage," as "Platonism without sodomy, which is to say, marriage without copulation" (p. 375). Martin says he might not be writing if Fiedler had not led the way, but adds:

Fiedler is not primarily interested in the sacred marriage as an alternative to dominant social patterns but rather as an evasion of them.... *Love and Death* was important for gay people in the same way the Kinsey Report was; it announced that we were there. At the same time, though, it instantly imposed the medical/scientific model which said, in effect, that we must be cured, just as American literature was to come to its senses and to create mature heterosexual models. [p. 9]

Here too I think Martin is accurate in characterizing Fiedler's implied standard, and I also think Fiedler's "mature heterosexual models" are the very ones Haberstroh continues to see Melville trying to emulate. Thus in the explicit terms of his divergence from Fiedler, Martin clearly if unknowingly joins the issue with Haberstroh too.

After an introductory chapter setting forth his thesis, from which all my quotations thus far have been drawn, Martin devotes his remaining four chapters to, respectively, *Typee*, *Redburn* and *White Jacket* together, *Moby-Dick*, and *Billy Budd*. In these chapters he explores the several variations within which the Hero/Stranger/Captain pattern is consistently visible, variations which also reflect Melville's progression from the hopefulness of *Typee*, for which Martin's chapter title is "The Quest for a Golden Island," to the disappointment of *Billy Budd*, for which the chapter title is "Losing Hope." In *Typee* there is no Captain to speak of, but Tom's and Toby's jumping ship at the outset, along with Tom's animadversions on Western colonialism, implies the exploitative culture of the Captain and directs our attention for most of the novel toward the encounter with the Stranger and the Golden Land. In *Billy Budd* the Hero's position is left blank, Billy being a Stranger who cannot become a Hero, and Billy's impressment at the outset directs our attention for most of the novel toward the Stranger's destruction in the world of the Captain. In *Typee* the Stranger's attractive function is doubled and shared by Toby and Marnoo, as it is again in *Redburn* by Harry Bolton and Carlo; in *Billy Budd* the Captain's repressive function is doubled and shared by Vere and Claggart, as it has been in *Redburn* by Riga and Jackson. Toby/Marnoo in *Typee*, Harry/Carlo in *Redburn*, Jack Chase in *White-Jacket*, and Queequeg in *Moby-Dick* are very different characters, yet all are described as dark and function consistently in attracting the Hero to a life of male friendship and masturbatory revery in contrast to the life of hierarchic authority and exploitative action represented by Captains as different as Riga, Claret, Ahab, and Vere. This account is comprehensive, flexible, and deeply responsive to the novels; it gives us reason to feel ourselves here put in touch with the full power of Melville's imagination.

The chapter on *Typee* is crucial in establishing the pattern, and here Martin identifies Melville's first novel with the overlapping genres of Polynesian travel narrative and Indian captivity narrative. In Melville's era of Western colonialism, the immensely popular travel narrative functioned not only as a medium of factual anthropology but also—and simultaneously—as both "genteel pornography" (p. 18) and utopian idealization: the Golden Island of the Noble Savage was characterized by undraped women whose images we still contemplate in the *National Geographic*, yet also by the social institution of male friendship which Dana had described in *Two Years Before the Mast* and which Melville came to know as *tayo*—and by both together as features of a culture devoted more to play and leisure than to work and purpose. The traditional Indian captivity narrative, meanwhile, was often characterized by a cultural ambivalence in which any tempting attractions of the "primitive" culture nevertheless threaten a loss of identity, symbolized in *Typee* by Tom's fear of tattooing no less than cannibalism. Thus Melville's first hero escapes the world of the captain only to encounter male friendship as the exotic feature of an external culture whose attractions are outweighed by its psychological threat.

A crucial link between the two cultures is Toby, a rebel like Tom from the rule of the captain and also a stranger in the world of the ship. Toby is described at the outset as a dark-skinned, dark-haired, black-eyed sailor given to revery—"already in some sense an islander" (p. 25); he becomes Tom's guide through the difficult entry into the Golden Island, and gives way first to Kory Kory, an assigned *tayo* friend whose grotesque tattoos make him nevertheless unacceptable, and then to Marnoo, whose Grecian beauty is not marred but enhanced by his single tattoo, a tree along his spine that suggests the tree of life. Marnoo has previously been uprooted from the island and taken to sea, then has returned; like Toby, he is a rover who mediates the two cultures, and eventually he helps Tom leave the island just as Toby helped him reach it.

From here the progression to *Moby-Dick* is unmistakable: within his own culture, and as an escape from its many aggressions ashore that are carried over symbolically in Ahab's quest and rule at sea, Ishmael makes a sustaining marriage with a grotesquely tattooed Polynesian cannibal, whose tomahawk, handed back and forth in connubial smoking, is an alternative phallic symbol to the darted harpoon of the whale hunter. In the figure of Queequeg, who is at home in Ishmael's world with all his strangeness intact, Toby, Kory Kory, and Marnoo coalesce; and in Ishmael's friendship with Queequeg the hero's vain external quest for the Golden Island is internalized to produce a pacific and communal alternative to the aggression and repression of the captain's world.

Martin opens his chapter on *Moby-Dick* with an account of its structure strictly according to the sexual politics of his Hero, Captain, and Stranger pattern. First Ishmael and Queequeg consummate their idealized marriage ashore, since that will be impossible on a ship dominated by Ahab's patriarchal values. Then on Ahab's ship the marriage sustains Ishmael intellectually and psychologically through Queequeg as an alternative model, and also facilitates his survival through Queequeg's love and sacrifice. Finally, Ishmael's survival completes a circular pattern in contrast to Ahab's linear path to self-destruction caused by the "imposition of exclusive white male power in its search for control over all that is nature or nonself" (p. 70). This emergence through plot of Ishmael's circle from Ahab's straight line entails both "the restoration of the feminine and maternal to a world that has forsworn all softness and affection" (p. 70), and at the same time a phallic self-sufficiency that Martin goes on to associate with masturbation.

In this connection he proposes a striking revaluation of Ishmael's famous opening allusion to the image of Narcissus as an image of "the ungraspable phantom of life." Invoking Marcuse's *Eros and Civilization*, Martin argues that Narcissus can be seen as a figure of generalized love whose self-embrace is an alternative to the "aggressive sexuality of possession" (p. 73). On this view the image of Narcissus combines revery and masturbation, and this image, Ishmael went on to say, "is the key to it all." His marriage to Queequeg is consummated by Queequeg's sharing not only his bed but also his money, which creates a political alternative to the institution of private property, and then by their smoking, which creates a sexual alternative to "phallic aggression.... The tomahawk that is both pipe and weapon is equivalent to the phallus that can be either a source of pleasure or an aggressive instrument of power. The tomahawk is thus the novel's synecdochic presentation of the transformation that is at its center: the rediscovery and reappropriation of the phallic" (p. 79). Martin explores several stages and variations in this reappropriation (Ishmael's proclivities for digressive narration and masthead revery, for example), which culminates in "A Squeeze of the Hand," where Ishmael's shift from solitary to mutual masturbation is accompanied by a "shift from the self to the community— a community erected by men working, and playing, together" (p. 82). The integration of work and play is here inseparable from the sexual union of self-sufficient individuals, and just this once in Melville's writing secures for the Hero the Stranger's political and sexual alternative to the culture represented by the Captain.

This summary does not do justice to Martin's enriching contributory arguments (e.g., for Ishmael's gradual emancipation from Ahab's language of aggression), or to some of his wrongheaded sub-arguments (e.g., for the novel as essentially a linear, patriarchal genre that Ishmael disrupts by his digressive procedure). But I hope it suggests the fundamental and comprehensive relevance of Martin's thesis to *Moby-Dick,* as well as Melville's actual progression from *Typee* to *Moby-Dick* in exemplifying the thesis. Part of Martin's persuasiveness is that his interpretations of these two novels are not conventionally "original," but in fact build on our conventional awareness of the novels' structure and characterization. By identifying hitherto unrecognized dimensions of the familiar, Martin deepens our already consensual understanding of both novels. That, I think, is the source of his book's originality and power.

The novels between *Typee* and *Moby-Dick, Redburn* and *White Jacket,* do not reflect self-evident stages in the progression, and on these works Martin is less compelling—more strained if yet interestingly problematic—than on *Typee* and *Moby-Dick.* In *White Jacket* Melville calls special friendships among sailors "chummying," and in his chapter called "Chums: The Search for a Friend," Martin begins unexceptionably by calling Melville's concern now with shipboard friendship a carryover from his concern with the *tayo* in his South Sea novels. But then Martin is faced with two disparate candidates for the office of chum, Harry Bolton in *Redburn* and Jack Chase in *White Jacket.* Harry seems unlikely to begin with; yet structurally he is more prominent than Jack as a forerunner of Queequeg; and by the time Martin has generalized his analysis to accommodate these and related disparities, he has also opened it to more qualification than perhaps he might wish.

The trouble with Harry, for all the consistency of his being described as a black-eyed brunette like Melville's other strangers, is his identification with the corrupt civilization from which the others stand apart. His personal history is not like the Stranger's but is very like the Hero's, and, insofar as he functions as a model or guide, he leads Redburn only to the iniquities of Aladdin's Palace, whatever they are, until Redburn reverses roles and leads him to the ship, here the necessary arena of male friendship. But even as a follower Harry is neither physically nor mentally robust enough to become a sailor on the way to becoming a chum, and finally it is hard to see how he can fit Martin's profile of the Stranger as an exceptional shipboard friend embodying an alternative culture.

Martin tries to reclaim Harry in several interesting ways. He argues for Harry's descent from the Restoration fop, whose "effeminacy" connoted not homosexuality but an undue interest in women that, Martin argues, is peculiarly susceptible of transformation into the enlightened androgyny appropriate to the homosexual couple. But he follows this subtle and resonant claim by suggesting that Aladdin's Palace, where Harry takes Redburn that night in London, is not only a gambling den but a male brothel, which is entirely plausible but which also makes Harry sound less like an agent of idealized androgyny than of the gross buggery that Martin first said is alien to Melville's sense of homosexual identity.

Finally, Martin sets over against Harry's shipboard ineptitude, symbolized by his inability to climb patriarchal masts, his power of song that turns the sailors into "charmed leopards and tigers" (Melville's words), just as the mythic Orpheus charmed the beasts while also introducing homosexuality into the world. Harry's musical alternative is then reinforced by Carlo, who Martin acknowledges is not a developed character but whose description, featuring the "hand organ" with which he charms his listeners, is "probably the most extravagant paean to masturbation to have appeared in respectable literature" (p. 55). Here again I think Martin's argument for Orphic homosexuality as a possible alternative for Melville's Hero is plausible in itself, but that it also lies askew of his main argument for the Hero, Captain, Stranger pattern. Insofar as it invites us to think of Harry and Carlo as singers associated concretely with buggery and masturbation, it also invites us to distinguish them from Melville's other Strangers—Toby, Marnoo, Jack Chase, Queequeg, and Billy—who are sexually idealized, physically active sailors and whose single phallic evocation is Queequeg's tomahawk-pipe, a very different affair from Carlo's hand organ or Aladdin's Palace.

Thus from Martin's perspective I would prefer to see the

Harry/Carlo image as a groping, erratic version of Melville's dark stranger, no doubt linked to the others by its place and function in the overall pattern, but also perhaps reflecting in Melville a direct homosexual impulse that resists the idealization intrinsic to the pattern—or even perhaps as a premature version of the pattern's collapse that reveals Melville's loss of hope in *Billy Budd*. Martin's final chapter acknowledges that Billy is not only a hero manqué but also a stranger manqué: that Billy's complexion is called "rose-tan" rather than the "intensely black" of the Handsome Sailor archetype; that "Billy's appeal is pederastic, and he is therefore inadequate as the locus of the erotic energy that Melville felt was necessary to combat tyranny" (p. 109); and that "the sexuality of *Billy Budd* is a sexuality divested of its subversive power: it is the sexual attraction between power and powerlessness, a sado-masochistic drama that contains all its energies and turns them inward" (p. 108). In these respects Harry Bolton's character and appeal can be seen as anticipating Billy's; and, insofar as in the absence of a hero, the authority figures themselves are here attracted to the stranger and need to destroy him—Claggart sexually and Vere politically—Billy's fate can be seen in key respects as an extension of Harry's. Indeed, Martin himself remarks at one point that Billy's ability to sing "links him to Orpheus . . . but we recall the fate of that earlier Orpheus, Harry" (p. 110).

On this view, however, Harry/Carlo's and Billy's feminine beauty, Orphic musicality, and pederastic appeal can also be seen structurally as an *ad hoc* exception to the very alternative represented by the idealized homosexuality of Melville's other dark strangers; thus as radical distortions of Martin's pattern, and lapses of his progression, in two of his five novels; and thus perhaps as calling into question his thesis itself. And here I think Haberstroh's rival argument for Melville's effort to invest his heroes with heterosexual identity can provide a relevant test for Martin's.

Haberstroh's analysis strongly implies a two-figure schema of hero and heterosexual role-model, in which the lost-child hero is looking for either (or both) a worldly success of a father-figure or a chum who exhibits already the signs of paternal maturity.

Melville's Sexual Politics

Their unreliable or absent fathers impel a series of orphaned, or impecunious, or declassé sons to look for models either to father substitutes such as Mehevi, Jack Chase, and Captain Vere, or to peers such as Long Ghost in *Omoo*, Harry Bolton, Queequeg, and even Ahab. Although attractive at first, some of these models (e.g., Long Ghost, Jack Chase, and Ahab) prove inadequate; one (Harry Bolton) proves even more lost than the hero himself; and one (Queequeg) proves so entirely adequate as to lie out of reach, and thus to fail the hero no less than the others. (Meanwhile Taji in *Mardi* and the prematurely fatherless Pierre fail disastrously in their direct attempts at relationships with women.) Only with Vere does the search succeed, and then its success can only consist of Billy's apotheosis in death. By the time Melville wrote *Billy Budd*, Haberstroh argues, he was too old to feel sexually threatened by his wife any longer, and he had enough money from family bequests to feel financially secure for the very first time. Thus he could accept now at last, and project onto Billy, his lifelong sense of lost-child impotence, accept as well the parental maturity of Vere's decision to sacrifice Billy to society's welfare, and seal his testament of acceptance by making Billy, in the destruction still appropriate to his impotence (and unlike Pierre in his similar destruction), forgive his father and become immortal.

Haberstroh's analysis thus appears more comprehensive and consistent than Martin's, in connecting not just five but virtually all of Melville's novels, and without requiring exceptions such as Martin seems to need for a Stranger like Harry Bolton, a missing Hero in *Billy Budd*, or a missing novel like *Omoo*. In effect Haberstroh collapses together Martin's Captain and Stranger in the single category of patriarchal role-model, and in so doing establishes a consistent Hero whose *Bildung* entails a single spectrum of models reaching from Long Ghost to Ahab. His analysis incorporates the heterosexual novels *Mardi* and *Pierre* with perfect coherence, and his account of *Billy Budd* identifies, no less than Martin's, a distinct final stage in Melville's progression. One might even argue that Haberstroh's argument does not contradict Martin's but subsumes it, in effect making the homosexual material with which Martin is concerned simply another evidence of Melville's struggle and failure to conceive heterosexual maturity.

Yet I think Haberstroh's comprehensiveness and consistency are achieved only at a level of generality above and beyond Melville's discrete narrative structures, so that his analysis in effect subsumes the novels in the sexual politics of Melville's personal life. His category of role-model is so broad, precisely in embracing such incommensurate figures as Long Ghost and Ahab, as to homogenize the novels themselves, and preclude the discriminating analysis by which Martin can explain both a total structure and an impressive variety of contributory detail. In *Typee*, for example, where Haberstroh can do little more than belabor the hero's passivity and the father-figure's inadequacy, Martin can account for the Dark Stranger gradations represented by Toby, Kory Kory, and Marnoo, which in turn helps him account for the total plot structure, and then to exhibit in relevant detail Melville's progression from this plot to the plot of *Moby-Dick*. In *Moby-Dick* Haberstroh and Martin are initially in accord that Ishmael is attracted to both Queequeg and Ahab. But then I think Haberstroh's argument that Queequeg's mature self-sufficiency is beyond poor Ishmael, and therefore that Ishmael must turn from Queequeg to Ahab, with whose lost-boy struggle he feels a kinship that makes Ahab's death leave him still lost even in surviving, overlooks rather than comprehends Melville's total structure. Queequeg's shipboard presence—in "The Mat-Maker," "The Monkey Rope," "Cistern and Buckets," and "Queequeg in His Coffin"—substantively fulfills the promise of his nourishing generosity ashore, and furnishes Ishmael with much of the material for reflection through which he finds an alternative "conceit of attainable felicity" to Ahab's, and thus finds himself instead of remaining lost. Martin's interpretation, as I have suggested, is built on this conventional understanding of the plot dynamics; for him Ishmael's marriage with Queequeg enables Ishmael to free himself from Ahab's struggle even while sympathizing with it, and Ishmael's survival, precarious as it is, precariously vindicates Queequeg as an alternative to Ahab in a sexual politics unique to this novel. To put it another way, Ishmael's survival via Queequeg's coffin is appropriate for Martin but a structural as well as symbolic anomaly for Haberstroh. Other examples might be given of the way in which Martin addresses and connects the individual novels in deeper, more varied detail than Haberstroh, but already I hope the grounds are clear for arguing that his analysis withstands "falsification" by Haberstroh's, and even indeed for turning the tables and arguing that Martin's analysis subsumes Haberstroh's and that Melville's inability to conceive heterosexual maturity is a by-product—if anything the result rather than the cause—of his persistent effort to conceive and dramatize the sacred homosexual marriage.

But I also think there is a third possibility, old-fashioned as it might be, that the politics embodied in Martin's structural pattern really transcends sexuality, and that even the homosexual impetus of Melville's novels is incidental to their idealized political drama. Amidst our culture's preoccupation with sexuality I think we can easily overlook two elements in Melville's culture that might have served to desexualize for him the very politics that Martin ascribes to him. One is the physical proximity of its everyday life. The kind of male bonding that transpires among us in military barracks or athletic locker rooms is not typically homosexual, and was presumably more common in a society with more single-sex occupations like whaling, and fewer beds to go round. That particular male bonding can also produce phallic jokes like Melville's in *Moby-Dick*, jokes whose homosexual bent and whose relevance to his thesis I think Martin is inclined to exaggerate.

A second desexualizing influence on Melville might have been the passionately idealized conception of "man" that he and his "Young America" colleagues eagerly imbibed from the Enlightenment and the French Revolution:

Men may seem detestable as joint stock-companies and nations; knaves, fools, and murderers there may be; men may have mean and meagre faces; but man, in the ideal, is so noble and so sparkling, such a grand and glowing creature, that over any ignominious blemish in him all his fellows should run to throw their costliest robes. That immaculate manliness we feel within ourselves, so far within us, that it remains intact though all the outer character seem gone; bleeds with keenest anguish at the undraped spectacle of a valor-ruined man. . . . But this august dignity I treat of, is not the dignity of kings and robes, but that abounding dignity which has no robed investiture. Thou shalt see it shining in the arm that wields a pick or drives a spike; that democratic dignity which, on all hands, radiates without end from God.

In this famous passage from the first of *Moby-Dick*'s two "Knights and Squires" chapters, Ishmael is idealizing Starbuck, with whom it has never been suggested he might have a homosexual connection, in terms no less intense than those given to Queequeg as his partner in sacred marriage. The passage rises to its climax by extending these same terms, with the idealization they entail, to Bunyan, Cervantes, and Andrew Jackson as "selectest champions [culled] from the kingly commons." Then the second "Knights and Squires" reaches its parallel climax by idealizing the Pequod's entire crew as "Isolatoes," and calling it "An Anacharsis Clootz deputation from all the isles of the sea, and all the ends of the earth, accompanying Old Ahab . . . to lay the world's grievances from that bar from which not very many of them ever came back"—just like the actual deputation for the Rights of Man at the French Assembly of 1790. The "Knights and Squires" passages in *Moby-Dick* are only the most familiar of Melville's many paeans to the idealized dignity of democratic "man," and in the light of Martin's claim for Melville's homosexuality as an idealized form of identity, such passages can lead us to ask whether the identity Melville idealizes is specifically rooted in any particular form of sexuality.

Let me propose in conclusion one more passage from *Moby-Dick* to test this asexual hypothesis as compared with Martin's and even Haberstroh's sexual theories. In "A Squeeze of the Hand" Ishmael's climactic expression of male interconnectedness—"Come, let us squeeze hands all round; nay, let us squeeze ourselves into each other; let us squeeze ourselves universally into the very milk and sperm of kindness"—constitutes for Martin the homosexual center of the book and virtually the keystone evidence for his entire argument. But neither Martin nor Haber-

Melville's Sexual Politics

stroh comments at all on what seems to me Ishmael's palpable *non sequitur* when he says immediately next:

> Would that I could keep squeezing that sperm for ever! For now, since by many prolonged, repeated experiences, I have perceived that in all cases man must eventually lower, or at least shift, his conceit of attainable felicity; not placing it anywhere in the intellect or the fancy; but in the wife, the heart, the bed, the table, the saddle, the fire-side, the country; now that I have perceived all this, I am ready to squeeze case eternally.

The activity in which Martin finds mutual masturbation and communal work inseparable nevertheless leads Ishmael immediately and unblinkingly to proclaim private property and heterosexual marriage as the only attainable human felicity. Here a proponent of Haberstroh's theory might simply say I told you so, that when all is said and done Melville's hero opts for bourgeois conventionality; but here again that conclusion would have to dismiss rather than confront the ecstatic paean to sperm-squeezing through which Ishmael arrives at his conceit of bourgeois comfort. Martin's theory, on the other hand, enables him not only to confront but to welcome the tension between Ishmael's momentary sperm-squeezing ecstasy and his long-range conceit of attainable felicity. Martin has argued all along that Melville could imagine the homosexual sacred marriage as a viable alternative only once even at sea, never ashore, and his argument could not be better served than by Ishmael's rejecting the sacred marriage at the moment he celebrates it most passionately and also tries to imagine a life ashore.

Yet I still think it possible for us to imagine that Ishmael moves without tension from the joy of squeezing sperm in communal male work to the further contentment of wife, table, and fire-side in a continuous domestic life. His *lowered* conceit of felicity is measured, after all, not by the fulfillment of squeezing sperm but by the heights of intellectual aggression to which he aspired with Ahab until he learned better (in part) from Queequeg; and now he repeats that he is ready to "squeeze case eternally" *after* he has enumerated his domestic felicities. All this can suggest that Ishmael's male friendships have had exactly the political force Martin ascribes to them, in creating an alternative to the destructive purpose of the Captain, and yet can leave open the possibility that such friendships are indifferently compatible with homosexual or heterosexual identity.

But that possibility remains at best and at last just barely open, and here I think Martin's argument earns the last word. Most readers would agree that Ishmael's precarious survival on Queequeg's coffin, to be picked up by the *Rachel* as yet another orphan, is not at all reassuring for his prospects ashore, and hardly a prophetic endorsement of the felicities of wife, table, and fire-side. The fragility of his survival can be read more readily as a retrospective endorsement of the homosexual felicity Ishmael found with Queequeg and must abandon ashore, so that the novel's muted ending can confirm in another dimension Martin's argument that the sacred marriage Melville idealized could only be sustained at sea. That entire argument, as I have tried to follow its logic here, is not quite in itself irresistible, and on occasion it is also distracted by a preoccupation with phallic detail. But it is beyond question an original and provocative argument whose explanatory power should make Melville's homosexuality now an unavoidable topic of reflection. With a daring worthy of Melville's daring, and a power of discrimination worthy of his daring, Martin has broken fertile new ground and put Melville scholarship deeply in his debt.

Strine Literature from Sydney Harbour

Miriam J. Shillingsburg

William H. Wilde, Joy Hooten, and Barry Andrews. *The Oxford Companion to Australian Literature.* New York: Oxford University Press, 1985. x, 760 pp.

> Q: Why is Australian literature filled with bushrangers instead of highwaymen?
> A: Because Australia has no highways.

An ordinary Yank visiting Australia (probably the most urbanized country in the world) is not likely to leave the cities, and so he will not appreciate how much of Australia is without "highways" or roads or even "tracks." But one who takes to the roads is rightly astonished by both the stark beauty and the apparent malevolence of the land. In Outback Queensland or the Northern Territory, survival itself bonds the human residents to the countryside with an ambivalent intensity that most Americans (or urban Australians) can scarcely imagine. This is one quality of the literature which is treated in *The Oxford Companion to Australian Literature.*

If ever there were a question about the contribution of Australian literature to English language studies, it certainly must have been laid to rest by Patrick White's 1973 Nobel Prize and by the continuing high quality of literature emanating from Down Under, especially the drama of the last decade. But this kind of achievement does not arrive full-blown from its author's forehead; it comes from a tradition of story-telling and writing as well as an environment which both inspires and cultivates a native literature. The *Companion* is especially good in illuminating this background.

Australia has had its problems in achieving a native literature—for that matter a national identity. Compare the following facts with the what we know of the origins of American literature. English America was colonized largely by religious zealots, entrepreneurs, and others whose vision for the New World was boundless; the first white Australians were convicts and their tyrannical keepers, both unwillingly shipped halfway around the world. Both nations' first Englishmen encountered stone-age natives whom they sought—with varying intensity of purpose—to exterminate since neither the Indians nor the Aborigines could understand the Englishmen's desire to stake out and possess the land. Hard as it was, Americans were able to travel west because they found navigable rivers. Free or freed Australians were hampered by a rim of mountains close to the sea and by rivers which were impassable. When the Appalachian mountains finally were crossed, Americans found a vast fertile well-watered potential breadbasket; while beyond the Blue Mountains and the Grampions Australians discovered that their arid land was a virtual wasteland. Whereas Lewis and Clark had crossed North America by 1805, Burke and Wills died in the desert in 1861 after making a successful but "useless" north-south crossing of Australia.

But there is more. The American colonial period occurred during the seventeenth and eighteenth centuries, a time not noted for humanitarian enterprise; the Australian colonies did not begin until 1788 with the arrival of the First Fleet, making the colonial period a nineteenth-century phenomenon, at least partly tainted with Victorian notions about social reform, respectability, and quite possibly "the white man's burden." In 1900 six Australian states and other territories were declared a Commonwealth without the bother of fighting a Revolution. This has been a significant handicap for Australians in their effort to develop a sense of "who they are" as a nation. Nor did they fight a War of 1812, nor did they enslave another race, nor did they fight a Civil War to reaffirm their sense of nationhood.

All these episodes in American history have been popular in literature and in consciousness-raising. What do the Aussies—who lack such instant identity—use as substitutes?

Here's where the *Oxford Companion to Australian Literature* offers guidance to the beginning reader in selecting topics which are prevalent, significant, typical, controversial, or popular, and, to the more accomplished scholar, assessments and analyses in a rich context. For example, war seems to get disproportionate attention from Australian writers, particularly since almost no wars have been fought on their native territory (except for brief Japanese forays into Darwin and Sydney Harbour in 1942). Most Australian war effort has been spent on behalf of Great Britain and other allies who had interests scattered around the globe. Gallipoli, a Turkish peninsula on which the Australians suffered over 27,000 casualties, holds the most mythic significance. Of that battle the *Companion* says, "That sacrifice was made in an imperial rather than national cause illustrates the paradoxes of Gallipoli in particular and Austrialian nationalism in general" (p. 287). Not only have authors turned to war for history, poetry, and fiction, but in recent years for screenplays and television dramas.

"Aboriginal in Australian Literature," a topic somewhat comparable to "Indian" or "Native American" and in other ways comparable to "Negro" in American literature, is an essay of nearly 7,000 words, a hefty article by the standards of most journals. It cites the factual accounts and reminiscences of the earliest white encounters with the native people (the kind of thing found in two centuries of Southern travel narratives, from Thomas Hariot to William Bartram). By the second half-century of colonization there appeared poetic and fictional treatments of the Aboriginal, most filled with stereotypes of violence and counter-violence, stock characters, and little sensitivity.

Twentieth-century literary treatments of the Aboriginal have affinities with some American treatments of the Negro or other racial minorities. Stereotypes have faded, and the Aboriginal is "the centre of the literature of social protest, either out of genuine concern for an underprivileged minority or because [he] is a ready-made device that writers can use to validate their own particular social or political causes" (p. 8). It is here that white writers have examined and/or exploited themes of interracial sex, racial prejudice, white guilt—the whole range of themes familiar to Americans who have read novels about Indians and blacks. And finally, since 1960, Aborigines like Kath Walker have begun to speak for themselves, especially in Queensland. Interspersed with all these general observations are plot summaries, character analyses, historical data, and thematic motifs to illustrate and support the major points.

A theme of continuing importance in Australian literature is man's relation to the natural environment. Almost everywhere the English went they found a hostility previously unknown. The literary treatment, both early and recent, depicts an ambivalence among the white settlers toward the land and sea, creatures and climate. Mere survival required heroic effort, and to anyone who managed it, the environment—particularly the "bush"—might take on a romantic mystique. For those who returned to the cities or country towns, it was often seen quite pessimistically, especially by the women who were left to manage rustic homes while their husbands sought work as shearers or drovers. These stories and poems reflect the "bush ethos" and were popular especially from 1850 until the First World War. And there is a whole body of literature about a place worse than the Outback; it's the literature of the Never Never, a place so isolated that those who escape "swear that they will 'never never' return" (p. 513).

The problem with a book like the *Companion* is that it is stuffed and overflowing with constantly fascinating and heretofore unknown information. Entries vary from 40 words to nearly 8000; most are in the 100 to 300 range. The reader is like a child at the carnival: he finds it extremely difficult to skip an entry for fear he might miss something exciting. And, if truth be told, he probably will. If the *Companion* reader continues reading straight through, for example, he will soon find another 6,000 words on "Aboriginal Song and Narrative in Translation."

The American reader finds out about things he doesn't already know: "Australian Rules, the only football game unique to Australia . . . spectacular, fast-moving . . . has contributed richly to the lexicon of Australian English" (p. 63). That language is often called "Strine," as in *Let Stalk Strine*; but the pronunciation is also used as an adjective, as in Strine Literature, or as a substantive, as in Strines. The American finds out that his Antipodean cousins have an "Australian Dream," but in literary treatments it tends more toward "mateship, democratic humanism, nationalism and radicalism" than toward the American dream of individualism and rags-to-riches success. He finds that *ryebuck shearers* are the masters of the trade while *backblocks shearers* are confident they will become better. And he discovers attitudes toward Aussie isolation in place names: Mounts Dreadful, Desolation, and Despair—all located in the dead heart of the continent—and Howlong and Beaudesert Stations in Queensland, for example.

But a good many words the American thought he knew don't mean the same things in Australian literature that they mean in American. For example, a *cornstalk* is a native-born white Australian male, particularly from New South Wales (NSW). This individual should be distinguished from the *croweater* born in South Australia (SA), the *sandgroper* from Western Australia (WA), the *sterling* born in England, the *remittance man* whose British family sent him an allowance to keep him from disgracing the family by coming back home, and the *new chum* (roughly equivalent to the American "greenhorn"). A *cornstalk* was the same, however, as a *native* or a *currency lad,* so-called from the time when promissory notes were issued instead of coin.

A *billy* is not a goat but a crude kettle used to boil tea while camping by a *billabong.* The *billabong* is, of course, a small water hole under a *collibah* tree frequented by *swagmen, jumbucks, squatters,* and *troopers* all (except the jumbuck) singing "Waltzing Matilda." With his curiosity piqued, a diligent user can also discover that a *matilda* in different locales and with slightly altered shapes and uses may be called a *swag, bluey, drum,* or the more highly specialized *shiralee,* shaped like a leg-o-mutton.

What is more, *Matilda, My Darling* (1983), a prizewinning novel by Nigel Krauth, originally called "The Jolly Swagman Affair," investigates the events surrounding the composition in 1895 of this ballad by Banjo Patterson. And when the National Anthem was changed in 1984 to "Advance Australia Fair," a national poll showed "Waltzing Matilda" placing second, well ahead of the former anthem "God Save the Queen." All above information may be found in the *Companion*, which, however, unfortunately omits *tucker bag*, leaving to his own devices the uninitiated American who might not be able to figure out why the *swagman* is planning to stuff the *jumbuck* into his *tucker bag*.

Unsuspecting Americans might also trip over *bastard* or *bastardization, pipes, squatters, selection* or *selectors, station* and other ordinary English words which take on extraordinary meanings when Australians get hold of them. A *ringer*, for example, is not a fake or imposter but was originally a champion shearer. The word now refers to anyone of exceptional ability; a literary critic who confused those two meanings might commit a serious literary *ockerism*.

Naturally, terms like *ocker, Speewah, larrikin, Jackeroo* or *Jilleroo* and *duffing* (which means *poddy-dodging*) would send a serious reader to the *Companion*. It might also be wise for him to look up *hatter* (a crazy person), *digger* (a soldier), *mates* (male companions), or *gumsucker* (a Victorian, i.e., a resident of Victoria). Unfortunately, however, one would not be able to identify *goanna, matily, totalizer* or *poddy-dodging*, from the alphabetical lists, though all are used in explaining other entries. The omission of *potch* is doubly unfortunate because ordinary American desk dictionaries do not include it and because it is in the title of a novel by Katharine S. Pritchard, *Potch and Colour*. While Australians do not need a definition, many American (and English) readers will not know that *potch* is the worthless grayish silica found alongside the precious opal which gets its value from what miners refer to as "colour."

One of the most enjoyable parts of reading entry after entry is the charming Australian vocabulary, not only the delightful Aussie slang, but especially the modifications from the Aboriginal. Many such words conjure up Mark Twain's scheme of collecting "curious names of Australasian towns, with the idea of making a poem out of them.... Those are good words for poetry. Among the best I have ever seen.... The best word in that list, and the most musical and gurgly, is Woolloomoolloo.... It has eight O's in it."[1] While the following examples might not be found in the *Companion's* alphabetical entries, they are used in biographies and plot summaries: Toowoomba, Cambaroora, Kalgoorlie, Dimboola, Ularu, Kurburu, Kunapipi, Gunwinngu, Gularabulu, and a myriad others. Many have the "gurgly" sound Twain identified, but others have a greater proportion of consonant sounds: Meanjin, Gundagai, Bunyip, Canberra, and what about *boomerang, dingo, kookaburra,* and *kangaroo*—all of which have passed into the wider languages of the world?

In among these hundreds of writers, titles, institutions, themes, motifs, characters, terms, and thousands of other tidbits of information guaranteed to garner points in any trivia game, are substantial essays on many subjects: the Australian Broadcasting Company, Australian English, Bushranger in . . . , Convict in . . . , Criticism, Feminism in . . . , Folk-Song and Ballad, on down to Science Fiction, Shearer in . . . , Transportation, and War Literature—the longest single essay in the volume—all merit 2,500 words or more. There are entries of similar length on individual figures—J. F. Archibald to Patrick White—and individual works—*Capricornia* to *Waltzing Matilda*—whose influence in Australian literature has been seminal or legendary.

While the *Companion* does present "received opinion," it also makes assessments of its own: "The *Bulletin*'s bush ethos and its contribution to the emergence of literary nationalism has sometimes been over-emphasized, with the result that the diversity of interests, attitudes and opinions expressed in the journal has been underestimated" (p. 123). A journal which sold an estimated 80,000 copies in the 1890s to a population which was already heavily concentrated in Sydney and Melbourne must (and did) have considerable urbane wit and humor, numerous book and theatre reviews, and much society and racecourse gossip, in addition to Lawson's and Patterson's bush ballads and stories. However, the *Companion* falls into the same trap that has snared many modern literary critics who assume that realistic literature is automatically somehow better than romantic, especially in fiction: Boldrewood's romances are "characteristically marred by stilted dialogue and self-conscious literariness" (p. 98), while such traits in the contemporary "bush balladists" are praised for language and tone similarly romanticized.

Is anything wrong with the *Oxford Companion to Australian*

Literature? Well, a few things, the most important being a possibly myopic view of Australia and perhaps of literature. All three of the compilers have been primarily interested in nineteenth-century literature in their other scholarship, and this no doubt accounts for the fact that the "Legend of the Nineties"—to borrow Vance Palmer's term—may be overemphasized. Many pages are devoted to the writers, editors, and publications of the late nineteenth century. This is appropriate, and, because much of the material—especially unpublished and newspaper material—is housed in the Mitchell Library (NSW), the nineteenth-century slant is heavily toward Sydney's influence. Perhaps this is unavoidable, and perhaps it is even correct; but one case may illustrate the *possibility* that other regions had more "culture" than appears from the *Companion*.

The Bulletin (established 1880) and the "*Bulletin* debate" merit about 1900 words. *Melbourne Punch* (founded 1856), the "best, most famous and longest-running of the colonial imitations on London *Punch*" (p. 476) receives less than 300 words while *Table Talk,* with which it merged, gets another 50. Adelaide's *Quiz* (begun 1889) occupies only 40 words and its mate *Lantern* is not even mentioned. All these papers were similar in reporting sports, society, politics, theatre, and in publishing original fiction, poetry, satire, and cartoons. The amount of space devoted to each may be determined not only by their relative influence but also by the difficulty of finding material about them. *Quiz,* for example, is not in the finding list of newspapers, nor does it seem to be available at the Australian National Library or the Library of NSW.

Likewise one could ask why *Bulletin* cartoonists Hop, May, and Low were included, but not Tom Durkin, a clever contemporary of the former two. And why so much less attention to journalists from the *Age* and the *Argus* in Melbourne than to those from equivalent Sydney papers? No mention is made of reporter Herbert Low, a precocious journalist who worked for papers in both Melbourne and Sydney and whose "Australian Press Reminiscences" provide an interesting and valuable sidelight on famous people he interviewed and on the state of journalism in turn-of-the-century Australia. Perhaps these items were considered and excluded, but surely the omission from the alphabetical listing of the Adelaide Festival was an oversight which will be corrected in future editions. And maybe it will be made clear that *brumby* is a horse.

A difficult problem in compiling such an ambitious work is setting its parameters. With this book the compilers are establishing the canon of Australian literature for many future readers. They had some previous guidance, especially H. M. Green's *A History of Australian Literature* (revised by Dorothy Green, 1984), and no doubt their coming late to the task has given them the opportunity to examine Companions to other literatures. But one does note a decided emphasis on prize-winning writers rather than on popular writers. The earlier authors get a disproportionate amount of plot summary and biography in comparison with, for example, Morris West, perhaps the most internationally famous of all modern Australian writers. Where Henry Handel Richardson gets more than 2000 words, plus entries on individual plots, Ethel Turner nearly 1000 plus individual plots, and Marcus Clarke nearly 1300 plus plot summaries, West merits slightly over 400 words. And not one of his works, not even the prize-winning *The Devil's Advocate,* is cross-referenced. Whether his books were considered too well known to need summaries, whether he was judged unpatriotic because he has mostly lived and published abroad, or whether his religious themes are not up to literary standards is not explained. In future editions a preface outlining the criteria for selecting "Australian Literature" would be a valuable addition, especially for a new reader. However, Americans will be relieved to know that Colleen McCullough, author of *The Thornbirds* (which Australians don't much like) and Rolf Harris, author of "Tie Me Kangaroo Down, Sport," are both included. But people all over the world will be puzzled that neither "Skippy the Bush Kangaroo" nor his creator, Eric Jupp, is listed. Pretty slack, mates!

Note

1. Mark Twain, *Following the Equator* (Hartford, Conn.: The American Publishing Co., 1897), pp. 328–330.

Whatever Self He Had: The Canonization of Stevens Continues

R. D. Ackerman

    Harold Bloom, ed. *Wallace Stevens.* Modern Critical Views. New York: Chelsea House Publishers, 1985. 196 pp.

    Albert Gelpi, ed. *Wallace Stevens: The Poetics of Modernism.* Cambridge Studies in American Literature and Culture. Cambridge: Cambridge University Press, 1985. x, 165 pp.

    Charles Doyle, ed. *Wallace Stevens: The Critical Heritage.* Critical Heritage Series. London: Routledge & Kegan Paul, 1985. xv, 503 pp.

    Milton Bates. *Wallace Stevens: A Mythology of Self.* Berkeley and Los Angeles: University of California Press, 1985. xiii, 319 pp.

    Joan Richardson. *Wallace Stevens: The Early Years, 1879–1923.* New York: William Morrow, 1986. 591 pp.

> And when she sang, the sea,
> Whatever self it had, became the self
> That was her song, for she was the maker.
> —"The Idea of Order at Key West"

The last two or three years have witnessed a burgeoning of Stevens scholarship, a veritable smorgasbord of Stevensiana—and this at a time when one might have expected a waning of interest in him as the darling of the New Critics and their heirs. Was he not a high modernist whose belated reputation surely had reached its apogee in the sixties and early seventies? Hadn't Frank Lentricchia (for instance) effectively buried Stevens by labeling him "the culmination and summary representative of . . . the conservative fictionalist tradition in modern poetics and philosophy," a tradition of "aesthetic isolationism" that was "radically dualistic and very often paranoid"?[1] And yet the scholarly interest in Stevens continues. The output of articles increases each year, and there are currently over fifty books in print in English on Stevens.

Are these efforts the worn-out leavings of a stale tradition, the mechanical products of a critical enterprise that grinds on—like so many academic industries—even when its subject has been reduced to an antiquarian interest? In view of all this output (and echoing the opening of Derrida's *Glas*): What really remains for us today of Wallace Stevens? The works examined in this review can help us to begin formulating an answer to that question—an answer, though, that can only be probative and partial since it remains integrally bound to our understanding of the larger issue of our relationship to the Romantic-modern tradition (or traditions) in general. And that understanding in turn depends, of course, upon our views of pivotal writers such as Stevens.

In fact, our view of Stevens not only influences our understanding of the nature of Romanticism and modernism; it also helps us navigate the troubled waters that have followed in the wake of modernism, since Stevens has variously been identified also with postmodernism, poststructuralism, and deconstruction. Perhaps Stevens will come to be viewed in retrospect as a large figure indeed, as a genre-creating master spanning the transition zone between the modern period and whatever we are now becoming. Perhaps we are today not at the end of the Stevens period but rather at the beginning of a second phase of our assimilation or appropriation of Stevens. Much will depend, I suspect, on the future of that pervasive mode of thinking we now misname deconstruction—and on the extent to which deconstruction shapes our future. For Stevens's ironic constructs and his emphasis on decreation and fictionality have proven especially congenial to deconstructive thought.

But it is more than this broad congeniality with deconstruction that poses difficulties for the scholarship under review here. It is also our ambiguous historical distance from the poet—who

The Canonization of Stevens

is neither quite present nor simply past—that diverts our approach to Stevens and his poetry into that disjunctive limbo that has been the special province of deconstructive thought. In other words, our efforts to negotiate Stevens's awkward temporal distance from us draws us into a problematics of appropriation that can then be seen to impede all our efforts to engage the past, whether individual or historical. This crucial difficulty surfaces most openly in the biographies by Bates and Richardson, but it also arises in various guises in most of the essays in the collections of criticism.

J. Hillis Miller's essay in the Bloom collection is an exception, however. "Stevens' Rock and Criticism as Cure" is the only basically deconstructive piece among the works reviewed here. Originally published in 1976, it was arguably the first major deconstructive essay on Stevens and remains the most influential. Thus it can help illuminate the disjunctive problematics and aporetic structure that deconstructive viewers are likely to find not only within Stevens's own poetry (in both its content and form) but also in their own efforts to reach out to this poetry (which oscillates uncannily between past and present). Miller's essay is a good place to begin because, in the process of setting itself apart from traditional approaches to Stevens, this essay provides the means of discerning certain questionable premises that surface repeatedly in much of the other work under review.

For Miller, Stevens's poetry—and all literature—remains a heterogeneous text that cannot be reduced to a ground (say in nature or reason or spirit) any more than it can be relegated to "an underlying system or code of terms, conceptual, figurative, 'symbolic,' mythical, or narrative" (p. 28). Instead of originating in and leading to a universal or univocal foundation, "The Rock," for instance, opens up the vista of an interpretive abyss, the infamous *mise en abyme*. This prospect of an undecidable oscillation displaces the metaphysical ground that once could anchor and provide coherence to our interpretations. This hermeneutic predicament, however, does not mean that "anything goes" or that texts are meaningless—but only that the meaning we do find or produce in a text is set against the metaphysical backdrop of a fundamental instability (an interplay of figure and ground, for example) or lack of fundament. On the other hand, this instability at the center is not without consequence. Determinations that we make in this oscillating textual environment share something of the unstable context from which they emerge.

Miller's deconstructive argument for textual heterogeneity and hermeneutic instability raises serious questions about the premises of traditional approaches to Stevens, readings that often begin with the assumption that human life is validly envisioned as a unity or wholeness, that the self is a stable presence or creative matrix, that acts of the mind can produce unified and unifying images, ideas, poems. Miller questions Stevens's allegiance to a certain reading of the Romantic-modern tradition that gives priority to the organic wholeness of life and selfhood, that maintains (in Emerson's words) that "'life . . . cannot be divided nor doubled,'" that "'invasion of [life's] unity would be chaos,'" that the "'great and crescive self . . . [is] rooted in absolute nature'" (pp. 42–43; quoted from Emerson). Against this view Miller argues that "The Rock" is a "thorough deconstruction of the Emersonian bedrock self." It is not a poem that asks to be read backward toward an authorial selfhood. Its "bleak impersonality of tone and locution . . . forbids thinking of it or feeling it as the autobiographical statement of a recognizable person, the man Wallace Stevens, vice president of the Hartford Accident and Indemnity Company, author of *Harmonium*" (p. 43).

The loss of encompassing grids of interpretation interferes with efforts to generate coherent readings of Stevens's poetry. It also frustrates our efforts to map a linkage between the poetry and the life of Stevens. Miller's essay is designed to reveal the obstacles that stand in the way of reading Stevens's poetry and his life through the lens of a Romantic-modern idealization of nature and author as creative origins capable of unifying and ordering both poem and life alike. Most readers of Stevens, however, have read and continue to read the poet in precisely this traditional way. There has been nearly unanimous agreement with Frank Doggett's early emphasis on Stevens's "preference for naturalistic thought and for ideas that lean on the imagery of organism," a preference that aligns Stevens with the

The Canonization of Stevens

"great tradition of romantic poets and . . . the matrix of thought that underlies their poetry."[2] Yet this unanimity says as much about the readers' own climate of interpretation as it does about Stevens. Perhaps Miller's essay can itself be read today as marking the beginning of a second phase in our understanding of the poet, a phase-in-process with premises which both contradict and clarify the enabling assumptions found in much of the work under review here.

Bloom's collection gathers together a group of solid essays on Stevens, most of which are not very recent and all of which have been published before. Helen Vendler's essay on "Like Decorations in a Nigger Cemetery" and "Thirteen Ways of Looking at a Blackbird" is from her book on Stevens, *On Extended Wings* (1969). Miller's essay, just discussed, has now been again republished in a slightly different form in his *The Linguistic Moment* (1985). Helen Regueiro's essay on Stevens and metaphor is from her 1976 book, *The Limits of Imagination*. Bloom's own contribution, "An Ordinary Evening in New Haven," is from his book on Stevens, *The Poems of Our Climate* (1977). Marie Borroff's study of the varieties of Stevens's poetic languages is from her *Language and the Poet* (1979). Patricia Parker's essay on Stevens's notion of inescapable figurality is from her 1979 book, *Inescapable Romance*. Charles Berger's essay on "The Owl in the Sarcophagus" and "To an Old Philosopher in Rome" is from his 1984 book on Stevens, *Forms of Farewell*. Two of the remaining essays—Isabel G. MacCaffrey on "Le Monocle de Mon Oncle" and John Hollander on the music of Stevens's poetry—are taken from a 1980 collection of essays on Stevens, while Eleanor Cook's study of Stevens's riddles is from a collection published in 1983.

There is both stature and variety in this gathering, and it would be unwise to seek a single guiding principle or premise of selectivity behind Bloom's choices. In his introductory essay (the only new piece in the collection) Bloom himself disavows the negative Stevenses of Miller and Vendler. And yet, and yet . . . (Stevens might have added), if there is no single guiding thread, there does emerge in this collection a general pattern of agreement, except for Miller, a vague consensus adumbrated perhaps by the view of the poet that Bloom extols in his introduction.

"The reader who loves Stevens learns a passion for Yes" (p. 2)—a passion that Bloom goes on to identify with that version of the Romantic tradition which he calls the American Sublime. The Stevens that Bloom celebrates (we should know by now) is the hugely imaginative poet of "defeated eroticism" who bursts through his impoverishment with a joyous vision that lies against time—and also against *otherness*. For this poet's longing is based on its erotic defeat by the world and *must* aspire beyond the world of mere being: "Stevens is uniquely the twentieth century poet of that solitary and inward glory we can none of us share with others" (p. 5). He "celebrates an apprehension that has no social aspect whatsoever. . . . His True Subject appears to be his own sense of glory, and his true value for his readers appears to be that he reminds us of our own moments of solipsistic bliss" (p. 6).

For Bloom, Stevens is the belated Romantic celebrant of his own gigantic Self, an identity secured in those "highest moments" when, in Emerson's words, "we are a vision." At such moments "the soul is raised over passion [which is doomed to 'erotic defeat']. It seeth nothing so much as Identity." In such moments the imagination discovers a oneness with itself—and with the world. But it does so only by *destroying* the world: "'Vast spaces of nature, the Atlantic Ocean, the South Sea; vast intervals of time, years, centuries, are annihilated in it [the soul]'" (p. 7; quoted from Emerson).

"American Romanticism found its last giant in Stevens," Bloom claims on p. 10. Probably he is right. The question is whether *this* Stevens is the Stevens that remains for us today. Do we need a poet whose principal power is to recall us to "solipsistic bliss"? Do we need a poet who leads us back into the Romantic dream or metaphysical nightmare from which we are trying to awake? Stevens is not only a poet of transcendent Identity. He is also—and crucially for us today—a poet who questions such visionary oneness, a poet whose awareness of lingustic mediation leads him to recognize the intrusion of otherness into the sanctum of the self. Compare Bloom's portrait of the visionary Stevens to Miller's view of "The Rock": "This dissolution [of selfhood], paradoxically, takes place not by a movement into a more and more vacuous solipsism . . . but precisely by incorporating that doubling of self and other which Emerson so resolutely . . . rejects. Stevens is more open to the existence of others . . . as Emerson and Whitman are not. . . . For Stevens the self-enclosed sphere of the self is broken" (p. 44).

I am not suggesting that the essays in this collection adhere rigidly to the specific credo espoused by Bloom. (Nor is there evidence here of the characteristic Bloomian gesture and tone.) But I am suggesting that the interpretive grids that inform much of the discussion in this collection—and indeed in much of the work under review—bear a family resemblance to each other, a resemblance traceable to an interrelated set of assumptions based on the key premise that Bloom openly acknowledges and celebrates—that is, an encompassing principle of Identity or vision of oneness that embraces the privileged but only apparent opposition between human self and natural world, between imagination and reality. The transcendent voice that Bloom valorizes as a response to the inevitable defeat of the imagination by the spatio-temporal limitations of nature is but the voice of nature made absolute as *Life*. Bloom's idea of the poetic Self is as rooted in "absolute nature" as is Emerson's idea of the subject. As Stevens says and Bloom quotes: " 'The indifferent experience of life is the unique experience, the item of ecstasy which we have been isolating and reserving for another time and place, loftier and more secluded' " (p. 12; quoted from Stevens). Large questions remain, however. Is Stevens's view of "life" compatible with Emerson's vision of Identity? Does Stevens fit as snugly into the Romantic-modern trajectory as Bloom claims?

These assumptions do not always surface openly in the other essays in this collection, but there are indications that these premises are widely shared even among critics with divergent styles and goals. I have space here only for a few illustrations. In "The Rejection of Metaphor" Helen Regueiro ably tackles the question of Stevens's view of the relationship between language and nature. Quite validly she maintains that although Stevens sometimes suggests the possibility of a correspondence between "poetic act" and "natural process" (p. 51), his usual approach to this problematic relationship is more complex. He emphasizes the distance between word and thing and argues that we do not live in a world of things but in a "world of words," that it is " 'never the thing but the version of the thing' " (p. 52; quoted from Stevens). Regueiro points out, however, that this recognition is counterbalanced by a strategy of decreation that remains aimed at the experience of a reality beyond metaphor. She concludes that Stevens seeks a "word that is uttered and not uttered," a "dual act of remembrance and forgetfulness." Here she is very close to describing the doubling of self and other that Miller emphasizes. Minus his valorization of the idea of language, though, Regueiro herself remains loyal to the Romantic paradigm of nature (and imagination) and concludes her essay by tracking the "dissolution of the self" into the "natural world"—and not into the world of *human* others, the world of language and history (p. 60). She does not seem to see that Stevens's rhetoric of nature is no more "natural" than his language of imagination.[3]

On the other hand, Marie Borroff's perceptive study of the languages of Stevens's poetry illustrates that a formal interest in poetic style is still no guarantee that the Romantic-modernist language/reality dualism will be avoided. Just the reverse. For here the whole of Stevens's vast linguistic undertaking is traced to the poet's quest for an extralinguistic reality: "Just as we see . . . Stevens . . . turning from one metaphor, one analogy, one symbolic setting, person, or event to another, so also we see him turning from one expressive means to another, trying out now this kind of language, now that, now this kind of word, now that, in the incessant attempt to express what remains perpetually 'beyond the rhetorician's touch' " (p. 103). Thus Borroff entitles her essay "An Always Incipient Cosmos" and joins league with the majority view of Stevens: "As everyone knows, the basic concerns and preoccupations of Stevens's poetry remained the same from first to last. His essential theme . . . [was] the interplay of imagination and reality"—where reality remains out there in the cosmos or in Vermont (as it is in the poem from which the title line is taken), and the imagination remains inside in the realm of "solipsistic bliss" (p. 101). And thus also where language serves but to mediate between two singular essences whose identities remain undisturbed by doubling.

Patricia Parker, however, does lead us in the right direction in

The Canonization of Stevens 249

her essay "Inescapable Romance," (from her book of the same title). She not only situates Stevens in a romantic tradition; she also points out that he "provides a restrospect on the meaning of romance for English poetry since Spenser" (p. 109). She sees that Stevens's decreative quest for a "neutral centre" or "pure reality" beyond "rotted names" leads him to the recognition that this "reduction . . . is not finally possible because figuration itself is part of the 'inescapable romance'" (p. 111). Thus his poetry develops out of a sense of "exile" from a "single center" or "abiding presence." His "imagination's locus is finally not the 'veritable ding an sich' . . . but something closer to that pregnant virtuality Keats called a 'shadow of reality to come,' the promise of 'the possibilities of things'" (pp. 112–13). Stevens's central concern comes to be with poetry not as the namer of reality but as an "affair / Of the possible," an affair of "seemings." One wonders, however, what happens to Parker's benign idea of romance once the distinction between reality and appearance (seeming) begins to disintegrate, once the romantic supplement invades the domain of primary reality. What can "pregnant virtuality" mean when one begins to believe that there is no "reality to come," since there has never been a reality that has come? What is the force of the idea of "exile" if there has never been a home to begin with?[4]

Unlike Bloom's volume, Albert Gelpi's collection for Cambridge University Press consists of essays that have not been published before. These essays, Gelpi notes in his preface, are by "six critics of twentieth-century poetry who have not previously published much, if anything, about Stevens—critics who are not, in any case, members of the Stevens critical establishment." Gelpi hopes that this gathering will "contribute to a new phase in Stevens criticism" and claims that these essays "are all engaged in a common venture: namely, specifying Stevens' place in the evolution of Modernest poetics in English" (p. vii). We might expect then that these essayists too, in aiming to situate historically a poet who is neither quite past nor present, will also find themselves contending with the disjunctive impasse that deconstruction has spotlighted, an impasse in this instance that concerns the very idea of Modernism. (Gelpi in fact emphasizes the "continuing presence of Modernism.") This volume is made up of essays on Stevens that address the following topics: Gelpi and Gerald L. Bruns on Modernism and the question of epistemology; Marjorie Perloff on the supreme fiction and the "pressure of reality"; Bonnie Costello and Charles Altieri on analogy, abstraction, and painting; Alan Golding on Louis Zukofsky; Michael Davidson on contemporary poetics.

Overall these are capable essays that raise a number of crucial issues for our current view of the poet, but the extent of their contribution to a "new phase in Stevens criticism" remains to be evaluated. Once again it is difficult to imagine a genuinely new phase without a deconstructive ingredient, and most of these essays avoid rather than confront the challenge of deconstruction. Indeed, minus the deconstructive influence, the approaches here tend to fall back into the "consensus approach" of the (putative) Stevens establishment that Gelpi claims they are writing against—that is, they focus (as Gelpi points out, surprisingly) on "strategies for fictionalizing the interaction of the imagination and reality" (p. vii).

Gelpi's own contribution, "Stevens and Williams: The Epistemology of Modernism," is a case in point. In his effort to distinguish Modernism from Romanticism, Gelpi ends up instead suggesting why Modernism looks to many viewers like a phase of Romanticism. For him, Stevens and Williams were of "profound importance to literary Modernism" because they "argued for, and premised their poetry upon, the primacy of the imagination" (p.4). Once he ascribes to this centering of the imagination (and therefore of strategies of relating it to reality), Gelpi is hard pressed to differentiate the Modern and the Romantic at this level and to avoid reading Stevens according to the "consensus approach." This is not the place to develop this point in detail, but I would suggest that even though the Modern poet (according to Gelpi) "does not reveal the divinity of nature," there yet remains a deep complicity between imagination and nature in Gelpi's account of and defense of Modernism—and that it is precisely this complicity that has informed most approaches to Stevens to date.

In "Stevens without Epistemology," on the other hand, Gerald

L. Bruns aims explicitly to find a way beyond epistemology, that is, beyond the question of "how the mind links up with reality" (p. 24). In order to do this, he sets out as his own enabling premise a narrative scheme of three moments or "turns" in the modern history of conceptual understanding: the "epistemological turn," beginning with Descartes; the "linguistic turn," marked, say, by analytic philosophy of language or by the later Heidegger; and the "hermeneutical turn," indicating the time when "questions about language . . . began to be reformulated as questions about social practice" (pp. 24–25). This scheme, though helpful, is suspect. It helps us to see more clearly that our approaches to Stevens are influenced—perhaps even determined—by our "philosophical" preconceptions. But it is suspect in that it suggests a false equivalence between these three moments and devises a misleading separation between the linguistic and the hermeneutical turns. But can we can leave epistemological or foundational questions about reality (say) completely behind us when dealing with Stevens? (Bruns is attacking a *realist* epistemology in the name of epistemology as such, although he does not say so.) I would agree, however, that the canonical approach to Stevens has been epistemologically simplistic in its reliance on the imagination-reality dichotomy it inherited from Romanticism, Modernism, and of course from Stevens himself.

The new phase of Stevens criticism initiated by critics such as Miller and the later Joseph Riddel locates the emergence of the other (social, political, psychoanalytic, historical, ethical) within and through the abyss of reflexivity opened up by both the epistemological and the linguistic turns. The linguistic and hermeneutical turns are inseparable, just as the later Heidegger, identified by Bruns with the linguistic turn, remains integrally related to the earlier Heidegger, identified by Bruns with the hermeneutic turn. Thus I believe that Bruns's main question— "What happens when one reads Stevens's poetry from the standpoint made available by the hermeneutic turn in human thinking"—remains misleading because it is only half a question. Just as in his earlier work, which he mentions, Bruns stressed the idea of language but placed it in the service of a Heideggerian or Ricoeurian hermeneutics of earth, so now he similarly seeks to transmute the linguistic turn into a hermeneutics of social practice. What is missing from the equation is the deconstructive dimension of the linguistic moment. Without it, Bruns might end up—as he does in this interesting essay—privileging a mystique of *voice,* in line with his earlier Orphic belief in earth, as a defense against the idea of *writing,* which lets us *see* language as well as hear it.

Before turning to a final illustration from this collection, I would like to note briefly another essay that seeks to open up the question of the social and historical dimension of Stevens's poetry. In "Revolving in Crystal: The Supreme Fiction and the Impasse of the Modernist Lyric," Marjorie Perloff juxtaposes a list of the violent historical events of the early forties with Stevens's preoccupation at the time with the idea of a "supreme fiction" and a "major man" (in the process of writing "Notes toward a Supreme Fiction"), claiming that Stevens's "ruling principal is *aesthetic detachment,*" that Stevens rejects the impure "pressure of reality" in favor of the clean "purity of art" (pp. 45–46). For her Stevens's poetry embodies the Romantic strain of modern poetry in that he remains committed to the "lyric paradigm" (p. 51). Perloff's charges against Stevens should be heard. But they are not the whole story. Like most Stevens critics she mistakes the Romantic theory of poetry that is lauded in Stevens's poems and prose for the actual poems that Stevens wrote— poems that are more meditative than lyrical, poems that do open routes of figuration for the "pressure of reality" to penetrate the interstices of their ironic reflexivity.

This last point helps to explain why Charles Altieri, in the most ambitious and interesting essay in this collection, "Why Stevens Must Be Abstract, or What a Poet Can Learn from Painting," can celebrate the "presentational force" of Stevens's poetry (p. 94), a poetry largely "devoted to abstraction" (p. 96) but not to insular detachment (as Perloff would have it). Altieri writes against the "suspicious impulse" of the "new historicists," including deconstructionists, but he does not seek simply to avoid this "critical spirit" (pp. 86–87). His argument is broad and intricate, and it is possible here only to point out a few of its major concerns. For Altieri, Stevens's "imperative to abstraction" parallels the "fundamental principles of the Modernist revolution established by the visual arts . . . [and] the philosophical enterprise of minimalist assertion typified by Wittgenstein" (p. 87). Stevens's valorization of abstraction is not simply opposed to historical reality. In "An Ordinary Evening in New Haven," for instance, "Stevens makes the process of abstraction the basic vehicle by which the life of poetry displays what can become the elements of a theory of life." Such abstraction opens a space through which the "*as* structure" of poetry becomes a connecting link between the "syntax of art . . . [and] a general theory of value." From this perspective we can understand that human identity "depends not on descriptions but on exponential indicators [the *as*] whose powers of imagination produce a dialectic of the real and unreal central to the possibility of there being distinctive human values" (pp. 105–106). Altieri both celebrates Stevens's contribution to the "Romantic quest" (p. 115) and understands the meditative dimension of that quest which destabilizes the lyric genre: "The theory of poetry—or better, poetry as theorizing—becomes the theory of life, because it puts within contemplative brackets the essential force that makes value possible, the interdependence of the unreal and the real" (p. 108).

Altieri makes a source of joy out of the disjunctive structures that deconstructive thinkers have found scandalous (recall Derrida's treatment of the scandal of metaphor in philosophical discourse). One wonders, however, if Altieri's leap into the *as* is too precipitous. Does he sufficiently register the tension and destabilization brought about by the necessary cohabitation of the theoretical and the lyrical, the philosophical and the poetic or metaphoric, the epistemic and the doxic—a tension that writers like Derrida and de Man have made the focus of their thinking? Perhaps, though, Altieri's wholly affirmative emphasis should be understood against what he perceives as the threatening despair of the "new historicists"—a threat that is now being redressed to an extent by a newly emerging affirmative deconstruction.[5]

Covering an area somewhere between the two preceding critical collections and the two biographical works to follow is the collection of (mostly) reviews edited by Charles Doyle for the Critical Heritage series of Routledge and Kegan Paul. Perusing this volume is like entering a time warp that allows us to participate in the gradual and variegated unfolding of Stevens's reputation over the years from 1916 to 1967. Although some of these pieces continue to be available elsewhere (eleven of them in the reprint of *The Achievement of Wallace Stevens*, edited by Ashley Brown and Robert S. Haller), the large number (123) and diversity of these reviews provide a unique glimpse of canon formation in the making. Also provided in this volume are helpful headnotes for most of the pieces, indexes of poems, topics, and names, as well as a list of reviews that are *not* collected here.

The items in this volume range from the insignificant or silly to the suggestive or ground-breaking—from the anonymous 1917 notice (no. 2) that "Carlos Among the Candles" is a "baffling monologue by Wallace Stevens, intended neither for the stage nor the library"—or the 1952 observation in the *Dallas Morning News* (no. 87) that Wallace Stevens is "one of our major poets, as 'major' goes these days"—to Alfred Kreymborg's prophetic observation of 1929 (no. 22): "To the yearning national question, where is our next major poet to come from, I always feel like responding: Out of Wallace Stevens, if Stevens would only let him come." Or there is the even earlier acclamation in 1922 (no. 8) by the twenty-one year old Yvor Winters acknowledging Stevens as the "greatest of living and of American poets"—an acknowledgment that contrasts sharply with his pronouncements on the "Hedonist's Progress" (no. 60) over twenty years later. Or consider these enthusiastic 1931 observations (no. 23) by Conrad Aiken on the poet he calls "the playboy of the western *word*": "He's perhaps the most remarkable *humorist* in poetry: I mean, he carries humor farther into terms of poetry than has perhaps ever been done.... Then, finally, there is of course the extremely keen critical awareness.... Ideas all over the place; but presented ... with rings in their noses and cockatoos on their wrists.... I think him as sure of a permanent place of importance as Eliot, if not surer. Eliot will go *down* ... and Stevens will, I feel sure, come up."

But beyond the province of historical curiosity, there are also many specimens here of criticism that remains valuable, especially for providing historical depth to our current studies.

The Canonization of Stevens

Witness as a final illustration the emergence of an atmosphere of genuine critical debate in the forties following the publication of *Parts of a World*, *Notes toward a Supreme Fiction*, and *Esthétique du Mal*. Among many others, the pieces by Horace Gregory (no. 53), Hi Simons (no. 54), R. P. Blackmur (no. 58), Yvor Winters (no. 60), and Wylie Sypher (no. 62) remain of critical interest. But note especially the 1946 review by Louis L. Martz (no. 64), "Wallace Stevens: The Romance of the Precise," a piece that crucially anticipates his better-known articles to come even as it tries to adjudicate claims in the current debate. In attempting to "define the genre of Wallace Stevens," Martz notes that Simon characterizes Stevens as an "intellectual poet" aligned with Donne, while Sypher stresses Stevens's "essential romanticism" in opposition to the "vogue of the metaphysical." Martz concludes that they are both "essentially wrong" and then goes on to explore, through Stevens's poetry and with reference to other critics, the distinction between an intellectual or metaphysical poetry and a *reflective* poetry based on "reverie," a genre he identifies ultimately with Herrick and Ben Jonson, and with their Roman and Greek predecessors, especially Horace.

The two biographical works under review—Milton J. Bates's *Wallace Stevens: A Mythology of Self* and Joan Richardson's *Wallace Stevens: The Early Years, 1879–1923*—face the profound dilemma accompanying all efforts today to negotiate the distance between historical fact and artistic creation. Ours is a period in search of paradigms or models of interpretation. Without such grids, efforts to map the relationship, say, between a biographical datum and a poem run the risk of a reductivity that endangers our response to both domains, the life as well as the art. And yet without such efforts both domains will even more certainly remain intransigent and opaque. At best, there can be an interplay between the research into the life of a poet and the development of a model through which to see the life and interpret the poems. At the least, there should be a careful effort made to reveal the paradigm or paradigms of interpretation that enable and guide the study. Both works under review fail in this respect. But that does not mean that they are unworthy of our attention.

Bates claims that his book is not biography at all but that it concerns instead "how one poet transcended biography by transforming it into fables of identity." And yet these fables do in fact have a biographical dimension since, as Bates goes on to inform us, they enabled Stevens to "create the self he would become" (p. ix). Bates's muddled expression in his preface of the relationship between Stevens's life and art foreshadows a certain fudging on this central issue throughout the book. Bates maintains that his approach is not biographical but rather "chiefly historical," but he does not in the least attempt to clarify this abstruse distinction. Instead, in his preface, he turns quickly to a defensive justification that he has indeed "benefited from . . . current inquiries into the nature of the self, language, and reality"—but that he has tried not to make Stevens "more sophisticated than he was"! The question, however, has nothing to do with Stevens's sophistication. It concerns the calibre of Bates's own approach to Stevens, an approach that is "particularly address[ed] . . . to students in and out of the university whose interest and good will have been balked by the difficulties of Stevens' poetry and the sometimes more formidable difficulties of Stevens criticism" (p. x). Fortunately Bates's book does not simply offer up the pabulum his preface promises.

Bates has chapters on Stevens's college years, his relationship with his wife-to-be Elsie, his *Harmonium* years, his views of "pure poetry," his resurgence during the thirties, his turn to the question of the "supreme fiction" and the "major man," and finally a chapter on some of the very late poems. Throughout there is an effort to set up reverberations between letters or other biographical data, some of it new, and the poems themselves. Often Bates comes up with interesting parallels, such as his discussion in Chapter 7 of Stevens's reading of Nietzsche in relationship to the figure of the major or central man. But sometimes Bates's overreliance on biographical data for his interpretation of the poems tends to render his readings superficial, as is the case for instance with his discussion of "Red Loves Lit" in Chapter 2.

Perhaps the difficulty with Bates's approach can be traced to his general resistance to theory (ideas about "self, language, and reality"), which he then proceeds to read as Stevens's own lack of motivation by ideas. Bates believes that there is a primary Stevens self—"the son of a lawyer, later a lawyer himself, living in comfortable middle-class surroundings in Pennsylvania, New York, and Connecticut"—to which are added in the poetry a series of "poses" of "dramatis personae" (p. 277). The biographical self remains the solid base from which the fictive poses emerge. And yet apparently, as we have seen, Stevens's secondary fictions somehow manage to infiltrate the primary self. How? How separable are they in the first place? Recall Miller's observation that Stevens's poetry "forbids thinking of it or feeling it as the autobiographical statement of a recognizable person." Which is to say that Bates's assumption of a primary biographical self as the basis from which to read the fictive poses of the poetry tends to ameliorate the danger and excitement of Stevens's poetry. The reason that there is interchange between "bedrock self" and fabled personae is that these domains are not clearly separable in the first place. The solid biographical foundation upon which Bates constructs his interpretations partakes of the insolidity of the fictive poses.

Bates's closest approach to the full implications of this question of multiple selfhood comes in Chapter 3 where he quotes from a cancelled manuscript passage from Stevens's lecture-essay "The Figure of the Youth as Virile Poet." Although this is a work that celebrates the singular unity of the poetic self, this particular passage raises questions about the solidity and separability of the biographical and poetic selves: "'We take a man like Picasso . . . and assume that here is Picasso and there is his work. This is nonsense. Where the one is, the other is. This son of an intellectual and antiquarian . . . may sit in his studio, half-a-dozen men at once conversing together. They reach a conclusion and all of them go back into one of them who seats himself and begins to paint. Is it one of them within him that dominates and makes the design or rather could it be? Can Picasso choose? Free will does not go so far' " (p. 92; quoted from Stevens). Bates admits that this passage "further complicates our sense of the relation between the man and his work" but then does not sufficiently explore this complication. His theoretical model of interpretation—which remains largely behind the scenes—provides Bates a simpler picture of the relationship between art and life than the model that Stevens spent his life attempting to articulate.[6]

Joan Richardson's ambitious two-volume *Wallace Stevens* may well turn out to be the "first full-scale biography" of the poet, as the prepublication advertisement promises. But there is little hope that this work will become the "definitive biography" of Stevens that Marjorie Perloff predicts on the book jacket. The reason is clear and commonplace. Stevens's poetry—not his life—is his claim to fame, and his poetry is largely a poetry of ideas, however "blooded." A definitive biography will have to begin there. It will have to be intellectual and critical and capable of following the pathways of Stevens's thinking as well as the events of his life. And it will have to be, in our time at least, extraordinarily sensitive to the complications impeding our efforts to establish causal connections between the domains of life and art, facts and ideas, emotions and thoughts.

The main virtue of Richardson's book lies in its detailed renderings of the personal and historical/social contexts of Stevens's life. Richardson takes meticulous care to portray the social environment and to trace the relationship between the changing times and the developing personality of the poet. Her book is valuable to us on this basis alone. In addition, there is a wealth here of new material garnered chiefly from the Wallace Stevens Collection at the Huntington Library (which Bates also draws on to a lesser degree), though by necessity Richardson relies mainly on already published material, especially the *Letters* and *Souvenirs and Prophecies*, to enable her to describe and narrate (sometimes day by day, sometimes month by month) the events of Stevens's early life. And this volume covers just that—the "early years," the years up to the publication of *Harmonium*. The second volume (covering the poet's mature years and most of his major poetry) is promised in a year (p.31). But compared to the first volume's eight chapters, the second installment will apparently make do with five (p. 29). This discrepancy need not be a shortcoming, but it does point up a potential drawback in trying to write a "life" of Stevens that avoids a full-scale exploration of his ideas. The large majority of the poet's published letters, for instance, were written after 1923. But they are more concerned with and more interesting for Stevens's idea-world than his life-world—and therefore less essential to the perspective this biographer brings to bear on her subject.

But Richardson is concerned with more than social milieux. She also aims to reveal the "evolution of Stevens's consciousness," and she begins with the same questionable premise that has informed most Stevens criticism to date: "The hero that emerges from his work is nature itself or, rather, consciousness as it understands itself to be part of nature" (p. 20). This broad assumption can lead at times even to the extreme position expressed on Richardson's book jacket that behind the mere "appearance" of "cerebral abstraction" of Stevens's poetry "lies the welter of common experience and strong emotion that are the true subject of his work." Stevens's work, then, comes to be for Richardson the site where the consciousness that is nature can fuse with the deep emotion that is the common social experience. Thus she claims that "in tracing the development of Stevens's consciousness," her biography is as much "a biography of America from 1879 to 1955 as it is of the poet who was so integrally bound to his time and place" (p. 20).

And yet Richardson knows that Stevens's poetry sprang also from the fact that he was unable simply to be "bound to his time and place." Her understanding of this crucial philosophical dimension of the poet, however, is the weakest aspect of her book. Her expansiveness on this subject betrays a limited comprehension: "Stevens's commitment to the use of reason belonged to the dominant tradition of the West, which had begun with the pre-Socratics and Plato and was passed down through time in different thinkers in different countries—a line that, in terms of the intellectual currents charging the air of the generation that produced the poet, was particularized in Charles Sanders Peirce. . . . Though Stevens did not claim familiarity with the work of Peirce, he was nonetheless heir to the same strains of thought that engendered in the philosopher a desire to justify God's ways to man by bridging the gap made by Darwin between the scientific outlook on the place of human beings in the world and the threatened religious view" (p. 21).

Likewise, Richardson's book is dedicated to mending this gap.

For her, "not to see the connection Stevens's poems have to the real 'facts' of his life is to miss what gave them their 'potency,' what made them part of the *res* and not about it" (p. 111). As for William James, whom she quotes in explanation, so for her it is only in "'the recesses of feeling . . . [that we can catch] real fact in the making, and directly perceive how events happen, and how work is actually done'" (p. 542n; quoted from James). The reductivity of this psychologistic approach to matters of thought and art is as debilitating to a biographer as to a critic. It leads to unwise hypothesizing of questionable causal connections based on deep emotion, to observations linking nature and poetry (Stevens's lines were longer in the summer than in late fall) or linking poetry and society (during wars the "sounds of his words were violent and strained") (p. 22).

Richardson imagines herself "breaking away from the New Critical tradition" (p. 26), but she forgets that despite their insistence on the autotelic nature of poetry, they too aimed to tie poetry to *life* (or to what both she and the New Critics imagine is life). She does break with the New Critics in one sense though: she forgets their warnings about facile identifications of art and life. Her valorization of nature and deep feeling are part of what she calls her "Kantian faith that the patterns emerging from consciousness uncensored reveal connections to things as they are in a way that mimics the object or subject—in this sense the two merge into one—of attention at deep structural levels" (p. 28). But contra Kant, Richardson's approach to Stevens allows for little critical distance. She tends to sentimentalize Stevens's relation to the world just as she does her own relation to Stevens. Reading him, she claims: "I gradually found myself becoming increasingly attentive to the quiverings of my own nature in response to the world around me. . . . I began to see again with an ignorant eye, the eye of a child. . . . I came to realize that what Stevens had managed to do was to preserve throughout his life the freshness of vision that belongs to the child" (p. 27). At the outset we asked what remains for us today of Stevens. This child Stevens of the ignorant eye is precisely what does *not* remain of Stevens. This is the remnant of a stale tradition once mistakenly called Romantic, a tradition still present behind the scenes of most New Criticism. Reading Richardson instead of Stevens, one might come to believe that above and beyond the poet's commitment to traditions of Western thought rises his belief in Zen Buddhism. But this largely imaginary connection, which Richardson makes on a number of occasions, reveals more about the biographer than the poet.

Richardson is at her best when she eschews the "deep structural levels" in favor of social context, but even here her dilations risk attenuation: "Poised between the slow step of the nineteenth century and the dash of the twentieth, Stevens arrived from Cambridge on Thursday, June 14, 1900, to seek his fortune in New York. The city moved as uncertainly as he. The young man walked through dimly lit nights and blazoned days. He followed shadowy streets crowded with clattering horse-drawn cabs, clanking elevated trains, and electric cable cars. He was at first dismayed. He saw it with a mind of simpler ways, educated by Pennsylvania's broad views and Cambridge's subtle arguments" (p. 105). Obviously Richardson wants us also to see with the "eye of a child," but in doing so she risks encouraging us to think with the mind of a child. Nonetheless, in this chapter she does go on to give us the "feel" of turn-of-the-century New York, its restaurants and apartment houses, the events of the time, even the honky-tonk of the newest "rags."

This desire to give the reader the "feel" or "freshness of vision" of a particular time and place, however, can also lead to sentimentalizations that belong in a cheap novel rather than in a scholarly biography. This is particularly true in Richardson's treatment of the relationship between Stevens and Elsie, which is the chief dramatic focus of this volume. What are we to make of such efforts as the following? "How did the young lawyer feel that deep green June night, back home in Reading, on being introduced to the most beautiful girl in town as a 'very fine poet' from New York? No doubt her blue eyes pierced him as the light playing on her golden hair created a mystic aurole around her head.... The exquisite young girl Stevens met that June night of summer-seeming had just turned eighteen. What were her dreams as she approached womanhood in the place she had never left at a time when becoming a woman did not mean becoming an autonomous being" (pp. 207–08)? How the reader responds to this novelistic style is likely to influence in large measure how the reader will respond to the entire book.

Yet these extreme instances of weak style do not add up to the whole book, and finally each of Richardson's observations and interpretations will have to be weighed on its own merits. There is much of value here: this volume will become a source book, an extensive collection of early Stevensiana. To illustrate, let me conclude my discussion with a brief list of representative topics that I found interesting and valuable: Stevens's reading interests, especially during his New York period, and their relation to his early poetry, particularly Robert Louis Stevenson (*The Silverado Squatters*, for example), Matthew Arnold, Goethe, Schopenhauer, and especially G. Lowes Dickinson and Paul Elmer More (whose references suggested a number of additional titles to Stevens); Bliss Carman's and Richard Hovey's *Songs from Vagabondia* and *More Songs*, which influenced a number of *Harmonium* poems, including "Peter Quince at the Clavier"; Stevens's extensive letters to Elsie, including material not previously published; Stevens's interest in modern art during the Armory Show period and afterward, along with his relationship to the Walter Arensberg circle (including Walter Pach); and finally Stevens's responses to the deaths of close relations, particularly his sister and mother.

Looking back over the works under review—what of Stevens remains for us today? One Stevens that remains is Stevens the writer, the Stevens who continues to raise the question of the *act of writing* itself. One approach to this issue, and thus to Stevens as well, comes in the form of the traditional Romantic glorification of the genius. Helen Vendler exemplifies this perspective in an interesting recent review, where she exalts the "extreme heroism of [Stevens's] poetic life—as he abandoned the received poetry of his century, vowed himself to an exhausting accuracy of registration and perception, tested his powers by examining and rejecting work he believed to be inferior, and persisted through solitude and overwork toward the creation of new forms of language." For her the "heroism of writing is an unthinkable venture into the unknown," and the biographer should approach the subject of Stevens, say, with "wonder, even amazement, that the wager of genius was won."[7]

This wonderment is not an attitude we can easily do without if we wish to continue raising the question of writing with the full array of implications that it deserves. But should we not also begin to extricate the theme of writing from the idea of genius, since this figure of the artist-hero serves ultimately to limit or contain the problematic of writing? That is one lesson Stevens can help us learn today. For his poetry is less the work of a visionary Romantic genius than the meditative unfolding of an understanding—or an effort to understand—the ramifications of the question of writing. His poetry calls into question the subjecthood of the writer, the very idea that the figure of the genius epitomizes. Stevens's writing-thinking raises profoundly the issue of the relationship between writing and thinking, between poetry and philosophy. Instead of approaching his poetry canonically as an "act of the mind," the doing of a subject, a genuinely fresh approach or new phase of Stevens criticism will consider reading these texts as a "deconstruction of thought as act" (in the words of Paul de Man[8]), as a persistent abyssing of whatever self Stevens had.

Notes

1. Frank Lentricchia, *After the New Criticism* (Chicago: Univ. of Chicago Press, 1980), pp. 31–33.
2. Frank Doggett, *Stevens' Poetry of Thought* (Baltimore: Johns Hopkins Univ. Press, 1966), pp. ix, xn.
3. See R. D. Ackerman, "Stevens' Skepticism: From Romantic Irony to Deconstruction," *Studies in Romanticism*, 22 (1983), 551–67.
4. See Paul de Man, "Conclusions: Walter Benjamin's 'The Task of the Translator,'" in *The Resistance to Theory* (Minneapolis: Univ. of Minnesota Press, 1986), p. 92.
5. See Jacques Derrida, *Memoires: For Paul de Man* (New York: Columbia Univ. Press, 1986), and R. D. Ackerman's forthcoming review-article of *Memoires* in *Philosophy and Literature*. Altieri's Wittgensteinian approach is not simply diametrically opposed to Derrida and deconstruction. For important parallels,

see Henry Staten, *Wittgenstein and Derrida* (Lincoln: Univ. of Nebraska Press, 1984).

6. For more on these complications, see Paul de Man, "Autobiography as De-Facement," in *The Rhetoric of Romanticism* (New York: Columbia Univ. Press, 1984).

7. Helen Vendler, "The Hunting of Wallace Stevens," *New York Review of Books*, 20 Nov. 1986, p. 46.

8. Paul de Man, *Allegories of Reading* (New Haven: Yale Univ. Press, 1979), p. 129. See also Derrida, *Memoires,* p. 134, passim.

On Leslie Stephen and the Art of Biography

Panthea Reid Broughton

Noel Annan. *Leslie Stephen: The Godless Victorian*. Chicago: University of Chicago Press, 1984. xiii, 432 pp.

Leslie Stephen thought James Boswell the model biographer. Late in his life Stephen wrote, "Boswell represents the original source not only of knowledge about Johnson, but of our knowledge of English literature in general. . . . We became members of the craft in spirit under Boswell's guidance."[1] Under Boswell's guidance, Stephen, as Lord Annan writes, "came into his own. He began to write biographies" (p. 110). A prolific member of the craft, Stephen wrote the lives of Swift, Pope, Johnson, George Eliot, and Hobbes for the English Men of Letters Series. He also wrote lives of Henry Fawcett, J. R. Green, and his brother Fitzjames Stephen. As the first editor of the *Dictionary of National Biography,* Stephen created a monument of Victorian comprehensiveness and established a new mode of succinct, non-eulogistic biographies offering "the greatest possible amount of information in a thoroughly business-like form."[2]

Stephen's opinions about biographical propriety were quintessentially Victorian (he thought the sexual implications in Froude's biography of Carlyle and in the Browning love letters inappropriate for print), but his opinions about biography's relation to historical context established standards for modern biography. Stephen titled a collection of his essays (first published in 1898) *Studies of a Biographer*. Any treatment of Stephen's life might properly concern itself with two major subjects: Stephen as biographer, and biography as hermeneutic. But Noel Annan's book on Stephen (a revision of his 1951 study) is only tangentially concerned with biography itself.

Though they illustrate changing biographical tastes, the major treatments of Stephen's life display little consciousness of the assumptions under which they were written. In 1903 Leslie Stephen wrote what he termed "Some Early Impressions" from his own life, but he insisted: "I have no reason to think that the story of my 'inner life' would be in the least interesting, and, were it interesting, I should still prefer to keep it to myself."[3] F. W. Maitland's 1906 commemorative biography of Stephen, a pre-Strachey portrait of a great man, in no way threatens the sanctity of that inner life. It epitomizes the Victorian assumption, promulgated by Leslie Stephen, that great works are produced by great men. In fulsome prose Maitland deprecates himself: "My meagre power of description I am glad to eke out by borrowing from Dr. A. W. Ward"; and he venerates Leslie Stephen who never wrote "'either a meaningless or an intentionally unfair word, never spoke a vapid or an unkind one.'"[4] Given the conviction that Stephen never said an unkind word, no wonder Maitland rejected Virginia Stephen [Woolf's] testimony about her father's verbal assaults on the women in his family.

When Noel Annan first began writing on Stephen, he was less interested in Stephen as a great man than as a representative one. Annan did not deprecate himself, but he seems to have so devalued biography that someone else had to suggest that he begin his intellectual study with a biographical introduction. He published *Leslie Stephen: His Thought and Character in Relation to his Time* in 1951. As the title suggests, Annan was then interested in Stephen primarily as an example of a type; thus his first sentence dealt, not with Stephen, but with the emergence of an "intellectual aristocracy" in Victorian times.[5] In 1951 Annan considered Maitland a model biographer who "did his work so well that a new biography would be superfluous." Therefore, Annan claimed to have written a "critical study" rather than a biography.[6]

Annan's 1984 book on Stephen begins much more dramatically with an analogy between a portrait of St. Jerome and a photograph of Leslie Stephen, each at "the end of his days" (p. 1). This beginning promises a new interest in Stephen as an individual and a new respect for the art of biography, but Annan claims, "The new book is still not a biography" (p. xii). Here Annan hedges. He revises an old book and describes it as a "new book." He writes a life but insists it is "not a biography." Annan's 1984 book is different, but not as "new" as it might have been. The illustrations are slightly different. He removes two family photographs and adds two more of Leslie Stephen's charming animal drawings and eight more pictures of individuals important in Stephen's life. He introduces much more material about Stephen's most famous daughter, Virginia Woolf, and exhibits considerable familiarity with Woolf scholarship. He cites more unpublished sources (many not available in 1951) and uses concrete detail adroitly. He is more sensitive to women's issues. He psychoanalyzes more freely and insightfully. And he introduces much fuller treatments of Stephen's work on the eighteenth century and of relations between British and German rationalism.

Unfortunately, however, Annan does not alter the basic structure of his work on Stephen. It remains a bifurcated treatment—first of the life, then of the intellectual currents important to that life. The first 145 pages of Annan's text provide the framework for what could have been an insightful and powerful biography. Annan's first three chapters ("The Early Years," "Making a Reputation," and "The Man of Letters") are a chronological survey of Stephen's life told in a style studded with metaphors. His tropes are derived from the visual arts and from card games, modern technology, science, horticulture, medicine, and finance; he recasts such stale metaphors as signing the warrant for his arrest (p. 322), biting the hand that fed him (p. 181), and discovering two sides of the same coin (p. 197). These metaphors are so various that they would call into question Ira Bruce Nadel's assumption that we can measure a biography by its tropes,[7] except that there is a common denominator in most of these tropes: competition. The trope of warfare is finally basic to Annan's way of seeing Stephen and intellectual history: "Kant had built for those who believed in God a new and formidable base camp but it was many years before Anglicans were willing to bivouac there" (p. 180); "[William] James's right-wing empiricism turned the flank of the rationalist position" (p. 249); "a battle was joined over [Stephen's] body which resembled in violence the struggle for the corpse of Patroclus on the plain of Troy" (p. 323).

If the battle metaphors are strained, the marriage/adultery metaphors are simply unfortunate. Annan writes: "Moral philosophy is a dignified matron and some elderly gentlemen such as Marcus Aurelius have led her to the altar; the rest of us require someone much more attractive if we are to resist temptation" (p. 316). Temptation, I gather, means the temptation to sleep around with illicit philosophies; the metaphor suggests that only sexy philosophies merit fidelity. Another metaphor of the same sort is even more outrageous; Annan writes, "The charms of mountaineering resemble those of a great courtesan. . . . Mountaineering makes it possible for the intellectual to experience things which would otherwise be impossible" (p. 91). These battle and adultery metaphors suggest a reductionist tendency in Annan's thinking.

But Annan does work much harder than he did in 1951 to explain such matters, large and small, as nineteenth-century university regulations, Stephen's resignation from the clergy, his living for a time with his mother, his affinity with James Russell Lowell, and his obsessive need to achieve. Annan praises Leslie Stephen for his opposition to Cambridge's "mania for testing ability," but faults him for being "subtly tainted with the English contempt for culture and the world of ideas" (p. 37). Annan also censures us: "To criticize a past generation for not accepting what we ourselves have only just accepted as normal is supercilious folly; and to argue that Stephen should have advocated open entrance examinations and have crusaded for the abolition, not only of the religious tests but also of the unspoken class tests, would be to ask him to step out of his own generation into our own" (p. 37). Annan explains: "Leslie Stephen was one of the very few intelligent Englishmen who found the United States sympathetic. . . . Stephen realized only too well that this [English] upper-class dislike of the North [American states] sprang from dread of democracy" (p. 52). Annan's summing-up reaffirms Stephen's status: "After Matthew Arnold's death in 1888 he was regarded as the first man of English letters and an eminent Victorian. His eminence can scarcely be in doubt" (p. 112). Only one third of the way into this book, Annan tallies Stephen's accomplishments and narrates his "last sad years." But what sort of biographical strategy would conclude a life-story on the 125th of 350 pages of text?

Probably the strategy was to modernize without substantially rewriting. After his first three chronological chapters, Annan adds a psychological chapter entitled "What Was He Really Like?" The very title acknowledges the failure of the biographical approach Annan began with. In this fourth chapter Annan examines Virginia Woolf's portrait of her father as Mr. Ramsay in *To the Lighthouse*, Stephen's own *Mausoleum Book*, the testimony of Leslie's sister Milly, the account of her father Woolf wrote for the *Times* on the centenary of his birth, and Woolf's final portrait of her father in "A Sketch of the Past" (1940). Annan writes:

In "A Sketch of the Past" Virginia drew her mother. But there was another draft which she never lived to incorporate in the [sic][8] her memoir in which she described her father. It was her last effort to come to terms with him before she killed herself and she categorized him as three fathers; the sociable father, the writer father; and the tyrant father. [p. 132]

The draft Annan refers to was bought at Sotheby's in 1981 by the British Library. It seems to be, not (as Annan describes it) an unincorporated draft, but a continuation and revision of part of the "Sketch" as published by Jeanne Schulkind in the 1976 *Moments of Being*.[9] Annan quotes two passages from this part of the "Sketch." I wish he had quoted more. Woolf begins, "June 19th 1940 I sit in my room at 37 M. S. [Mecklenburgh Square] and turn to my father."[10] She turns to him after narrating the story of the death of her half-sister Stella (with which the 1976 Schulkind text ended), "because it was during the seven years between Stella's death in 1897 and his death in 1904 that Nessa [her sister Vanessa Stephen Bell] and I were fully exposed without protection to the full blast of that strange character."[11] Woolf sets a standard for Stephen biography:

He was a little early Victorian boy, brought up in the intense narrow, evangelical yet political, highly intellectual yet completely unaesthtic [sic], Stephen family, that had one foot in Clapham, the other in Downing Street. Such is the obvious first sentence of his biography.[12]

Woolf goes on to judge her father: "Roger Fry said that civilization means awareness; he [Leslie Stephen] was uncivilized in his extreme unawareness. He did not realize what he did. No one could enlighten him. Yet he suffered."[13] She concludes with the vision of greatness she inherited from Leslie Stephen and his generation:

Greatness still seems to me a positive possession; booming; eccentric; set apart; something to which I am led up dutifully by my parents. It is a bodily presence; it has nothing to do with anything said. It exists in certain people. But it never exists now. I cannot remember ever to have felt greatness since I was a child.[14]

Woolf scholars will wish that Annan had explored these materials further, for today Leslie Stephen is known only to specialists as the foremost Victorian man of letters after Matthew Arnold. For most of us he is the father of Virginia Woolf.

To his credit, Annan does examine the vexed issue of Virginia Woolf's education. Virginia "resented the fact that no money was spent on sending Vanessa and herself to school. She resented being excluded from that great male preserve [the university]" (p. 119). Annan acknowledges that "for many years to come British parents of the professional classes to their shame were to save on their daughters' education" (p. 121), but he does point out the advantages Woolf, with her free run of her father's library, had over the typical undergraduate.

Annan also quotes from an early exchange between Julia Duckworth (before she was Julia Stephen) and Leslie Stephen that suggests that she, not he, was the parent hostile to female education. In 1877 Leslie had written to her that he hated "to see so many women's lives wasted because they have not been trained well enough to take an independent interest in any study or have a profession." On the next day Julia replied that it required "all my faith in you to believe with such views on female education you can care for me." She continued, "I am quite sure you have no idea how utterly uneducated I am—it is almost impossible for you to imagine any one so uneducated." And she ended her letter, "I feel more & more how much less there is in me of every kind of thought & power than in you—except love— I think I have no want of that." Leslie, of course, asked for her forgiveness and assured her that for a woman a "noble character" was much more important than that "she should learn anything whatever."[15] Sadly enough, Stephen's discussion of "professions for women" (to use his daughter's phrase) had reference to his retarded daughter Laura, the one child of his first marriage to Thackeray's daughter Minnie and the child who, Annan wisely concludes, suffered most for being her father's offspring. That Stephen was not able to acknowledge Laura's debility and fantasized a career for her suggests a well-developed denial syndrome. But however much Stephen denied Laura's infirmity, these passages, which I have quoted somewhat more fully than Annan does, establish that Stephen (at least until Julia demurred) did not deny that a woman needed an education and a profession. These unpublished letters suggest that, had Julia lived, she would have stifled the careers of Vanessa Bell and Virginia Woolf in ways that Leslie Stephen did not.

Annan's fourth chapter compares what we know about the psyches of Leslie Stephen and Virginia Woolf. As Katherine Hill has shown most fully in a Columbia University dissertation which Annan consults, they both were manic depressives. (Sadly, though, in the late Victorian era, masculine depression was considered sensitivity; feminine depression was labeled insanity.) Annan's psychological chapter offers genuine insight into Leslie Stephen's character, but the topics seem mostly to have been thrust upon Annan by the work of others, chiefly Woolf scholars. Because the chapter is more reactive to others than productive of a fully-worked out hypothesis, it does not finally answer the question ("What was he really like?") posed by its title.

Annan follows his first four chapters with nine more: "Evangelicalism," "British Rationalism," "The Rhetoric of Truth," "The Revelation of the Eighteenth Century," "Agnosticism,"

"The Moral Society," "Morality through Biography," "Morality and Literature," and "Conclusion." The first six of these offer effective summaries of the nineteenth-century intellectual currents that influenced Leslie Stephen. Annan claims he has higher ambitions than biography-writing: "I have tried to contribute more to the history of ideas itself and this time set Stephen in a wider constellation of ideas: in particular those of the German Renaissance of the eighteenth and nineteenth centuries which has been as important for Europe today as the Italian Renaissance was in the sixteenth and seventeenth centuries" (pp. xii–xiii). Annan asks questions: "Stephen prophesied the secularization of society. Was he right?" (p. 259). He points out such inconsistencies as "the power of religion over the very minds which denied it" (p. 290). He praises: "Such insight reassures the reader and implies that Stephen will not take a man at face value" (p. 309). He judges: "It was, however, this reluctance to discuss what human beings are really like which diminishes Stephen's worth as a moralist" (p. 316). He testifies: "But on one issue he made his mark. Stephen was determined to separate ethics from religion" (p. 350). And he concludes: "Leslie Stephen was, then, a representative, not an aberrant, figure" (p. 343).

Annan finally does not make a well-integrated book, principally because he separates his study of ideas from his story of Stephen's life. Of course, one might argue that a philosopher's work is abstract and hence has fewer connections with his life than, say, a politician's or poet's life does. I disagree and so, I think, would Leslie Stephen. Annan says Stephen "will be remembered longest for declaring that you could not judge literature unless you had related it to the times" (p. 321). He adds that "few biographers have been more intent than Stephen to place their subject in his age" (p. 301), but Annan's structure, first diachronic then synchronic, separates his subject from his age.

Annan's diachronic structure takes its narrative from the history of Leslie Stephen's ancestors through his life to his death. The synchronic structure collapses time and progression into a discussion of intellectual currents. Sometimes in the latter part of the book, Annan's collapsing of time schemes provokes interesting analogies: "Bloomsbury, like Clapham, was a coterie"

(p. 159); at others, it almost creates anachronisms: "On one matter [Stephen] differed from [Desmond] MacCarthy and Bloomsbury" (p. 336). Furthermore, each structure suffers from its isolation from the other. The diachronic narrative of Stephen's life lacks much of the story of Stephen's intellectual development, while references to Stephen seem oddly tacked onto the intellectual history. For example, in the chapter "British Rationalism," referring to Benjamin Jowett who became Master of Balliol in 1870, Annan says, "Stephen thought Jowett an intellectual coward" (p. 187). Annan's notes establish that this was an 1897 opinion, but that in 1870 Stephen had praised Jowett for stimulating "'the intellect of the rising generation'" (p. 383). Such a shift in opinion is not particularly important to a study of British Rationalism, but it would have been very important to a study of Leslie Stephen's emerging values. Similarly, Annan ends his excellent analysis of Darwin by straining to connect it with Stephen: "Stephen read Darwin as *evidence* confuting orthodox metaphysics" (p. 201). In the chapter "The Rhetoric of Truth," Annan makes a similarly gratuitous reference to Stephen: "How was it that in England open opposition to Christianity was so long delayed and left to men of Stephen's generation to make?" (p. 211). In the chapter "Agnosticism" Annan tells us that Stephen attributed to atheists and materialists much of the work for the prevention of cruelty to animals. Then Annan remarks, "It is hard to believe that he did not know that this honour belonged to the Evangelicals" (p. 237). If Annan had been working within the diachronic structure he could have gone on to speculate about reasons for Stephen's misattribution of good works to non-believers.

Annan's chapters "Morality through Biography" and "Morality and Literature" deal more explicitly with Stephen's own ideas, but they are weakened by being divorced from the treatment of Stephen's life. Annan says that, to Stephen, manliness was the supreme virtue. He adds, "The opposite of masculine is not feminine but morbid" (p. 305). Such comments would gain resonance within the stories of Stephen's marriages. Annan tells us that as a biographer Stephen "could never bring himself to admit that great writers are often horrible men. It was too painful a contradiction" (p. 315). Twentieth-century literary biography explicitly rejects Stephen's assumptions about greatness, but Annan seems unconcerned with Stephen's place in the development of biographical theory. And he is less than alert to the ways in which carrying the art of biography beyond Boswell shaped the life of that man who "came into his own" by writing biography.

Annan's "ambition" not to write biography but to write the history of ideas suggests a residual disrespect for the art of biography. Such disrespect, forgivable in the 1950s, is not in the 1980s, an age which Donald Greene proclaims is at last "the golden age of English biography."[16] As I suggest early in this review, the various treatments of Leslie Stephen's life exemplify shifts in biographical assumptions and expectations. In revising his 1951 study of Stephen as representative man, Lord Annan had an opportunity to bring the biographical standards of the 1980s to bear on Stephen's life. But despite his considerable knowledge and talent, Annan found it easier to preserve his 1951 bifurcated format than to take up the gauntlets thrown down by such writers of holistic biographies as W. Jackson Bate, Richard Ellmann, Michael Holroyd, Leon Edel, A. J. P. Taylor, John Grigg, James Pope-Hennessy, and Leslie Stephen's grandson Quentin Bell. Writing a holistic biography that placed Stephen's life within (rather than before) the context of his times would not only have made a more aesthetically satisfying biography, it would also have been a fuller testimony to the influence of Leslie Stephen.[17]

Notes

1. "Johnsoniana," in *Studies of a Biographer*, I (London: Duckworth and Co., 1904), p. 108.
2. "A New 'Biographia Britannica,'" *Athenaeum*, December 23, 1882, p. 850.
3. *Some Early Impressions* (London: Hogarth Press, 1924; reprinted from *The National Review*), pp. 9–10.
4. Frederic William Maitland, *The Life and Letters of Leslie Stephen* (London: Duckworth and Co., 1906), p. 438.

5. Noel Gilroy Annan, *Leslie Stephen: His Thought and Character in Relation to his Time* (London: Macgibbon and Kee, 1951), p. 1.

6. Ibid., p. v.

7. See his chapter "Biography and Theory: Steps Toward a Poetics," in *Biography: Fiction, Fact and Form* (London: Macmillan, 1984).

8. This and the odd punctuation in the rest of this passage are the only typographical errors I have found in this text, but I believe Annan misdates Stephen's discovery of St. Ives as 1881 rather 1882. See BL Add. MS 57920, p. 52.

9. Virginia Woolf, *Moments of Being*, ed. Jeanna Schulkind (Sussex: Sussex Univ. Press, 1976). The unpublished version used by Annan was incorporated into the second revised and enlarged edition (London: Hogarth Press, 1985).

10. BL Add. MS 61973, p. 1. Permission to quote from this manuscript granted by Quentin Bell.

11. Ibid.

12. Ibid., p. 2.

13. Ibid., p. 59.

14. Ibid., p. 78.

15. BL Add. MS 57922, p. 78. Permission to quote from this manuscript granted by Quentin Bell.

16. Donald Greene, "'Tis a Pretty Book, Mr. Boswell, But—,'" *Georgia Review*, 32 (1978), 17.

17. Research used in this review was conducted while on a grant (for a related project) from the National Endowment for the Humanities. I am most grateful to the Endowment for its support.

Chaucer's Debts in *Troilus and Criseyde*

Colin Wilcockson

Winthrop Wetherbee. *Chaucer and the Poets: An Essay on Troilus and Criseyde*. Ithaca and London: Cornell University Press, 1984. 249 pp.

Winthrop Wetherbee's study of *Troilus and Criseyde* is the most detailed analysis we have of Chaucer's use of poetic sources for that work. Wetherbee is deeply informed about the source material, is sharp in observation, sensitive in interpretation—and admirably clear. His book is an important contribution to Chaucer studies.

We know from the closing stanzas of the *Troilus* that Chaucer self-consciously writes in the tradition of the great poets of the past:

> But litel book, no makyng thow nenvie,
> But subgit be to alle poesie;
> And kis the steppes, where as thow seest space
> Virgile, Ovide, Omer, Lucan, and Stace. [V. 1789–92]

In addition, of course, and of direct influence, are Dante, Boccaccio, Boethius and the authors of the *Roman de la rose*. Wetherbee picks up in particular the word *poesie* from the above quotation (and elsewhere in Chaucer) and contrasts it with Chaucer's use of the word *making*. In pursuing this discussion, as he acknowledges, he is indebted to the studies of several recent critics. The most persuasive of these, to my mind, is Anne Middleton in her 1980 essay in *Literature and Society*.[1] In that essay, she demonstrates that Chaucer uses *poetrie* (*poesie*) to indicate composition with a serious moral or philosophical content, whereas *making* is applied to works of lighter weight such as *fabliaux*.

Wetherbee argues that Chaucer is specifically aware of writing in a tradition of *poetae* who acknowledge that they have derived enlightenment from their predecessors: this is exhibited in a recurrent pattern of movement within their poems of initial sympathy with weakness followed by its exposure, and the poet's subsequent disillusionment. This sort of movement is seen in the *Roman de la rose* and notably in Dante, guided by Vergil from his misleading sympathy with Francesca, and in his account in the *Purgatorio* of Statius' transformation from pagan poet to purified Christian soul. The references to the *poetae* in the *Troilus* are often, Wetherbee maintains, of this revelatory nature: the Neo-Platonic movement, the growing vision of the divine beyond and above earthly experience, is underscored by suggestive reference to the works of great poetic predecessors.

To take an example: the possibility of an incestuous relationship between Pandarus and Criseyde may be inherent in the stanzas that follow soon after the description of the sexual consummation of the love between Troilus and Criseyde. Pandarus comes to Criseyde's bed and makes sexually loaded innuendoes about the stormy night and the difficulty Criseyde may have experienced in getting any sleep. She tells him that he is a cunning contriver ('fox that ye ben') and then hides under the sheet.

> And Pandarus gan under for to prie,
> And seyde, 'Nece, if that I shal be dede,
> Haue here a swerd, and smyteth of myn hede.'
> With that his arm al sodeynly he thriste
> Under hire nekke and at the last hire kyste. [III. 1571–75]

In the following stanza, the narrator tells us that he won't say any more except that she willingly forgave her uncle (for devising the opportunity to sleep with Troilus), and finally she 'gan to pleye' with him and 'Pandarus hath fully his entente' (III. 1555–82). Perhaps Wetherbee might have added that the word *thrust* was used much earlier in the poem in an account of a playful encounter between Pandarus and Criseyde (II. 1155). There, Pandarus delivers a letter to Criseyde from Troilus, 'And in here bosom the letter doun he thraste.' Many critics (C. S. Lewis among them) have regarded the relationship between Pandarus and his niece as unexceptionable, as informed by innocent playfulness.[2] I think that a darker undertone is intended and am further persuaded by Wetherbee's pointing out that Chaucer's modelling of the greeting of the day after the night of consummation on some lines from the *Purgatorio* carries a sinister implication:

> And Lucifer, the dayes messager,
> Gan for to rise, and oute hire stremes throwe,
> And estward roos, to him that koude it knowe,
> Fortuna Major.... [III. 1417–20]

The *Purgatorio* passage reads:

> quando i geomanti lor Maggior Fortuna
> veggiono in oriente, innanzi a l'alba,
> surger per via che poco le sta bruna....

This is a prelude to Dante's dream of the Siren. She is ugly, but made beautiful in the sensuous imaginations of those who desire her. Any unease we may feel about Criseyde's behavior with Pandarus immediately after this (and, indeed, more generally about Criseyde) becomes more poignant if we accept the lurking implication of the reference to the Siren.

Wetherbee acknowledges the danger that one can take too far the implication of these references. There are occasions when I think he does strain the argument: the problem is, of course, to what extent Chaucer's quotations from other poets are intended to activate a *total* context; and, to put a further tantalizingly unanswerable question, how much of the context could he count on his audience to recognize? When they hear the news that they must be parted, Troilus and Criseyde are deeply distressed:

> So bittre teeris weep nat, as I fynde,
> The woful Mirra thorugh the bark and rynde. [IV. 1138–39]

The reference is to the story in Ovid of Myrrha's incestuous desire for her father which is gratified by the scheming of her nurse (by then, against Myrrha's better judgement). The weeping Myrrha is changed into a tree, which forever weeps its resin. One could reasonably take the reference to Myrrha simply to be the ultimate example of unending grief which the narrator assumes the lovers will feel.[3] Or one could take it further, as Wetherbee does. He argues that Troilus is sexually innocent, that he is manipulated by Pandarus to fulfill Pandarus' "vicarious needs" against his better judgement. Wetherbee contends that Troilus was drawn from the sexually naive tradition of the Lorris portion of the *Roman de la rose* while Pandarus derived from the tradition of cynical sexuality of de Meun: "Pandarus becomes, in effect, the appetitive element lacking in Troilus's feelings toward Criseyde" (p. 75). If we accept that, and I do not think it is so clear-cut, we are then forced to assume that the act of sexual union in itself is presented as *unnatural* if the Myrrha parallel is taken to its ultimate. It could certainly be countered that the sin lies not in their love but in replacing with their partial love Love itself—that is, the love of God. Their lack of perspective is wrong; they try to make one little room an everywhere. Herein lies the Neo-Platonism.

But to wrench isolated examples from the book is, of course, to distort. Even if I am right in suggesting that on occasion Wetherbee's enthusiasm for the thesis overstretches the argument, it would be quite wrong for the impression to be given that the book is unbalanced in its views. It is marked throughout by deep scholarship and by steadiness of judgement. It is marked, too, by a sense of critical humility, by acknowledgement that it is a worrying matter if ever we think we have sewn up the meaning of a great work of art. *Chaucer and the Poets* is an admirable and stimulating book.

Notes

1. Anne Middleton, "Chaucer's 'New Men' and the Good of Literature in the *Canterbury Tales*," *Literature and Society*, ed. Edward W. Said, *Selected Papers from the English Institute*, n.s. 3 (Baltimore: John Hopkins Univ. Press, 1980), pp. 15–56.

2. C. S. Lewis, *The Allegory of Love* (Oxford: Oxford Univ. Press, 1936), pp. 193–94: "In the banter with which he greets Cryseide next morning, there is humour of a familiar avuncular or parental type, somewhat now discredited."

3. Ovid, *Metamorphoses*, X. 298–502. The conclusion stresses the immortality of the grief: "est honor et lacrimis, stillataque robore murra / Nomen evile tenet nulloque tacebitur aevo."

Classical Psychoanalytic Criticism

Andrew Gordon

Daniel Weiss. *The Critic Agonistes: Psychology, Myth, and the Art of Fiction*. Eric Solomon and Stephen Arkin, eds. Seattle: University of Washington Press, 1985. xii, 270 pp.

The Critic Agonistes is an example of old-fashioned Freudian literary criticism at its best; like a classic car, it still works rather well. The book is worthwhile for those interested in psychoanalytic criticism or for anyone who enjoys literary criticism distinguished by learning both wide and deep, provocative insight, humanistic sensitivity, and elegant style. Daniel Weiss, who died in 1976 at the age of fifty eight, was known for his psychoanalytic study of D. H. Lawrence, *Oedipus in Nottingham* (1962), and for a few classic essays, such as those on Stephen Crane and Saul Bellow. But Weiss wrote a great deal that never saw print. After his death, Eric Solomon and Stephen Arkin, his colleagues at San Francisco State University, discovered in his desk files a thousand pages of manuscript. From them, they gleaned this memorial to the critical talents of Daniel Weiss. Five of the essays—on Crane, Bellow, Faulkner, Lawrence, and Frank O'Connor—have been previously published, but the remaining six—two on Freudianism and the critic, and others on Sherwood Anderson, Hemingway, and Dostoevsky—are printed here for the first time. The editors chose the essays based on excellence, "finished contribution to the general theme of mythic, philosophical, and psychoanalytic literary theory; and concentration on the art of the novel" (p. x). They had to omit essays on Kafka, Fitzgerald, James, Mansfield, Shakespeare, Yeats, and Joyce, which suggests both the range of Weiss's scholarship and the possible need for a companion text.

The publication of this memorial volume raises a few obvious questions. First, since the essays were written between 1959 and

1975, have they been superseded by the enormous bulk of scholarship on these particular novelists and by the rapid evolution of literary criticism—particularly the psychoanalytic variety—in the interim? Second, have the editors really done the writer a service by printing some material which the author either intended to revise or never meant to publish?

As to the possible obsolescence of the material, Weiss was never a critic to tack with current fashion. His approach is that of "classical" psychoanalysis: make the unconscious motivations conscious, and identify the core fantasies and neurotic symptoms supposedly at work in the text. He focuses on the characters or the author, rather than attempting to psychoanalyze the transaction between the reader and the text. Richard Ellmann, in his foreword, says that Weiss's criticism "alternated between penetrating analysis of authors' minds and brilliant close readings of their texts" (p. v). And the editors note: "If he does not seem to show signs in these pages of being overly involved in contemporary debates about psychoanalytic procedure or criticism, if he seems indifferent to object theory, French tailoring of Freud, and the various structures . . . the clever interpreter can deconstruct down to, it is because Weiss was classical by temperament and, having staked out a problem area that fascinated him, stayed within it" (p. xii). This is not to say that Weiss is a dogmatic or programmatic psychoanalytic critic. His interest in philosophy, for example, makes him attempt to square Schopenhauer and Nietzsche with Freud. His interpretations are always tempered by his wide reading and awareness of the cultural and historical context in which literature is produced. And he is not afraid to move from psychoanalytic interpretations to aesthetic value judgments. Some of the pioneering essays—especially those on Crane, Bellow, and Lawrence—are filled with a sense of intellectual discovery and so well wrought that they remain a pleasure to read. Such writing does not date badly.

As to the second question, the publication of posthumous, sometimes incomplete or unrevised material is a common practice in both literature and criticism: witness the continued scavenging of Hemingway and the recent edition of Nabokov's lectures. Solomon and Arkin have chosen to publish the essays with only minor editorial corrections and "a few omissions to avoid redundancy" (p. x). There is, however, some repetition Weiss might have wished to remove had he known that the essays would be published together. Some of his metaphors and puns are recycled: "as regular and predictable as the life cycle of the housefly" (p. 175 and p. 242); "the skeleton in the closet has become the bat in the belfry" (p. 52 and p. 229); "between the devil and the bourgeoisie" (p. 42 and p. 234). And several sentences about the work of art as sublimation and compensation are repeated twice (p. 49 and p. 122). But these are minor cavils. Even the previously unpublished material seems polished and reads well. The editors have done both Weiss and the reader a service by collecting these essays in book form.

The first two essays concern "Freudianism and the Critic," and constitute Weiss's defense of psychoanalytic criticism and his acknowledgment of its limitations. The opening essay, "The Critic Agonistes," was written last: in 1975, just a year before his death. Unfortunately, it is so heavily metaphoric that the style sometimes overwhelms the substance. Weiss cannot resist a pun, even a bad one: "ideologues, demagogues, and gog magogs" (p. 6), and "Oedipus Rex—or oedipal wreckage" (p. 23). Such lapses are a pity, particularly since his usual prose style is positively elegant. The argument, however, remains worthwhile. Weiss admits that he was wary of psychoanalysis for a long time but finally decided that it was not simply a new sort of tool for the literary critic but something describing the conditions that have formed the consciousness of both artist and critic. Psychoanalysis is therefore inescapable for both the writer and his interpreter. The artist is close to the vivid fantasy life of the infantile psyche; in objectifying his unconscious, he presents a mirror to us and becomes our "alter ego, alter id, alter superego and all the interstices between" (p. 11).

Weiss distinguishes between three concentric circles in his approach to a text: the outer circle is the text as aesthetic phenomenon, belonging to the world; the middle circle is the text as a product of individual consciousness and craft; and the inner circle is the text as a product of unconscious urgencies. He contrasts Joyce's *Portrait of the Artist*, which develops its hero from the inner circle outward, with Mann's *Death in Venice,* which moves in the opposite direction, from the level of aesthetics downward into the inner circle of the psyche.

Next, Weiss dismisses the Freudian theory of art as disease, which he finds inadequate to account for the power of art, preferring instead Nietzsche's conception of art as moral protest, a crime against society. The artist as criminal represents our urge toward freedom. In perhaps the central statement of the essay, Weiss says: "There is no such thing as an unbound, entirely free mind. What one admires as a free mind, one that explores the alternatives of existence in life and art, represents simply the struggles of a bound mind to free itself from the tyrannies of culture" (p. 18). Thus the title, "The Critic Agonistes," evoking Milton: what Weiss admires in both the artist and the critic is the heroic impulse to struggle against our inherent limitations, the chains of both the unconscious and culture. He also seems to be suggesting that, like Samson, we all work in the dark.

Weiss explains that the Freudian critic approaching a tragic action "must first clear the immediate foreground of its apparent claim to a realistic motivation, and reestablish the drama's relations with the underlying fantasy" (pp. 23–24). The tragic hero, he believes, is obsessive, dominated by his superego, and usually unaware of his unconscious aims. But Weiss doesn't find such possibility for writing tragedy today. Because the modern writer has had to accept the notion of the unconscious, "his business is exposure.... He turns his violated personality inside out and shows us its lining" (pp. 29–30). This self-contemplation leads more toward comedy than tragedy.

The second essay, "The Black Art of Psychoanalytic Criticism," considers the relevance and limitations of psychoanalysis applied to literature. Weiss skims briefly over the various psychological assumptions of different historical periods. He sees William James and Freud reacting against the biologically deterministic psychology of the late nineteenth century: James, by emphasizing the importance of the conscious mind, and Freud, by asserting the significance of the unconscious. Freud shifts the focus from the conflict between man and his environment to the conflict within the mind. The artist has a special role in Freud's system, as "the comedian of reality," transcribing intrapsychic dramas into conscious form: "The unconscious does tell the conscious mind the truth, but it tells it, especially in poetry, in the form of a beautiful lie" (p. 44).

Weiss does not deviate here very much from the standard Freudian line: the artist successfully overcomes neurotic symptoms, sublimating his drives in a work in which others may participate. Through his art, he also possesses or incorporates the world and experiences a sense of "oceanic reunion." The price he pays for his greater sensitivity is greater susceptibility to trauma.

Weiss admits the faults of psychoanalytic criticism: it is perhaps too committed to explaining present action through past events, too free with the catchwords of neurosis, and too ready to reduce art to infantilism. The primary virtue of such criticism is that it reaffirms the subjective nature of experience. Moreover, because psychoanalysis has affected contemporary art, so that works tend increasingly to imitate psychic reality rather than "literal observed reality," psychoanalytic criticism has become indispensable. "We must, in order to interpret works of art whose stage is the mind itself, become experts in the natural history of the mind. If this be a black art, then we critics must make the most of it" (p. 54).

After the two essays establishing his psychoanalytic framework, the next six are practical applications of his approach to American fiction. In his study of Stephen Crane, Weiss takes issue with John Berryman's excessively "biocentric" interpretation of Crane's fiction. Where Berryman sees parricidal impulses everywhere in the fiction, Weiss sees instead "hostility directed against an older sibling, for the mother's love" (p. 63). Weiss's argument seems persuasive, considering that Crane's father died when he was eight, that Crane had thirteen older siblings, and that the father figures in his fiction are usually distant, weak, or absent. Unlike Berryman, Weiss prefers to begin with the psychological dynamics of the work and only then return to the author's life for corroborative data.

Weiss interprets *The Red Badge of Courage* as a study of fear, of anxiety-defense mechanisms working under the pressure of war.

He draws on psychoanalytic observations concerning war stress and the fear of death by Freud, Gregory Zilboorg, Abram Kardiner, Herbert Spiegel, and others. In Weiss's view, young Henry Fleming wants to liberate himself from his overprotective mother and prove himself to his dead father. The army becomes his substitute parents, providing him with a temporary sense of invulnerability. But the first time the army proves vulnerable, Henry flees from battle in panic. For the rest of the action, Henry swings between oral passivity and oral aggression, but his natural tendency is to revert to passivity. By becoming a flagbearer in battle at the end, Henry moves from actor to spectator and overcomes his fear. The flag is a trophy of his "new invulnerability, a renewed reunion with the parents" (p. 94).

In Crane's "The Blue Hotel," Weiss also reads a fixation at the oral phase, but exaggerated in the Swede into full-blown manic-depressive psychosis. Like Henry, the Swede is in battle and swings violently between passivity and activity. But the battle is in the Swede's mind, a defense against his own homosexual aggressions. In his paranoid delusions of persecution, he provokes the very threat he fears.

"Shedding His Sickness in Books: Sherwood Anderson's Literary Case History" interprets Anderson as a sort of poor man's D. H. Lawrence. Both Lawrence and Anderson are "prophets of sexual hygiene" and both seem arrested in a permanent adolescence. However, Weiss strongly prefers Lawrence. He finds Anderson's works much too symptomatic of the author, filled with unassimilated and poorly understood neurotic elements. Only occasionally is Anderson capable of transforming neurotic symptoms into symbolic action, as in the story "The Man Who Became a Woman," where he demonstrates that he could be "an intuitive psychological writer of fiction on a level of achievement equal to Mann and Lawrence" (p. 132). Weiss's comparison of Anderson and Lawrence illuminates the work of both authors. This is a critical strategy he favors; elsewhere in the volume he compares Joyce with Mann, Bellow with Kafka, Crane with Hemingway.

"Ernest Hemingway: The Stylist of Stoicism" is an appreciation written in 1962, shortly after Hemingway's death. Weiss admires his style but dismisses his stoic philosophy as "a masochistic version of Christian doctrine denied the unction of salvation" (p. 135). Weiss does not believe that Hemingway's traumatic wound in World War II was as crucial to the development of his character and art as Philip Young would have it. Hemingway was predisposed to machismo, masochism, and morbidity because of his boyhood idealization of his cruel father and his contempt and hostility for his mother. His war wound merely reconfirmed Hemingway's attraction to violence. War was always the norm for Hemingway, which made him a superb artist for wartime but constitutionally incapable of retooling for peace.

The Hemingway style Weiss sees as a defense, a form of emotional detachment, "a sort of insulation around a core of lacerated nerves" (p. 159). And the Hemingway hero is a version of Hemingway's earliest image of his father, until, "in the end, Hemingway's sense of his separate identity . . . coalesced absolutely with that of his father" (p. 151). Finally, Weiss partially excuses Hemingway's "imbalances" by referring to the strange imbalances of his literary epoch. "He, along with his contemporaries, was a man walking in a tilted world" (p. 159).

The two essays on Faulkner which follow are myth criticism, not particularly psychoanalytical, so they sit a little awkwardly with the rest of the book. "Lyrical Darwinism and the Mythical World of Faulkner's *The Hamlet*" deals with the general topic of "the distasteful" in the modern novel and Faulkner's way of rationalizing such material "into the province of art" (p. 161). The seamy side of life began to be emphasized in fiction through the rise of literary naturalism in the late nineteenth and early twentieth century, but such fiction was eventually rejected because it valued heredity and environment over human character. When twentieth-century anthropology, folklore, and myth reaffirmed the tragic dignity and ritual significance of "the simplest, the basest, even the most sordid human action," it inspired a literature that transformed naturalism into what Weiss calls "lyrical Darwinism" (p. 166), as in Joyce's *Ulysses*. Weiss finds this mythicizing tendency also at work in Faulkner's fiction, redeeming a novel like *The Hamlet* from "its picayune squalors and corruptions" (p. 169). Faulkner observes a period of decline and fall in the South, similar to that observed by the Greek poet

Hesiod, a time "when all the heroes and demigods are gone from the land" (p. 168). "William Faulkner and the Runaway Slave" applies myth criticism to two stories, "Was" and "Dry September," both of which exhibit the black in the role that Faulkner often ascribed to him, as "ritual object" and sexual totem.

Weiss's pioneering study, "Caliban on Prospero: On Saul Bellow's *Seize the Day*," is one of the first indepth psychoanalytic interpretations of Bellow's fiction. He considers *Seize the Day* as an important contribution to the theme of father-son conflict in fiction, and he introduces the term "moral masochism" (from Bernhard Berliner) to the discussion of Bellow's protagonists. According to Weiss, there has always been a psychological ambivalence in father-son relationships, but in the post-Freudian era that ambivalence has come to occupy center stage. He compares the neurotic relationship between Tommy Wilhelm and his father with the father-son tensions that appear in Kafka's "Letter to His Father." And he describes Wilhelm as a moral masochist, for whom suffering has become a way of life. Whereas Freud thought of masochism as an *intrapersonal* problem, Berliner redefined it as a disturbance in *interpersonal* relationships; the character must suffer to be worthy of the love of a sadistic and rejecting parent. Wilhelm turns himself into a sacrificial victim and degrades himself in front of his father and everyone else. But he is filled with repressed hostility toward his father which is choking him: Wilhelm is chronically short of breath. The novel's moving but ambiguous final scene, in which Wilhelm weeps at the funeral of a total stranger, has provoked perhaps more different readings than any other incident in Bellow's fiction. Weiss reads the dead man in the coffin as "the symbolic fulfillment of two alternatives—the wish to destroy the hated father and the wish to be destroyed" (p. 210), and he claims that through Wilhelm's weeping he is purged of both wishes. This is a persuasive reading, although not one that I necessarily endorse: Bellow's novels are characteristically open-ended and encourage the reader to project his own desires onto the action. Here is one possible instance where reader-response criticism could build on Weiss's classical psychoanalytic reading.

The book concludes with three essays on European fiction.

Classical Psychoanalytic Criticism

"D. H. Lawrence: The Forms of Sexual Hunger" is an excerpt from *Oedipus in Nottingham*. Weiss interprets Lawrence as a man torn, in both his life and his art, between his mother and his father. For Lawrence, his mother represented the mind and his father the blood. Thus Weiss equates "Lawrence's rejection of mental consciousness with his rejection of his old incest fixation on his mother" (p. 220). In contrast to critics who consider Lawrence the high priest of heterosexual copulation, Weiss sees a driven quality in Lawrence's obsessive heterosexuality, as if, in fleeing from the image of the father, he became a slave to women. And he notes the constant coitus anxiety in Lawrence's imagery, in which sex is always violent annihilation and carries an underlying fear of being destroyed or castrated. This anxiety culminates in Lawrence's fascination with martyrdom and mutilation, with the crucified and resurrected Christ and the mutilated but still phallic Osiris.

In "Freedom and Immortality: Notes from the Dostoevskian Underground," Weiss returns to his philosophical interest in the idea of freedom, as expressed in the opening essay, "The Critic Agonistes." He begins with a general question: "Why is it that philanthropy and material progress have always drawn catcalls from the artist?" (p. 234) And he cites the example of Dostoevsky: Freud admired Dostoevsky but was disappointed that Dostoevsky "apparently turned his back on freedom" (p. 230). Weiss decides that there is no real quarrel between Dostoevsky and Freud—they approach the same psychological truths, the one as an artist and the other as a scientist. Both value human freedom and define that freedom as "the possession of one's own unfettered consciousness, for better or for worse" (p. 231). Dostoevsky opposed nineteenth-century scientific positivism and unearthed "out of his own dark impulses" a psychology which anticipates Freud's (p. 240). Because Dostoevsky was a pessimist about himself and about humanity, he refused to believe in disinterested brotherly love and "could find everything in his psychology except utopia" (p. 240).

"Freudian Criticism: Frank O'Connor as Paradigm," composed first (1959), as the first essay was composed last, brings the book full circle, back to the opening concern with the merits and pitfalls of psychoanalytic criticism. Weiss begins this essay by stressing the problems of such criticism: psychoanalysis tends to ignore the aesthetic qualities of works and to reduce all art to endless repetitions of a few basic acts. It is too directed to the artist rather than to the work, and it seems to treat art as evidence of disease. Weiss cautions against "the temptation to ditch the aesthetic altogether," or, as he wittily puts it, to "throw out the baby with the birth trauma" (p. 244). How then should the critic proceed? "At its best, then, psychological criticism should constitute a bureau of tragic or comic weights and measures, testing in the work of art for the organic, psychologically valid material. . . . Its amateur function should be analytic rather than reductive and therapeutic" (pp. 247–48).

Having considered the critic's role, he then wonders about "the artist's complicity in this psychoanalysis of art" (p. 250). Weiss decides that the artist can neither ignore Freud's findings nor consciously delve too far into his unconscious. He illustrates his premise by discussing two stories by O'Connor, "My Oedipus Complex" (1952) and "Judas" (1948). The former is a consciously contrived Oedipal comedy, but mere slapstick, whereas the latter Weiss considers far superior, a more moving and true, because more psychologically profound, Oedipal comedy. Curious as to the genesis of the stories, Weiss wrote O'Connor, who replied that he was unaware when he wrote "Judas" that it dealt with an Oedipal situation, even though he had the same sort of intense attachment to his mother that his hero had, but that "My Oedipus Complex" was deliberately written as a parody of Freudian notions. This seems to prove Weiss's point: too much conscious tampering with the unconscious will weaken the work; "the writer must pursue his unconscious bents in blindness" (p. 250). So we return to the image of blind Samson, of the artist (and presumably the critic) working in the dark.

The Critic Agonistes reemphasizes the complex and tricky relationship between the conscious and the unconscious, and the ways in which the best art is a shot in the dark. The book is a welcome reminder of the continuing value of classical psychoanalytic interpretation, especially when such criticism is applied with caution and wit, deep scholarship, delight in aesthetic effects, and humanistic concern. Daniel Weiss's work is worth preserving: like a classic car, its value may well appreciate with time.

The Satirists Swift and Pope Reassessed

Vincent Carretta

Allan Ingram. *Intricate Laughter in the Satire of Swift and Pope*. London: St. Martins, 1986. x, 206 pp.

Ellen Pollak. *The Poetics of Sexual Myth: Gender and Ideology in the Verse of Swift and Pope*. Chicago: University of Chicago Press, 1985. xii, 239 pp.

Allan Ingram's object in *Intricate Laughter in the Satire of Swift and Pope* is to answer the questions he raises at the end of "The Uneasy Chair: Laughter, Satire and The Eighteenth Century," the first of the five chapters that compose his book: "What do we do when we laugh? what do we do to others? what do we do to ourselves? Above all, what care can we observe in the art of the writer who would attempt to handle the laugh?" (p. 39).

Ingram sees the eighteenth-century satirist faced with a dilemma framed by the opposing views of Thomas Hobbes and Anthony Ashley Cooper, the 3rd Earl of Shaftesbury, on the cause of laughter. For Hobbes, laughter results from the "sudden glory" we experience when we recognize the inferiority of others to ourselves. Laughter, prompted by self-interest and vanity, promotes the separation of members of society and is essentially vicious in nature. For Shaftesbury, however, laughter leads to the fellowship of man because the recognition of folly in others helps us to recognize it in ourselves and thus to correct it. We can change our behavior because we operate in a world of divine benevolence. Shared laughter polishes social intercourse and helps us accept the reality of a greater unity presiding over our daily action. To Hobbes, the laugh is a signal of pessimism, to Shaftesbury of optimism.

The distinction will be familiar to most of the readers of this book. Familiar, too, will be Ingram's brief discussion of the treatment of Horatian vs. Juvenalian satire in John Dryden's *Discourse Concerning the Original and Progress of Satire*. Dryden, too, is seen as in a dilemma, which he unsatisfactorily tries to escape by positing an ideal victim who shares with the satirist the pleasure of the attack, the "fine raillery." From the attention Ingram pays to Hobbes, Shaftesbury, and Dryden one might expect that *Intimate Laughter* will be a book about the conscious intentions of satirists who, as they sat down to write, chose either a Hobbesian or Shaftesburyian approach. Fortunately, Ingram does not believe that satirists operate in so clumsily deductive a way. Unfortunately, however, Ingram almost completely ignores satirists' direct statements about their own intentions. Or when he does consider such statements, as in Dryden's case, he chooses not to test the statement against the practice.

Indeed, as becomes clearer in Chapter 2, "Acts of Exclusion: Laughter and the Satiric Victim," Ingram's main interest is in arguing that Swift and Pope's satires illustrate later theories of developmental psychology, particularly those of Henri Bergson, Sigmund Freud, and R. D. Laing. The approach will not startle many readers, as Ingram occasionally acknowledges. But at times Ingram goes too far, as in his argument that the reader's watching Corinna disassemble herself in Swift's "A Beautiful Young Nymph Going to Bed" is equivalent to the reader's raping her: "To laugh at is to violate as completely as to rape, for both insist on treating the person as object" (p. 46). Ingram shows little interest in the effect of tradition on the satires of Swift and Pope. Nor does he consider the intriguing problem of why some people, particularly Colley Cibber, seemed to feel a compulsion to become satiric victims. Cibber even played a role satirizing himself in an early Popean dramatic farce.

In Chapter 3, "Showing the Teeth: Laughter in Society," Ingram turns from victim to audience to argue that "the group that laughs together stays together" (p. 89) because shared laughter unifies them against the excluded victim. When satirists seem to attack groups rather than individuals, "we are being shown apparent unity within groups which becomes, on closer examination, an array rather of disunity as each individual blindly follows his own inclination and fights for his own individual ends" (p. 94). The satirist is the optimistic Shaftesburyian mocking the selfish Hobbesians. The satirist, Ingram says in the next chapter, "The Playground of the Mind," remains Shaftesburyian because his attack is basically ludic, in the sense in which John Huizinga uses the term. The dangerous is rendered controllable, and any authority undercut is replaced by the alternative authority of the satirist. Swift, for Ingram, is a more sophisticated satirist than Pope in his use of play:

> Swift's poems of self-negation, therefore, are also, in a way in which Pope's poetry is not, poems of genuine self-effacement, for the reader is being asked to respond not to the satirist putting his own case, but to him standing in for the reader. When we affirm, then, when we laugh, it is the signal not of our endorsement of this or that political or personal attack striking home, but of our having been successfully brought close to the unthinkable for ourselves. The sound of this laughter is not the clink of the coins of bribery, but the celebration of childhood play properly transferred to the adult world. [p. 151]

The satirist becomes a father-figure, "the steadying adult" (p. 152), for the reader. Consequently, "with satire, and with satiric poetry especially, we should expect to experience the harmony of form coinciding with the harmony of a psychological steadying, and to express our experience through laughter" (p. 153).

In his final chapter, "Glory, Jest and Riddle," Ingram nominates Democritus, the laughing god, as the archetype of the ideal satirist. The god-like side of the actual satirist thinks about life and finds it comic; the human side feels and finds life sad. Hence, another dilemma: "The satirist's duty [is] to feel as a man while judging as a god" (p. 164). Laughter allows the father-figure, the god-like satirist, to perform his duty and reassure his "created readers" (p. 154) that this is a Shaftesburyian world after all: "The laugh . . . means we have been brought close to our own human nature, seen its corruption, its absurdity, its tenderness, and now laugh not with contempt but in affirmation of its value and in the certainty that life, despite its corruptions and absurdities, will go on" (p. 181).

Ingram offers us the sunny side of satire. Ignored are the Pope who wrote the last book of the *Dunciad* and the Swift who wrote these lines in *An Epistle to a Lady*:

> If I can but fill my Nitch,
> I attempt no higher Pitch.
> . . .
> Let me, tho' the Smell be Noisom,
> Strip their Bums; let CALEB hoyse'em;
> Then, apply ALECTO's Whip,
> Till they wiggle, howl, and skip.

Ignored, too, are all articles and books written on Swift and Pope since 1973.

No one can accuse Ellen Pollak of not being up-to-date in *The Poetics of Sexual Myth: Gender and Ideology in the Verse of Swift, and Pope*. Published in 1985, Pollak's book not only cites but obviously uses works as recent as several that appeared in 1984. I approached this book with trepidation because the dust-jacket comments label it *brilliant*, a contemporary codeword which often indicates that a book is written in the kind of hyper-critical newspeak incomprehensible to most readers. Pollak's book, however, is clearly written. The only time I ran into trouble was in Chapter 6, "The Difference in Swift," which opens with a mention of Derrida, a name whose mention I generally find equivalent to invoking cloud-compelling Dulness.

Pollak uses the term *myth* "to refer specifically to the representational forms that ideology takes—to the literary and epistemological structures by which certain propositions about the phenomenal world (in this case, women) are made to seem the outgrowth of a strict necessity, consistent with the laws of natural order" (p. 5). Pollak investigates the influence of the myth of passive womanhood, first fully outlined by Mary Wollstonecraft in *A Vindication of the Rights of Woman*, on the poetry of Swift and Pope. Pollak seeks to analyze "the relationship of their writing to their culture's ideological imperatives regarding gender" (p. 19), imperatives that went largely unexamined by authors in the eighteenth century.

Pollak's own unexamined "ideological imperatives," accepted *a priori* as universal verities, are tenets of marxism, Freudianism, and twentieth-century feminism, selectively chosen. We should read Pope and Swift as reflectors of bourgeois values that are more economically than religiously determined; Freud's concept of fetishism (but certainly not his notion of penis envy) is applicable to the eighteenth century; and since the texts of Pope and Swift are "the products of a phallocentric culture and of its authorizing sign-systems and codes" (p. 182), there is little doubt that they are misogynistic.

Although she considers Pope the better poet, Pollak finds Swift the better thinker because he struggles, albeit unsuccessfully, to question his cultural imperatives:

> Meaning, in Swift's texts, is generated not—as it is in Pope's—at the point of poised reconcilation between the contrary terms of a single epistemological or mythic structure (such as between the contradictory nature of Belinda as goddess and tease, or of man as glory and jest); it is produced, rather, at the point where two or more heterogeneous systems of signification meet, engage, and in interacting become the mutual critics of the logic of one another's terms. Conceiving culture as a relative phenomenon, Swift did not presume, with Pope, that anarchy would reign in the absence of social myths and conventions he considered valid or valuable, but rather recognized the potential efficacy of other kinds of orders. [p. 17]

The heart of Pollak's book is her feminist readings of *The Rape of the Lock*, *Epistle to a Lady*, and *Cadenus and Vanessa*, each of which is treated in a separate chapter. Many readers will be irritated by the author's deterministic approach, but they will be irritated in the right way. Granted her premises, Pollak makes a strong case for seeing the *Rape* as a tale about the futility of trying to subvert the myth of passive womanhood, the *Epistle* as a counsel of compromise and domestication to Martha Blount, and *Cadenus* as an inconclusive challenge to the myth. Pope's deceptively easy reconciliations are expressed in heroic couplets; Swift's indeterminate challenges occur in works of "metaphysical and narrative collapse" (p. 151). Form follows content. The arguments are too detailed to be recounted here, but they are well worth considering, even if ultimately one does not totally accept them. If we do embrace Pollak's assumptions, however, we are left with a remarkably passive Pope, at best an unquestioning advocate of a false myth and at worst the prisoner of an evil ideology. Either way, Pollak's Pope is very unlike the poet and the man Maynard Mack describes in his recent biography. Mack's Pope is a complex example of what sociologists call a *marginal* man, relegated to the outskirts of society by his appearance, his religion, his profession of satirist, and his politics. Such *marginality*, for Mack, enables Pope to treat those excluded by their gender with sympathy, if not empathy.

Ingram and Pollak share an interest in the differences between Swift and Pope, and both encourage us to revise upward our evaluation of Swift the poet, even though Ingram's poet is a laughing philosopher while Pollak's is more often a brave desponder. Not every reader will accept all of their premises, arguments, or conclusions, but we should welcome their attempts to get us to reconsider the relative merits of two of the greatest poets of eighteenth-century Britain.

Watching Our Language

David Simpson

Cleanth Brooks. *The Language of the American South*. Athens: University of Georgia Press, 1985. x, 58 pp.

Dennis Baron. *Grammar and Gender*. New Haven: Yale University Press, 1986. 238 pp.

These are two very different books. The one, by Cleanth Brooks, contains hardly a single documented fact of the historical sort, very little that we could call "research," and extends to less than sixty pages. Not surprisingly, then, it is graciously written and punctuated by strategic expressions of modesty. Along with the absence of detailed evidence and close argument, there is a strong narrative line sustaining a clear political mythology. The other book, by Dennis Baron, is almost devoid of a narrative dimension, and it is packed with facts. Its ambitions are encyclopaedic, and its wealth of documentation urges us inevitably towards an understanding of the assumptions about gender that seem to reside both in the conventions of the English language and in most people's ideas about it.

I begin with Baron's book, about which there is less to say, largely because it is exhaustively scholarly and convincing. By organizing his chapters topically rather than historically, the author avoids raising the spectre of an evolutionary model according to which our generation is more or less enlightened than others. But his method is relentlessly historical in another sense, as he documents the forms and varieties of arguments about and instances of the relation between language and gender in such detail as to suggest that he must have spent half a lifetime gathering his materials. Baron sifts through some five hundred years of grammatical and etymological speculation, and demonstrates that these apparently disinterested fields of enquiry have often been places where socially instituted sex roles have been defined and refined. The story, for anyone with feminist sympathies, is not an encouraging one. Indeed, the term "feminist" itself fulfils the logic that Baron describes. Can we, in our present world, imagine a need for such a term as "masculinist"? Obviously not, despite the loud cries of some defensive and beleagured males. For Baron shows that the masculine has traditionally existed as the unmarked norm within the English language, against which other entities have had to define themselves. We may laugh at James Harris's eighteenth-century confidence in the justness of this state of affairs, but we have not substantially changed the rules. We no longer credit the derivation of *woman* as *man's woe*, except at drunken dinner parties; and our generation would not find itself significantly motivated to etymologize *femina* as *less faith* (p. 29). But we might feel rather more implicated in other processes that Baron identifies, for example the "double bind" criticism of women as either dangerous innovators (being more susceptible to fashion, etc.), or as linguistic conservatives slowing the development of the language (p. 88); and the litany of instances whereby terms that begin as neutral or positive (*lady, wench, woman*) have rapidly become derogatory (p. 154f.).

Baron, to his credit given the nature of the encyclopaedic enterprise and its claims of credibility, is not given to self-righteous statements of his own enlightened position. In this book the facts speak for themselves. The list of the various attempts since around 1830 to introduce an epicene pronoun into the language is four and a half pages long (pp. 205–09). None of these terms has succeeded in being adopted, and if we are tempted to snigger at the ungainliness or improbability of some of these inventions, then Baron reminds us politely but firmly of the dark significance of this compendium of failed causes, its relation to the "deep antifeminist tradition" that underlies our language and our reflections upon it. He bravely hopes, by way of conclusion, that we may become more sympathetic to "woman's position as a visible and independent linguistic partner in the creation and perpetuation of English" (p. 220). But the logic of his examples points to another probability: that until women conquer men as the Normans did the Saxons, or find some more peaceable but equally powerful access to the male imagination (analogous perhaps to the historical role of international commerce?), things will remain much as they have always been. Guardians of the language are always complaining about the ways in which it is changing. On the matter of gender, Baron's account suggests that the language is monotonously enduring. One might conclude from Baron's book that language reproduces power but does not create it. The power that is in place may be reflected and reinforced by language, but cannot be displaced by an alternative language working alone. This is not to say that we should not try to substitute "chair" or "chairperson" for "chairman"; but it is to suggest that to rest content with merely doing this is not going to change the world. If women do ever share power with men, then men may find it to their advantage to adopt an epicene pronoun. The extension of this argument to the situations of other minorities in the English-speaking world must be obvious to all, even as few will be disposed to ponder it.

Baron's book very clearly invites all sorts of applications to urgent contemporary debates, and it is to his credit that he does not pursue them to the extent of distracting us from the weight of his facts. Cleanth Brooks writes a very different prose, in which salient facts are either ignored or passed over lightly. The insouciance of this very slim volume might be justified by accepting that we have here the text of three lectures, a written record of an impermanent spoken event. If the author of the foreword speaks authoritatively for the nature of these events, they were received as landmarks in the tradition of celebrating southern gentility. Michael Cass tells us that Brooks was "by strictest and warmest definition a gentleman" (p. ix), and a speaker whose "diction was a joy to hear, a worthy vehicle for his ringing peroration, toward the end of the third lecture, against the ugliness that dominates so much of contemporary speech and writing" (p. x).

Brooks's own words are modest and measured by comparison to the foreword, but they do not in any way unsettle what one imagines to have been the hopes and expectations of any audience properly typified by Mr. Cass. Language, for Brooks, embodies "the soul of a people" (p. 2), and most of all in the

American South. Following an introductory burst of modesty—"I am still trying to find out where the Southern dialect really came from" (p. 4)—Brooks passes on to an enthusiastic exposition of his own favorite myth of origination in "the country dialects of southern England" (p. 7). By page 13 this has become a conviction: "The language of the South almost certainly came from the south of England."

The evidence for this idea does not come in the form of a careful scholarly argument, but by way of a few hopeful examples. Prominent among them is the transcription, offered as an analogy to Joel Chandler Harris's literary reproduction of black English, of an 1860 pamphlet purporting to print *The Song of Solomon* as it would have been spoken by "a countryman or villager of Sussex." This pamphlet begins thus: "De song of songs, dat is Solomon's" (p. 8). Brooks's conjecture is that the white settlers arriving in the American South spoke like this, and taught their speech to the black population, which preserved the form longer than did the educationally and socially more volatile whites.

There is an egalitarian surface to Brooks's case here. He contends that the English nobility in the sixteenth century would have almost certainly spoken in dialect, thus implying that what was imported into the American South was a socially cohesive language. This is what the black population learned and continued to reproduce. According to Brooks's model, we may imagine Uncle Remus speaking an English rather close to that of Sir Walter Raleigh. Or at least he might have pronounced some of his words in the same way. Among the many factors that Brooks is unwilling or unable to consider is the question of grammar. He thus sidesteps completely the case put forward, most famously by J. L. Dillard, that Plantation Creole is the origin of modern black English, and that it was and is consistent enough to warrant the attribution of its own separate grammar.[1] Against Dillard's model of separate development, Brooks offers that of a "democratic" paternalism. It seems to me plausible that elements of both these explanations, in the realms of grammar and pronunciation, might be convincingly applied to an account of black English (granting Brooks, for the moment, the benefit of the doubt about his basic premise); Brooks's dishonesty consists in presenting his contribution without giving any sense of the complex whole to which, if valid, it might belong. He thus implies that the most essential characteristic of black English (the only one he bothers to mention) is what it took from the original, linguistically classless white settlers. But if the prototype of southern English were indeed classless, and if language is really the soul of a people, then one cannot fail to wonder how the old South developed a society so vividly marked by class and race consciousness.

Professional linguists will surely have a host of objections to Brooks's conclusions. How would he explain the degree to which American English as a whole is marked by the tendency to pronounce *t* and *th* as *d*, not in uniquely frontal positions, giving us Wallace Stevens's "noble rider"? How did this habit pervade those parts of America definitely not settled by the people of Sussex? Most critically, why does Brooks assume without question that what he reads in literature is an accurate rendering of speech? Perhaps it often is an accurate rendering, but how do we know, and when? Far too often, the Snopeses and Remuses of fiction are judged "real" just because they are different; the writer sets up a narrative norm and then departs from it for specific, local effects. I would not myself advance the extreme case that such transcriptions are never truthful; but I would be even more reluctant to assume that they always are.

What we have here is a model of social cohesion insinuated by way of an incomplete and unsubstantiated account of language. This becomes even clearer as Brooks goes on to discuss southern writers, whose strength, he contends, "stems from their knowledge of and rapport with the language spoken by the unlettered"; thus the best of them "have never held in contempt the speech of the folk or used it only for comic effects" (p. 17). I would happily concur with Brooks's definition of the best, discounting those writers who *have* used dialect for comic effect. But I would find it hard to endorse the idea of an essentially southern literature whose defining feature is a critical dismantling of the boundaries of class and race. At the most literal level, Brooks's case is that differences are *represented* by these writers, whether or not they agree with them; but beyond this fairly acceptable idea (itself open to criticism: which differences? all of them?), Brooks indulges in a romantic populism that some may find implausible and others objectionable. In approving southern writers' disdain for the fastidiously polite, for "foolishly incorrect theories of what constitutes good English" (p. 53)—Brooks stands in the tradition of nineteenth-century Whig populism, for which a measure of demotic color could hide a multitude of inegalitarian propositions. His scorn for "an insistence on spelling pronunciations," for example, fails to acknowledge that for Noah Webster, the most famous exponent of the policy of conforming spelling to speaking, the purpose of the project was to make the language more available to others besides the better educated members of the ethnically dominant group. It would be hard not to share in Brooks's disapproval of the jargon of professionalism and special interest in modern American English—"the propagation of bureaucratese, sociologese, and psychologese" (p. 53)—or in his distaste for the strenuous grandiloquence of so much American public speaking, which seldom chooses to "help along" when it can "facilitate." I at least have some sympathy for the idea that "the occasional use of *ain't*" is less offensive than "the bastard concoctions from a Latinized vocabulary produced by people who never studied Latin" (p. 53). But the alternative to the modern condition that Brooks harks back to is an organicist, agrarian ideal in which all serious investigation of (as opposed to recognition of) difference is suppressed. No writer swaggered more vociferously and located himself more insistently as one of the boys than Walt Whitman (not, of course, a figure within the parameters of Brooks's topic); and, arguably, no American writer is more ignorant or repressive of the empirical dynamics of social interaction in the America of his time. It takes more than a racy vocabulary to make a real man of the people; not can it be assumed that every superficially fastidious speaker is an élitist. Brooks makes the problems of his position yet more apparent in selecting Yeats as "the great poet of our century" (p. 53), and in defining this greatness in terms of Yeats's commitment to "the unwritten literature of the folk." He quite fails to perceive or communicate the tensions apparent in Yeats's romantic alliance between the "peasantry" and the "hard-riding country gentlemen,"[2] an alliance designed to cover over the real state of sublunary Ireland, with its struggles between Protestant landowners and Catholic peasants. This "great poet of our century" either ignored or scorned, in pursuit of his conservative social model, the unstable middle ground in which emerging and declining factions were struggling for self-definition and power in something we may loosely call the "middle class." Brooks's diatribe against the language of professionalism is mounted in this same Yeatsian spirit, and one does not have to be a defender of professionalism to suggest that its problems call for an analysis very different from that here offered. At least since Samuel Johnson and probably before, commentators have been lamenting the rise of factions and special interests and their effects upon the language. But the plea for a prelapsarian standard of "common" language is merely an obfuscation. I doubt very much whether peasants and aristocrats ever spoke the same language; but the idea that they might have is appealing to conservative minds because it is an easy image of identity and common interest imposed upon the historical facts—and they are facts—of a near-absolute social, economic and cultural distinction. Brooks's "bureaucratese" and "psychologese" exist because there are factions that speak them, some of which have become powerful and are thus able to persuade others that there are advantages to speaking their languages. We may wish that some of these factions did not exist, or were not as powerful as they are, but wishing will not make it so. No one is more tired than I am of hearing about "softwear" and "bite," but the computer revolution will not go away, nor can I hope to understand it and those caught up in it by mere disdain.

The crucial mythological construct that holds together Brooks's narrative is that of the South, *the* South. The first lecture does confess its limitations in this respect, declaring its focus as "Coastal or Lowland Southern" (p. 6) rather than other dialects of the region. But this qualification is forgotten as we go on to read about *the* South. Brooks's choice of paradigm is itself significant. His early, prominent examples come from Charleston, South Carolina, a city whose region is perhaps less marked than any other, besides tidewater Virginia, by the Scots-Irish immigrations that have surely had more effect than most in forming the cultures and characters, and perhaps the languages, of so many parts of the southern states. Brooks writes as if there were no non-plantation South: and the non-English white population whose prominence is apparent in every southern telephone directory is even more tellingly displaced from this account than are the speakers of black English. Brooks claims to describe "our common language, in all its variety, complexity, and richness" (p. 54), but the language he details is anything but varied and complex. All too often Brooks lays claim to whatever is colorful, regardless of detail. The transcription of Willie Stark's speech in *All the King's Men* looks to me like a version of mid-nineteenth-century "tall-talk," associated with the western (Kentucky-Missouri) frontier; but it satisfies Brooks as "intensely Southern" (p. 26). Similarly, Longstreet's *Georgia Scenes* is here described without any reference to its use of locutions that were, in the nineteenth century, widely associated with New England, perhaps reflecting the New England origins of many of the early settlers of Georgia. To admit this would perhaps strain the image of *the* South. On other occasions, terms that are or were verifiably pan-American are cited as distinctively southern. Allen Tate's use of "critter" is, for Brooks, "intensely local" (pp. 36–37). But this word in one or another of its various forms has been a stereotype in the literary depiction of common speech since at least the early 1800s, and it is not restricted to or associated particularly with the southern states.[3]

As I have said before, Brooks tends to equate literary sources with the language that was actually spoken, thus missing entirely any sense of the problems raised by the existence of conventions for the representation of demotic speech. Does it not make a difference to our reading of Burns, for example, to learn that he employed a literary version of the common speech, rather than the thing itself?[4] But this is a minor problem, compared to Brooks's near-total investment in the image of a unitary South, *the* South. We wonder in vain, unenlightened by Brooks's pages, about the linguistic status of the Louisiana French, and about how many of the Mississippi Choctaw are monoglot, or bilingual, or completely anglicized; about the relations between Gullah and "polite" Charleston speech; about the different kinds of English spoken by blacks *and* whites in the southern states. If these be thought of as over-strenuous demands to be made upon a slim volume of sixty or so pages by a literary critic, then let the reader ponder the pretensions of this book's title, *The Language of the American South*. The definite articles are spurious; there is no such language, and no such entity. No one would contest the idea that some southern speakers might have learned some locutions from speakers of southern British English, but to focus exclusively upon this paradigm must seem a gross misrepresentation of the linguistic state of affairs. What we need, above all, is facts, facts of the sort that can be learned, for example, from a recent anthology of essays titled *Language in the British Isles*.[5] Note the absence of the definite article. Here, among many other such facts, we learn that in 1971 there were over half a million native speakers of Welsh, and some 90,000 of Scottish Gaelic (p. 257); that the speaking of the second was on the increase in the lowland counties in the period 1961–1971, while declining in its traditional homeland (p. 499); that inflected Romani is still spoken by two to five hundred people in north-central Wales (p. 367). We read of Punjabi and Urdu speakers, of West Indian creole and British black English, as well as of speakers of other languages that most English people have never heard of: Manx, Shelta, Polari, and so on. To discover these things is an education in all the things that our upbringing within the dominant faction of our culture—whether British or American—has excluded.

Perhaps a similar compendium exists for the southern states of America. If not, it could surely be compiled. These matters are not irrelevant to literary criticism; they are the basic materials without which a literary critic ought to be ashamed to speak about common languages, the soul of language, the social cohesiveness of language, and so forth. Some detailed understanding of the interactions that differentiate one southern speaker from another in terms of origin, race, class and occupation is surely a necessary preliminary to sound literary judgments. To conduct even simple literary criticism, we cannot just read literature; for how, then, could we ever discover what was *not* written about, but could have been? The unitary identity of the southern states is a favorite motif in the rhetoric of northern prejudice; unfortunately, it is a concept shared by some southerners. Neither seems to me to do much of a service to the peoples of the southern states, and neither advances an understanding of their languages.

Notes

1. J. L. Dillard, *Black English: Its History and Usage in the United States* (New York: Random House, 1972).
2. *The Collected Poems of W.B. Yeats*, 2nd ed. (London: Macmillan, 1950, 1969), p. 400.
3. See the *Dictionary of American Regional English*, ed. Frederic G. Cassidy, Vol. 1, A–C (Cambridge: Harvard Univ. Press, 1985), p. 852.
4. See Raymond Bentman, "Robert Burns' Use of Scottish Diction," in *From Sensibility to Romanticism: Essays Presented to Frederick A. Pottle*, eds. Harold Bloom and F. W. Hilles (New York: Oxford Univ. Press, 1965), pp. 239–58.
5. *Language in the British Isles,* ed. Peter Trudgill (Cambridge: Cambridge Univ. Press, 1984).

Providence and Poststructuralism

Roger B. Henkle

Barbara Hardy. *Forms of Feeling in Victorian Fiction.* Athens: Ohio University Press, 1985. 215 pp.

Thomas Vargish. *The Providential Aesthetic in Victorian Fiction.* Charlottesville: University Press of Virginia, 1985. xi, 250 pp.

These are times in which we seem to be engaged in two separate dialogues in the criticism of Victorian fiction. Thomas Vargish's *The Providential Aesthetic* and Barbara Hardy's *Forms of Feeling in Victorian Fiction* come before us in a context of critical works such as Catherine Gallagher's *The Industrial Reformation of English Fiction,* J. Hillis Miller's *Fiction and Repetition,* Peter Brooks's *Reading for the Plot,* and the several studies of nineteenth-century novels in Terry Eagleton's "Rereading Literature" series. The latter join with the vital works in feminist criticism of Victorian culture to constitute a dialogue in which literature is understood to be an expression of complexly inscribed ideology, and in which configurations of desire, repression, gender, and class relations account not only for characterization and imagery, but for structure and strategy. The Vargish and Hardy books address Victorian fiction from a markedly different set of assumptions: Vargish is concerned with the operations of the aesthetic derived from Providential order, without considering that order as a function of a particular class or gender orientation; Hardy is interested in examining the articulation of feeling in the novels, without reference to psychological categories.

There is no reason, of course, why we should all talk about fiction in the same sets of terms; pluralism is one of the foundations of the critical enterprise. Still, the disjuncture of approaches seems all the more striking in a time when we are self-conscious about the jousting of methodological "schools" or "trends"; one recalls George Levine's determination to position himself with reference to Derrida and Barthes and Miller at the outset of *The Realistic Imagination*. And, of course, it is possible to dismiss books that eschew the various poststructuralist and psychoanalytic methods as "old-fashioned," or to condemn those that concentrate upon those methods as "unscholarly" or "ahistorical." Indeed, one's first reaction to Vargish's exploration of the important element of belief in the Providential scheme in the early nineteenth century, and to Hardy's subtle examinations of authorial craft, is to acknowledge that they serve as healthy "correctives" to our tendency to apply our own ideologically coded methodologies to the expressions of another era. But is it possible to believe that we can go home again to a study of structures of religious belief, and to representations of subjectivity, without bringing into play our consciousness of, say, the ways in which even the most strongly held beliefs serve the causes of class and gender? To "review" these two books, then, as I propose to do, from a point of view somewhat inconsonant with their own programs, is not to perpetuate that common reviewer's sin of faulting an author for not writing the book as I would have written it, but rather to interrogate each of these scholars with that "other" dialogue in mind. The purpose is to ask how the two approaches problematize each other.

Vargish is not free of that critical self-consciousness that I mentioned; he opens his discussion by sizing up the formidable task of interesting readers in a topic—providential intention—that "they let . . . go either as an essentially uninteresting anachronism or as an aesthetic convention so monolithic and opaque as to be inaccessible to lively critical discourse" (p. 2). Besides presenting us with many instances of the open reference to Providence in Victorian novels, Vargish addresses his task by analyzing works by Charlotte Brontë, Charles Dickens, and George Eliot in which providential order becomes the structuring principle of the text, and by demonstrating that the providential scheme of belief is immanent in the characterization of many of those works. The providential worldview, in which no action or event occurs without its being related to the overarching plan of God, manifests itself in nineteenth-century fiction in the frequent use of coincidence, in "inconsequent actualization" through which a desire or fear of a character is realized "by causal sequences which the characters do not initiate or control" (p. 10), by poetic justice, and by the direct and proportional relationship between outside occurrences (as, say, in Nature) and the spiritual state of the protagonist. The assumptions of the time about providential design acquire such weight and density that they constitute an organization of convictions, "a flexible paradigm of relationships, a sense of the true underlying order of things, a center of value" (p. 24) that creates its own "decorum." The providential decorum thus alludes to a "system of co-ordinates" against which to read the significance of the human action and the progress of events in the novelistic worlds.

As one might expect, Vargish adduces numerous instances of direct reference to the workings of Providence and of the providential decorum in Victorian texts. While this would appear to be the least disputable evidence of the importance of the decorum in a literary text, it is not without its own problematic aspects. The invocation of Providence and even the overt assertion of it in resolving situations may, in fact, betray an equivocal attitude toward the concept. Catherine Gallagher has shown that many novels of the 1840s often use providential design at cross-purposes with other organizing principles of human life. We are also now suspicious of overdetermined texts or passages in texts; feminist criticism has alerted us, for instance, to the implications of profuse elaborations upon female beauty or purity. One of the indicia of a second-rate novel is the frequent recourse to moralizing or philosophizing, often as a means of imposing or resynthesizing the values or worldview that is becoming more difficult to dramatize in convincing psychological or social terms. Vargish runs up against that issue when discussing Dickens's heroines, for though he argues that their function is to provide proof that the true order of things is benign, he acknowledges that their characterizations are so arbitrary that they threaten "conventional concepts of selfhood and defy even minimal requirements for credibility of character in fiction" (p. 111). Are we not then almost compelled at this point to turn to other ways of interpreting these problems of characterology, (such as, say, Fredric Jameson's in *The Political Unconscious*) rather than remain stuck at the critical impasse of saying that a great and complex writer firmly adhered to the providential aesthetic but couldn't render it?

A similar kind of critical problem arises with respect to reading novelistic structures in terms of the providential order. Vargish argues, compellingly, I think, that the resolutions of Dickens's *Bleak House* bring it into accord with providential design, in which there is not only a reward for goodness demonstrated to us, but an assertion of order against the urban chaos. To pose this reading against that of Steven Connor in *Charles Dickens* (published by Basil Blackwell in the Rereading Literature series in 1985) is to contrast most starkly our two contemporaneous modes of critical discourse on the Victorian novel. For Connor comes to the opposite assessment; drawing on Derrida's theory of supplementarity and on analyses of metonymy, he concludes: "The internal deconstruction of the title of the novel echoes that movement which is continually at work within the novel itself, in which the prospect of unity and totality is set up by binary opposites which prove impossible to maintain because of the disrupting, dispersing play of difference which constitutes them, and constitutes the text itself" (p. 88). Connor pays the providential aesthetic no mind, and gives us a reading that too often does not take into account Dickens's involvement—his inscription, if you will—in the beliefs of his time. Thus Vargish's reading provides us with a "corrective." Yet Vargish seems to fail to allow for the effects of the novel. Connor's approach comes much closer to accounting for that powerful retrograde pull of disintegration and constant (failed) reconstitution of centers of order and being that dominate Dickens's great social novels. Even to acknowledge, as Vargish does, that Dickens asserts his providentially inspired scheme of order against the social chaos he presents does not furnish us with a critical procedure for understanding the dynamics of the contradictory effects of these texts.

The Providential Aesthetic does provide us, nonetheless, with an intriguing avenue of literary analysis through the doctrine of immanence. Under this theological reemphasis, providential workings were sought less in outward design than in individual consciousnesses; God was in-dwelling, and His scheme could be perceived in His attention to and care for His creatures. "The concept of providence itself becomes progressively less an image of order, regulation, grand planning, and more an intimate solicitude for individual lives" (p. 21). Vargish argues that Victorian novelists such as Brontë and Dickens, who believed deeply in Providence, yet found it hard to discover providential order in a social world that they perceived to be "corrupt, indifferent, untrustworthy," turned to the psychologies of individuals as the sites of immanent providential design. Since, I believe, Dickens attempts to arrest the deconstructing play of difference that Connor observes in *Bleak House* by constituting a center in the subjectivity of Esther, deferring, in a classic bourgeois maneuver, social issues into the realm of subjectivity, the discovery of immanent providential design in the heroine furnishes us with a source of order that implicitly transcends the individual.

It is within the analysis of providential immanence that the two dialogues of contemporary criticism could be usefully counterposed. When, for example, Vargish discusses *Villette,* he dwells upon the apprehensions of providential immanence that one can discern from Lucy Snowe's accommodation of desire and circumstance, and from the correlatives of that spiritual struggle in nature and in the settings of the novel. As important as it is to trace such a pattern, one misses the insights that psychological theory would provide. *Villette* has proven to be a particularly rich text for feminist analysis, *vide* the work of Sandra Gilbert, Susan Gubar, and Elaine Showalter, and it is ripe for a Lacanian reading, *vide* Christina Crosby. Were one to apply these critiques, when looking at instances of providential immanence in Victorian texts, one could examine the intertwining of influential belief systems and gender psychology. The full force of spirituality in shaping feminine subjectivity in the early nineteenth century remains to be gauged. It is simplistic to say that spirituality functions simply as a reinforcement of patriarchal power—although it surely serves as that. Spirituality provides an extrasocial space for psychological formation, a space that is important to the development of woman's subjectivity in a patriarchally determined culture. Providential immance mystifies the self's struggles within the social order, in ways that create those auratic qualities of subjectivity that resist socializing and politicizing. The woman is so important in Victorian literature because she seems to harbor those qualities of selfhood that cannot be socially coded; her stereotyping as the Angel of Death is not as banal as it might seem. Providential immance also displaces female subjectivity from the social moment; Barbara Hardy points out in her book that Brontë's frequent inclusion of religious allegory in her narrative generalizes moments of emotion, enabling feeling to appear to transcend the particular social occasion that gives rise to it. Such effects, essential to realization of female subjectivity in the time, are not possible without the presence of an ordering belief system such as the providential, which is so pervasive, so structured, so deeply embedded in its historical provenances, that it is as naturalized as the counterveiling social/patriarchal system. Indeed, it took a radical formulation such as Nietzsche's theory of *ressentiment* to abstract it sufficiently to critique it. Vargish's book reminds us that we are in danger of misperceiving the power of the providential belief system when we treat it as merely another strategem played by the dominant social order.

So pervasive is the providential belief system that, as with all such integrated schemes, the fending off of it produces a new set of dynamic structures. Vargish observes that the providential design has an afterlife that persists long after common adherence to it has faded. George Eliot furnishes his case in point; she "took the chief thematic and structural convention of the English novel and adapted it to the representation of a reality uninformed by the premises upon which that convention was founded. In her work we can see the late tendency of Christian providentialism to diffuse and disguise itself in other moral and philosophical paradigms or systems" (p. 165). Somewhat surprisingly, Vargish does not argue that Eliot plays off of the form of providential design in structuring her novelistic worlds, even in *The Mill on the Floss* and *Romola*, but rather he finds evidence of the providential aesthetic in the manner in which characters "structure" their lives. Such "structuring" reaches its most complex stage in *Middlemarch*, where variations on the providential scheme interweave. Bulstrode, Casaubon, Lydgate, and Fred Vincy each believes that he can possess the key to the secret order of things, a "pattern that gives significance to the cosmos" (p. 217). Lydgate's premise, for instance, that science can ultimately discover the nature of life through "primitive tissue," replicates the providential habit of mind in secular terms, and engenders a disposition that produces his schematically false readings of individuals. By Eliot's time, belief in providential immanence has been so corrupted that it produces only egocentricity. As provocative as such an observation may be, it is presented to us detached from analytical or historical explanation. Yes, we can observe a tendency in that direction through Vargish's descriptions of the manifestations of providential thinking in Dickens's late novels, but unless we understand the ways in which providential immanence has actually affected human psychology, we are confronted with scarely more than generalizations. *Middlemarch* literally *invites* us to discriminate among kinds of ordering mentalities, from the fundamentalist evangelical mode of Bulstrode's thinking, to that scientific disposition of Lydgate's. Such a discrimintion can take place only when a critic is willing to consider the ideological formations of nineteenth-century English society. In addition, we cannot possibly fully appreciate George Eliot's treatment of so influential an ordering scheme as the providential, unless we come to terms with her own historical perspective—or, more likely, the several historical perspectives with which she grapples. To do this properly, one needs to bring to bear the historiographical critiques of people such as Stephen Bann in his *The Clothing of Clio*, or Hayden White in *Metahistory*. Again, what I am calling for is not an eclectic salad, in which all the avant garde critical schools are sliced up and mixed in, but an engagement of them to pose the crucial questions about process, dynamics, and context. Without such engagement, the manifestations of a mode of thought as crucial as the providential will appear only as *symptoms* in literary texts.

Barbara Hardy's critical program in *Forms of Feeling in Victorian Fiction* directs us away from those aspects of the novel, such as the worldview, that are manifestly ideological or ideational, and toward the rhetoric of fiction as it presents *feeling*. She examines the modulations of emotional expression in works by Dickens, the Brontës, Thackeray, Eliot, Thomas Hardy and Henry James.

With the authority and lucidity that is Barbara Hardy's special gift, she takes us carefully through passages in the text to demonstrate how effectively the novelist situates an emotional moment in a continuity of interacting feelings, moderating its drama, balancing pathos off against humor or anger. In the most successful exercises of craft, a writer manipulates the affective experiences of reading so that feeling embodies value—it enlarges the expressions of a dramatic moment into an understanding of the complexities of human nature. When Sir Leicester Dedlock lies half-paralyzed in a late scene in *Bleak House,* Dickens's narrator steps back from his often-maligned character to remark:

His formal array of words might have at any other time, as it often had, something ludicrous in it; but at this time it is serious and affecting. His noble earnestness, his fidelity, his gallant shielding of [Lady Dedlock], his general conquest of his own wrong and his own pride for her sake, are simply honourable, manly, and true. [Ch. LVIII]

Hardy observes that "this is mature Dickens, controlled and subtle. Wit and hyperbole are subdued to the occasion.... Sir Leicester's gentlemanliness and formality (images of the legal and legalistic forms which colour the language of the novel) are expressed in his controlled and elaborate crescendo, parenthesis, inversions, and legal phrases. It is not a dead or deadlocked language any more; Dickens uses it to express a 'manliness' larger than 'gentlemanliness'" (p. 55). In noting the modulations of tone and mood, Hardy shows us how emotive affect evokes not simply the poignancy of a moment in an individual character's life, but draws us out into consideration of the values at issue in the entire novel: fellow feeling, courage, integrity. The finest instances of representation of feeling in Victorian writing have that quality.

As for those passages that do not meet such a standard, Hardy's exclusive attention to rhetoric and craft puts her in a position in which she has restricted her own interpretive maneuvering room. Thus, when dealing with the notorious sentimentality of the death of Little Nell, Hardy's only course seems to be to finesse it:

It is hard to accept Huxley's comment in *Vulgarity in Literature* (1930) that Dickens's sentimentality is caused by a failure to think, 'just to overflow, nothing else'. On the contrary, he seems in full control of a quasi-biblical style and a manipulative structure.... The causes of stylistic excess seem matters for conjecture only, though it is true that Dickens usually over-reaches himself when he expresses religious sentiment. The 'momentum of feeling' in the death-bed scene of Nell is not artless. I do not suggest that we can always put our finger on artifice: it seems impossible to decide whether the gross repetitions and solemn appeals in these episodes from *The Old Curiosity Shop* are the accumulated and overcharged results of self-indulgence, or arrangements made in the hope of wringing readers' hearts. There seems to be indulgence and persuasion here. [pp. 67–68]

Once again, an engagement with other critical dialogues would take even such analyses of rhetoric into more profitable directions. John Kucich's *Excess and Restraint in the Novels of Charles Dickens* reframes our discussion of sentimentality in a more generative way; he notes how it both localizes loss (in this case perhaps a felt loss of innocence) to enable it to be safely comprehended, and at the same time elicits a community of feeling. Kucich explores as well the erotic dimension of emotional excess—a particularly crucial consideration in Dickens's treatment of his heroines. By the same token, Hardy's treatment of repetition in Dickens and other Victorian novelists stops at the symptom without finding ways to discover the cause. Perhaps she would find the psychoanalytical accounts of repetition in Peter Brooks and J. Hillis Miller uncongenial, but such approaches yield more nuanced readings of authorial procedure than do conclusions based on failures of craft.

Barbara Hardy is, of course, one of the High Practitioners of New Criticism with all that implies in terms of close readings of texts, adherence to the premise that the novel should be considered as a wholistic entity, sensitivity to the reflexive properties of great art, and allegiance to the liberal school of novel criticism embodied in figures such as W. J. Harvey and E. M. Forster. There are few practitioners as adept as she is; reading her latest book produces, once again, the admiration that one feels when a discriminating, informed, judicious mind applies itself to a sophisticated text. Few critics can analyze George Eliot as ably as Barbara Hardy has, in book after book, and her latest is no exception. One example will have to suffice; speaking of Bulstrode's crisis of conscience over the dying Raffles in *Middlemarch*, Hardy writes:

> [The] rhetoric draws attention to a disintegration which marks and judges secret habits of mind and feeling. Bulstrode has taken over the Christian theological abstractions, to invent and perform the false drama of the hypocrite, and also to play tricks on himself: he is not candid and whole in his inner life. George Eliot's is no common study of hypocrisy, since she does not show a break between the private and public lives, but a break and deception within the consciousness. Bulstrode's desire is segregated from conscience, his passions deceptively imitate a holy choir, his conscience is protected by secrecy, which is no angel. The habit of impersonation is perfectly figured through the act of abstraction. [p. 132]

Hardy goes on, in a shrewd analysis of Eliot's *Quarry for Middlemarch*, to show how the novelist created a pattern of feeling and judgment in the narrative voice. "The narrator's emotions, implicit and explicit, fill in the spaces between the feelings of the characters. The novelist devises a rhetoric for the development and differentiation of these characters, and invariably supplements the drama of her characters' emotional life by the fluent ironies and sympathies of the omniscient but reticent narrative voice. This narration ensures emotional continuity, marks development and openly manipulates the reader's response" (pp. 143–44). Hardy thus accounts for the interplay between characterological "emotion," the informing quality of narrative sensibility, and reader response.

After witnessing such criticism, can we ask for more than that? Or, rather, *should* we ask for more than that? Shouldn't we allow such new critical analysis to coexist with other approaches, without attempting a joinder? Or should we avoid our common temptation to segregate critical approaches, and ask, instead, what a "new critical reading" poses for us in terms of other kinds of approaches? There have to be means of interrogating "new critical" modes of literary analysis without recourse to loaded (and deceptive) generalities about "humanistic" and "liberal."

I want to close, then, by suggesting one line of consideration that arises from Barbara Hardy's examinations of the representation of feeling in Victorian texts. What Hardy's approach enables us to register is the elaboration of narrative consciousness with reference to (or in interplay with) a specific reading consciousness. Her demonstrations of the modulations of depictions of feeling show that this interplay of consciousness at times takes us out to ahistorical generalization of emotive responses, and at other times into a highly particularized expression, so that the movement of the text is constantly denying the historicity of the instance of emotion. As solidly grounded as Bulstrode's mentality is in evangelical variations of providential thinking, for example, the representation of it seems persistently to dehistoricize it, and, correspondingly, to detach it from its ideological base. What we are witnessing, of course, is the specific discourse of the English novel in the nineteenth century, and we have long been familiar with its disposition to lift situations and emotive expressions out of the immediate social context in order to give them a universality of meaning. The sources for this lie in the generic roots of the novel, in the concept of high culture in the nineteenth century, and in assumptions about aesthetics—the nature of "great art." Hardy does, in fact, argue that second-rate novels do not achieve the patterns of modulation she discerns in the great works.

We are examining, then, a particular kind of *ecriture*, as it were, that determines not only the affective patterns of great novels in the Victorian period, but also may constitute what we consider to be aesthetic effect. Coming to terms with aesthetic effect has been the bane of most poststructuralist and psychoanalytic criticism, the most difficult element to describe. Concepts of defamiliarization or displacement do not prove sufficient. While we may justifiably argue that the concept of aesthetics is a mystification that serves middle and upper class purposes, we have not accounted for its affect. By locating the discursive operation that produces certain kinds of aesthetic effect specifically in the representation of feeling—in the evocation and modulation of the emotive responses that have traditionally been so intimately inscribed into aesthetic effect (as in Walter Benjamin's concept of aura), Barbara Hardy opens up avenues for discovering how the aesthetic is made to work. The development of a continuity and play of feeling at the narrative level, that relation of specific emotional states to larger cultural patterns, and that sense of formal rhythm produced by conscious reflexivity, which Hardy maps out in George Eliot's craft, direct us toward an apprehension of the nature of aesthetic effect. The procedures of a more traditional new critical approach, and the problematics of literary interpretation which have been most effectively posed for us by poststructural approaches, can be finally engaged.

John Smith Whole

Everett Emerson

The Complete Works of Captain John Smith. Edited by Philip L. Barbour. 3 vols. Chapel Hill and London: Published for the Institute of Early American History and Culture by the University of North Carolina Press, 1986. lxxii, 447; xii, 488; xi, 513 pp.

Captain John Smith is widely recognized as the first American writer, even though he lived in America for only two-and-a-half years. The man himself is readily pictured, since the first edition of his *Description of New England* (1616) includes a portrait of him in his thirty-seventh year. He was the savior of the Jamestown colony, and he deserves to be called the first American hero. Scholars are seldom thought of as heroes, but Smith was fortunate to have had in our time an heroic scholar who devoted many years, first, to writing an authoritative biography, and then to providing historians, literary scholars, and general readers with this splendid edition of Smith's writings. Unfortunately the editor did not live to see the publication of his work. Philip L. Barbour died on 21 December 1980, his eighty-second birthday. But the publisher of the edition, recognizing Barbour's achievement, celebrated its appearance in April 1986 with a superb conference on Smith.

Armed not with the learning associated with advanced degrees but instead with training as an intelligence officer, familiarity with east European languages, remarkable energy, and great care for precise detail, Barbour produced in 1964 *The Three Worlds of Captain John Smith,* a book that ends with the emphatic declaration, "Let it only be said that nothing John Smith wrote has yet been found to be a lie." In his biography of Smith, Barbour announced his intention to undertake an edition of the complete works; originally the project was to have been the work of Barbour and Lawrence Towner. (It was not Towner but the eminent British scholar David Quinn who served as Barbour's expert consultant in all of his researches.) Barbour's Hakluyt Society edition of *The Jamestown Voyages under the First Charter, 1606–1609,* appeared in 1969 and included Smith's *A True Relation* and *A Map of Virginia.* In 1971 Barbour began work on his complete edition of Smith's writings, under the auspices of the Jamestown-Yorktown Foundation, the National Endowment for the Humanities, the Newberry Library, and the Institute of Early American History and Culture, with other agencies providing additional grants. It was a costly project, and the task was not finished when Barbour died. Part of Thad Tate's foreword is worth quoting both to indicate how much Barbour was able to do and what procedures were followed in the editing:

At the time of Mr. Barbour's death, each of the three volumes in the set was in a different stage of editing. . . . Volume II had been prepared by the compositor first. By fall 1980 this volume was in page proof, and Mr. Barbour had a chance to make final corrections. Volume I and Volume III had not yet been typeset, but for both of these volumes Mr. Barbour's editorial work was basically complete. In the case of Volume I, the manuscript had already been perused by a recognized authority on John Smith's period, and Mr. Barbour had responded to detailed criticisms and had been able to make appropriate changes. He had also approved of the copy editing that had been done on the volume.

More work remained to be done on Volume III after Barbour's death, but the three volumes are properly his, and his name alone appears on the title page. The twenty-six Smith-related items by Barbour in the bibliography suggests something of Barbour's specialized learning.

The Complete Works of Captain John Smith is a magisterial edition, beautifully produced. It is not only a distinguished edition of Smith but also a model for those who would undertake other editions, especially editions of seventeenth-century works. Preliminary matter includes a statement of editorial method, an excellent brief biography of Smith, a general introduction that examines Smith as writer, autobiographer, compiler, geographer, ethnographer, soldier and governor, sailor and admiral, and the like, and a biographical directory. For each of Smith's substantial works, the edition provides at least an introduction, the text, textual annotation, and a bibliographical note. What is most impressive is the judiciousness with which the selection of materials was made. The introductions are models of their kind, concise, precise, and readable. The explanatory notes, at the foot of each page of the text, are economical; they are never gratuitous displays of learning. I had wondered whether Smith's rather eloquent description of history in *Advertisements for the Unexperienced Planters of New England, or Any Where* was original: "History is the memory of time, the life of the dead, and the happiness of the living." Barbour explains, to my satisfaction, "Smith's aphorism on history seems to be his own, though it may have been influenced by John Florio, commenting on Cicero: 'History . . . is the testimony of Tyme, the light of veritie, the life of memory, the guide of tyme, the messenger of antiquity'" (*Florio his Firste Fruits* [London, 1578], p. 52). Any matter which might occasion an excessively long note is taken up instead in the introductory essay or in an appendix. Repetition is avoided by the provision of cross-references and referral to the biographical directory.

In addition to these virtues, Barbour's edition includes much important material not appearing in the edition that it supercedes, the Edward Arbor edition of 1884. Besides the *Sea Grammar* (1627), which Arber had chosen to omit, Barbour includes a dozen documents of great interest, several of which explore the complicated relationship between Smith and Samuel Purchas, the successor of Richard Hakluyt as publisher of accounts of travels. Although Barbour provides many corrections of the historical record, he always shows respect and gratitude for his predecessors: Barbour was very much a southern (specifically Kentucky) gentleman.

When Barbour undertook his biography of Smith, it was the question of verifying Smith's account of his travels in Hungary—across the Black Sea to Muscovy and back to England via the heart of Europe—that was most crucial. Anyone who had read Smith's autobiographical *True Travels* was likely to consider suspect anything Smith had written that was not corroborated elsewhere. Barbour's remarkable detective work in his biography made sense of Smith's story of his continental travels and, by extension, made Smith's accounts of his Virginia adventures, which some scholars judged to be the work of an egotistical, lying braggart, much more creditable. But the *True Travels* still remained practically unreadable. In this new edition, Barbour's explanatory notes make Smith's autobiography intelligible, and this is one of the most important achievements of the new edition. I do regret that Barbour chose not to offer his latest thoughts on Smith's account of his rescue by Pocahontas. Instead, he simply refers the reader to his explanation in his biography of Smith and the explanation I hazarded in my *Captain John Smith* (1971).

The editorial method employed is set forth fully and explicitly, and the text should meet the needs of both general readers and specialists. Whereas the spelling is not modernized, misprints are corrected, with the original erroneous spelling recorded in the textual notes. Appearing in two columns on a page, the textual notes take up little space. No time was given to determining which copy of a work by Smith should be used as copy-text; variations from copy to copy are said to be "invariably extremely minor." Variations that Barbour had identified in his years of research are, however, recorded. In the preparing of the text, intelligence and common sense ruled.

In fact, Barbour departed from the announced editorial method in the very first work included, *A True Relation*. Often identified as "the first American book," it is a letter that Smith wrote in late spring 1608. It was published without its author's permission in a very badly edited and poorly printed form. Nothing, not even the text of the *True Travels*, made such heavy demands on an editor. For his edition of this work, Barbour provides on verso pages a photo-reproduction of the British Library copy of the *Relation*, which has annotations perhaps by Samuel Purchas; on the recto pages is "a specially edited transcription," characterized by "editorial suggestions" intended to increase intelligibility. Substantive annotations are to be found at the end of the text, with the "footnote space . . . reserved for transcription and discussion of the handwritten marginal comments on the facsimile leaves." Again, Barbour's editing is admirable. I wish I could report that this edition now makes Smith's letter an attractive contribution to the American literature canon, but I cannot. However valuable this edition, it is clear that only a determined specialist will attempt to understand *A True Relation*. What writing by Smith is available and significant for those who want to see the first American writer represented in the standard American literature anthologies? Barbour agrees with me that Smith's *Advertisements* is the most attractive work. I would urge that it be given greater recognition; it can usefully serve as a representative of Smith's work. It is not too long to be offered whole. The one objection I can imagine is that it deals with New England and thus would appear next to writings by William Bradford, Anne Bradstreet, and Edward Taylor, New Englanders all. No early work about the South would remain. So be it.

In addition, Barbour's volumes have a great many special features; I have not been able to think of anything that I would want to have added. The endpapers consist of splendid maps of the Atlantic coast from southern North Carolina to northern Maine, with Indian place-names located. Also to be found here are carefully selected facsimiles of each of the original title pages and other valuable front matter, such as maps; a facsimile of the letter of presentation Smith wrote in the Huntington Library copy of *The Generall Historie*; a map of John Smith's European travels, and as a frontispiece a most attractive color reproduction of the armorial bearings of Smith as recorded at the College of Arms, London, in 1625. These volumes are unusually handsome, though all of the attractive features can be defended by strictly utilitarian criteria.

Philip L. Barbour's edition of *The Complete Works of Captain John Smith* is a landmark in the editing of American literature; there has been heretofore no complete edition of an early American author to appear in full dress. It deserves attention and praise, though only specialists may be able to justify the purchase of this expensive set.

New Puzzles over the Editing of *Tristram Shandy*, A Response

Ian Campbell Ross

Professor Melvyn New's eighteen-page puff for his own Florida edition of *Tristram Shandy* is so evidently self-regarding that it is tempting to allow it to find the oblivion it deserves.[1] As his article masquerades as a review of my own edition of the same work and since it contains very substantial errors of fact, I feel, albeit reluctantly, obliged to reply. Since the article also glosses over weaknesses in the (often valuable) Florida edition and, in so doing, raises wider questions about editing and annotating, it is hoped that this reply may interest even those readers who have not edited *Tristram Shandy*, besides setting the record straight.

The first three pages of New's article make a couple of simple points from which New draws a quite false conclusion. First, the "Oxford World Classics" [sic?] edition of *Tristram Shandy* ($4.95) and the hardback version ($55.00) are identical except for the size of page and type.[2] Second, that in one advertisement Oxford University Press described my work as a "scholarly edition" and, in a catalogue, as containing "full explanatory notes." The first of these points is true; for the second, I will take Professor New's word. Some commentary on the false conclusion he draws will quickly overturn the error on which his subsequent review-article is based.

In 1979, I undertook to produce an edition of *Tristram Shandy* for the Oxford World's Classics [sic] series. Some time before publication in February 1983, but after I had read final proofs, Oxford University Press informed me of their intention to bring out a hardback version of my text. This version's origin as a World's Classic is indicated in the bibliographical information given on the verso of the title-page. I was not told the hardback would appear under the Clarendon imprint. I received no payment in addition to the flat fee I received for my commissioned work for the World's Classics edition. I was not shown any advertising copy, either for the *PMLA* advertisement New mentions, nor for the O.U.P. catalogue.[3]

In other words, my work was *never* intended to produce a full-scale critical edition, as New repeatedly implies, nor did I personally make a single one of the claims for it in the advertising as New quite falsely alleges. Had New been in any doubt about these facts, they could have been easily checked by a simple enquiry. That no such enquiry was made in itself suggests the dubious nature of New's much-professed concern with "scholarly" accuracy. Much more disturbingly, however, New was demonstrably aware that mine was a textbook edition. In his introduction to the third volume of the Florida edition of *Tristram Shandy* (1984), he referred to "Ian Campbell Ross's textbook edition for Oxford University Press" (p. 30). In other words, New is guilty, at best, of the most careless and unscholarly misrepresentation in alleging mine to be a failed scholarly edition in his *Review* article.

I have no desire, however, merely to hide behind Oxford University Press. If the charges New subsequently lays against my work were true I should still feel I had failed in the task of producing a reliable text with helpful annotation for the World's Classics series. The charges, however, are demonstrably false.

Professor New's first complaint is that he found the advertising (over which I had no control) misleading. His second complaint, apparently, is that the jacket-blurb (of which I was shown a first draft) is accurate. The blurb states that mine is the "first single-volume edition to take as copy-text for volumes I and II the York edition, now established as pre-dating the London edition." "What an odd statement," comments New. Yet it is simply true. It is a statement designed to acknowledge the priority of the Florida edition (two volumes of text and a third volume of annotation, this last then not published), which is, as New well knows, cited in my bibliography. Why this should be an admission of the "scholarly and economic culpability" of the O.U.P. edition is not easy to guess.

The Editing of *Tristram Shandy*, A Response

But if New would damn the blurb equally for being accurate or, as he implies, inaccurate, he is no less perverse in his attitude to the use a later editor might make of the Florida edition. New avers that "it is this edition that Ross either used to establish his own text . . . without giving adequate credit—or did not use, in which case his claim that he is a 'scholarly' editor is highly suspect" (p. 2). I shall pass over without comment the sly elision by which the claim to be producing a scholarly edition becomes mine and not the publisher's. Most damaging is New's repeated insinuation that my text is based on his. This is simply untrue. And not only is it untrue but New again *knows* it to be untrue, or else he is a reader with the most curious blind-spots.

In my "Note on the Text" (p. [xxv]), to which New elsewhere refers, I state clearly, "The present text follows the first editions of the several volumes of *Tristram Shandy*. . . . For Volumes I and II, the British Library copy of the first edition catalogued as Ashley 1770 was used; for the remaining volumes, the Bodleian set Godw. subt. 111–16, 118." New, for reasons of his own, withholds this information. It was, however, from a photocopy of these volumes, carefully emended, that the text of the World's Classics *Tristram Shandy* was set. The general similarity between my text and that of the Florida edition, then, derives from our use of copies of the same editions as copy-text.

This won't do for New, of course, because similarities are to be explained only by my having copied the Florida text, while differences—and there are many minor ones—must derive from copying it badly. The truth, of course, is quite different. Each of my emendations of copy-text was principled (though this need not mean that readers must agree with them). Each was made with a view to presenting the reader with a text which represents the author's final intentions.

Let me examine carefully New's own, carefully selected, examples. I draw attention in my notes to the two states of the dedication to Volume I. Professor New implies that since the Florida edition mentions these two states that this must be the source of my note. But on what evidence? None at all. Mr. Kenneth Monkman, in his important and well-known essay, "The Bibliography of the Early Editions of *Tristram Shandy*," published in 1970, draws attention to the two states of the dedication.[4] So, too, does he in "Towards a Sterne Bibliography" in A. H. Cash and J. M. Stedmond, eds., *The Winged Skull*, published in 1971.[5] I was well aware of these two states without ever having set eyes on the Florida edition. Moreover, I *examined* the two states by comparing Volumes I and II of my chosen copy-text with a set in my own possession which reveals the alternative state. (Almost exactly the same may be said of the variant states of the dedication to Volume IX, which Mr. Monkman also mentions in his 1970 essay.)[6]

If it is easy to demonstrate that Professor New's more offensive insinuations are baseless, then the questions of collation and variant readings remain. As to the first, I did collate, so far as I was able. I did not make a full collation of the kind evidenced by the voluminous textual apparatus of the Florida edition. Such collation would have been both inappropriate for the World's Classics edition I was preparing and quite beyond my resources of time and finance. I did not have a decade in which to work, nor did I receive the "delightful surprise" of grants from the National Endowment for the Humanities and the American Philosophical Society. I did not enjoy the services of a co-editor who is given shared credit for the Florida text, nor the assistance of a distinguished advisory board, nor the expertise of Mr. Kenneth Monkman "without whose assistance this edition [i.e. the Florida edition] would not have been possible" (Florida II:812).

And yet. . . . Lest the reader may have forgotten, New's complaint is *not* that my text is markedly inferior to his but that it is very largely the same. How was this achieved? Not by copying the Florida text but by accurately reproducing my copy-text (from a marked-up xerox of the first editions, as described above), *carefully emended*.

Emendations worry Professor New. They needn't, for the general principles by which I worked are easily explained. In *From Writer to Reader* (1978), Philip Gaskell describes the production of a critical edition and continues: "The copy-text is therefore converted into a critical text by means of a technique of controlled eclecticism whereby the editor, in the light of all the evidence, emends the copy-text by substituting readings from

The Editing of *Tristram Shandy*, A Response 333

another text or by supplying new ones himself; he does this where he believes that the alterations represent the author's intended text more closely than the copy-text readings, because they correct errors, omissions, or unauthorized alterations."[7] In fact, this is very much how New works. He acknowledges that the editor's job is to choose "'superior'" readings. Every choice, however, he finds "embarrassingly problematic." As a result, he follows the thorough procedure his grants permit by recording "every substantive variant in the lifetime editions" (II:832).

I do not find every choice "embarrassingly problematic." Of course, there *are* problems. It may be, to restrict myself to examples New selects, that to change the first edition's "nicity" to "nicety" (p. 18) is an unwarranted change, though the spelling occurs (I think) nowhere else and "nicety" is the reading of the second edition.

New's second example of my emendation merits closer examination. I change "gentlemen" to "gentleman" (p. 19). New wonders why. Perhaps a look at the context will help him. In the following extract, Tristram is speaking of Yorick; the text is that of the first edition: "I have the highest idea of the spiritual and refined sentiments of this reverend gentlemen, from this single stroke in his character. . . ." New points out that the emendation of "gentlemen" to "gentleman" is listed in "Apendix [sic?] Two" of the Florida edition. Fortunately, this example of what New implies to be unacknowledged dependence on his edition is so absurd as to set any table in a roar. The decision to correct an instance of what, in my "Note on the Text," I call "obvious errors," that is, to make a noun agree with a singular adjective in order to turn nonsense into sense, New finds "embarrassingly problematic." I, by contrast, do not, and am happy to leave readers to adjudicate between us.

The charge of plagiarism that hangs always on New's eager lips is not left there, however. "On page 56," New writes, "Ross emends the copy-text reading 'come cast away' to 'comes cast away,' an interesting emendation that modern editors before the Florida edition have not made; the emendation is explained in the Florida edition" (p. 5). What could be clearer, insinuates New, than that Ross copied the Florida edition. But again, I didn't. What the Florida's textual note reveals is that the copy text "shows 'come' but most copies examined, otherwise unmarked, have an 's' added in manuscript, indicating a correction in the printing house" (II:845). And so too does the British Library copy "Ashley 1770." It seemed to me to produce a superior reading. I checked it against the second edition which has the reading "comes" and preferred it as the reading for my text.

There is not space to go into all the instances of emendations to the respective copy-texts made both by the Florida editors and by me, though most of New's objections are equally silly and all my changes equally easily accounted for. Let me look instead at a case New cites where he emended and I didn't. In Volume II, a passage appears in the first edition and in my edition as "but it was a little hard to male-treat him after, and plunder him after he was laid in his grave" (p. 113). New prints "male-treat him before . . ." (I:167). New tells us that this emendation follows James Work's "suggested reading" (p. 6). In fact, it follows Work's unindicated alteration of the second edition of Volume II he used as copy-text. It thus falls into the category of an "indubitable error" which Work licensed himself to correct silently. New finds my category of "obvious errors" unscholarly but Work's "indubitable errors" he apparently thinks acceptable as the basis for emending copy-text. And this even though I emend (in the instance quoted above) to produce a reading which makes grammatical sense, whereas Work emends to produce merely a reading he finds preferable. New, meanwhile, finds "male-treat him before" to be "clearly the intended meaning of the passage" (II:848). I have no real quarrel with Work's decision; if he thought that "before" rather than "after" represented Sterne's intention he was right to change it. It is, to be sure, an easier reading but it was not one which was made in *any* edition in Sterne's lifetime. In other words, Sterne apparently found nothing unacceptable in the original reading and neither did contemporary readers. New's text, therefore, represents rather less 'clearly' the intended meaning of the passage. New produces what, for the twentieth-century reader is the easier reading; it is not necessarily the correct one.[8]

The Editing of *Tristram Shandy*, A Response 335

So far, this reply has of necessity been little more than a demonstration of the absurdity of Professor New's arguments, and the inconsistency of his own position. Yet it would be proper, first, to acknowledge that he does occasionally point out a genuine error and, second, raise questions about editing *Tristram Shandy* that are of more general interest.

First, let me confess my error. In emending the copy-text for the printers by inserting the sentences Sterne added to the second edition of Volume V, I inadvertently omitted four words. I wish I hadn't but I did, and I didn't notice the error until Professor New pointed it out. Yet the fact that he does so also pleases me. He has evidently searched diligently for errors in a text which, in my World's Classics edition, extends to 529 pages, and has found four missing words. The text should read: "But the auxiliaries, my brother is talking about, answered my uncle *Toby*,—I conceive to be different things.—" I was wrong and Professor New was. . . . But, wait a minute. *What* does New tell us the text should be? "But the auxiliaries, my brother is talking about, answered by [sic?] uncle *Toby* [sic?]—I conceive to be different things.—" (p. 7). It doesn't look right to me. If this is really the reading of New's edition it may not be a text worth so much self-praise. What the reading more likely tells us, of course, is that in the transmission of texts mistakes do occur, even to Professor New.

The point of genuine interest that arises from New's comparison of the World's Classics and Florida texts surprisingly seems to escape New completely. "Surprisingly," not because New seems especially astute but because I alluded to it in my brief "Note on the Text."

Tristram Shandy is a book which makes a great show of learning, often for parodic purposes. At times, the learning Sterne displays is real; at others, he merely copies from sources which readers and scholars from John Ferriar onwards have enjoyed locating. Since these sources are often identifiable beyond reasonable doubt, a particular problem arises where Sterne apparently miscopied. In such cases, do we assume that he did not *intend* to miscopy and, in respecting authorial intentions, correct the error? Or do we say that Sterne's intentions are best represented by admitting the parodic use he makes of the display of learning, mistakes and all?

In preparing his edition, New evidently thought about the issue. In Appendix Six (II:939–45), for example, he argues for his decision to take as copy-text of the "MEMOIRE presenté a Messieurs les Docteurs de SORBONNE" not the "Mémoire" as it appears in the first edition of *Tristram Shandy* but as it is printed in Sterne's source, Deventer's *Observations Importantes sur le Manuel des Accouchemens* (1734).[9] New argues that Sterne probably copied out the text himself, "introducing a few substantive changes and considerably more accidental variants; the compositor then introduced further variants into the text" (II:940), or, less likely, that Sterne provided the printed pages of Deventer for the printer to use as copy. New further suggests that it is important to separate Sterne's function as a copyist from his function as an artist by distinguishing between copying errors and deliberate emendations.[10] I suggested my conflicting view in my "Note on the Text": "No attempt has been made to 'correct' errors arising from Sterne's over-hasty copying from sources such as Chambers's *Cyclopaedia* or Burton's *Anatomy of Melancholy* as the retention of such minor errors best indicates Sterne's relationship to the tradition of learned wit on which such borrowing depends" (p. [xxv]). Despite Professor New's arguments, I continue to believe my decision superior and hence, in this respect, the World's Classics text to be decidedly preferable to that of the Florida edition.

At times, of course, it is impossible to be certain whether an error derives from Sterne's miscopying or a printer's misreading. Where I decided on the latter, I emended the copy-text; where I thought the former, I did not. Hence, I left the copy-text reading of "*Aldergate-street*" (instead of "*Aldersgate-street*" [O.U.P., p. 57]) partly because the reading may derive from an edition of a book Sterne actually saw and partly because Sterne's error may result from an understandable ignorance of London. New calls Aldersgate-street "well-known." But *was* it to Sterne who was not familiar with London before the success of the first instalment of *Tristram Shandy* in which the mistake occurs? The second edition reading could be not an authorially-inspired correction but a

The Editing of *Tristram Shandy*, A Response 337

deliberate or even unintentional change by a London compositor who did know the capital and Aldersgate-street.

In the case of the reading "Alquife" for the copy-text's "Alquise" (O.U.P., p. 122) I decided that the more likely explanation of the original error was a compositorial misreading of the long 's' in a name unknown to him, though familiar to Sterne if not through *Don Belianis of Greece* then through *Don Quixote*. (New, as his textual note reveals, here reasoned in a similar fashion.)

In the first case, I may be right and New wrong or vice versa. In the second, we stand or fall together. I don't mind if New disagrees with my "Aldergate-street" reading, nor if a third reader disagrees with our shared "Alquife." What, once more, I do object to is New's arrogant and groundless suggestion that I did not think about the issues involved, merely because I had no opportunity to present the reader with my entire line of reasoning.

What is most surprising about New's conclusions, however, is that he neither sees that they are as applicable to his text as to mine, nor that they represent the logical result of the textual principles he and I espouse. "At times," he writes, "spellings are corrected, at times not, at times punctuation is altered, at times not, at times proper names are corrected, at times not, at times changes from the second edition are admitted into the text, at times not" (p. 6). These observations apply equally to the Florida text. And rightly so, for as Philip Gaskell has written: "Every textual situation is unique, and the editor must base his procedures on his own critical judgement as much as on critical principles" (op. cit., p. 6). The luxury New enjoyed was that of noting and often explaining the reasons behind every decision. But the Florida edition has *besides Sterne's text* (which is surely the important thing) no fewer than 727 pages of textual commentary and annotation. My edition, *including Sterne's text*, runs to just 614 pages. I would, ideally, have liked to record at least all verbal emendations of copy-text but felt that, in the absence of explanatory notes, this would have been of scant use to my intended readers.

Perhaps my decision was wrong but the text itself is principled and accurate. But New is not really interested in this. Though he comments that "the text of the Oxford *Tristram Shandy* is indeed based on the correct copy-texts, and is an accurate transcription" (p. 4), and elsewhere remarks that my World's Classics text "is better than other textbook editions" (p. 3), he then asserts, breathtakingly, that "for students the differences are of minimal significance" (p. 3). In other words, while making enormous play of the proper choice of copy-text and the accuracy of his own edition, he says that my correct choice and accurate transcription are of no account. New's apparent indifference to scholarly accuracy in textbook editions is something I do not share.

What does interest New? He is, by his own admission, "in especial suspense over the question of the relationship of his [i.e., Ross's] text to the Florida text" (p. 6) and insinuates my text's dependence upon his. This insinuation is (if possible) even more foolish than offensive. I studied his edition but my text was established, as clearly stated, from the specified copies of the first editions of the various volumes of *Tristram Shandy*. The frequent agreement of the two texts may be attributed not only to a shared choice of copy-texts, but, like the disagreements, to different, but always thoughtful, editorial decisions, about when, or when not, to emend those copy-texts.

New's charges about the text, then, are as false as his attribution to me of claims I nowhere made about my edition. Is there, finally, any substance to his remarks on my annotation? Here, New stands on the shakiest ground of all. His own major decision in annotating—i.e., to adopt many readings verbatim from James A. Work's edition—is not only (so far as I am aware) unique among editors with scholarly pretensions; it leads him also into the repetition of some of Work's own errors and imprecisions.

Professor New's own selectivity makes it tempting to point equally unfairly to all the weaknesses of his own edition. Lack of space persuades me to restrict myself principally to the particular examples *he* selected. First, though, we can agree. We both admire the admirable labours of Work. The Florida edition uses its space to pay generous tribute to Work. I confine myself to citing his edition in a Select Bibliography while assuming everyone at all interested in the history of annotating *Tristram Shandy* will recognize both my own considerable debt to Work's edition, and the numerous places at which I emend information Work supplies by reference to more up-to-date sources or offer fresh information. I did not feel it any more appropriate to have cited what I learned (but always independently checked) from Work or others than Work felt it necessary to cite the pioneering labours of John Ferriar or his nineteenth-century successors.

What are New's objections to my annotations? His first reveals him in a rarefied world of his own, so lost in 'scholarship' as to be unable to read. New quotes this passage:

My way is ever to point out to the curious, different tracts of investigation, to come at the first springs of the events I tell;—not with a pedantic *Fescue,*—or in the decisive Manner of *Tacitus,* who outwits himself and his reader (I:74/p. 54).

Pedantic fescue in hand, New indicates at an entire page's length the annotations of Work, Watt, Petrie, Anderson, and myself, in relation to Tacitus.[11] Work comments on a Tacitus whose style "proverbial for its brevity, is occasionally obscure and affected, and whose interpretation of actions appears sometimes to be over-subtilized" (Work, p. 66, n. 4). Watt, Petrie, Anderson and I are equally criticized on two points: 1) giving a note along Work's lines but not quoting Work direct, and 2) omitting the reference to "over-subtilized" interpretation of actions. I can only speak for myself but, as to the first point, I find the verbatim quotation of a previous editor an inadmissible dereliction of any annotator's duty; in this case, too, I provide a different date for Tacitus's birth, and add an extra piece of information about Tacitus, while using only twenty-four words to Work's twenty-eight. As to the second point, I think Work and New are simply wrong to lay stress on the "over-subtilized" interpretation. Sterne speaks of the "decisive Manner" of Tacitus and I am unable to reconcile "decisiveness" with "over-subtilization." I *am* able to reconcile it with Tacitus's style which Work notes to be "proverbial for its brevity" and which I call "elliptical." Nothing in New's commentary makes me change my mind.

New's next example is, more than unconvincing, simply risible. He indicates that in Volume II, Watt, Anderson, and I offer, like Work, a note to the passage where Walter and Toby remain "like *Brutus* and *Cassius* at the close of the scene making up their accounts" (I:134/p. 93), indicating that Sterne had Shakespeare's *Julius Caesar* in mind. We all fail, however, to spot that Walter's reference to "this rash humour which my mother gave me" (I:133/p. 92) is also quoted from *Julius Caesar*. Again, I speak only for myself. I admit to failing to spot this allusion and I am glad to have it pointed out to me. But to suggest that, in noting the other reference, I (or Watt or Anderson) must have copied Work is grotesque. My familiarity with the complete text of *Julius Caesar* evidently leaves something to be desired, but when Brutus and Cassius are united in my mind with the idea of a play, then *Julius Caesar* pops in as well, without Work's aid.

Again, though, logicality is not New's strong point. He thinks it wrong to follow the lead of previous editors but equally culpable not to. So I am to be blamed for not spotting another Shakespearean allusion, this time from *Henry VIII*, noted by Watt and "appropriated" (New's slight) by Anderson. "The fact is," New avers, "that Ross never looked at the Watt or Anderson editions in compiling his notes." This is simply false. I consulted those editions as I did Work's. But, unlike New, I did not compile my annotations with those editions, or any other, open on the desk before me. I noted on as careful a reading of the text as possible what I thought required annotation for the World's Classics audience. I then set about providing the annotation from the best sources available to me. It is certainly true that my sense of what might be annotated was influenced by my knowledge of other editions. I first read *Tristram Shandy* as an undergraduate student in Petrie's Penguin edition and my own knowledge of the novel's many allusions was undoubtedly influenced by this. What I fail to annotate may be attributed, however, not only to my own (freely acknowledged) failure at times to pick up submerged allusions but also to a reluctant discarding of information in my possession as not being appropriate to the kind of edition I was preparing.

Professor New wonders, for instance, why I annotate only one

The Editing of *Tristram Shandy*, A Response 341

proverbial phrase. The answer is that, as I worked, I became aware of the very great number of proverbs cited or alluded to in *Tristram Shandy*. It became clear to me that to uncover them all would be an enormous labour and one whose fruits could not be incorporated in a World's Classics edition. The one proverb New notes is merely a vestigial trace of much discarded work (and should have been discarded likewise). How, though, does the Florida edition fare on proverbs? In Volume I of *Tristram Shandy*, there are at least fifty-six proverbs quoted or alluded to of which the Florida edition notes seven; in Volume II at least fifty-five of which the Florida edition finds seventeen. No fewer than seventy-three may be traced in Volume III of which again the Florida edition notes seventeen, as they do in Volume IV, which contains at least sixty-nine.[12] To which of New's preferred categories are we to attribute this selectivity: carelessness or capriciousness?

Of course, all annotators are open to criticism. They are certain to include too much material for some readers, too little for others. Hence many of the omissions of which New complains. Others, certainly, stemmed from my own ignorance, and New is right to point out an error which indeed resulted from a misreading of an awkward sentence in Arthur H. Cash's *Laurence Sterne: The Early and Middle Years*. I regret having made the error. I do not, *pace* New, regret having read the first volume of Cash's biography nor having made use of it.

The principal difference between the Florida edition and the World's Classics in its annotation is a natural one. The Florida editors attempt comprehensiveness; I attempt conciseness. Lest, in pointing out the errors in New's article, I sound impolite, I will pay proper tribute to the Florida edition's annotation. It is far in advance of anything so far attempted and will provide a valuable commentary for all seriously interested in *Tristram Shandy*. The annotation is also, however, variously redundant, incomplete, and wrong.

Redundancy is perhaps the least grievous (if massively present) fault. It's difficult, though, to imagine the reader who will simultaneously welcome the extensive and learned treatment of certain topics—two pages on Sterne's refusal to separate wit and judgement, for instance (III: 237–9)—and need to be told, *tout court,* that *"Pardonnez moi"* means "Pardon me" (III:488) or "diable," "the devil" (III, 456). Nor, if the purpose of annotation is to illuminate the text, rather than display the editors' erudition, is it obvious how New's learned monoglot will benefit from being referred, in relation to a very familiar eighteenth-century phrase like "gives the wall," to *Romeo and Juliet* (III:466).

Such superfluity in annotation is everywhere in evidence. Many of the Florida edition's notes go on for pages, often to little real purpose.[13] Most, indeed, are too long to discuss adequately here but a very short note will indicate the scale of the problem. In Volume IX, mention is made of a "black-pudding." The Florida edition's note reads: "American readers may need to be informed that black-pudding is a kind of sausage made of blood and suet, sometimes with the addition of meat" (III:546). Far from being an appropriate note, this should not even have been the first draft of a note; it is, rather, a thought of the kind that necessarily passes through any annotator's mind. The assumptions it reveals, though, are interesting. British and Irish readers—New's logic presumably goes—know what a black-pudding is. That leaves American readers. (Whatever happened to non-native speakers of English or native speakers from other cultures we can only surmise.) If New doesn't annotate "black-pudding" he may face criticism from those who are ignorant of its nature. If he simply describes a black-pudding, though, he may be charged with redundancy by those British readers who don't know he is here annotating for Americans, and those American scholars who will be insulted by the assumption that they don't know about black-puddings. In order, so New hopes, to guard himself against any criticism whatever, the note has to read "*American* readers *may need* . . . [my italics]." As it happens, this insecure agonizing is wholly unnecessary because the entire note is redundant. New has already elaborately justified his non-annotation of certain words: "Our second rule . . . was to define no word recorded in the *Shorter Oxford English Dictionary (SOED),* which we took to be the desktop dictionary of a scholarly audience" (III:10–11). "Black-pudding," of course, appears in the *SOED,* as indeed it does in the *Concise Oxford Dictionary.* If any

The Editing of *Tristram Shandy*, A Response 343

annotation *had* been required, however, "Sausage made of blood and suet" would have fully covered the case. It would have used six words instead of twenty-five without losing anything of value. Had similar savings of space occurred throughout, the Florida notes might have been more helpfully readable and the resulting volume rather less expensive.

At times, moreover, excessive annotation may be genuinely counterproductive to the business of enabling the reader fruitfully to approach Sterne's text. The first note to Volume II of *Tristram Shandy* is a good example. This note occupies three and a half pages, and includes a map of Namur. Of course, Ian Watt had also included in his edition a note on fortification and a map of Namur, while trying to indicate where uncle Toby was wounded, so New cannot claim precedence. Instead, he strangely argues that Watt's information on fortification is "superfluous"! The Florida edition contains vastly more such information (including an eight-page glossary) but this is apparently appropriate while Watt's is superfluous.

Why might excessive annotation of terms of fortification be unhelpful? The Florida edition argues that it "seem[s] superfluous— perhaps even counter—to Sterne's purpose, which is to bewilder both Toby and the reader" (III:127). A good argument but one strangely familiar to this editor. In my World's Classics edition, I wrote: "Terms from the science of fortification are annotated, here and subsequently, only when they do not appear in the *Concise Oxford Dictionary*. In *Tristram Shandy*, uncle Toby's use of such terms is partly intended to baffle the reader as it baffles other characters" (p. 548). I was the first annotator of *Tristram Shandy* to make this point. New follows it virtually verbatim. If his annotations had not appeared a year and a half *after* mine, would he have accused me of plagiarism? I do not so accuse him. Rather, I leave it to the reader to decide whether New copied me without acknowledgement or whether the similarity of thought and expression may not derive from similar perceptions about this aspect of Sterne's novel, open to any conscientious annotator.

Leaving aside for a moment the misrepresentation of my intentions in preparing the World's Classics edition, I still have differences with New over the proper responsibility of an annotator. The examples of my annotation to which New objects are so varied that it is hard to know how to respond briefly. If I follow a previous writer I am copying him; if I don't, copying him badly. I have already indicated that to quote a previous annotator verbatim seems unacceptable to me. Even in matter of translations, the Florida edition just copies out Work's versions of, for example, the long passage including the submission to the doctors of the Sorbonne concerning baptism in the womb and their reply (I, xx) and the longish extracts from Baillet (IV, x). There is nothing especially wrong with Work's versions but it seems strange to imply that they could not *possibly* be improved on. I did my own translations; the Florida editors relied on the existing translations of an earlier scholar.

The least one could hope, however, of annotators who decided to copy a predecessor is that they would check the accuracy of the information copied. Occasionally, they do so and emend Work's note. Elsewhere, they retain his imprecisions and even errors as they stand.

Two simple errors to begin with. Work tells us that Niccolò Tartaglia was the author of *Questi et inventioni diverse*; the Florida edition repeats this verbatim (III:138), as a note 'we are unable to improve on' (III:30). Perhaps so. But it *could* be improved on. By anyone, for instance, with a rudimentary knowledge of Italian, or even anyone prepared to check Work's note. The former would know that the title as given makes no sense, while the latter would easily find that the first word should be "*Quesiti*." Second, Work calls the Earl of Angus killed at Steinkirk "James Hamilton"; so do the Florida editors. His name was, in fact, James Douglas.

Not that the Florida edition falls into error merely when copying from Work. On page 196 of Volume III, it quotes Work verbatim on "Thomas Bartholine (1616–1680), an eminent Danish physician." On page 198, they paraphrase from another source and tell us learnedly that "many of the great works of anatomy were indeed written by the Dutch during this period, including Thomas Bartholin." So Bartholin changes not only the spelling of his name but also his nationality within the space of three pages of the "scholarly" edition. Spelling of names is very inconsistent throughout the Florida text, often because of the editors being unable to improve on Work. They may be able, for instance, to indicate Work's source for christening the Italian engineer Lorini "Buonajute" but Italian sources simply give "Buonaiuto."

Dates seem similarly to have perplexed the Florida editors. In the list which includes Lorini's name, Work gives dates for all the engineers mentioned except Girolamo Cataneo; the Florida editors make no attempt to rectify this anomaly. Samuel Marolois is described by Work as "(fl. early 17th C.)"; drawing on more up-to-date sources I am able to suggest tentative dates for his birth and death. Such instances could be multiplied many times over. Work's dates for classical figures, for instance, are very occasionally emended by the Florida editors who seem to draw principally on the *Oxford Classical Dictionary* (2nd ed., 1970), cited in their Key to the Notes. But there is no consistency whatever. Why, for instance, not emend the dates of Quintilian or Longinus (*TS*, I, xix)? Why add the dates of Zeno of Citium in line with the *OCD* but leave Chrysippus's dates unaltered, though they are mentioned together (*TS*, II, xix)? Or the dates of Seneca, Pantaenus, or Titus Flavens Clemens (*TS*, III, iv)? Why follow Work in dating the code Hermogenianus to 324 A.D. when the *OCD* thinks it written around 293/4 A.D.? (If New and his colleagues have done the original research necessary to correct the dates suggested by their regular source of information, why not say so, as they do elsewhere?) In most cases, the changes are slight but—to adapt New—"what do 'scholarly' annotators do if not pursue the minutiae of the text they annotate?" (p. 7).

Despite the voluminous evidence that it is the Florida editors, not I, who followed Work without checking his information, New would like it to be otherwise. "In the note on bridges," he writes, "Ross follows Work so closely that he too omits the dates for the Marquis de l'Hôpital while providing those for Bernouilli, even though both men are named in the same sentence" (p. 12). It is true that here I am inconsistent. But are the Florida editors never inconsistent in the same manner? For an answer, we may look not at just any note but the *very note* (III:260) in which they (properly) give the Marquis de l'Hôpital's dates. The bridges to which Sterne refers are, in his text, at "Spires" and "Brisac." Work identifies "Brisac" as the modern Breisach but fails to tells us that "Spires" is now Speyer. Astonishingly, the Florida editors identify "Brisac" as Breisach while ignoring "Spires" completely (III:260). This information, besides the location of the two cities, is found only in the World's Classics textbook.

The Florida edition's own inconsistency based on closely following Work is apparent throughout. In *Tristram Shandy* (III, xii), Justinian and Tribonian are mentioned in the same sentence. Work gives dates for the former but not the latter; so too does the Florida edition (III:226). When Hadrian's grief for Antinous is mentioned (*TS*, V, iii), Work gives Hadrian's dates but not those of Antinous; the Florida edition follows suit (III:347). In *Tristram Shandy*, V, iii, Work does not annotate a list of names beginning "*Plato*, or *Plutarch*, or *Seneca*, or *Xenophon*, or *Epictetus*, or *Theophrastus*, or *Lucian*." The Florida edition helpfully tells us that the "classical names . . . are well known" (III: 346). Unlike, presumably, the name of Petrarch, which is glossed immediately afterwards in the same paragraph in the usual Florida manner. Still in the same note, though, the Florida editors tell us (and tell us only) that St. Augustine is a "major ecclesiastical figure." (Oh, *that* St. Augustine.) Other "major ecclesiastical figures" are St. Cyprian and St. Bernard. Perhaps such lists don't require annotation but they are annotated by the Florida editors in most instances. The least one might subsequently expect in a "scholarly" edition is consistency and an absence of fatuity. In these cases, consistent and helpful annotation is found only in the World's Classics edition.

So too in other passages, even within a single chapter. A list of cities—once flourishing, now decayed—in Volume V, Chapter iii, contains names which many readers may find need a note. Work offers none; neither does the Florida edition. Sterne mentions some celebrated last words of the dying, and Work rightly tells us that Sterne's source was the essay "Of Death" by Francis Bacon. He doesn't tell us what Bacon's sources were; neither does the Florida edition. For all this information, you'll need the World's Classics edition.

The Editing of *Tristram Shandy*, A Response 347

It's not just that the Florida edition follows Work. Sometimes it omits information entirely. Why, in *Tristram Shandy*, VI, v, no note on St. Ambrose? ("Another major ecclesiastical figure," perhaps?) Or Julian the Apostate? Or Gregory of Nazianzum? In this last case, the reader is advised in the Florida edition (III:439) to consult a note on page 404. But anyone who does so will find no information, just an irrelevant anecdote.

The pattern is similar elsewhere. Sterne twice uses "campaign" in the sense of "open country." Work apparently missed the first usage and annotated only the second; the Florida's gloss also occurs at the second usage, a cross-reference appearing the first time. Work accidentally annotated the name Hugh Mackay twice and, despite its elaborate system of cross-referencing, so too does the Florida edition.

Lack of space prevents any comprehensive reply to New's charges, as he doubtless was aware when throwing them out so recklessly. To look at just one charge, however, may both correct errors in New's article and reveal the limitations of his own principles of annotation.

New says that my notes inspire no confidence that I read Ephraim Chambers's *Cyclopaedia*. In my note 13 to Volume II, chapter xix of *Tristram Shandy* (O.U.P., p. 556), I point out that the list of names of those supposedly born by Caesarian section is taken from the entry "Caesarian section" in the *Cyclopaedia*. No previous annotator—Work, Watt, Petrie, or Anderson—had indicated this; nor, I believe (though my purpose was never to claim priority), had anyone before me. The Florida editors note this borrowing, of course, but their annotations appeared after mine. In addition to the information I provide, however, they add a note in which error competes vigorously with redundancy. Unable to comment on anything without quoting from an authority, Florida cites Chambers to "explain" why Mrs. Shandy might have paled at her husband's suggestion she undergo a Caesarian section without anaesthetics. The Florida editors then comment on section by quoting from a book, by John Glaister, published in 1894. To this source, they manage to add an error [in scholarly square brackets] by knighting Fielding Ould eighteen years before he was in fact so honoured (1760 *not* 1742). What Glaister describes, however, is Fielding Ould's understanding of the history of section—something irrelevant to *Tristram Shandy* because unknown to Sterne and unhelpful to the reader because, in its historical aspects, partly inaccurate. "Finally," the Florida edition says, after more than a page, "it might be noted that the first recorded successful caesarean operation in England, i.e., with the mother recovering [lest we should think otherwise], took place in 1793" (III:203). Well, it *might* be so noted but to what possible purpose? If anything along these lines is to be added why not refer instead to the discussion by John Burton, in a book Sterne *did* know, of alleged instances of successful Caesarian section performed in Ireland, in Sterne's lifetime, and recorded in contemporary medical literature?[14]

Having stuck to examples selected by New, I cannot forbear reference to one final example of my own. It is one of those instances where the Florida edition draws on my own annotation. Because, despite his failure to mention the fact in his article, New does take information from the World's Classics edition. "From Ian Campbell Ross's textbook edition for Oxford University Press (1983) we have made use of one or two suggestions" (III:30). (The reader will notice how the concern for scholarly accuracy here gives way to a curious imprecision.) How does the scholarly Florida edition get on copying from the textbook edition? In Volume IX of *Tristram Shandy* we are informed of uncle Toby's way of courting Widow Wadman: "When he had told Mrs. Wadman once that he loved her, he let it alone, and left the matter to work after its own way" ("𝕿𝖍𝖊 𝕰𝖎𝖌𝖍𝖙𝖊𝖊𝖓𝖙𝖍 𝕮𝖍𝖆𝖕𝖙𝖊𝖗," O.U.P., p. 525). Walter thinks this a system which "if there was faith in a Spanish proverb" would win Toby the hearts of "half the women upon the globe."

What is the Spanish proverb? The Florida editors don't know and take only eight lines to admit it. On the way, they quote two quite inapt proverbs ("a buen entendedor, pocas palabras"—"to the good listener, few words are required" and "en boca cerrada no entran moscas"—"a shut mouth catches no flies"). Neither of these, they engagingly admit, "is quite as appropriate as one might wish" (III:546). They then add:

See also Ian Campbell's [sic?] suggestion (*Tristram Shandy* [Oxford: Oxford University Press, 1983], p. 594) of a line [sic?] from Caldéron

The Editing of *Tristram Shandy*, A Response 349

[sic?]: "En las venturas de amor/dice más el que más calla" ("In affairs of love, the less said the better").

In following my suggestion, in other words, they manage to miscopy my name and, more importantly, that of Calderón [sic], perpetrate an error of their own, and omit the source of the lines, which I give (*Ni amor se libra de amor*, III, iii). (My surname is also incorrectly given in the index—despite being correctly given elsewhere in the text—but since neither Calderón nor even Calderón makes the index at all, I can scarcely grumble.)

What, then, can we conclude from New's article, except that he greatly admires his own work and is not afraid to go into print to say so? First, that he is wrong to insinuate that mine is a failed attempt to produce a full-scale critical edition such as his, although I worked to scholarly standards of accuracy. Second, that he is, at best, culpably negligent, even to suggest that I was attempting a full-scale critical edition since his own introduction to the third volume of the Florida edition makes it clear that he knows mine is a textbook edition, and I nowhere make any other claim for it. Third, New is wrong to insinuate the dependence of my text on his, as indicated above, and proved by the marked-up xeroxes of the first editions of the several volumes of Sterne's novel, from which the World's Classics text was set, coupled with our many different emendations of copy-text. Fourth, he is wrong to imply that there is no fresh annotation in the edition. Finally, while he is at liberty to object to what I chose to annotate, it is demonstrable that his own edition suffers from errors, imprecisions, and omissions while adding frequent redundancy.

I am grateful to the editors of *Review* for allowing me to correct New's errors. They tell me he will be invited to comment on this reply. He might care to address himself to these particular questions: 1) Why, knowing that mine was a textbook edition, did he write otherwise in his *Review* article? 2) Why did he falsely attribute to me claims I nowhere made for my work? 3) Why, given his emphasis on his own scholarship, does his edition contain the verbatim repetition of the errors of Work (among others), when these could easily have been checked?

Professor New has taken a textbook edition, whose text and annotation he acknowledges to be accurate, costing $4.95, as a standard by which he may measure the success of his own three-volume edition, costing $112.50, and produced over fifteen years by two textual editors and three annotators, with the aid of an advisory board, and grants from the University of Florida, the National Endowment for the Humanities, and the American Philosophical Society. At least Professor New and I can agree on one thing:

☞ A dwarf who brings a standard along with him to measure his own size—take my word, is a dwarf in more articles than one.

Notes

1. Melvyn New, "Whim-whams and Flim-flams: The Oxford University Press Edition of *Tristram Shandy*," *Review*, 7 (1985), 1–18.
2. The hardback version was priced at £25 in the United Kingdom; Oxford University Press in England inform me that their American branch is wholly responsible for pricing policy in the United States.
3. The wording of the *PMLA* advertisement was again the responsibility of the American branch of O.U.P., and quite outwith my control. If Professor New was shown all the promotional material for his own edition he was very fortunate, though in that case one might wonder why the University of Florida Press thinks he spells his name "Melvin "
4. Kenneth Monkman, "The Bibliography of the Early Editions of *Tristram Shandy*," *The Library*, 5th series, 25 (March 1970), 23.
5. Kenneth Monkman and J. C. T. Oates, "Towards a Sterne Bibliography," in Arthur H. Cash and John M. Stedmond, eds., *The Winged Skull: Papers from the Laurence Sterne Bicentenary Conference* (London: Methuen, 1971), p. 291.
6. Op. cit., 29.
7. Philip Gaskell, *From Writer to Reader: Studies in Editorial Method* (Oxford: Clarendon, 1978), pp. 4–5.
8. It is relevant here to note that neither of the modern translators of *Tristram Shandy*, in two languages, whose versions sit on my shelves, found the original reading impossible, though both are free elsewhere in their translations. Charles Mauron, in *Vie et Opinions de Tristram Shandy, Gentilhomme* (1946; repr. Paris: Flammarion, 1982), has "mais il était un peu dur de le maltraiter encore après et de le piller quand il gisait dans sa tombe" (p. 139); Antonio Meo, in *La vita e le opinioni di Tristram Shandy gentiluomo* (1958; repr. Milan: Arnoldo Mondadori, 1983), has "però, maltrattarlo anche dopo, saccheggiarlo persino quand'era morto e sepolto, fu un'azione piuttosto ingenerosa" (p. 105).

The Editing of *Tristram Shandy*, A Response 351

9. The flaws in New's procedure in doing this are indicated by O. M. Brack, Jr., in "A Book for a Parlour-Window," *Review*, 8 (1986), 280 (though I should add that, unlike me, Brack appears to approve of New's decision to use Deventer as copy-text). I am grateful to the editors of *Review* for making Brack's review available to me.

10. Unfortunately, New is unable to be consistent. In a parodic discussion of polytheism, for example, Sterne refers to the gods who "as *Varro* tells me ... made no less than thirty thousand effective beards upon the pagan establishment" (III, xi). In fact, it was not Varro but Hesiod who reckoned up 30,000 gods; Varro counted 300 Jupiters. Sterne's mistake arose, as all editors agree, from a misreading of his source, Robert Burton's *Anatomy of Melancholy* (6th ed. 1651; 3.4.1.3). Did Sterne *intend* to miscopy? There is no reason to think so but New does not follow the logic of his position and substitute "Hesiod" for "Varro." (Neither does he "correct" the error Sterne made in copying from the *Anatomy* [3.1.1.2] in Volume VIII, chap. xxxiii, although again there is no suggestion that Sterne intended to miscopy.)

11. Laurence Sterne, *The Life and Opinions of Tristram Shandy, Gentleman*, ed. James Aiken Work (Indiana: Odyssey Press, 1940), Ian Watt (Boston: Houghton Mifflin, 1965); Graham Petrie (Harmondsworth: Penguin, 1967), Howard Anderson (New York: W. W. Norton, 1980).

12. For permission to quote these provisional figures, I am grateful to Ms. Noha Nasser, at present completing a thesis on proverbs in *Tristram Shandy* for the degree of M. Litt., under my supervision.

13. For a differently focused discussion of the Florida edition's redundant annotation, see O. M. Brack, Jr., op. cit., 290–92.

14. John Burton, *An Essay towards a Complete New System of Midwifry* (London, 1751), p. 271.

Correspondence

TO THE EDITORS:

Thank you for the opportunity to respond to Ian Campbell Ross's defense of his indefensible "whim-wham," but I have never thought it probable that one could respond to a negative review without appearing nasty, petulant, and self-serving—a pitfall Mr. Ross should have contemplated before responding to my harsh but deserved review of his efforts. Indeed, he was quite unable to avoid not merely the appearance but the actuality of becoming all three.

We have now both spoken our minds. Posterity will judge which edition of *Tristram Shandy* will "swim down the gutter of Time" with the original and which will drown.

Melvyn New
University of Florida

Contributors

R. D. ACKERMAN is a Visiting Scholar in the Interdisciplinary Graduate Program in the Humanities at The Pennsylvania State University.

A. OWEN ALDRIDGE is Professor Emeritus of French and Comparative Literature at the University of Illinois.

MORRIS BEJA is Professor of English at Ohio State University.

PANTHEA REID BROUGHTON is Professor of English at Louisiana State University.

RICHARD A. BURT is Assistant Professor of English at the University of Massachusetts at Amherst.

VINCENT CARRETTA is Associate Professor of English at the University of Maryland.

ARTHUR D. CASCIATO is Assistant Professor of English at Miami University of Ohio.

EVERETT EMERSON is Professor of English at the University of North Carolina, Chapel Hill.

RICHARD J. FINNERAN is Professor of English at Tulane University.

DONALD GALLUP is Curator Emeritus of the American Literature Collection at the Beinecke Library, Yale University.

ANDREW GORDON is Associate Professor of English at the University of Florida.

ROGER B. HENKLE is Professor of English at Brown University.

U. C. KNOEPFLMACHER is Professor of English at Princeton University.

GEORGE P. LANDOW is Professor of English and Art at Brown University.

JULIAN MARKELS is Professor of English at Ohio State University.

MICHAEL O'BRIEN is Phillip R. Shriver Professor of American History at Miami University of Ohio.

ROBERT L. PATTEN is Professor of English at Rice University.

PAUL L. SAWYER is Associate Professor of English at Cornell University.

MIRIAM J. SHILLINGSBURG is Professor of English at Mississippi State University.

PETER L. SHILLINGSBURG is Professor of English at Mississippi State University.

DAVID SIMPSON is Professor of English and Comparative Literature at the University of Colorado, Boulder.

ALBERT J. VON FRANK is Associate Professor of English at Washington State University.

COLIN WILCOCKSON is Director of Studies in English at Pembroke College, Cambridge.